Fourth Edition

Teaching Students To Be Peacemakers

David W. Johnson and Roger T. Johnson

Interaction Book Company
7208 Cornelia Drive
Edina, Minnesota 55435
(952) 831-9500; FAX (952) 831-9332
www.co-operation.org

Copyright © 1987, 1991, 1995, 2005 by David W. Johnson

This book is dedicated to our wives, Linda Mulholland Johnson and Anne Earle Johnson, who keep our conflict skills in practice.

ISBN: 0-0939603-30-6

Johnson, D. W., & Johnson, R. (2005). **Teaching Students To Be Peacemakers** (4th Ed.). Edina, MN: Interaction Book Company, (952) 831-9500.

Table Of Contents

Johnson, D. W., & Johnson, R. (2005). **Teaching Students To Be Peacemakers** (4th Ed.). Edina, MN: Interaction Book Company, (952) 831-9500.

Preface

This book is about teaching students to be peacemakers. Despite the amount of time teachers and students waste in dealing with destructively managed conflicts, and despite the considerable research evidence indicating that the constructive management of conflict will increase the productivity of the classroom, teachers receive very little training in how to (a) use conflict for instructional purposes and (b) teach students the procedures and skills involved in constructive conflict management. In essence, teachers have been implicitly taught to avoid and suppress conflicts and to fear them when they burst forth and cannot be denied. Trying to suppress or deny conflicts only makes them worse.

Included in this book are practical exercises to teach students the strategies and procedures they need to be peacemakers. Teaching students to be peacemakers is not easy; it takes training, perseverance, and support. The training that has been planned to go with this book will provide a good start, but it may take a year or two of actual experience before teaching conflict procedures and skills becomes a natural part of your teaching. The results for you and your students are well worth your efforts.

It has taken us nearly 40 years to build the theory, research, and practical experience required to write this book. In the 1960's we began by reviewing the research, conducting our initial research studies, and training teachers in the classroom use of constructive conflict (Johnson, 1970). Since then our work has proliferated. Our writings on constructive conflict include **Reaching Out** (Johnson, 1972/2003), **Joining Together** (Johnson & F. Johnson, 1975/2003), and **Productive Organizational Conflict** (Tjosvold & Johnson, 1983). We have made a video to accompany this book. Related work in cooperative learning includes **Cooperation in the Classroom** (Johnson, Johnson, & Holubec, 1984/1998), **Learning Together and Alone** (Johnson & Johnson, 1975/1999) and **Circles of Learning** (Johnson, Johnson, & Holubec, 1984/2003). Yet the concept of constructively managed conflict is older than our work. Our roots reach back to Morton Deutsch and then to Kurt Lewin. We wish to acknowledge our indebtedness to the work of these social psychologists. We are also indebted to our two sisters, Edythe Johnson Holubec and Helen Johnson Misener, who have significantly contributed to our understanding of conflict. We wish to thank David W. Johnson Jr. for doing the boring computer stuff.

Many teachers have taught us procedures for training students to be peacemakers and have field tested our ideas in their classrooms with considerable success. We have been in their classrooms and we have taught beside them. We appreciate their ideas and celebrate their successes. We have had many talented and productive graduate students who have conducted research studies that have made significant contributions to our understanding of conflict. We feel privileged to have worked with them. We wish to thank Thomas Grummett for most of the drawings in this book. Some of the drawings were contributed by Nancy Waller to whom we are also grateful.

Johnson, D. W., & Johnson, R. (2005). **Teaching Students To Be Peacemakers** (4th Ed.). Edina, MN: Interaction Book Company, (952) 831-9500.

Chapter One: Teaching Students How To Resolve Conflicts Constructively

Introduction

A few years ago, two high school students made a plan to kill over 250 people in their school (Aronson, 2000). They prepared ninety-five explosive devices and placed them in strategic places. The first set of devices they placed a few miles from the school to explode first and distract police by keeping them busy away from the school. The second set was intended to explode in the cafeteria, killing a large number of students and terrorizing the rest to evacuate the school where they would be shot down as they exited. The third set was planted in the two students' cars and timed to explode after the police and paramedics had arrived at the school to create more chaos and casualties. Fortunately, the explosive devices failed to go off because of an electronic malfunction. The two students (Eric Harris and Dylan Klebold), however, entered Columbine High School in Littleton, Colorado on April 20, 1999 with assault weapons and explosives. They killed a teacher and thirteen of their fellow students, and then committed suicide. Twenty-three other students were hospitalized, some with severe wounds. It was the worst school massacre in American history. But it was not an isolated case. During a two and one-half year period, nine multi-victim school shootings took place in the United States.

In retrospect, trying to determine the reason why Harris and Klebold engaged in such extreme violence, Columbine students suggested that the two had suffered greatly by being severely taunted, mocked, humiliated, and excluded by the Columbine's in-group of students. One member of the in-group (i.e., a football player), in an interview a few weeks after the tragedy, stated:

> *"Columbine is a good clean place except for those rejects. Most kids didn't want them there. They were into witchcraft. They were into voodoo. Sure we teased them. But what do you expect with kids who come to school with weird hairdos and horns on their hats? . . . If you want to get rid of someone, usually you tease them. So the whole school would call them (names). . . ."*

(**Time**, Gibbs, N., & Roche, T. [1999, December 20, p. 154])

Clearly, the students at Columbine High School did not address their conflict with Harris and Klebold constructively. Conflicts are constructively resolved when all the individuals involved are satisfied with the resolution, the relationship among the individuals has improved (or at least not damaged), and the individuals' ability to resolve conflicts with each other in the future has been improved. At Columbine, however, members of the "in-

Johnson, D. W., & Johnson, R. (2005). **Teaching Students To Be Peacemakers** (4th Ed.). Edina, MN: Interaction Book Company, (952)831-9500.

group" considered taunting "outsiders" an appropriate thing to do. They believed that schoolmates who dress differently, wear their hair differently, or behave differently *deserve* to be teased, taunted, and rejected. The students at Columbine High School had never been taught how to manage conflicts constructively. The overall school environment, furthermore, seemed to encourage competitive, cliquish, exclusionary ways of resolving conflicts.

As destructive as this conflict at Columbine was, there are many examples of conflicts being constructively resolved. Two of the most influential English writers in the 20th Century were J. R. R. Tolkien and C. S. Lewis. Tolkien was a philologist who wrote great myths, such as **The Lord of the Rings**. Lewis was an historian who wrote theology (i.e., **The Four Loves)** and minor myths (i.e., the Narnia Series). Each is recognized as a genius. Both were professors at Oxford University at the same time and had intense conflicts with each other. Tolkein was a converted Catholic who believed deeply in Christianity. Lewis was an atheist, insisting that no god existed. He had been raised in Northern Ireland in a Protestant family who had taught him to hate Catholics. As a converted Catholic, Tolkien tended to challenge Protestantism. Lewis believed that although myths had great power, they were ultimately untrue. Myths are "lies and therefore worthless, even though breathed through silver," Lewis explained to Tolkien. "No," Tolkien said, "They are not lies." Tolkien believed that myths were the best way of conveying truths that would otherwise be inexpressible. Tolkien created the story of **The Hobit** for his children and developed **the Lord of the Rings** for his own and his children's amusement. Lewis insisted that Tolkein finalize the stories and publish them. Whenever these two men met conflicts would flair.

The result of these and other conflicts between the two men had profound effects. They became close friends, deeply involved in each other's work, and greatly influenced each other's thought and writing. Tolkein had a major part in converting Lewis to Christianity. It if were not for Tolkein, Lewis may never have become a Christian, let alone a great Christian theologian. Lewis convinced Tokein to write down and publish **The Hobit** and **The Lord of the Rings**. If it were not for Lewis, those books may never have been published. Tolkein once said, "*I wrote **the Lord of the Rings** to make Lewis a story out of **The Silmarillion**.*" Tolkein's books inspired Lewis to write the Narnia series. Without Tolkein, **The Lion, The Witch, and The Wardrobe** and the other books in the series may never have been written. The two become such close friends that Lewis made friendship one of the **Four Loves** (one of his most famous and influential books on Christian Theology). Their conflicts with each other were not only a source of their inspiration, hard work, and creativity, their conflicts literally changed the world.

Whether a conflict is resolved constructively and destructively is largely determined by (a) the participants having learned procedures for constructively managing conflicts, (b) the participants being skilled in the use of the procedures, and (c) the norms of the organization supporting the use of the procedures. Everything hinges on students learning the procedures for resolving conflicts constructively. Without the procedures, skills cannot be developed and the organizational norms can have no influence.

Johnson, D. W., & Johnson, R. (2005). **Teaching Students To Be Peacemakers** (4th Ed.). Edina, MN: Interaction Book Company, (952)831-9500.

The purposes of this book are to instruct teachers to (a) train students in the procedures they need to resolve their own and their schoolmates' conflicts constructively, (b) structure guided practice sessions so that students become skillful in the use of these procedures, and (c) ensure the school environment supports the use of these procedures. In this chapter the nature of the **Teaching Students To Be Peacemakers Program** (TSP) will be presented, the benefits for implementing the program will be discussed,

Power Of Education

The proverb, "The hand that rocks the cradle rules the world," is a metaphor for understanding that whoever educates children shapes the future. Children, youth, and young adults may be educated in ways that leaves them egocentric, socially immature, unable to form caring and committed relationships with others, and unconcerned about the well being of their society and the world. Or they may be educated in the systems of knowledge, social and emotional competencies, attitudes, and values that are needed to be contributing citizens and happy human beings concerned about the well being of society, empathetic and able to take the perspective of others, competent in managing their emotions and interactions with others constructively, and able to form and maintain meaningful and fulfilling relationships. If the latter is desired, one of the most important aspects of education is teaching children, adolescents, and young adults how to manage conflicts constructively.

Nature Of Training Students To Be Peacemakers Program

Establishing the comprehensive **Teaching Students To Be Peacemakers Program** involves three major components:

1. Creating a cooperative context.

2. Implementing the TSP Program.

3. Supplementing the TSP Program with the instructional use of academic controversies.

Step 1: Creating A Cooperative Context

The best way I know how to defeat an enemy is to make him a friend.

Abraham Lincoln

Johnson, D. W., & Johnson, R. (2005). **Teaching Students To Be Peacemakers** (4th Ed.). Edina, MN: Interaction Book Company, (952)831-9500.

The constructive resolution of conflict requires participants to recognize that their long-term relationship is more important than the result of any short-term conflict. They must recognize and value their long-term mutual interests and be invested in each other's long-term well-being. The first step, therefore, in managing conflicts constructively is to establish a cooperative environment. The more cooperative the relationships among the individuals involved, the more constructively conflicts will be managed. The easiest way to create a cooperative environment is to use cooperative learning procedures the majority of the day (Johnson, Johnson, & Holubec, 1998). This is discussed in Chapter Three.

Step 2: Implementing The TSP Program

The second step is to implement the Teaching Students To Be Peacemakers Program. Students are taught to recognize the potential positive nature of conflicts, master the five primary strategies for managing conflicts, master the problem-solving negotiation procedure, master the mediation procedure, and as a last resort seek out a teacher or administrator to arbitrate when negotiation and mediation have failed.

Recognizing The Potential Value Of Conflict

Students are taught to recognize that conflicts are inevitable, healthy, and potentially valuable. Rather than suppressing conflicts, conflicts should be faced and even encouraged given that all students, faculty, and staff are skilled in resolving conflicts constructively. It is a fallacy to try to eliminate all conflict from the school through suppression and avoidance. This is discussed in Chapter Two.

Mastering The Five Strategies For Managing Conflicts

Students are trained to keep two concerns in mind when resolving conflicts: (a) the importance of the goals they are trying to achieve and (b) the importance of the relationship with the other person. When those two concerns are present, there are five strategies available for managing a conflict: Withdrawal, forcing, smoothing, compromising, and problem-solving negotiations. In long-term, ongoing relationships maintaining a high quality relationship is usually more important than is achieving one's goals on any one issue. This is discussed in Chapter Four.

Teaching Students The Problem-Solving Negotiation Procedure

Students must be taught how to negotiate constructive resolutions to their conflicts. When conflicts of interests occur, settlements must be negotiated. Broadly, there are two negotiation procedures: Win-lose and problem solving. In long-term, ongoing relationships the problem-solving negotiation problem tends to be more effective. Students master the steps of problem solving negotiations, practice them with their classmates, and use them in actual conflicts. This is discussed in Chapter Five.

1 : 4

Johnson, D. W., & Johnson, R. (2005). **Teaching Students To Be Peacemakers** (4th Ed.). Edina, MN: Interaction Book Company, (952)831-9500.

An important aspect of negotiating to solve a problem is the management of anger. Like conflict, it is not the presence of anger that is the issue, it is how anger is expressed and reacted to. This is discussed in Chapter Six.

Teaching Students To Mediate Schoolmates' Conflicts

When problem-solving negotiations fail, students must be able to mediate a constructive resolution to schoolmates' conflicts. A mediator listens carefully to both sides and helps the disputants move effectively through each step of the problem-solving negotiation sequence in order to reach an agreement that both believe is fair, just, and workable. Mediating schoolmates' conflicts teaches students the importance of each step of the negotiation procedure as well as many other important lessons. All students, therefore, are given the opportunity to be a mediator. This is discussed in Chapter Seven.

Implementing Peer Mediation Program

When students have received the initial negotiation and mediation training, the peer mediation program is implemented in the school. Each day pairs of students are chosen to serve as class or school mediators. The responsibility is rotated so that all students serve as mediator an equal amount of time. The implementation procedure is discussed in Chapter Eight.

Refining And Extending Students' Negotiation And Mediation Skills

Each week further lessons on using negotiation and mediation procedures are taught to refine and upgrade students' skills. Whenever possible, the procedures are integrated into academic lessons. Overlearning the procedures is emphasized so that students go through the procedures many, many times. Students can continue to sharpen and refine their skills in using the problem-solving and mediation procedures when guided practice is incorporated into academic lessons and integrated into the fabric of school life. The conflict resolution training is a 12 year spiral curriculum so that the procedures are taught every year at a more sophisticated and complex level. This is discussed in Chapter Eight.

Arbitrating Students' Conflicts

When students are unable to negotiate an agreement and mediation has failed, a faculty member or administrator may arbitrate the conflict. An arbitrator carefully listens to both sides and makes a decision. This is discussed in Chapter Eight.

1 : 5

Johnson, D. W., & Johnson, R. (2005). **Teaching Students To Be Peacemakers** (4th Ed.). Edina, MN: Interaction Book Company, (952)831-9500.

Step 3: Instructional Use Of Academic Controversies

It's best that we should not all think alike. It's difference of opinion that makes horse races.

Mark Twain

The TSP Program optimally is supplemented by the instructional use of the constructive controversy procedure. Intellectual conflicts can be utilized to increase the quantity and quality of academic learning (Johnson & Johnson, 1979, 1989, 1995b, 2003). Engaging in an academic controversy tends to increase student achievement and retention, critical thinking, use of higher-level reasoning strategies, motivation to learn, and conflict skills. Controversies promote conceptual conflicts that are resolved through engaging in what Aristotle called deliberate discourse (i.e., the discussion of the advantages and disadvantages of proposed actions) aimed at synthesizing novel solutions (i.e., creative problem solving). Teaching students how to engage in the controversy process begins with randomly assigning students to heterogeneous cooperative learning groups of four members. The groups are given an issue on which to write a report and pass a test. Each cooperative group is divided into two pairs. One pair is given the con-position on the issue and the other pair is given the pro-position. The cooperative goal of reaching a consensus on the issue (by synthesizing the best reasoning from both sides) and writing a quality group report is highlighted. Students then (a) research and prepare the best case for their assigned positions, (b) present the positions, (c) engage in an open discussion in which they criticize the opposing position while defending their own, (d) reverse perspectives and present the best case for the opposing position, and (e) arrive at a synthesis including the best reasoned judgment of the students involved. Engaging in academic controversies demonstrates the value of conflict, promotes positive attitudes toward conflict, and promotes the skills used in negotiation and mediation.

Benefits Of Conflict Resolution Training

There are many reasons why all students need to be taught to manage their conflicts constructively. Learning how to be a peacemaker benefits students, the school, the students' families, the community, and the society. There are so many benefits, only a few can be discussed here.

Personal Benefits

When students become peacemakers, they improve their psychological adjustment, gain a developmental advantage, achieve their goals more often, achieve higher academically, become engaged in more positive and supportive relationships with peers, and become more successful in future career and personal life.

Johnson, D. W., & Johnson, R. (2005). **Teaching Students To Be Peacemakers** (4th Ed.). Edina, MN: Interaction Book Company, (952)831-9500.

Psychological Adjustment

The more constructively students manage their conflicts, the happier they will tend to be, the more optimistic their view of the future, the higher their self-esteem, the lower the stress levels in their life, and the greater their sense of personal efficacy. They tend to be more assertive, have more self-control, are more able to communicate effectively, and are more able to cooperate with others. Learning how to manage conflicts constructively tends to increase prosocial behavior that enhances students' relationships and popularity while decreasing anti-social, inappropriate behavior (such as bullying, teasing, excluding others, challenging the authority of teachers and administrators).

Developmental Advantage

Learning how to resolve conflicts constructively, and being skilled in doing so, gives students a developmental advance over those who never learned how to do so. The developmental advantage includes positive effects on actualizing one's potential, improving the quality of one's relationships, and enhancing life success. Individuals skilled in resolving conflicts constructively tend to make and keep more friends, and be more liked by and popular with peers. They tend to be more employable, be more successful in their careers, have a more fulfilling family life, be better parents, and better able to maintain life-long friends. Teaching students to be peacemakers may be one of the most valuable competencies that can be given to students, benefiting them throughout their lives.

Achieve Goals

The more constructively students resolve their conflicts, the more likely they are to achieve their goals and the more likely other individuals will support their efforts. When students manage their conflicts destructively, the other individuals will tend to sabotage, obstruct, and interfere with the students attempts to achieve their goals.

Academic Achievement

When the Peacemaker Training is integrated into the academic curriculum, student achievement tends to increase for at least two reasons. The first is that the problem-solving negotiation procedure tends to act as a cognitive framework for processing information and learning and retaining academic content. The problem-solving negotiation framework provides the type of step-by-step guidance that helps students more thoroughly and effectively analyze, synthesize, evaluate, and remember academic material. A cognitive framework is created when students organize academic content into what each side of the dramatic, historical, or scientific conflict wants and feels, the specific interests underlying each side's position, and the alternative ways in which the conflict may be resolved so that both sides achieve their goals and improve the quality of their relationship with each other. The second reason the integration of the Peacemaker Training into

1 : 7

Johnson, D. W., & Johnson, R. (2005). **Teaching Students To Be Peacemakers** (4th Ed.). Edina, MN: Interaction Book Company, (952)831-9500.

academic units increases achievement is through the impact of role playing and simulations, which tend to increase understanding of the characters and positions being portrayed, change attitudes toward the issues being discussed, and facilitate the long-term retention of the material being studied. As one high school student who participated in the curriculum-integrated Peacemakers training wrote:

> *We have been studying conflict managing and negotiating along with World Civilization. Now at first, I was a little skeptical about the whole thing, but after all kinds of practice and studying and applying to real-life historical situations, I came to the conclusion that these steps could really work in real life. The only problems are that not many other people know them or even care enough to use them. To put yourself in the other's shoes can be a great way to solve conflict. I really think that these steps should be taught to all kids. I really believe that they could be used to stop even wars. (Stevahn, Johnson, Johnson, & Schultz, 2002, pp. 326-327)*

Positive Peer Influences

The more skillful students are in resolving conflicts constructively and working with others cooperatively, the more positive their relationships will be. There is considerable evidence that positive peer relationships are the keys to psychological health, cognitive and social development, prosocial attitudes and values, and many other important aspects of productive and successful lives (Hartup, 1976; Johnson, 1981). Resolving conflicts constructively, furthermore, tends to create more supportive relationships (both personal support and academic support) with both peers and teachers. Having peers and teachers who will support students on a personal level and provide the help and assistance they need to be successful in school tends to increase students' productivity and achievement, physical and psychological health, ability to cope with stress and adversity, and many other positive outcomes.

Appropriate Aggression In Relationships

Aggressiveness is not necessarily destructive or "bad" behavior. Aggressiveness in achieving goals is often desirable and admirable. Social development requires the engagement in some squabbles with peers in order to learn how to navigate life's inevitable confrontations. Peer conflict contributes to children's development and represents an important form of social interaction (Rende & Killen, 1992; Ross & Conant, 1992). A certain amount of conflict among children and among adolescents is not only expected, but is critical for learning how to get along with others, how to interact appropriately, and how to have fun. Conflicts are maturing, and it is very common for children and adolescents to say and do things that may be hurtful as they are learning what is acceptable in relationships and what is not, and where the lines are between entertaining repartee and hurtful teasing. It is important for children and adolescents to learn to negotiate these conflicts without adult intervention.

Johnson, D. W., & Johnson, R. (2005). **Teaching Students To Be Peacemakers** (4th Ed.). Edina, MN: Interaction Book Company, (952)831-9500.

Career Success

Learning how to engage in problem-solving negotiations and peer mediation may especially impact later employability and career success. Individuals who are skillful in managing conflicts may be first to be hired and last to be laid off. A recent survey of vice presidents and personnel directors of 100 of the nation's 1,000 largest corporations found that the people who manage America's leading corporations spend over four working weeks a year dealing with the problems caused by employees who cannot resolve their conflicts with each other. The American Management Association reported that about 24 percent of manager's time is spent dealing with conflict. School and hospital administrators, mayors, and city managers report that conflict resolution commands nearly 49 percent of their attention. Individuals who are skillful in managing conflicts may be promoted to higher management positions because competencies in conflict resolution become more and more important the higher the position in the corporation.

Meaning And Sense Of Accomplishment

Mediating classmates' conflicts may give students a sense of purpose and meaning in life. Helping others work through their problems often results in feelings of meaning and purpose that are unavailable in most of school life. Being a mediator is often described as a "transformative" experience in which individuals become more prosocially oriented and academically oriented.

Conclusions

Learning the problem-solving negotiation and peer mediation procedures and thereby being able to resolve conflicts constructively tends to affect positively students' interpersonal and intergroup relations throughout the rest of their life, increase their appropriate behavior and prosocial actions while decreasing their inappropriate behavior and antisocial actions, increase their academic achievement, and promote their career success. By resulting in such personal benefits, the Peacemaker Training tends to transform schools into optimal interpersonal and intellectual learning communities.

School Benefits

Promoting students' competencies in managing conflicts has positive benefits for the school and reduces the severity of many problems. Teaching students how to manage conflicts constructively can decrease discipline referrals, bullying, social rejection, social withdrawal, and the dropout rate. The more positively students manage conflicts, the higher will tend to be their academic achievement, positive attitudes toward school and learning, positiveness of the classroom and school climate, and the overall quality of life within the school community.

Johnson, D. W., & Johnson, R. (2005). **Teaching Students To Be Peacemakers** (4th Ed.). Edina, MN: Interaction Book Company, (952)831-9500.

Discipline Problems

The more competent students are in managing conflicts, the fewer the discipline problems faculty and administrators may have to deal with. Teaching is different from what it used to be. Fifty years ago the main disciplinary problems in schools were running in halls, talking out of turn, and chewing gum. Today's transgressions include physical and verbal violence, incivility to the teacher and schoolmates, taunting and teasing schoolmates, cheating, rowdiness, truancy, cutting class, being late for class, and, in some schools, drug abuse, physical fighting, robbery, assault, and murder. The result is that many teachers spend an inordinate amount of time and energy dealing with conflicts, discipline problems, general incivility, and lack of motivation to learn. Many teachers complain about the "tyranny of the few" as considerable time is taken away from instruction to deal with recurrent offenders. A few students can create a distracting and disrespectful atmosphere. When students manage their conflicts poorly, aggression tends to result, which is usually punished with detentions, suspensions, and expulsions. Many teachers consider leaving the profession because of intolerable student behavior. Many discipline problems are prevented when students are taught how to resolve their conflicts constructively.

Bullying

The more skilled students are in managing conflicts constructively, the lower will tend to be the frequency of bullying. **Bullying** occurs when a student or group of students repeatedly engages in behavior that is intended to harm or disturb a less powerful schoolmate. The bullying can be physical (hitting), verbal (teasing, name calling), or psychological (shunning). Bullying is a serious issue in many schools. A nationwide study found that bullying affects nearly one of every three U.S. children in sixth through tenth grades. Children who reported being bullied tended to be lonely and had difficulty making friends; as adults they tend to be more prone to depression and low self-esteem. Bullies were more likely to have poor grades, smoke and drink alcohol, and engage in criminal behavior as adults. Males were more apt to resort to hits, slaps, or pushing, while bullying for females more typically entailed making sexual comments, spreading rumors, and social ostracism. Social ostracism can have serious negative psychological consequences. Verbal taunting often focused on the victim's looks or speech, as opposed to race or religion. Teaching students how to manage conflicts constructively will tend to reduce the incidence of bullying and change students' responses to being bullied.

If bullies do not learn how to manage conflicts in constructive ways, their future is not bright. Bullies tend to increasingly get in more serious trouble (Aronson, 2000). By their mid twenties, for example, males who were bullies in elementary school were convicted of at least one felony. One-third of the males who were bullies in middle school were convicted of three or more crimes, often violent ones, and had already done prison time. It could be concluded that allowing a student to bully others is tantamount to giving aggressive children training for a life of crime.

1 : 10

Johnson, D. W., & Johnson, R. (2005). **Teaching Students To Be Peacemakers** (4th Ed.). Edina, MN: Interaction Book Company, (952)831-9500.

Social Rejection

The more competent students are in resolving conflicts constructively, the less likely they are to be socially rejected. Students are often socially rejected if they engage in coercive, bullying, or antisocial behavior or if they act in ways that are outside peer group norms. There is consistent research that indicates socially rejected students show poor academic achievement, spend less time on task, tend to be deficit in academic skills, and tend not to complete homework assignments (Patterson, DeBaryshe, & Ramsey, 1989). They may, however, join a deviant peer group which encourages their antisocial behavior.

Social Withdrawal

The more competent students are in resolving conflicts constructively, the less likely they will be isolated or withdrawn from the other people in the school. **Social engagement** involves positive relationships with other students, faculty, and staff. People who live in social isolation are very rarely happy. Social isolation may result from withdrawal from relationships due to shyness or other causes, or social ostracism due to schoolmates withdrawing from and avoiding interaction with a student. While both forms of social isolation can have serious psychological consequences, social ostracism may especially have negative consequences. Social isolation cues a basic human drive: the need to belong. Belonging is a fundamental human motivation that increases individuals' chances for survival and well being. People need frequent personal contacts with others and positive interpersonal relationships marked by stability, emotional concern and continuity. Being isolated and feeling lonely contribute powerfully to problems in psychological and physical well-being. While the psychological consequences include depression, anxiety, and anger (resulting in extreme behaviors such as suicide and violence towards others), the physical consequences are as detrimental as such factors as cigarette smoking, obesity, and high-blood pressure. Constructive conflict management can contribute to enhancing the relationships students need to develop in order to stay in and succeed in school.

Academic Engagement

The more competent students are in resolving conflicts constructively, the more engaged students will be with the academic program. The more students are engaged in the school, the more effective instruction and the quality of school life tend to be. **Academic engagement** involves being interested in what one is learning and being committed to completing academic assignments. Not all destructive conflicts are characterized by anger and aggression. There are quiet conflicts characterized by withdrawal and disengagement from school life. Disengagement is reflected in tardiness, class cutting, and truancy, all of which may lead to suspension, which results in further disengagement. When conflicts are managed constructively, however, students (and faculty) tend to become more engaged academically, increasing student and faculty success and the success of the school.

Johnson, D. W., & Johnson, R. (2005). **Teaching Students To Be Peacemakers** (4th Ed.). Edina, MN: Interaction Book Company, (952)831-9500.

Dropping Out Of School

The more competent students are in resolving conflicts constructively, the lower the dropout rate will tend to be. Dropping out of school is less a matter of indifference or having something better to do than it is of feeling angry, victimized, disappointed, and failure (all of which are aspects of destructively managed conflicts). A high school student drops out every nine seconds according to the Children's Defense Fund (2002). If these students do not eventually graduate from high school and go on to post-secondary education of some sort, they will likely end up as part of the working poor, in prison, or on welfare. Every student who does **not** drop out is a success for the school and may save society considerable resources. Teaching students to manage their conflicts constructively will tend to decrease the frequency of students' dropping out.

Conclusions

The frequency of destructive conflicts among students and the increasing severity of the violence make managing conflicts very costly in terms of the faculty, administrator, and student time and energy. Considerable instructional, administrative, and learning efforts are lost. In order to make schools orderly and peaceful places in which high quality education can take place, conflicts must be managed constructively without physical or verbal violence. This requires that all students are trained in how to manage conflicts constructively.

Societal Benefits

There are numerous advantages for our society if all children, adolescents, and young adults are trained in how to engage in problem-solving negotiations and mediation of others' conflicts. When citizens are skilled in resolving conflicts constructively, they have the potential to be more productive and responsible, and the society will tend to be more cohesive with more cooperative relations among citizens and groups. Organizations will function more smoothly and effectively. Families will be more cohesive and caring. Fewer citizens will be involved in legal disputes. There are so many benefits to society that it is impossible to list them all here.

Nature Of Conflict Resolution

Conflict resolution focuses on a set of procedures and skills designed to assist individuals and groups in better dealing with the conflicts that arise in all aspects of their lives. Conflict resolution does not focus on eliminating conflict. Conflicts are both inevitable (i.e., they occur no matter how hard people try to avoid them) and potentially constructive (i.e., they can have positive outcomes). Conflict resolution deals with:

1 : 12

Johnson, D. W., & Johnson, R. (2005). **Teaching Students To Be Peacemakers** (4th Ed.). Edina, MN: Interaction Book Company, (952)831-9500.

Conflict Resolution

1. The antecedents to conflict (i.e., the barriers to resolving conflict and the events that trigger conflicts).

2. The issues the conflict is about. Issues may be classified as being of low or high intensity. **Low intensity issues** are not very important to the disputants or are easily managed, such as wanting to use a book someone else is using or needing to borrow a pencil day after day. **High intensity issues** are very important to the disputants and are difficult to manage, such as spreading rumors about someone or bullying. Issues may also be classified as involving morality (such as physical harm and individual rights) and social order (such as rules for activities).

3. The social context in which the conflict occurs. There are two types of contexts: competitive and cooperative. A competitive context tends to result in destructive management of conflicts based on a desire to win. A cooperative context tends to result in constructive management of conflicts based on a desire to maximize joint outcomes. The context includes interested audiences such as peers, faculty and staff, parents, and community members. Audiences may be passive (thus allowing destructive conflicts to continue) or active (thus either encouraging the conflict or intervening to ensure that the conflict is managed constructively).

4. The strategies and related procedures used to manage conflicts. Strategies typically may be classified as withdrawing, forcing, smoothing, compromising, and problem solving (see Chapter Four). In addition, students may seek faculty intervention to resolve a conflict. Each of these strategies is reflected in a procedure that includes both physical and verbal actions. The strategy used may determine the outcome of the conflict. Conciliatory behaviors are associated with peaceful outcomes and with continued interaction following the conflict. Physical domination often leads to ending the interaction. Violence is one type of the forcing strategy for resolving conflicts. When physical or verbal violence is used to manage a conflict, it becomes high-intensity, especially if it involves a weapon. Violence prevention programs focus on creating conditions in which violence cannot occur (such as eliminating all weapons, increasing surveillance, increasing penalties) so that students will resolve their conflicts using more constructive strategies.

5. The skills required to engage in the strategies and procedures effectively. Skills may include communication skills, cognitive reasoning skills, perspective taking, trust-building, and so forth.

6. The outcomes or consequences of the conflict. Outcomes may be classified as being (a) positive and constructive or (b) negative and destructive. Alternatively, outcomes may be classified as being adult-imposed or participant determined. Participants may leave the situation unresolved (they simply drop the issue and withdraw, finding alternative activities), give one participant what he or she wants at the expense of the other participants (this may involve either submission or

Johnson, D. W., & Johnson, R. (2005). **Teaching Students To Be Peacemakers** (4th Ed.). Edina, MN: Interaction Book Company, (952)831-9500.

kindness), compromise, or derive a mutually agreed-on solution achieved through problem-solving negotiations.

Table 2.1: Components of Conflict Resolution

Antecedents	Issues	Context
Barriers To Resolving	Low Intensity	Competitive
Triggering Events	High Intensity	Cooperative
	Morality (Physical Harm and Individual Rights)	Audiences
	Social Order (Rules for Activities)	

Strategies	Skills	Outcomes
Withdrawing	Communication	Positive, Constructive
Forcing	Reasoning	Negative, Destructive
Smoothing	Perspective-Taking	
Compromising	Trust-Building	
Problem Solving		

Issues often determine the strategies disputants use. When the issue is control over a physical object (both children want the same toy), for example, the strategy may be physical resistance (both children try to pull the toy away from the other), although as children grow older they begin to use verbal protest more frequently, compromise, and negotiation (Ross & Conant, 1992).

Two Purposes Of Conflict Resolution Programs

There are two central purposes for implementing conflict resolution programs in schools. The **immediate purpose** is to make schools safe places where students relate to each other in constructive ways and can learn. The **long-term purpose** is to socialize children, adolescents, and young adults into the competencies and attitudes they need to resolve conflicts constructively for the rest of their lives. The intent is to develop an adult who can

Johnson, D. W., & Johnson, R. (2005). **Teaching Students To Be Peacemakers** (4th Ed.). Edina, MN: Interaction Book Company, (952)831-9500.

resolve conflicts constructively in career, family, job, neighborhood, and societal settings. The two purposes are complementary. To achieve both purposes, children, adolescents, and young adults must be:

1. Exposed to positive models for constructive conflict management. This means that faculty and staff need to learn and consistently use the procedures for managing conflicts constructively. In addition, during academic lessons (especially in language arts and social studies) exemplary models of resolving conflicts constructively should be pointed out and discussed.

2. Taught the procedures and skills required to manage conflicts constructively. Students need to be given the tools to manage conflicts constructively.

3. Given the opportunity and time to resolve their conflicts without adult intervention. Letting students resolve conflicts on their own promotes more healthy social and cognitive development than does adult intervention in which adult-generated resolutions are imposed (Killen & Turiel, 1991; Ramsey, 1991). This is important, as traditionally, many teachers have (a) tried to suppress conflict among students out of a belief that conflicts are inherently destructive or (b) quickly intervene in students' conflicts to ensure that the conflicts are short lived and do not escalate.

When students are exposed to positive models, given the tools to manage conflicts constructively, and given the freedom to do so, classrooms become places where destructive conflicts are prevented and constructive conflicts are encouraged, structured, and utilized to improve the quality of instruction and classroom life. In addition, students tend to master the competencies and inculcate the attitudes they need to deal constructively with conflict for the rest of their lives, thus significantly improving the quality of their lives, the quality of the lives of those they work and live with, and the quality of life throughout their society and world.

Approaches To Conflict Resolution Training

Conflict resolution training may be classified as taking a cadre approach or a total school (i.e., comprehensive) approach. Both can be effective, and both have their strengths and weaknesses.

The **cadre approach** involves training a small number of students to be peer mediators. The goal is to provide well-trained peer mediators to help schoolmates resolve conflicts more constructively. This approach is based on the assumption that a few specially trained students can defuse and resolve constructively the interpersonal conflicts taking place among members of the student body. The training of a cadre of mediators may consist of a one or two day workshop or a semester-long class. The cadre approach is typically less time consuming and less costly than is the total school approach.

Johnson, D. W., & Johnson, R. (2005). **Teaching Students To Be Peacemakers** (4th Ed.). Edina, MN: Interaction Book Company, (952)831-9500.

The **total school or comprehensive approach** emphasizes training every student, faculty member, and staff member in the school (and often parents) to manage conflicts constructively. The goal of the comprehensive approach is to ensure that all members of the school community skillfully use the same procedures for resolving conflicts. The assumption is that every student in the school needs to learn how to manage conflicts constructively and help schoolmates to do likewise. The training may extend over several years and the use of problem-solving negotiations and peer mediation may be integrated into the curriculum, the school's mission statement, and the school's policies and procedures. Adult modeling of effective conflict management is emphasized. The total school approach is more time consuming and costly than is the cadre, but is generally more effective in achieving the two objectives of creating a safe school environment and socializing students into the attitudes and competencies they need to resolve conflicts constructively for the rest of their lives. The **Teaching Students To Be Peacemakers Program** is an example of this approach.

Planning For Implementation Of The TSP Program

Over the past 35 years, preschool, primary, intermediate, middle-school, high-school, and university faculty members and administrators have been trained in how to implement the **TSP Program**. The training has occurred throughout North America and in Central and South America, Europe, the Middle East, Asia, the Pacific Rim, and Africa. There are two long-term training goals. The first is for teachers to use the TSP program with (a) durable fidelity so that the program maintains its effectiveness and (b) appropriate flexibility so the program can be adapted to changing conditions. The second training goal is to institutionalize the program in the school and district.

Implementing the Teaching Students To Be Peacemakers Program in your school involves:

1. Clarifying the goals for the program: While there are two general goals for the **TSP Program** (make schools safe places where students can learn and relate to each other in constructive ways and socialize students into the competencies and attitudes they need to resolve conflicts constructively for the rest of their lives), members of the school community may wish to set more specific school or classroom goals. The goals may include (a) reducing fights, bullying, teasing, and social rejection of stigmatized students, (b) reducing expulsions, and suspensions, (c) reducing the amount of time faculty and staff spend dealing with conflicts among students or discipline issues, or (d) enhancing the quality of life within the school community by preventing violence and increasing the respect, honesty, and good citizenship of everyone involved. To get the most out of its effort to implement a conflict resolution program, faculty and staff must first identify their specific goals and objectives for the program.

2. Creating a planning team: A planning team or advisory group may be organized to implement the program goals and objectives and to coordinate the design and

implementation of the school's TSP Program. The team may include representatives from all parts of the school community (i.e., teachers, administrators, students, parents).

3. Conducting a needs assessment: A needs assessment may focus on the types of conflicts that occur in the school, how the conflicts are managed by students, faculty, and staff, and the training and resources needed to ensure conflicts are managed constructively. The needs assessment can be conducted through surveys or small group discussions. Input from all parts of the school community is recommended to ensure that the program meets the school's current needs and is consistent with the school's mission and overall improvement plans.

4. Identifying the budget for the program: The resources available for program design and implementation need to be identified. Funding and other resources affect the program design (i.e., who is trained, how much training can be offered, and who conducts the training).

5. Developing an action plan: An action plan explains how the program will operate to meet its goals and objectives. The plan usually includes (a) the tasks or steps that need to be taken to implement the program, (b) the individuals responsible for carrying out the tasks, and (c) a time line for completing each task.

6. Implementing the plan: The plan is implemented, the effectiveness of the implementation is assessed, and the implementation is modified accordingly.

Typical Action Plan

A typical action plan includes a combination of bottom-up and top-down strategies. First, an awareness session is given for all staff members so that everyone shares a common understanding of the TSP Program. Interested teachers are then asked to volunteer to participate in the program. The best teachers who volunteer are included in the training and they are given considerable support and assistance to ensure their implementation is successful. If the initial implementation efforts fail, the entire faculty may be inoculated against the training. The initial teachers trained may be used as demonstration sites for other faculty who wish to see the TSP Program in action.

The first year, teachers who volunteer (Cohort One) receive four to six days of training (either distributed throughout the school year or may be a multi-day intensive session) in the TSP Program and meet weekly in colleagial teaching teams to help each other implement what they have learned. Team members and the trainers provide support by giving demonstration lessons, helping members' prepare lessons, observing implementation efforts, providing feedback, and integrating the TSP training into ongoing academic curriculum units. Administrators may encourage and support faculty member's implementation of the Program.

Johnson, D. W., & Johnson, R. (2005). **Teaching Students To Be Peacemakers** (4th Ed.). Edina, MN: Interaction Book Company, (952)831-9500.

The second year, a new group of teachers (Cohort Two) receive the initial TSP training. Cohort One teachers (a) act as mentors and provide help and assistance, (b) continue their weekly colleagial teaching team meetings to help each other improve their implementation of the TSP program, and (c) receive a 30 to 40 hour training in cooperative learning. They meet with the trainers periodically to solve implementation programs and plan advanced training activities for their students.

The third year, a new set of teachers (Cohort Three) receives the initial TSP training with the help and assistance of the teachers trained the first two years. The most interested teachers from Cohort One enter a leadership training program focusing on how to (a) conduct the TSP training program, (b) give inclassroom help and support to teachers being trained, and (c) organize and facilitate the functioning of colleagial teaching teams. These teachers then conduct the above sequence of training for their own and other schools in the district. In addition, the Cohort One teachers receive the academic controversy training. The Cohort Two teachers receive the cooperative learning training.

This sequence continues until all teachers in a school and district have been trained.

TSP As A Classroom Management Program

Discipline problems are by definition disruptions to the overall cooperative nature of the school (Johnson & Johnson, 2005). Typically, most discipline problems involve either conflicts among students or conflicts between students and (a) teachers or (b) standards concerning appropriate and acceptable conduct. Approaches to manage such disruptions may be placed on a continuum. At one end are discipline programs based on teacher administrated external rewards and punishments that control and manage student behavior. Faculty control and manage student behavior. At the other end are programs based on teaching students the competencies and skills required to regulate their own and their schoolmates' behavior. Students control and manage their own and their schoolmates' behavior. Peer mediation programs anchor the self-regulation end of the continuum.

Most discipline programs are clustered at the adult administering external rewards and punishment end of the continuum. Thus, it is up to the staff to monitor student behavior, determine whether it is or is not within the bounds of acceptability, and force students to terminate inappropriate actions. When the infractions are minor, the staff often arbitrate ("*The pencil belongs to Mary, Jane be quiet and sit down.*") or cajole students to end hostilities ("*Let's forgive and forget. Shake hands and be friends.*"). If that does not work, students may be sent to the principal's office for a stern but cursory lecture about the value of getting along, a threat that if the conflict continues more drastic action will ensue, and a final admonition to "*Go and fight no more.*" If that does not work, time-out rooms may be used. Eventually, some students are expelled from school. Such programs teach studen that adults or authority figures are needed to resolve conflicts. The programs cost a great deal in instructional and administrative time and work only as long as students are under

1 : 18

Johnson, D. W., & Johnson, R. (2005). **Teaching Students To Be Peacemakers** (4th Ed.). Edina, MN: Interaction Book Company, (952)831-9500.

surveillance. This approach does not empower students. Adults may become more skillful in how to control students, but students do not learn the procedures, skills and attitudes required to resolve conflicts constructively in their personal lives at home, in school, at work, and in the community.

Figure 1.2: Continuum Of Classroom Management Programs

Competition	Cooperation
Instruction Emphasizes Direct Teaching, Lecturing Management Programs Emphasize Faculty Administrated External Rewards And Punishments	Instruction Emphasizes Learning Groups, Active Engagement, Social Construction Management Programs Emphasize Teaching Students The Competencies They Need To Regulate Own And Schoolmates' Behavior

1—2—3—4—5—6—7—8—9—10

Disciplinary Interventions Include Faculty Being A Police Officer, Judge, Jury, And Executioner; Faculty Monitor Student Behavior, Judge Its Appropriateness, Decide Which Consequence To Administer, And Give The Reward Or Punishment	Disciplinary Interventions Include Strengthening Five Basic Elements of Cooperation. Students Monitor The Appropriateness Of Their Own And Their Groupmates' Behavior, Assess Its Effectivene And Decide How To Behave.

At the other end of the continuum are programs aimed at teaching students self-responsibility and self-regulation. **Self-regulation** is the abilities to (a) act in socially approved ways in the absence of external monitors and (b) initiate and cease activities according to situational demands. Self-regulation is a central and significant hallmark of cognitive and social development. To regulate their behavior, students must monitor their own behavior, assess situations and take other people's perspectives to make judgments as to which behaviors are appropriate, and engage in the desired behavior. Students have to monitor, modify, refine, and change how they behave in order to act appropriately and competently. If students are to learn how to regulate their behavior they must have opportunities to (a) make decisions regarding how to behave and (b) follow through on the decisions made. Allowing students to be joint architects in matters affecting them promotes feelings of control and autonomy.

IMP.

Summary

One of the most important aspects of education is teaching students how to manage conflicts constructively. The procedure for doing so consists of (a) creating a cooperative

Johnson, D. W., & Johnson, R. (2005). **Teaching Students To Be Peacemakers** (4th Ed.). Edina, MN: Interaction Book Company, (952)831-9500.

context, (b) implementing the Teaching Students To Be Peacemakers Program, and (c) supplementing the TSP Program with the use of academic controversies. The TSP Program involves teaching students to recognize the value of conflict, master the five strategies for managing conflicts, learn the problem-solving negotiation procedure, learn the peer mediation procedure, implementing the program, and refine and extend their negotiation and mediation skills throughout the school year. The personal benefits for the students include improved psychological adjustment, a developmental advantage, frequent goal achievement, higher achievement, more positive and supportive relationships, greater career success, and a happier personal life. The benefits for the school include fewer discipline problems, less bullying, less social withdrawal and academic disengagement, more academic engagement, and fewer dropouts. The societal benefits include having a citizenry skilled in managing conflicts constructively.

Conflict resolution deals with the antecedents to conflict, the issues, the social context, the strategies and related procedures, the skills required to engage in the procedures, and the outcomes. The purposes of conflict resolution programs include making schools safe places where students relate to each other in constructive ways and socializing students into the competencies and attitudes they need to resolve conflict constructively for the rest of their lives. Achieving these purposes requires that students be exposed to positive models, taught the required procedures and skills, and given the opportunity and time to resolve their conflicts without adult intervention. While both the cadre and the whole-school approaches are effective, teaching all students in the school to manage conflicts has considerable advantages. Planning to implement the TSP Program involves clarifying the school goals for the Program, creating a planning team, conducting a needs assessment, identifying the budget for the Program, developing an action plan, and implementing the plan. Finally, the TSP Program may be viewed as a classroom management program emphasizing teaching students the competencies they need to be self-regulating.

1 : 20

Johnson, D. W., & Johnson, R. (2005). **Teaching Students To Be Peacemakers** (4th Ed.). Edina, MN: Interaction Book Company, (952)831-9500.

CREATIVE CONFLICT CONTRACT

Write down your major learnings from reading this chapter and participating in training session one. Then write down how you plan to implement each learning. Share what you learned and your implementation plans with your base group. Listen carefully to their major learnings and implementation plans. You may modify your own plans on the basis of what you have learned from your groupmates. Volunteer one thing you can do to help each groupmate with his or her implementation plans. Utilize the help groupmates offer to you. Sign each member's plans to seal the contract.

MAJOR LEARNINGS	IMPLEMENTATION PLANS

Date: _____ Participant's Signature: _____

Signatures Of Group Members: _____

_____

1 : 21

Johnson, D. W., & Johnson, R. (2005). **Teaching Students To Be Peacemakers** (4th Ed.). Edina, MN: Interaction Book Company, (952)831-9500.

CREATIVE CONFLICT PROGRESS REPORT

Name: _____ School: _____

Subject Area: _____ Grade: _____

Date	Lesson	Successes	Problems

Describe Critical Or Interesting Incidents:

Johnson, D. W., & Johnson, R. (2005). **Teaching Students To Be Peacemakers** (4th Ed.). Edina, MN: Interaction Book Company, (952)831-9500.

Chapter Two: The Positive Nature Of Conflict

The Nature Of Constructive Conflict

In his play, **King Lear**, Shakespeare describes a conflict in which King Lear (who has three daughters) decides to give his wealth and kingdom before he dies to the daughters who love him. So he holds a public ceremony in which he asks his three daughters to show how much they love him. The two oldest daughters, who do not love their father, profess deep abiding love for him and flatter him elaborately. The youngest daughter, who does love her father, refuses to participate, saying simply that she loves him as much as any daughter would love her father. In this conflict, the father gets angry because the younger daughter will not flatter him to get her inheritance. The youngest daughter is angry because she thinks her father is a fool to believe flattery under such circumstances. How they resolve their conflict will largely determine the course of the rest of their lives. If you were King Lear, or if you were his youngest daughter, Cordelia, what would you do to make sure the conflict had constructive outcomes?

Conflicts are inevitable, healthy, and potentially valuable. Rather than avoiding conflicts, individuals should face and even encourage conflicts, given that all students, faculty, and staff are skilled in resolving conflicts constructively. It is misguided to try to eliminate all conflict from the school through suppression and avoidance. In order to create a conflict positive school, educators must understand:

1. What is and is not a conflict.

2. How to determine whether a conflict is resolved constructively or destructively.

3. The positive outcomes of constructively managed conflicts.

What Is Conflict?

Storms are a natural and unavoidable aspect of the earth's weather system. Storms range in intensity from mild rainstorms to hurricanes. Some storms are accompanied by gentle rain, others by thunder and lightning. Conflicts are the storms between individuals. They are a natural and unavoidable part of human relationships. And they vary in intensity from mild to severe and can be as small as a disagreement or as large as a war. According to the **World Book Dictionary**, a conflict is a fight, struggle, battle, disagreement, dispute, or quarrel. A prominent psychologist, Morton Deutsch (1973), defines **conflict** as existing

Johnson, D. W., & Johnson, R. (2005). **Teaching Students To Be Peacemakers** (4th Ed.). Edina, MN: Interaction Book Company, (952)831-9500.

whenever incompatible activities occur. An activity that is incompatible with another activity is one that prevents, blocks, or interferes with the occurrence or effectiveness of the second activity. Incompatible activities may originate in one person, between two or more people, or between two or more groups.

Figure 2.1: Creating A Conflict Positive School

Understand What Conflict Is

Know The Difference Between Destructive And Constructive Conflicts

Understand The Value Constructive Conflicts Contribute To The School

Ensure All School Members Are Co-Oriented In How To Manage Conflicts

Train All School Members How To Manage Conflicts Constructively By:

1. Establishing Cooperative Context

2. Establishing Peacemaker Program

    a. Teach The Potential Positive Nature Of Conflict.

    b. Teach The Five Strategies For Managing Conflicts of Interests.

    c. Teach The Integrative Negotiation Procedure.

    d. Teach The Mediation Procedure.

    e. Implement The Peer Mediation Program

    f. Teach Follow-Up Lessons To Refine And Upgrade Students' Negotiation And Mediation Skills

    g. When All Else Fails, Teachers Arbitrate

3. Enhancing Instruction With Academic Controversies

The truth is, conflicts are inevitable. Students might as well try to stop the earth from turning on its axis as to try to eliminate conflicts from their lives. The inevitability of conflicts, however, need not be a cause for despair. Conflicts have many positive outcomes if they are managed constructively. The occurrence of conflicts indicates people have goals they care about and are involved in relationships they value. The absence of

Johnson, D. W., & Johnson, R. (2005). **Teaching Students To Be Peacemakers** (4th Ed.). Edina, MN: Interaction Book Company, (952)831-9500.

conflict often signals a dysfunctional situation where neither the goals nor the relationship are valued. The absence of conflict, therefore, is often a cause for concern.

Table 2.1: Conflict Positive And Negative Organizations

Conflict Negative Organization	Conflict Positive Organization
See Conflict As Unitary	Recognize Different Types Of Conflicts
Sees Conflict As The Problem	Sees Conflict As Part Of The Solution
Avoids Conflicts	Seeks Out And Encourages Conflicts
Believe Conflict Is Inherently Destructive	Believe Conflict Management Determines Destructive Or Constructive Outcomes
Sees No Value To Conflict	Sees Many Values To Conflict
Conflicts Create Fear, Anxiety, Apprehension, Insecurity, Defensiveness	Conflicts Create Excitement, Interest, Concentration, Sense Of Promise
Competent Management Suppresses, Avoids, Contains Conflict	Competent Management Encourages And Supports Conflicts
Isolates And Separates Individuals To Avoid Conflicts	Organizes Individuals Into Teams To Promote Conflicts
Establishes Procedures For Preventing Conflicts	Establishes Procedures For Managing Conflicts
Sees Training As Encouraging Conflicts	Trains All Members To Ensure Co-Orientation And Normative Support
When Involved In A Conflict, Individuals Go For A "Win"	When Involved In A Conflict, Individuals "Solve The Problem"

There are at least four important types of conflicts for schools: (a) **controversy** (which occurs when one person's ideas, information, conclusions, theories, and opinions are incompatible with those of another and the two seek to reach an agreement), (b) **conceptual conflict** (which occurs when incompatible ideas exist simultaneously in a person's mind or when information being received does not seem to fit with what one already knows), (c) **conflict of interests** (which occurs when the actions of one person attempting to reach his or her goals prevent, block, or interfere with the actions of another person attempting to reach his or her goals), and (d) **developmental conflict** (which occurs when recurrent incompatible activities between adult and child, based on the opposing forces of stability and change within the child, cycle in and out of peak intensity as the child develops cognitively and socially).

Johnson, D. W., & Johnson, R. (2005). **Teaching Students To Be Peacemakers** (4th Ed.). Edina, MN: Interaction Book Company, (952)831-9500.

Quiz 2.1: Understanding The Nature Of Conflict

Demonstrate your understanding of the following concepts by matching the definitions with the appropriate concept.

Answer	Concept	Definition
	1. Conflict	a. When recurrent incompatible activities between adult and child, based on the opposing forces of stability and change within the child, cycle in and out of peak intensity as the child develops cognitively and socially
	2. Controversy	b. When the actions of one person attempting to maximize his or her wants and benefits prevent, block, or interfere with another person maximizing his or her wants and benefits
	3. Conceptual Conflict	c. When one activity prevents, blocks, or interferes with the occurrence or effectiveness of a second activity
	4. Conflict of Interests	d. When incompatible ideas exist simultaneously in a person's mind or when information being received does not seem to fit with what one already knows
	5. Developmental Conflict	e. When one person's ideas, information, conclusions, theories, and opinions are incompatible with those of another and the two seek to reach an agreement

In this book we will focus primarily on conflicts of interests and the related developmental conflicts. To understand a conflict of interests, you must first understand what wants, needs, goals, and interests are. There are many things each of us want. A **want** is a desire for something. Each person basically has a unique set of wants. A **need** is a necessity for survival. Needs are more universal. Every person needs to survive and reproduce (water, food, shelter, sex), belong (loving, sharing, cooperating), have power, have freedom, and have fun (Glasser, 1984). On the basis of our wants and needs we set goals. A **goal** is an ideal state of affairs that we value and are working to achieve. Our goals are related through social interdependence. When we have mutual goals we are in a cooperative relationship; when our goals are opposed we are in a competitive relationships. Our **interests** are the potential benefits to be gained by achieving our goals.

Within schools and classrooms the interests of students, teachers, and administrators at times are congruent and at times are in conflict. A **conflict of interests** exists when the actions of one person attempting to reach his or her goals prevent, block, or interfere with

Johnson, D. W., & Johnson, R. (2005). **Teaching Students To Be Peacemakers** (4th Ed.). Edina, MN: Interaction Book Company, (952)831-9500.

the actions of another person attempting to reach his or her goals (Deutsch, 1973). Most conflicts of interests are over:

1. Use of something (computer, book, clothes, car).

2. Obtaining something (money, clothes, computer games, power). Scarcity may occur naturally, or be created (i.e., in many classrooms teachers create a conflict of interests among students by having them compete for grades that are artificially limited).

3. Agreeing on something (what movie to see, where to eat, what to do).

Quiz 2:2: Understanding Conflicts Of Interests

Demonstrate your understanding of the following concepts by matching the definitions with the appropriate concept.

Answer	Concept	Definition
	1. Want	a. Desired Ideal State Of Future Affairs
	2. Need	b. The Actions Taken By Person A To Achieve Goals Prevent, Block, Or Interfere With The Actions Taken By Person B To Achieve Goals
	3. Goal	c. A Process By Which Persons Who Have Shared And Opposed Interests And Want To Come To An Agreement Try To Work Out A Settlement
	4. Interests	d. Universal Necessity For Survival
	5. Conflict of Interests	e. Potential Benefits To Be Gained By Achieving Goals
	6. Negotiation	f. Desire For Something

Student Views Of Conflict

Most students have a **negativity bias**, that is, they tend to describe conflict as resulting in (a) anger, hostility, animosity, and violence, (b) personal pain and sadness, and (c) broken friendships, divorce, lawsuits, and war. They do not usually recognize conflicts as such when conflicts result in laughter, insight, learning, and problem solving. While negative affect may or may not be present in a conflict, when students are asked to complete questionnaires, are interviewed, or asked to recall past conflicts (from two weeks to

Johnson, D. W., & Johnson, R. (2005). **Teaching Students To Be Peacemakers** (4th Ed.). Edina, MN: Interaction Book Company, (952)831-9500.

months), they tend to confuse conflict with anger, fighting, and quarreling. Conflicts that involve anger and violence, furthermore, are more salient and more likely to be remembered and, therefore, the incidents of constructive conflicts tends to be under-estimated (Collins & Laursen, 1992). The most common types of conflicts in American schools tend to be verbal harassments (name-calling, insults), verbal arguments, rumors and gossip, physical fights, and dating/relationship issues (Johnson & Johnson, 1996). While there tend to be more physical and verbal aggression in urban than in suburban schools, it almost never involves serious altercations or violations of law.

There is reason to believe that students tend to overestimate the frequency of conflicts involving anger and violence. Susan Opotow (1991) interviewed 40 inner-city seventh graders (50 percent male; 52 percent Hispanic, 43 percent Black, 5 percent White). She found that when asked about their conflicts with peers, more than two-thirds of the students described conflicts that occurred in school. This is not surprising, as school is the center of adolescent's social life (Coleman, 1961). While students described their in school conflicts as being violent, in actual fact the contact fights were most often infrequent scuffles that caused no or only minor injury. Lee (1990) conducted a study of school violence in New York City schools and found that essentially all violence and drug use ascribed to students after school occurred or was initiated by nonstudents.

Garofalo, Siegel, and Laub (1987) analyzed the National Crime Survey for school-related victimizations among adolescents. Such data tend to be skewed toward extreme incidents reported to the criminal justice system. But they did not find calculated assaults or violence. Instead they found quarrels, threats and arguments. Seventy-nine percent of the incidents were committed by offenders well-known to or acquaintances of the victim. Thefts involved such diverse items as pencils, books, meal tickets, baseballs, and jackets. Knives were used in a quarter of the robberies, but 40 percent of the weapons were available items grabbed on the spur of the moment, such as rocks, baseball bats, metal bars, spray-paint cans, scissors, or screwdrivers. Resulting injuries, sustained by 72 percent of the sample, were relatively minor bruises, black eyes, cuts, scratches, and swellings. Thus school conflicts tend to be teasing, bullying, and horseplay that got out of hand. The authors conclude that the alarm about rampant violence in schools is not justified, but the frequency with which adolescents victimize each other is of concern, even though the victimizations are more bothersome than injurious. They conclude that the key to prevention is providing juveniles with the attitudinal and behavioral tools they need to prevent the escalation of conflict into violence.

Schools need to be safe havens, and since homicides often result from spontaneous arguments among acquaintances (Prothrow-Stith, Spivak, & Hausman, 1987), schools could offer students greater safety by providing them with the procedures and skills to manage constructively their inevitable conflicts.

Johnson, D. W., & Johnson, R. (2005). **Teaching Students To Be Peacemakers** (4th Ed.). Edina, MN: Interaction Book Company, (952)831-9500.

Students View Violence As Constructive

In interviewing inner city, seventh-grade, lower class, minority students in New York City, Opotow (1991) surprisingly found that the students perceived fights as being more constructive than destructive. The students viewed fights as necessary and desirable to maintain valued social norms, deter harmful behavior, provide protection from victimization, gain status, increase self-awareness, clarify personal identity, clarify others' identities, clarify dominance hierarchies, initiate friendships, and provide enjoyable and entertaining experiences. In conflicts, students found opportunities for (a) modifying the status quo and the behavior of troublesome peers, (b) increasing self-protection, social advancement, personal worth, interpersonal insight, conflict resolution, and excitement, (c) providing heroic drama that generated an oral history of danger, heroism, and good versus evil, and (d) providing moral discourse and clarification of values and codes of behavior. Opotow concludes that these inner-city seventh-graders were clearly fascinated by and drawn to conflicts--they liked to start them, watch them, hear about them, and discuss them. Thus, telling students not to fight obviously will not be an effective strategy to pursue.

Summary

Conflicts are an avoidable part of human life. Conflicts of interests are especially frequent and often resolved destructively. While conflicts are potentially highly constructively, students tend to have a negativity bias, that is, they tend to see conflicts as typically involving anger and violence and tend to overestimate the frequency with which violent conflicts occur. Interestingly, students also tend to see violent conflicts as necessary and desirable to achieve many positive outcomes. The key to prevention is providing juveniles with the attitudinal and behavioral tools they need to prevent the escalation of conflict into violence. Students do need to learn what makes a conflict constructive or destructive.

Conflicts Can Be Destructive Or Constructive

It is not the presence of conflicts, but the way in which they are managed, that determines whether conflicts are destructive or constructive. **Conflicts are constructive to the extent that they:**

1. Result in an agreement that allows all participants to achieve their goals. The agreement is constructive when it maximizes joint outcomes, benefits everyone, and is in all participants' best interests.

2. Strengthen the relationship among participants by increasing their liking, respect, and trust for each other.

Johnson, D. W., & Johnson, R. (2005). **Teaching Students To Be Peacemakers** (4th Ed.). Edina, MN: Interaction Book Company, (952)831-9500.

3. Increase participants' ability to resolve future conflicts constructively.

What You Need To Know About Conflicts

First, you need to understand what is and is not a conflict. Conflicts may involve struggles, disagreements, disputes, or quarrels. More precisely, **conflicts** occur as the actions of one person attempting to reach his or her goals prevents, blocks, or interferes with the actions of another person attempting to reach his or her goals (see Deutsch, 1973).

Second, you must accept conflicts as a natural part of life that must be faced and resolved in constructive ways. You might as well try to stop the earth from turning on its axis as to try to eliminate conflicts from your life. Conflicts arise no matter what you do. Conflicts are especially frequent whenever you have goals you care about and are involved in relationships you value.

Third, whenever conflicts occur, destructive or constructive outcomes may result. Obtaining constructive outcomes requires (a) a set of procedures for managing conflicts constructively, (b) the opportunity to practice, practice, practice the procedures until real skill and expertise in their use is attained, and (c) the support and encouragement to use the procedures by the norms and values of the school (and home).

Fourth, if conflicts are to be managed constructively, everyone needs to use the same procedures to resolve them and be skilled in their use. All members of an organization (such as a school, business, or family) must use the same procedure.

Fifth, a constructive agreement has resulted when (a) the agreement maximizes joint benefits and everyone goes away satisfied and pleased, (b) disputants are better able to work together cooperatively and have more respect, trust, and liking for each other, and (c) disputants are better able to resolve future conflicts constructively.

Sixth, because conflicts occur continually, and because so many people are so unskilled in managing conflicts, learning how to resolve conflicts constructively is one of the best investments you can make. Once learned, conflict skills go with a person to every situation and every relationship. Knowing how to resolve conflicts with skill and grace will increase career success, quality of relationships with friends and colleagues, more fulfilling family life, and happiness in general.

2 : 8

Johnson, D. W., & Johnson, R. (2005). **Teaching Students To Be Peacemakers** (4th Ed.). Edina, MN: Interaction Book Company, (952)831-9500.

The Value Of Conflict

The Chinese character for crisis represents a combination of the symbol for danger and the symbol for opportunity. Inherent in any conflict is the potential for destructive or constructive outcomes. The issue is not whether conflicts occur, but rather how they are managed. On the destructive side, conflicts can create anger, hostility, lasting animosity, violence, pain, and sadness. Destructively managed conflicts are highly costly, decreasing the school's effectiveness by decreasing student learning by sabotaging the needed concentration and cognitive processes, damaging the relationships among students and between students and faculty, and interfering with teaching and learning efforts (Janz & Tjosvold, 1985). Ill managed conflicts result in faculty and students spending time brooding and fighting rather than teaching and learning.

Conflicts also carry the potential for many important positive outcomes. When managed constructively, conflicts tend to have many desirable outcomes (Deutsch, 1973; Johnson, 1970; Johnson & F. Johnson, 2003; Johnson & Johnson, 1979, 1995). **First**, conflicts can increase the quantity and quality of achievement, higher-level reasoning, and creative problem solving. **Second**, conflicts can increase the quality of decision making and problem solving. Higher level moral reasoning results from conflicts. Conflicts tend to improve decision quality and strategic planning, leading to innovation, re-evaluation of the status quo, and adaptation to the current situation. Without dissenting viewpoints, superior alternatives may be overlooked and thus decisions may be suboptimal.

Third, conflicts are essential for healthy cognitive, social, and psychological development. It is through conflicts that relationship issues are resolved at various stages of growth. Many times, there are developmental imperatives that require conflicts between children and adults. It is within conflicts that children learn to take the perspectives of others and become less egocentric. Successfully resolving conflicts increase feelings of self-esteem, self-efficacy, self-agency, and ability to cope with adversity and stress. Competence in managing conflicts constructive, furthermore, results in adolescents being more cooperative (as opposed to disruptive), more proactive and involved (as opposed to withdrawn), and generally more psychologically healthy.

Fourth, conflicts energize individuals to take action. Awareness of conflict can trigger a great deal of physical energy and an intensity of psychological focus, which in turn result in a strong motivation to resolve the conflict and put one's plans into action. The energy that students put into being angry and upset could be focused on resolving conflicts constructively.

Fifth, skills in managing conflicts constructively make students more employable, enhancing their career success, and generally increasing the quality of their lives. Individuals skillful in managing conflicts constructively tend to be more readily hired, retained, and promoted in career situations. Through experiencing numerous conflicts and perfecting the procedures and skills required to manage them effectively, students will be

Johnson, D. W., & Johnson, R. (2005). **Teaching Students To Be Peacemakers** (4th Ed.). Edina, MN: Interaction Book Company, (952)831-9500.

more able to maintain high quality friendships, family relationships, and relationships on the job with superiors, peers, and subordinates.

Sixth, conflicts are essential to promoting caring and committed relationships. Conflicts can deepen and enrich relationships, strengthening each person's conviction that the relationship can hold up under stress, communicating the commitments and values of each person that the other must take into account, and generally keeping the relationship clear of irritations and resentments so that positive feelings can be experienced fully. Resolving conflicts creates a sense of joint identity and cohesiveness within the relationship. A good conflict may do a lot to resolve the small tensions of interacting with others. Like all communities, classrooms and schools are cooperative enterprises within which diverse and heterogeneous individuals work together to achieve mutual goals. Conflicts will occur, and when they are constructively managed, the quality of community life within schools is enhanced.

Seventh, conflicts increase awareness that there is a problem that needs to be solved. Conflicts increase our awareness of what the problems are, who is involved, and how the problems can be solved.

Eighth, conflicts promote change. Conflicts create incentives to challenge and change outmoded procedures, assignments, structures, habitual patterns of interacting with others, and personal habits. **Ninth**, conflicts help students understand what they are like as a person and how they need to change. There are times when things need to change, when new skills need to be learned, when old habits need to be modified. What makes them angry, what frightens them, what is important to them, and how they tend to manage conflicts are all highlighted when students are in conflict with others. Being aware of what they are willing to argue about and how they act in conflicts can help them learn a great deal about themselves. Such self-awareness encourages change. **Tenth**, conflicts help students understand what others are like as individuals. Knowing what people are willing to fight about increases students' awareness of what they are like as individuals and their values, attitudes, and perspectives.

Eleventh, conflicts are essential for having an interesting and fun life. Being in a conflict often sparks curiosity and stimulates interest. Arguments about politics, sports, work, and societal problems make interpersonal interaction more intriguing and less boring. Skillful bargaining is a form of entertainment. Because they are enjoyable, many persons seek out conflicts through such activities as competitive sports and games, movies, plays, books, and teasing.

Need For Co-Orientation

Different students have quite different ideas about how conflicts should be resolved. Some rely on physical dominance through threats and violence. Other students use procedures such as verbal attack, the cold shoulder, giving in, or getting back at the other person in

Johnson, D. W., & Johnson, R. (2005). **Teaching Students To Be Peacemakers** (4th Ed.). Edina, MN: Interaction Book Company, (952)831-9500.

some way in the future. The multiple procedures for managing conflicts within the classroom create some chaos. This is especially true when students are from different cultural, ethnic, social class, and language backgrounds.

In order for education to proceed and learning to occur, students need to be **co-oriented** so that everyone uses the same procedures for managing conflicts. All students need to operate under the same norms and adhere to the same conflict resolution procedures. **Norms** are shared expectations about the behavior that is appropriate within the situation. School norms need to create clear and public expectations about what procedures and actions are appropriate when conflicts occur. Norms should make it clear that students (and faculty) are **not** to engage in physical violence against themselves or others, public humiliation and bullying of others, or lying and deceit. Conflicts among students should be skillfully. The norms for appropriate social conduct that students (and school personnel) are expected to follow without exception need to include negotiating to solve problems and maintain good relationships.

Ensuring that all students use the same conflict resolution procedures is especially important when students are from different cultures, ethnical groups, and backgrounds. America has always been a nation of many cultures, races, languages, and religions. The school is the meeting ground for children from different cultural, ethnic, social class, and language backgrounds. They come to know each other, appreciate the vitality of diversity, and internalize a common heritage of being an American. While this diversity represents a source of creativity and energy, it also provides a series of problems concerning how conflicts are managed in the classroom. Differences may need to be recognized and adjusted to. All students need to use the same set of procedures to resolve conflicts so that their goals are achieved, the relationship is strengthened, and their ability to manage future conflicts is improved.

Managing Conflicts Constructively

If we are to reach real peace in the world we shall have to begin with children; and if they will grow up in their natural innocence, we won't have to struggle; we won't have to pass fruitless ideal resolutions, but we shall go from love to love and peace to peace, until at last all the corners of the world are covered with the peace and love for which consciously or unconsciously the whole world is hungering.

Gandhi

To make schools conflict positive organizations, students must be trained how to manage conflicts constructively. The training program and the conflicts need to take place within a cooperative context. Creating a cooperative context is discussed in the next chapter. Students then need to be trained in the positive potential of conflicts, the five strategies for managing conflicts of interests, how to negotiate to solve problems, and how to mediate schoolmates' conflicts. The peer mediation program is then implemented. In addition,

2 : 11

Johnson, D. W., & Johnson, R. (2005). **Teaching Students To Be Peacemakers** (4th Ed.). Edina, MN: Interaction Book Company, (952)831-9500.

lessons need to be taught throughout the year to refine and extend students' negotiation and mediation skills. What results is that students face their conflicts, try to negotiate mutually beneficial resolutions, if that fails they seek the help of a peer mediator, if that fails they seek out the teacher who mediates, if that fails the teacher arbitrates, if that fails the students see an administrator who mediates, and if that fails the administrator arbitrates.

Points To Remember

Given below are a series of points about conflict and conflict resolution. For each statement, indicate your degree of agreement from "1" (strongly disagree the statement is true) to "10" (strongly agree the statement is true). Then meet in a group of four. Come to agreement as to the degree of true contained in each statement.

Statement Is False 1--2--3--4--5--6--7--8--9--10 Statement Is True

1. Conflicts arise no matter what you do. They are inevitable.

2. The more important your goals the more conflicts you will be involved in; the more important a relationship, the more likely you are to be involved in conflicts.

3. Any conflict has the potential for destructive or constructive outcomes.

4. Whether a conflict is constructive or destructive depends on your skill in managing conflicts in positive ways.

5. Ideally, you seek to resolve a conflict in a way that maximizes beneficial results for both yourself and the other persons involved.

6. To manage conflicts with skill, finesse, grace, and class, you need to know a conflict resolution procedure and be skilled in its use.

7. When two individuals involved in a conflict are using different procedures, destructive outcomes typically result. If conflicts are to be managed constructively, everyone needs to use the same procedures to resolve them.

8. Since the procedures for resolving conflicts effectively are not learned in most families or from television, movies, or novels, you must learn how to resolve conflicts as part of your education at school.

9. Knowing how to resolve conflicts with skill and grace will increase your career success, quality of relationships with friends and colleagues, and happiness.

Johnson, D. W., & Johnson, R. (2005). **Teaching Students To Be Peacemakers** (4th Ed.). Edina, MN: Interaction Book Company, (952)831-9500.

Training All Students

There is a great diversity of conflict resolution / peer mediation programs in schools, but generally they can be described as either cadre or total student body programs. The **cadre approach** emphasizes training a small number of students to serve as peer mediators. The training usually consists of a one or two day workshop or a semester-long class. A peer mediation program is then implemented with the small number of trained students serving as mediators for the whole school for the whole year. The cadre approach is based on the assumption that a few specially trained students can defuse and constructively resolve the interpersonal conflicts taking place among members of the student body. It is a relatively easy and inexpensive program for a school to adopt. It has not been clearly demonstrated, however, how the existence of a cadre of peer mediators decreases the severity and frequency of interpersonal conflicts among the general student population.

The **total student body approach** emphasizes training every student in the school to manage conflicts constructively. This approach is based on the assumption that all students need to be empowered to regulate their own behavior and resolve their interpersonal conflicts constructively. Empowering students involves (a) training all students in the school to negotiate integrative agreements to their conflicts and mediate schoolmates' conflicts, (b) implementing a peer mediation program in which the responsibility for peer mediation is rotated throughout the entire study body so that every student gains experience as and expects to be a mediator, and (c) ensuring the norms, values, and culture of the school promote and support the use of the negotiation and mediation procedures. Training the whole student body and faculty in the same negotiation and mediation procedures requires considerable time and commitment by the faculty and administration and is, therefore, relatively costly. Yet it changes the school and its learning climate in ways that few other programs can do (see Appendix A).

Your Challenge

Your challenge is to teach students how to make conflicts go well. Most people spend a lot of time and energy in conflicts. They often do not understand what causes conflicts or how they can be settled. People worry about the conflicts they are in and are afraid when conflicts take place. What they do not realize is that conflicts offer the chance to see a problem more clearly, see things in a new way, get new ideas, make better friends, and motivate change for the better. History is filled with many exciting examples of constructive conflicts. It is not possible to eliminate conflict from school life. It is, however, possible for students to learn how to make conflict enrich rather than disrupt their life. If they are to do so, a comprehensive conflict-resolution training program has to be established.

Johnson, D. W., & Johnson, R. (2005). **Teaching Students To Be Peacemakers** (4th Ed.). Edina, MN: Interaction Book Company, (952)831-9500.

Summary And Concluding Note

The first set of lessons focuses on the nature of conflict, the nature of constructive conflict resolution, the potential positive outcomes of conflict, and self-awareness of how one reacts in conflicts. Rather than avoid conflicts, students should increase the frequency of constructively managed conflicts. Conflicts occur all the time. They are a natural, inevitable, potentially constructive, and normal part of school life. Students disagree over who to sit by at lunch, which game to play during recess, when to work and when to play, when to talk and when to listen, and who is going to pick the paper up off the floor. Schools and classrooms become conflict negative organizations when conflicts are denied, suppressed, and avoided. The potential constructive outcomes of conflicts are lost due to the educators' fear and anxiety about how conflicts may be managed. The procedures most students use to manage their conflicts are most frequently inadequate and destructive, making things worse rather than better. Different students often have different ideas about how conflicts should be resolved. Students may get angry, fight, hurl verbal abuse at each other, verbally harass each other, ignore the conflict, take their anger out on someone/something else, play head-games, or fantasize how to get revenge. These methods generally provide little chance of resolving any problems and often result in alienating students from their peers and the school staff. Students, furthermore, generally have received very little training in how to manage conflicts constructively. In order to create a conflict positive school, in which conflicts are sought out, encouraged, and managed constructively, all students must be taught the same procedures for constructively resolving conflicts. A conflict has been resolved constructively when it solves the problem, strengthens the relationships among participants, and increases their ability to constructively resolve their conflicts in the future. Such constructively managed conflicts promote learning, problem solving, healthy social development, life success, and make life more interesting and fun. Students learn how to achieve these outcomes when (a) a cooperative context for relationships is created through the extensive use of cooperative learning, (b) academic controversies are structured by the teacher, and (c) a peer mediation program in which all students learn a basic negotiation procedure, all students learn how to mediate their schoolmates' conflicts, and teachers arbitrate as a last resort.

2 : 14

Johnson, D. W., & Johnson, R. (2005). **Teaching Students To Be Peacemakers** (4th Ed.). Edina, MN: Interaction Book Company, (952)831-9500.

CREATIVE CONFLICT CONTRACT

Write down your major learnings from reading this chapter and participating in training session one. Then write down how you plan to implement each learning. Share what you learned and your implementation plans with your base group. Listen carefully to their major learnings and implementation plans. You may modify your own plans on the basis of what you have learned from your groupmates. Volunteer one thing you can do to help each groupmate with his or her implementation plans. Utilize the help groupmates offer to you. Sign each member's plans to seal the contract.

MAJOR LEARNINGS	IMPLEMENTATION PLANS

Date: _____ Participant's Signature: _____

Signatures Of Group Members: _____

Johnson, D. W., & Johnson, R. (2005). **Teaching Students To Be Peacemakers** (4th Ed.). Edina, MN: Interaction Book Company, (952)831-9500.

Steps Of Managing Conflict

1. **Create A Cooperative Context:** The constructive resolution of conflict within an ongoing organization such as a school and classroom requires participants to recognize that their long- term relationship is more important than the result of any short- term conflict. In order for long-term mutual interests to be recognized and valued, individuals have to perceive their interdependence and be invested in each other's well-being. To teach students the procedures and skills they need to manage conflicts constructively, furthermore, a cooperative classroom environment must be established. The easiest way to do so is to use cooperative learning procedures at least 60 percent of the day. Since cooperative learning increases achievement and promotes a number of other important instructional outcomes, there will be little objection to doing so.

2. **Structure Academic Controversies:** In order to maximize student achievement, student critical thinking, and student use of higher-level reasoning strategies, engage students in intellectual conflicts within which they have to prepare intellectual positions, present them, advocate them, criticize opposing intellectual positions, view the issue from a variety of perspectives, and synthesize the various positions into one position.

3. **Teach Students To Be Peacemakers:** All students must be taught how to seek out conflicts and resolve their constructively, thereby capitalizing on the positive potential of most conflicts.

   a. Teach students to understand the nature and the positive potential of conflicts.

   b. Teach students to master the five strategies (withdrawing, forcing, smoothing, compromising, problem-solving negotiating) for managing conflicts of interests.

   c. Teach students how to engage in problem-solving negotiations. Students must practice the six-step negotiation procedure sufficiently to integrate the procedure into their behavioral repertoire (i.e., achieve automaticity).

   d. Teach students how to mediate schoolmates' conflicts: When students cannot successfully negotiate a constructive resolution to their conflicts, mediators should be available to assist. Experience as a mediator will increase negotiation skills.

   e. Arbitrate Student Conflicts: When mediation fails, the teacher or administrator arbitrates the conflict. As a last resort, when students cannot negotiate their conflicts and a mediator is unable to assist them to negotiate effectively with each other, the teacher or principal will have to decide. This is a last resort because typically it involves deciding who is right and, therefore, at least one student may be left with resentment and anger toward the arbitrator.

Johnson, D. W., & Johnson, R. (2005). **Teaching Students To Be Peacemakers** (4th Ed.). Edina, MN: Interaction Book Company, (952)831-9500.

Pair Reading of the Chapter

Your **task** is to read and comprehend the material in the chapter. To do this you must establish the meaning of each paragraph and then integrate the meaning of the paragraphs into the meaning of the chapter (and book) as a whole.

Form pairs. Work **cooperatively**. Ensure that both you and your partner become experts on the material. Agree on the meaning of each paragraph. Formulate one summary from the two of you. Both must be able to explain the meaning of the assigned material. Use the following procedure:

1. Read all the section heads in the chapter to get an overview.

2. One of you will be the **summarizer** and one will be the **accuracy checker**. These roles are rotated after each paragraph.

   a. Both members silently read the first paragraph.

   b. The **summarizer** summarizes in his or her own words the content of the paragraph.

   c. The **accuracy checker** listens carefully, corrects any misstatements, and adds anything left out. Then he or she tells how the material relates to something they already know.

   d. Move on to the next paragraph, switch roles, and repeat the procedure. Continue until you have read the whole chapter.

3. Work **cooperatively with other groups**. Whenever it is helpful, check procedures, answers, and strategies with another pair.

Johnson, D. W., & Johnson, R. (2005). **Teaching Students To Be Peacemakers** (4th Ed.). Edina, MN: Interaction Book Company, (952)831-9500.

∞ **Conflict Journal** ∞

You are to make a conflict journal in which you record what you are learning about yourself and how you behave in conflict situations. A **journal** is a personal collection of your significant thoughts about conflict. Include specific information you have learned about conflict resolution, effective behavior in conflict situations, and the extent to which you have mastered the conflict skills. Personalize it with art, poetry, cartoons, and creative writing. The most important thing about journal writing is to express your ideas freely without judging them. Whatever you write is OK. Spelling, grammar, and neatness do not count. The only thing that matters is writing freely about your experiences and ideas.

The purposes of the journal are to collect (a) thoughts that are related to the book's content (the best thinking often occurs when you are riding to or from school, about to go to sleep at night, and so forth) and (b) newspaper and magazine articles and references that are relevant to resolving conflicts constructively.

Entries

1. Each day find a conflict in the newspaper or on television and describe it in your journal.

2. Each day describe one conflict you were involved in during the day:

   a. What was the conflict about?

   b. Who was involved?

   c. What strategies did you use to manage the conflict?

   d. How did you feel?

   e. How was it resolved?

   f. What did you learn about managing conflicts constructively?

(Note: If you publish your journal as did John Holt, Hugh Prather, and others, all we ask is a modest 10 percent of the royalties.)

Johnson, D. W., & Johnson, R. (2005). **Teaching Students To Be Peacemakers** (4th Ed.). Edina, MN: Interaction Book Company, (952)831-9500.

Journal Entry One

Conflicts always occur, and you can profit from them if you have the necessary skills. It is important, therefore, to master the skills necessary for resolving conflicts constructively. The first step for doing so is to become more aware of your most frequently used strategies for managing conflicts.

Think back over the interpersonal conflicts you have been involved in during the past few years. These conflicts may be with students, administrators, parents, or colleagues.

1. Describe a recent conflict with a schoolmate, teacher, administrator, or parent.

2. What kind of emotional reaction do you have to these or other classroom or school-related conflicts? Check the ones that are appropriate.

___ Anger   ___ Resentment   ___ Depression

___ Frustration   ___ Fear   ___ Excitement

___ Annoyance   ___ Exasperation   ___ Sadness

___ Resignation

3. What were the strategies you used to resolve the conflicts?

4. Compare your answers with those of the person next to you.

Johnson, D. W., & Johnson, R. (2005). **Teaching Students To Be Peacemakers** (4th Ed.). Edina, MN: Interaction Book Company, (952)831-9500.

2 : 19

CONFLICT DETECTIVE

Conflicts go on continually everywhere. As a conflict detective you need to investigate conflicts daily. The two major sources of conflicts are the newspaper, TV entertainment programs, and TV news programs.

1. **Investigate the newspaper each day.** Find an example of a conflict in an article. It can be a small conflict (neighbors quarreling about a barking dog) or a large conflict (nations disagreeing). Bring in the article for the Conflict Bulletin Board. Or you can put the article in your Conflict Journal.

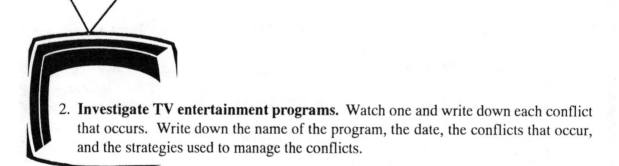

2. **Investigate TV entertainment programs.** Watch one and write down each conflict that occurs. Write down the name of the program, the date, the conflicts that occur, and the strategies used to manage the conflicts.

3. **Investigate TV news programs.** Watch one and write down each conflict that is discussed. Write down who is involved in the conflict and what strategies they are using to resolve it.

Johnson, D. W., & Johnson, R. (2005). **Teaching Students To Be Peacemakers** (4th Ed.). Edina, MN: Interaction Book Company, (952)831-9500.

What Is Conflict?

Working as a pair, write out your answers to the following questions. When you have finished, find another pair and compare answers. Take some of their ideas and make your answers better.

1. Conflict begins when two people want the same thing. When one person says, "I want the ice cream bar" and another person says, "I want the ice cream bar," a conflict exists. What do you think a conflict is? Define the word **conflict** in your own words, using your own ideas.

2. Give two examples of good conflicts. Give two examples of good conflicts and two examples of bad conflicts. Then list two small and two large conflicts you know about. Finally, list two conflicts at home and two conflicts at school.

	Good	Bad
1.		
2.		
	Small	**Large**
1.		
2.		
	Home	**School**
1.		
2.		

3. What is more important:
   _____ Getting what you want or _____ Maintaining a good relationship with the other person.
   (What lasts longer, a cookie or a friend?)

Johnson, D. W., & Johnson, R. (2005). **Teaching Students To Be Peacemakers** (4th Ed.). Edina, MN: Interaction Book Company, (952)831-9500.

Map Your Associations With Conflict

Individualistic Task:

Think of what the word "conflict" means and what associations and memories it evokes. When you think of conflict, do negative or positive, scary or delightful, hostile or caring images come to mind? Each time you think of something write it down in one of the circles. Then write down all the words you associate with each of the new words. Add additional circles as needed.

Cooperative Task:

Compare your associations with those of the other members of your group:

1. What words did you associate with the concept "conflict."

2. What elements do all conflicts have in common?

3. What causes conflict?

4. What makes conflicts destructive?

5. What makes conflicts constructive?

Individualistic Task:

Write down answers to the following:

1. What did you learn about your associations with conflict.

2. What did you learn about the nature of conflict and how most people perceive it.

Johnson, D. W., & Johnson, R. (2005). **Teaching Students To Be Peacemakers** (4th Ed.). Edina, MN: Interaction Book Company, (952)831-9500.

Conflict Self-Assessment

1. Rate your ability to resolve conflicts constructively on the criteria given in the table below.

Low 1--2--3--4--5--6--7--8--9--10 High

2. Then rate the ability of your classmates (students) to resolve conflicts constructively.

Low 1--2--3--4--5--6--7--8--9--10 High

3. Share ratings with partner. Compare your ratings of yourself and others.

Rating of Me	Criteria	Rating of Others
	Engage In Conflicts Frequently	
	Knowledge of Negotiation Procedure	
	Overall Level of Negotiation Skills	
	Able to Negotiate Agreements That Achieve Both Own And Other's Goals	
	Able to Negotiate So That Relationship Is Improved (Liking, Trust, Respect Increased)	
	Able to Improve Negotiation Skills Every Time A Conflict Is Resolved	

I am _____ / am not _____ satisfied with the way I now solve conflicts.

I would _____ / would not _____ like to learn ways to solve conflicts.

Johnson, D. W., & Johnson, R. (2005). **Teaching Students To Be Peacemakers** (4th Ed.). Edina, MN: Interaction Book Company, (952)831-9500.

Dividing Our Money Exercise

Some conflicts begin because there is only so much of something several people want, and no one can have as much as he or she would like. Salaries, promotions, office space, supplies, and even food are often the sources of such conflicts. Where there is only so much money and several people have definite plans about how it should be used, not everyone has his or her plans adopted by the total group. This exercise focuses on such a conflict. It requires three people to divide some money two ways. If you participate actively in this lesson, you will become more aware of how you manage such conflicts. You will also be able to give other participants feedback on how they act during such conflicts. The specific procedure is as follows.

1. Divide into groups of three.

2. **Each person contributes one dollar to the group**; the three dollars is placed in the center of the group.

2. **The triad decides how to divide the money between two people.** The majority rules. Only two people can receive money (one person must receive no money). It is all right for one person to end up with all the money. A clear decision must be reached as to how the money is to be divided between not more than two people. The group has fifteen minutes to decide who will receive how much of the money.

   a. The group cannot use any sort of "chance" procedure such as drawing straws or flipping a coin to decide which two people get what amounts of money.

   b. The group cannot make side agreements (I will receive the money and use it to buy a cup of coffee for everyone).

3. **The purpose of this exercise is to get as much money for yourself as you can.** Try to convince the other two members of your triad that you should receive all the money. Tell them you are broke, poor, smarter than they are, or more deserving of the money. Tell them you will put it to better use or will give it to charity. If the other two people make an agreement to divide the money between themselves, offer one of them a better deal. For example, if they agree to split the money fifty-fifty, tell one person that you will let that person have two dollars and will take only one dollar if he or she agrees to split the money with you.

Johnson, D. W., & Johnson, R. (2005). **Teaching Students To Be Peacemakers** (4th Ed.). Edina, MN: Interaction Book Company, (952)831-9500.

4. **The majority rules.** Whenever two people make a firm agreement to split the money a certain way, the decision is made. Be sure, however, to give the third person a chance to offer one of the two a better deal.

5. As soon as a decision is made, write your answers to these questions. Work by yourself.

   a. What were my feelings during the negotiations?

   b. How would my conflict strategies be described? Did I give up? Did I try to persuade others to my point of view? Did I try to take the money by force?

   c. What strategies did the other two individuals use in trying to get the money?

   d. What did I learn about how I manage conflicts?

6. In your triad, describe how you saw each other's actions during the decision making. Use the rules for constructive feedback. Make sure all members of your triad receive feedback.

7. Combine into a group of six and discuss the following questions.

   a. How did you feel during the decision making?

   b. How did members act in each triad during the decision making?

   c. What strategies did each member use during the decision making?

   d. What did we learn about conflict from the lesson?

2 : 25

Johnson, D. W., & Johnson, R. (2005). **Teaching Students To Be Peacemakers** (4th Ed.). Edina, MN: Interaction Book Company, (952)831-9500.

Abe Absentmind can't find his history book. He is convinced that Harry Findandkeep has two books and one of them is Abe's. Harry denies having Abe's book. In history class Abe walks by Harry's desk and suddenly grabs the history book in Harry's hands. Harry jumps up and tries to grab the book back, but Harry holds tight to the book and insists that it is his. Harry shoves Abe and demands the book back. Abe starts yelling that he is going to "get" Harry if he does not stop it.

Abe and Harry are in your class. In order to restore peace to the class without getting Abe and Harry in serious trouble, you wish to mediate the conflict. Your **task** is to explain how you would do so.

This is a **cooperative** assignment. Formulate one plan from the three of you, everyone must agree, everyone must be able to explain the group's plan.

NONVERBAL CONFLICTS Exercise

Thumb Wrestling: Lock fingers with another person with your thumbs straight up. Tap your thumbs together three times and then try to pin the other's thumb so that the other cannot move it.

Slapping hands: Person A puts her hands out, palms down. Person B extends his hands, palms up, under Person A's hands. The object of the exercise is for Person B to try to slap the hands of Person A by quickly moving his hands from the bottom to the top. As soon as Person B makes a move, Person A tries to pull her hands out of the way before Person B can slap them.

2 : 26

Johnson, D. W., & Johnson, R. (2005). **Teaching Students To Be Peacemakers** (4th Ed.). Edina, MN: Interaction Book Company, (952)831-9500.

What Might YOU Do?

Here are three problems. You are to pretend you are the person in the conflict. You are to guess what you might do in the same situation. Write out your answer.

1

Another student is playing with a ball you would really like to use. You ask him nicely if you can have the ball and he says "no." You still want to play with it. What might you do?

2

You are reading a book. A classmate wants you to join their game. You want to be left alone. What might you do?

3

During lunch a classmate calls you "stupid." Your feelings are hurt. What might you do?

Form pairs. Share your answers. Come to an agreement as to what the person in each conflict should do. Write out your answers. One member will be choosen at random to present the pair's answers to the class.

2 : 27

Johnson, D. W., & Johnson, R. (2005). **Teaching Students To Be Peacemakers** (4th Ed.). Edina, MN: Interaction Book Company, (952)831-9500.

How Conflicts Should Be Managed

1. Working with a partner, write out five rules for resolving your conflicts. There should be one set of answers for the two of you, both of you have to agree on the answers, and both of you have to be able to explain your answers to the teacher or the entire class.

    1.

    2.

    3.

    4.

    5.

2. Combine with another pair. Share your rules. Listen carefully to theirs. Use their ideas to improve your list.

    1.

    2.

    3.

    4.

    5.

Here is a list from another class:

1. Deal with the present, not the past (ancient history does not count).
2. No name calling (it only makes things worse).
3 No pushing, shoving, or hitting (physical violence makes things worse).
4. Stand up for yourself (You have a perfect right).
5. Talk to each other face-to-face (not behind each other's back).
6. Do not spread the conflict (keep it between the two or you).
7. Attack problems, not people.

2 : 28

Johnson, D. W., & Johnson, R. (2005). **Teaching Students To Be Peacemakers** (4th Ed.). Edina, MN: Interaction Book Company, (952)831-9500.

What Are The Four Types Of Conflicts?

Working with a partner, write out in your own words the definitions of the types of conflict.

1. Conflict:

2. Controversy:

3. Conceptual Conflict:

4. Conflict Of Interests:

5. Developmental Conflict:

Name the type of conflict each of the following examples represents:

1. The same amount of water is poured into two glasses. One glass is tall and skinny and the other glass is short and fat. The student knows that each glass holds the same amount of water but at the same time believes that the tall glass has more water in it.

2. The grade is "A" is given to the "best" students in the class. Each student attempts to prove that he or she is a better student than the other students in the class.

3. Students are placed in groups of four. Two students argue that all nuclear energy plants should be closed. The other two students argue that nuclear energy is vital to meet our nation's energy needs in a safe way. The group must write one report on nuclear energy giving their best thinking on the subject.

4. One year a child is dependent on the teacher and wants to be noticed and approved of by the teacher all the tiime. The next year the child feels independent and does not want the teacher to express approval or liking.

Johnson, D. W., & Johnson, R. (2005). **Teaching Students To Be Peacemakers** (4th Ed.). Edina, MN: Interaction Book Company, (952)831-9500.

Name _____ **Date** _____

YOU'VE WON!!

Congratulations!

Your group has just won an all-expense-paid field trip for one week to the destination of your choosing. It can be anywhere in the world. Since it is a field trip, you will have no school for that week. Now comes the hard part -- where will your group choose to go?

1. Think of three places you would like to go. Write down your reasons for wanting to go there.

	Place	Reason
Place 1.		
Place 2.		
Place 3.		

2. In order to make that choice, form pairs. Each pair will think up a list of three places that would be special to them to visit. The pairs will write down their choices and talk over reasons why they think their choices are wise ones. (A trip to someone's grandparent's house may be a fine choice, if that person can suggest things that all the group members would enjoy there.)

   a. Person A states where he or she wants to go. Person B states where he or she wants to go.

   b. Person A states his or her reasons. Person B states his or her reasons.

   c. The two reach an agreement as to where they would like to go as a pair and why.

3. After each pair has made its selection of places, two pairs combine to make a group of four. The group meets to choose a field-trip destination. The group must reach consensus in order to claim their prize.

4. Divide into two pairs. Working as a pair, define the words negotiate, negotiating, and negotiations.

2 : 30

Johnson, D. W., & Johnson, R. (2005). **Teaching Students To Be Peacemakers** (4th Ed.). Edina, MN: Interaction Book Company, (952)831-9500.

Chapter Three: Creating A Cooperative Context

Introduction

The context within which conflicts occur largely determines whether the conflict is managed constructively or destructively (Deutsch, 1973; Johnson & Johnson, 1989; Tjosvold & Johnson, 1983; Watson & Johnson, 1972). There are two possible contexts for conflict: cooperative and competitive (in individualistic situations individuals do not interact and, therefore, no conflict occurs).

Competitive Context

Conflicts usually do not go well in a competitive context. For competition to exist, there must be scarcity. I must defeat you to get what I want. Rewards are restricted to the few who perform the best. In a competitive situation, individuals work against each other to achieve a goal that only one or a few can attain. You can attain your goal if and only if the other people involved cannot attain their goals. Thus, competitors seek outcomes that are personally beneficial but detrimental to all others in the situation. Within competitive situations (Deutsch, 1973; Johnson & Johnson, 1989; Tjosvold & Johnson, 1983; Watson & Johnson, 1972):

- Individuals focus on differential benefit (i.e., doing better than anyone else in the situation). In competitive situations, how well a person is doing depends on how his or her performance compares with the performances of the others in the situation. There is a constant social comparison in which the value of one's outcomes depends on how they compare with the outcomes of others.

- Individuals focus on their own well-being and the deprivation of the other participants. In striving to "win," individuals focus not only on what is good for them but also what will deny others what they need to win. There is a vested interest in others doing less well than oneself.

- Individuals adopt a short-term time orientation where all energies are focused on winning. Little or no attention is paid to maintaining a good relationship. In most competitions, there is an immediate finishing line on which all attention is focused with little or no concern with the future relationship with the other competitors.

Johnson, D. W., & Johnson, R. (2005). **Teaching Students To Be Peacemakers** (4th Ed.). Edina, MN: Interaction Book Company, (952)831-9500.

Figure 3.1 Creating A Cooperative School Environment

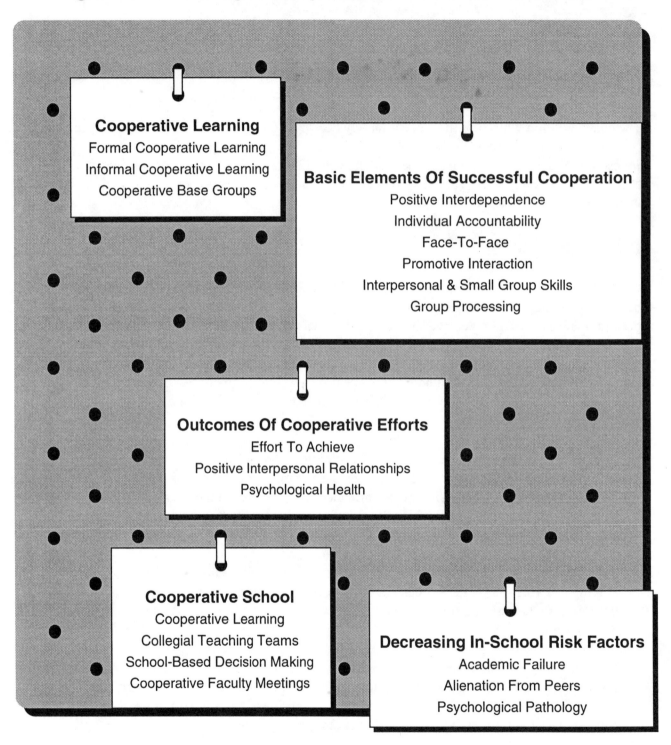

Cooperative Learning
Formal Cooperative Learning
Informal Cooperative Learning
Cooperative Base Groups

Basic Elements Of Successful Cooperation
Positive Interdependence
Individual Accountability
Face-To-Face
Promotive Interaction
Interpersonal & Small Group Skills
Group Processing

Outcomes Of Cooperative Efforts
Effort To Achieve
Positive Interpersonal Relationships
Psychological Health

Cooperative School
Cooperative Learning
Collegial Teaching Teams
School-Based Decision Making
Cooperative Faculty Meetings

Decreasing In-School Risk Factors
Academic Failure
Alienation From Peers
Psychological Pathology

- Communication tends to be avoided and when it does take place it tends to contain misleading information and threats. Threats, lies, and silence do not help students resolve conflicts with each other. Competition gives rise to espionage or other techniques to obtain information about the other that the other is unwilling to communicate, and "diversionary tactics" to delude or mislead the opponent about oneself.

- There are frequent and common misperceptions and distortions of the other person's position and motivations that are difficult to correct. Students engage in self-fulfilling prophecies by perceiving another person as being immoral and hostile and behaving accordingly, thus evoking hostility and deceit from the other person. Students see small misbehaviors of opponents while ignoring one's own large misbehaviors (mote-beam mechanism). Double standards exist. Because preconceptions and expectations influence what is perceived, and because there is a bias towards seeing events in a way that justifies one's own beliefs and actions, and because conflict and threat impair perceptual and cognitive processes, the misperceptions are difficult to correct.

- Individuals have a suspicious, hostile attitude toward each other that increases their readiness to exploit each other's wants and needs and refuse each other's requests.

- Individuals tend to deny the legitimacy of others' wants, needs, and feelings and consider only their own interests.

Cooperative Context

Conflicts usually go well in a cooperative context. For cooperation to exist there must be mutual goals that all parties are committed to achieving. I am not successful unless you are successful. The more successful you are, the more I benefit and the more successful I am. In a cooperative situation students work together to accomplish shared goals. Students seek outcomes that are beneficial to everyone involved. They are committed to each other's, as well as their own, well-being and success. Within cooperative situations (Deutsch, 1973; Johnson & Johnson, 1989; Tjosvold & Johnson, 1983; Watson & Johnson, 1972):

- Individuals focus on mutual goals and shared interests.

- Individuals are concerned with both self and others' well being.

- Individuals adopt a long-term time orientation where energies are focused both on achieving goals and on building good working relationships with others.

- Effective and continued communication is of vital importance in resolving a conflict. Within a cooperative situation, the communication of relevant information tends to be open and honest, with each person interested in informing the other as well as being informed. Communication tends to be more frequent, complete, and accurate.

3 : 3

Johnson, D. W., & Johnson, R. (2005). **Teaching Students To Be Peacemakers** (4th Ed.). Edina, MN: Interaction Book Company, (952)831-9500.

- Perceptions of the other person and the other person's actions are far more accurate and constructive. Misperceptions and distortions such as self-fulfilling prophecies and double standards occur less frequently and are far easier to correct and clarify.

- Individuals trust and like each other and, therefore, are willing to respond helpfully to each other's wants, needs, and requests.

- Individuals recognize the legitimacy of each other's interests and search for a solution accommodating the needs of both sides. Conflicts tend to be defined as mutual problems to be solved in ways that benefit everyone involved.

Conclusions

Conflicts cannot be managed constructively within a competitive context. When competitive and individualistic learning dominates a classroom and school, conflicts will inevitably be destructive. Instead of trying to solve interpersonal problems, students will think short-term and go for the "win." In order to resolve conflicts constructively, an instructor first has to establish a cooperative context, primarily through the use of cooperative learning. A complete and thorough discussion of cooperative learning may be found in Johnson, Johnson, and Holubec (1998a, 1998b).

What Is Cooperative Learning?

Cooperation is working together to accomplish shared goals. Within cooperative activities individuals seek outcomes that are beneficial to themselves and beneficial to all other group members. **Cooperative learning** is the instructional use of small groups so that students work together to maximize their own and each other's learning. In cooperative learning situations there is a positive interdependence among students' goal attainments; students perceive that they can reach their learning goals if and only if the other students in the learning group also reach their goals (Deutsch, 1962; Johnson & Johnson, 1989). Cooperation is commonly contrasted with **competition**, which exists when individuals work against each other to achieve a goal that only one or a few may attain. In competitive learning situations there is a negative interdependence among students' goal attainments; students perceive that they can reach their learning goals if and only if the other students fail to reach their goals (Deutsch, 1962; Johnson & Johnson, 1989). In addition, students may work **individualistically**, where the outcomes of each person are unaffected by others' actions. In individualistic situations there is no interdependence among students' goal attainments; students perceive that reaching their goals does not affect the likelihood of other students achieving their goals.

Johnson, D. W., & Johnson, R. (2005). **Teaching Students To Be Peacemakers** (4th Ed.). Edina, MN: Interaction Book Company, (952)831-9500.

When lessons are structured cooperatively, students work together to accomplish shared learning goals (Johnson, Johnson, & Holubec, 1998a). Students are assigned to small groups and given two responsibilities—to learn the assigned material and to make sure that all other group members master the assignment. Students seek outcomes that are beneficial to all those with whom they are cooperatively linked. A criteria-referenced evaluation system is used.

Teachers can structure lessons cooperatively so that students work together to achieve shared learning goals (Johnson, Johnson, & Holubec, 1998a). There are three types of cooperative learning: formal cooperative learning used to teach specific content, informal cooperative learning used to ensure active cognitive processing of information during a lecture, and cooperative base groups used to provide long-term support and assistance for academic progress. In formal cooperative learning students work together, for one class period to several weeks, to achieve shared learning goals and complete specific tasks and assignments (such as decision making or problem solving, completing a curriculum unit, writing a report, conducting a survey or experiment, or reading a chapter or reference book, learning vocabulary, or answering questions at the end of the chapter). Any course requirement or assignment may be reformulated to be cooperative. In formal cooperative learning groups teachers (Johnson, Johnson, & Holubec, 1998a):

- **Specify the objectives for the lesson**. In every lesson there should be an academic objective specifying the concepts and strategies to be learned and a social skills objective specifying the interpersonal or small group skill to be used and mastered during the lesson.

- **Make a number of preinstructional decisions**. A teacher has to decide on the size of groups, the method of assigning students to groups, the roles students will be assigned, the materials needed to conduct the lesson, and the way the room will be arranged.

- **Explain the task and the positive interdependence**. A teacher clearly defines the assignment, teaches the required concepts and strategies, specifies the positive interdependence and individual accountability, gives the criteria for success, and explains the expected social skills to be engaged in.

- **Monitor students' learning and intervene within the groups to provide task assistance or to increase students' interpersonal and group skills**. A teacher systematically observes and collects data on each group as it works. When it is needed, the teacher intervenes to assist students in completing the task accurately and in working together effectively.

- **Evaluate students' learning and help students process how well their groups functioned**. Students' learning is carefully assessed and their performances are evaluated. Members of the learning groups then process how effectively they have been working together.

3 : 5

Johnson, D. W., & Johnson, R. (2005). **Teaching Students To Be Peacemakers** (4th Ed.). Edina, MN: Interaction Book Company, (952)831-9500.

© Johnson & Johnson

Informal cooperative learning consists of having students work together to achieve a joint learning goal in temporary, ad-hoc groups that last from a few minutes to one class period (Johnson, Johnson, & Holubec, 1992; Johnson, Johnson, & Smith, 1991). During a lecture, demonstration, or film they can be used to focus student attention on the material to be learned, set a mood conducive to learning, help set expectations as to what will be covered in a class session, ensure that students cognitively process the material being taught, and provide closure to an instructional session. Informal cooperative learning groups are often organized so that students engage in three-to-five minute focused discussions before and after a lecture and two-to-three minute turn-to-your-partner discussions interspersed throughout a lecture.

Cooperative base groups are long-term, heterogeneous cooperative learning groups with stable membership (Johnson, Johnson, & Holubec, 1992; Johnson, Johnson, & Smith, 1991). The purposes of the base group are to give the support, help, encouragement, and assistance each member needs to make academic progress (attend class, complete all assignments, learn) and develop cognitively and socially in healthy ways. Base groups meet daily in elementary school and twice a week in secondary school (or whenever the class meets). They are permanent (lasting from one to several years) and provide the long-term caring peer relationships necessary to influence members consistently to work hard in school. They meet to discuss the academic progress of each member, provide help and assistance to each other, and verify that each member is completing assignments and progressing satisfactorily through the academic program. Base groups may also be responsible for letting absent group members know what went on in class when they miss a session. The use of base groups tends to improve attendance, personalize the work required and the school experience, and improve the quality and quantity of learning.

What Makes Cooperation Work?

Simply placing students in groups and telling them to work together does not in and of itself result in cooperative efforts. There are many ways in which group efforts may go wrong. You can have competition at close quarters or individualistic efforts with talking. The essential elements of cooperation need to be understood if teachers are to be trained to implement cooperative learning successfully. The five essential elements are (Johnson & Johnson, 1989).

1. **Positive Interdependence**: Positive interdependence is the perception that you are linked with others in a way so that you cannot succeed unless they do (and vice versa), that is, their work benefits you and your work benefits them. It promotes a situation in which students work together in small groups to maximize the learning of all members, sharing their resources, providing mutual support, and celebrating their joint success. Positive interdependence is the heart of cooperative learning. Students must believe that they sink or swim together. Within every cooperative lesson positive goal interdependence must be established through **mutual learning goals** (learn the assigned material and make sure that all members of your group learn the assigned material). In order to strengthen positive

3 : 6

Johnson, D. W., & Johnson, R. (2005). **Teaching Students To Be Peacemakers** (4th Ed.). Edina, MN: Interaction Book Company, (952)831-9500.

interdependence, **joint rewards** (if all members of your group score 90 percent correct or better on the test, each will receive 5 bonus points), **divided resources** (giving each group member a part of the total information required to complete an assignment), and complementary roles (reader, checker, encourager, elaborator) may also be used. For a learning situation to be cooperative, students must perceive that they are positively interdependent with other members of their learning group.

2. **Individual Accountability**: Individual accountability exists when the performance of each individual student is assessed and the results given back to the group and the individual. It is important that the group knows who needs more assistance, support, and encouragement in completing the assignment. It is also important that group members know that they cannot "hitch-hike" on the work of others. The purpose of cooperative learning groups is to make each member a stronger individual in his or her right. Students learn together so that they can subsequently perform higher as individuals. To ensure that each member is strengthened, students are held individually accountable to do their share of the work. Common ways to structure individual accountability include (a) giving an individual test to each student, (b) randomly selecting one student's product to represent the entire group, or (c) having each student explain what they have learned to a classmate.

3. **Face-To-Face Promotive Interaction**: Once teachers establish positive interdependence, they need to maximize the opportunity for students to promote each other's success by helping, assisting, supporting, encouraging, and praising each other's efforts to learn. There are cognitive activities and interpersonal dynamics that only occur when students get involved in promoting each other's learning. This includes orally explaining how to solve problems, discussing the nature of the concepts being learned, teaching one's knowledge to classmates, and connecting present with past learning. Accountability to peers, ability to influence each other's reasoning and conclusions, social modeling, social support, and interpersonal rewards all increase as the face-to-face interaction among group members increase. In addition, the verbal and nonverbal response of other group members provide important information concerning a student's performance. Silent students are uninvolved students who are not contributing to the learning of others as well as themselves. Promoting each other's success results in both higher achievement and in getting to know each other on a personal as well as a professional level. To obtain meaningful face-to-face interaction the size of groups needs to be small (2 to 4 members).

4. **Social Skills**: Contributing to the success of a cooperative effort requires interpersonal and small group skills. Placing socially unskilled individuals in a group and telling them to cooperate does not guarantee that they will be able to do so effectively. Persons must be taught the social skills for high quality cooperation and be motivated to use them. Leadership, decision-making,

3 : 7

Johnson, D. W., & Johnson, R. (2005). **Teaching Students To Be Peacemakers** (4th Ed.). Edina, MN: Interaction Book Company, (952)831-9500.

trust-building, communication, and conflict-management skills have to be taught just as purposefully and precisely as academic skills. Procedures and strategies for teaching students social skills may be found in Johnson (1991, 2003) and Johnson and F. Johnson (2003).

5. **Group Processing**: Group processing exists when group members discuss how well they are achieving their goals and maintaining effective working relationships. Groups need to describe what member actions are helpful and unhelpful and make decisions about what behaviors to continue or change. Students must also be given the time and procedures for analyzing how well their learning groups are functioning and the extent to which students are employing their social skills to help all group members to achieve and to maintain effective working relationships within the group. Such processing (a) enables learning groups to focus on group maintenance, (b) facilitates the learning of social skills, (c) ensures that members receive feedback on their participation, and (d) reminds students to practice collaborative skills consistently. Some of the keys to successful processing are allowing sufficient time for it to take place, making it specific rather than vague, maintaining student involvement in processing, reminding students to use their social skills while they process, and ensuring that clear expectations as to the purpose of processing have been communicated.

Well-structured cooperative learning lessons are differentiated from poorly structured ones on the basis of these elements. With a thorough mastery of the essential elements of cooperation, teachers can (a) tailor cooperative learning to their unique instructional needs, circumstances, curricula, subject areas, and students and (b) diagnose the problems some students may have in working together and intervene to increase the effectiveness of the student learning groups. These essential elements, furthermore, should be carefully structured within all levels of cooperative efforts. Each learning group is a cooperative effort, but so is the class as a whole, the teaching team, the school, and the school district.

Outcomes Of Cooperation

Between 1897 and 1989, over 550 experimental and 100 correlational studies were conducted by a wide variety of researchers in different decades with different age subjects, in different subject areas, and in different settings (for a detailed review of the research on cooperative, competitive, and individualistic efforts, see Johnson & Johnson [1989]). In our own research program at the Cooperative Learning Center (University of Minnesota) over the past 30 years we have conducted over 90 research studies to refine our understanding of the nature of cooperation and how it works. Many different researchers have conducted the research with markedly different orientations working in different settings, countries, and decades. Research participants have varied as to economic class, age, sex, nationality, and cultural background. A wide variety of research tasks, ways of structuring cooperation, and measures of the dependent variables have been used. The research on cooperation has validity and generalizability rarely found in the educational literature.

Johnson, D. W., & Johnson, R. (2005). **Teaching Students To Be Peacemakers** (4th Ed.). Edina, MN: Interaction Book Company, (952)831-9500.

Effort To Achieve

Cooperation tends to promote considerably greater effort to achieve than do competitive or individualistic efforts (effect sizes = 0.67 and 0.64 respectively). Effort exerted to achieve includes such variables as achievement and productivity, long-term retention, on-task behavior, use of higher-level reasoning strategies, generation of new ideas and solutions, intrinsic motivation, achievement motivation, continuing motivation, and greater transfer of what is learned within one situation to another. Thus, more successful coping with academic challenges occurs within cooperative than within competitive or individualistic situations.

Interpersonal Relationships

There have been over 175 studies that have investigated the relative impact of cooperative, competitive, and individualistic efforts on quality of relationships (Johnson & Johnson, 1989). Cooperation generally promotes greater interpersonal attraction among individuals than do competitive or individualistic efforts (effect sizes = 0.67 and 0.60 respectively).

In addition to friendly, caring, and committed relationships among collaborators, there has been considerable research on social support. Since the 1940's there have been 106 studies comparing the relative impact of cooperative, competitive, and individualistic efforts on social support. Cooperative experiences tended to promote greater social support from peers and from superiors (i.e., teachers) than did competitive (effect-size = 0.62) or individualistic (effect-size = 0.70) efforts.

Psychological Health

Asley Montagu (1966), a famous anthropologist was fond of saying that with few exceptions, the solitary animal in any species is an abnormal creature. Karen Horney (1937), a renowned psychoanalyst often stated that the neurotic individual is someone who is inappropriately competitive and, therefore, unable to cooperate with others. Montagu, Horney, and many others have recognized that the essence of psychological health is the ability to develop and maintain relationships in which cooperative action effectively takes place. With our students and colleagues, we have conducted a series of studies relating cooperative, competitive, and individualistic efforts and attitudes to various indices of psychological health. The samples studied included middle-class junior-high students, middle-class high school seniors, high-school age juvenile prisoners, adult prisoners, Olympic ice-hockey players, and adult step-couples. The diversity of the samples studied and the variety of measures of psychological health provide considerable generalizability of the results of the studies. A strong relationship was found between cooperativeness and psychological health, a mixed relationship has been found with competitiveness and psychological health, and a strong relationship has been found between an individualistic orientation and psychological pathology.

3 : 9

Johnson, D. W., & Johnson, R. (2005). **Teaching Students To Be Peacemakers** (4th Ed.). Edina, MN: Interaction Book Company, (952)831-9500.

More specifically, in our studies we found that the more positive a person's attitudes toward cooperating with others, the less likely they are to engage in antisocial behaviors such as drug abuse and criminal activities, the less their tension and anxiety, the less their depression and dejection, the less their anger and hostility, the less forceful and demanding they are, and the less rebellious and egoistic they are (see Johnson & Johnson, 1989). In addition, the more cooperative individuals are, the more they use socially appropriate and approved ways of meeting environmental demands, the more they see reality clearly without distorting it according to their own desires and needs, the greater their emotional maturity, the greater their ability to resolve conflicts between self-perceptions and adverse information about oneself, the higher their self-esteem and self-acceptance, the greater their basic trust in others and optimism, the more aware they are of their feelings, the more they can control their anger and frustration and express them appropriately, the more they take into account social customs and rules in resolving interpersonal and personal problems, the more willing they are to acknowledge unpleasant events or conditions encountered in daily living, the more their thinking is organized and focused on reality and free from confusion and hallucinations, the greater their leadership ability and social initiative, the more outgoing and sociable they are, the greater their sense of well-being (which includes minimizing their worries and being free from self-doubt and disillusionment), the greater their common sense and good judgment, and the more conscientious and responsible they are (see Johnson & Johnson, 1989). All of these qualities relate to coping successfully with stress and adversity.

The Cooperative School

In a cooperative school, students work primarily in cooperative learning groups, teachers and building staff work in cooperative teams, and district administrators work in cooperative teams (see Johnson & Johnson, 1994). The use of cooperation to structure faculty and staff work involves (a) colleagial support groups, (b) school-based decision making, and (c) faculty meetings. Just as the heart of the classroom is cooperative learning, the heart of the school is the colleagial support group. **Colleagial support groups** are small cooperative groups whose purpose is to increase teachers' instructional expertise and success. The focus is on improving instruction in general and increasing members' expertise in using cooperative learning in specific. A colleagial support group consists of two to five teachers who have the goal of improving each other's instructional expertise and promoting each other's professional growth (Johnson & Johnson, 1994). A school-based decision-making program may be created through the use of **task forces** that plan and implement solutions to schoolwide issues and

problems such as curriculum adoptions and lunchroom behavior and **ad-hoc decision-making groups** that are used during faculty meetings to involve all staff members in important school decisions. Faculty members listen to a recommendation, are assigned to small groups, meet to consider the recommendation, report to the entire faculty their decision, and then participate in a whole-faculty decision as to what the course of action should be. The use

Johnson, D. W., & Johnson, R. (2005). **Teaching Students To Be Peacemakers** (4th Ed.). Edina, MN: Interaction Book Company, (952)831-9500.

of these three types of faculty cooperative teams tends to increase teacher productivity, morale, and professional self-esteem. Cooperation is more than an instructional procedure. It is a basic shift in organizational structure that extends from the classroom through the superintendent's office.

Decreasing Inschool Risk Factors

An important principle in teaching students how to manage conflicts constructively is to use cooperative learning the majority of the school day to decrease the risk factors that influence children and adolescents to use violence and other destructive strategies in managing conflicts. Three factors that place children and adolescents at risk for using violence are (a) poor academic performance (with an inability to think through decisions), (b) alienation from schoolmates, and (c) psychological pathology. The more schools do to reduce these factors, the less violence and destructively managed conflicts schools should experience.

Children and adolescents who academically fail in school are more at risk for violent and destructive behavior than are students who achieve academically. Sociologists Gold and Osgood (1992) have identified patterns of school-induced delinquency caused by school failure. Unable to secure self-esteem in positive ways, some students seek status through antisocial behavior. Schools should accomplish what they are supposed to do—ensure that every student achieves up to his or her ability. Cooperative learning results in higher achievement and greater competence in using higher-level reasoning strategies than do competitive or individualistic learning (Johnson & Johnson, 1989). The more students know and the greater their ability to analyze situations and think through decisions, the more able they will be to envision the consequences of their actions, understand and respect differing viewpoints, conceive of a variety of strategies for dealing with conflict, and engage in creative problem-solving.

Children and adolescents who are disliked by or alienated from their schoolmates are more at risk for violent and destructive behavior than are students who are integrated into strong caring and supportive relationships in the school. The most powerful restraints on violent and antisocial behavior are healthy human attachments. Usually these originate in early relationships of parental affection and guidance where children learn trust, competence, self-management, and prosocial behavior. Peer relations are, however, a very powerful influence. Bonding with a set of constructive peers is one of the most powerful influences on a person's behavior. Cooperative efforts result in more positive and supportive relationships than do competitive or individualistic experiences (Johnson & Johnson, 1989). In order to create an infrastructure in schools of personal and academic support, long-term caring and committed relationships need to be promoted. Procedures for doing so include (a) the use of cooperative learning (including cooperative base groups that last for a number of years) (Johnson, Johnson, & Holubec, 1998a, 1998b) and (b) assigning teams of teachers to follow cohorts of students through several grades (instead of changing teachers every year) (Johnson & Johnson, 1994).

Johnson, D. W., & Johnson, R. (2005). **Teaching Students To Be Peacemakers** (4th Ed.). Edina, MN: Interaction Book Company, (952)831-9500.

Children and adolescents who have high levels of psychological pathology are more at risk for violent and destructive behavior than are students who are psychologically well adjusted. Cooperative learning promotes more healthy psychological adjustment, higher self-esteem, and greater social competence than do competitive and individualistic learning, (Johnson & Johnson, 1989). David Hamburg, the president of Carnegie Corporation, states that the reversal of the trend of violence among the young depends on teaching children how to work cooperatively with others, share, and help others. Children who develop socially, cognitively, and psychologically in healthy ways tend to manage conflicts constructively. The more children and adolescents work in cooperative learning groups, the greater will be their psychological health, self-esteem, social competencies, and resilience in the face of adversity and stress. Consequently, they will be less likely to use violence and other destructive strategies in managing their conflicts with others.

Conclusions

Experts on organizations such as W. Edwards Deming constantly remind us that behavior is 85 percent determined by organizational structure and 15 percent determined by the individual (Johnson & Johnson, 1994). It makes no sense to talk of constructive conflict management in schools structured competitively. The first step in teaching students the procedures for managing conflicts, therefore, is creating a cooperative context in which conflicts are defined as mutual problems to be resolved in ways that benefit everyone involved. Creating a cooperative context requires that teachers use cooperative learning the majority of the day. This requires that a number of essential elements must be carefully structured into each lesson. The effort is worth it, however, because of the superior achievement, positive relationships, and psychological health generally found in cooperative situations.

Once a cooperative context has been established, students may be directly taught the procedures and skills required to manage conflicts constructively. There are two ways in which conflict resolution procedures are essential to high quality education. Faculty may use intellectual, academic conflicts as an inherent part of the instructional program (Johnson & Johnson, 1995). Students may negotiate resolutions to their conflicts of interests and mediate schoolmates' conflicts when negotiations fail. While each procedure stands on its own, the two support and enhance each other's effectiveness.

3 : 12

Johnson, D. W., & Johnson, R. (2005). **Teaching Students To Be Peacemakers** (4th Ed.). Edina, MN: Interaction Book Company, (952)831-9500.

CREATIVE CONFLICT CONTRACT

Write down your major learnings from reading this chapter and participating in training session one. Then write down how you plan to implement each learning. Share what you learned and your implementation plans with your base group. Listen carefully to their major learnings and implementation plans. You may modify your own plans on the basis of what you have learned from your groupmates. Volunteer one thing you can do to help each groupmate with his or her implementation plans. Utilize the help groupmates offer to you. Sign each member's plans to seal the contract.

MAJOR LEARNINGS	IMPLEMENTATION PLANS

Date: _____ Participant's Signature: _____

Signatures Of Group Members: _____

_____

Johnson, D. W., & Johnson, R. (2005). **Teaching Students To Be Peacemakers** (4th Ed.). Edina, MN: Interaction Book Company, (952)831-9500.

The Instructor's Role in Cooperative Learning

Make Pre-Instructional Decisions

Specify Academic and Social Skills Objectives: Every lesson has both (a) academic and (b) interpersonal and small group skills objectives.

Decide on Group Size: Learning groups should be small (groups of two or three members, four at the most).

Decide on Group Composition (Assign Students to Groups): Assign students to groups randomly or select groups yourself. Usually you will wish to maximize the heterogeneity in each group.

Assign Roles: Structure student-student interaction by assigning roles such as Reader, Recorder, Encourager of Participation and Checker for Understanding.

Arrange the Room: Group members should be "knee to knee and eye to eye" but arranged so they all can see the instructor at the front of the room.

Plan Materials: Arrange materials to give a "sink or swim together" message. Give only one paper to the group or give each member part of the material to be learned.

Explain Task And Cooperative Structure

Explain the Academic Task: Explain the task, the objectives of the lesson, the concepts and principles students need to know to complete the assignment, and the procedures they are to follow.

Explain the Criteria for Success: Student work should be evaluated on a criteria-referenced basis. Make clear your criteria for evaluating students' work.

Structure Positive Interdependence: Students must believe they "sink or swim together." Always establish mutual goals (students are responsible for their own learning and the learning of all other group members). Supplement, goal interdependence with celebration/reward, resource, role, and identity interdependence.

Structure Intergroup Cooperation: Have groups check with and help other groups. Extend the benefits of cooperation to the whole class.

3 : 14

Johnson, D. W., & Johnson, R. (2005). **Teaching Students To Be Peacemakers** (4th Ed.). Edina, MN: Interaction Book Company, (952)831-9500.

Structure Individual Accountability: Each student must feel responsible for doing his or her share of the work and helping the other group members. Ways to ensure accountability are frequent oral quizzes of group members picked at random, individual tests, and assigning a member the role of Checker for Understanding.

Specify Expected Behaviors: The more specific you are about the behaviors you want to see in the groups, the more likely students will do them. Social skills may be classified as **forming** (staying with the group, using quiet voices), **functioning** (contributing, encouraging others to participate), **formulating** (summarizing, elaborating), and **fermenting** (criticizing ideas, asking for justification). Regularly teach the interpersonal and small group skills you wish to see used in the learning groups.

Monitor and Intervene

Arrange Face-to-Face Promotive Interaction: Conduct the lesson in ways that ensure that students promote each other's success face-to-face.

Monitor Students' Behavior: This is the fun part! While students are working, you circulate to see whether they understand the assignment and the material, give immediate feedback and reinforcement, and praise good use of group skills. Collect observation data on each group and student.

Intervene to Improve Taskwork and Teamwork: Provide **taskwork assistance** (clarify, reteach) if students do not understand the assignment. Provide **teamwork assistance** if students are having difficulties in working together productively.

Assess and Process

Assess Student Learning: Assess and evaluate the quality and quantity of student learning. Involve students in the assessment process.

Process Group Functioning: Ensure each student receives feedback, analyzes the data on group functioning, sets an improvement goal, and participates in a team celebration. Have groups routinely list three things they did well in working together an done thing they will do better tomorrow. Summarize as a whole class. Have groups celebrate their success and hard work.

3 : 15

Johnson, D. W., & Johnson, R. (2005). **Teaching Students To Be Peacemakers** (4th Ed.). Edina, MN: Interaction Book Company, (952)831-9500.

COOPERATIVE LEARING LESSON PLANNING

Grade Level: _____ Subject Area: _____ Date: _____

Lesson: _____

Objectives: _____Academic _____Social Skills

Group Size: _____ Method Of Assigning Students: _____

Roles: _____ Materials: _____

Academic Task:	**Criteria For Success:**

Positive Interdependence:	**Individual Accountability:**	**Expected Behaviors:**

Montoring: _____ Teacher _____ Students _____ Visitors

Behaviors Observed: _____

Assessment Of Learning: _____

Small Group Processing:	**Goal Setting:**	**Whole Class Processing:**

Celebration: _____

Other: _____

3 : 16

Johnson, D. W., & Johnson, R. (2005). **Teaching Students To Be Peacemakers** (4th Ed.). Edina, MN: Interaction Book Company, (952)831-9500.

CONTEST OF THE CODES:
Who'll Be the Best?

Your **task** is to solve the following codes. You have a set of coded messages and the same messages decoded. Your task is to identify the pattern so that you are able to write a message with the code.

This is a **competitive** activity. Work by yourself. Try to break the codes faster and more accurately than the other students. At the end of this activity you will be ranked from best to worst in breaking codes.

NEHWEHTGNITTESSIEVITITEPMOCIMIWS

WHENTHESETTINGISCOMPETITIVEISWIM

DNAUOYKNISROIKNISDNAUOYMIWS.

ANDYOUSINKORISINKANDYOUSWIM.

The pattern for this code is _____.

VA N PBBCRENGVIR TEBHC, GUR ZBER FHPPRFFSHY LBH NER

IN A COOPERATIVE GROUP, THE MORE SUCCESSFUL YOU ARE

GUR ZBER V ORARSVG NAQ GUR ZBER FHPPRFFSHY V NZ.

THE MORE I BENEFIT AND THE MORE SUCCESSFUL I AM.

The pattern for this code is _____.

GM DHA6J A9C K 79C6A10C2 10H MH K9 J

MY GOALS ARE UNRELATED TO YOURS

L 4C7 LC LH9F E 72 E11E 2 KA6EJ10EBA66M

WHEN WE WORK INDIVIDUALISTICALLY.

The pattern for this code is _____.

Johnson, D. W., & Johnson, R. (2005). **Teaching Students To Be Peacemakers** (4th Ed.). Edina, MN: Interaction Book Company, (952)831-9500.

Conquering the Codes Together

Your **task** is to solve the following codes. You have a set of coded messages and the same messages decoded. Your task is to identify the pattern so that you are able to write a message with the code.

This is a **cooperative** activity. Work together. Encourage and assist each other's learning. Agree on one answer to each question. Every member must be able to explain what the code is and be able to write a message with the code.

---

18 5 13 5 13 2 5 18   20 8 1 20   9 14   1   3 15 15 16 5 18 1 20 9 22 5   7 18 15 21 16
R E M E M B E R   T H A T   I N   A   C O O P E R A T I V E   G R O U P

23 5   1 12 12   19 9 14 11   15 18   19 23 9 13   20 15 7 5 20 8 5 18
W E   A L L   S I N K   O R   S W I M   T OGET HE R.

The pattern for this code is _____.

HDFK   LQGLYLGXDU   PXVQ   EH   DFFRXQWDEUH   IRU   KLV/KHU
EACH   INDIVIDUAL   MUST   BE   ACCOUNTABLE   FOR   HIS/HER

RZQ   SHUIRUPDQFH   ZKHQ   ZRUNLQJ   FRRSHUDWLYHOB.
OWN PERFORMANCE WHEN WORKING COOPERATIVELY.

The pattern for this code is _____.

WHN   W   WRK   CPRTVLY,   W   HLP,   SHR,
WHEN WE WORK COOPERATIVELY, WE HELP, SHARE,

ND   NCRG   CH   THR   T   LRN.
AND ENCOURAGE EACH OTHER TO LEARN.

The pattern for this code is _____.

Johnson, D. W., & Johnson, R. (2005). **Teaching Students To Be Peacemakers** (4th Ed.). Edina, MN: Interaction Book Company, (952)831-9500.

When Are You Interdependent?

You can take a walk by yourself. You can only play tennis with another person. Some things we can do by ourselves. Some things can only be done through a joint effort. When a joint effort is required, you are interdependent. You are dependent on others to do their part, they are dependent on you to do your part.

Given below are a sets of activities. Some can be done separately. Some can only be done as part of a joint effort. Classify each activity as being "independent" or "interdependent." Then write down **why** you classified the activity as you did. Finally, name three things you can do by yourself. Add them to the above list. Name three things that require the efforts of you and several other people to accomplish. Add them to the above list.

This is a cooperative task. Work as a pair. Both persons must agree on and be able to explain the answers.

Activity	Separate	Mutual
Win a lottery		
Score a touchdown		
Follow a map from A to Z		
Play in a band		
Run a mile		
Negotiate		
Kick a ball		
Mediate		
Pilot a jet airliner		
Sing in choir		
Form a human circle around a tree		
Have a friend		
Play soccer		
Jump rope 25 times		
Play catch		
Lift 500 pounds		
Get married		
Be a hermit		
Teach math		
Be a family		

3 : 19

Johnson, D. W., & Johnson, R. (2005). **Teaching Students To Be Peacemakers** (4th Ed.). Edina, MN: Interaction Book Company, (952)831-9500.

Establishing Positive Interdependence

Jim can't find his lunch. It contains two ham sandwiches, a banana, and a plain chocolate candy bar. Jim sees Roger sitting at a lunch table with two ham sandwiches, a banana, and a plain chocolate candy bar. Roger has often grabbed and eaten parts of Jim's lunch in the past. Jim has let it go, but this is too much. Jim says, "Hey! That's my lunch! Give it back!" Roger insists the lunch is his. Jim and Roger start yelling at each other over whose lunch it is.

1. Whenever you are involved in a conflict, your first step is to establish the cooperative context. What can Jim do to remind Roger to take a long-term cooperative perspective on the relationship and therefore help find a solution to the conflict?

2. Role play the following methods of establishing positive interdependence. Alternate roles of actor and listener. The actor plays Jim and presents the appeal for interdependence. The listener plays Roger and responds to the appeal.

3. After all situations have been role played, write down three recommendations for establishing a perception of positive interdependence with the opponent.

Appeals For Interdependence

1. "We share a common fate. We can solve this problem in a way that we both benefit."

2. "You can not succeed without my help and I can't succeed without your help."

3. "Look. We are going to be classmates for years. Let's think about the future as well as about this issue."

   a. "We have more to gain by staying friends and working this out than we have to gain by trying to win over each other. Let's not try to take advantage of each other. Let's solve this problem and stay friends."

   b. "We are in the same classes. Our lockers are near each other. We see each other all the time. And we are going to keep seeing each other for the next three years. We have a long- lasting relationship. We interact frequently. Let's work together to solve this problem."

4. "We are both basketball players. We live in the same neighborhood."

5. "Remember all the times we celebrated our successes? We accomplished a lot together in the past. We can do it again in the future."

Johnson, D. W., & Johnson, R. (2005). **Teaching Students To Be Peacemakers** (4th Ed.). Edina, MN: Interaction Book Company, (952)831-9500.

BREAKING BALLOONS

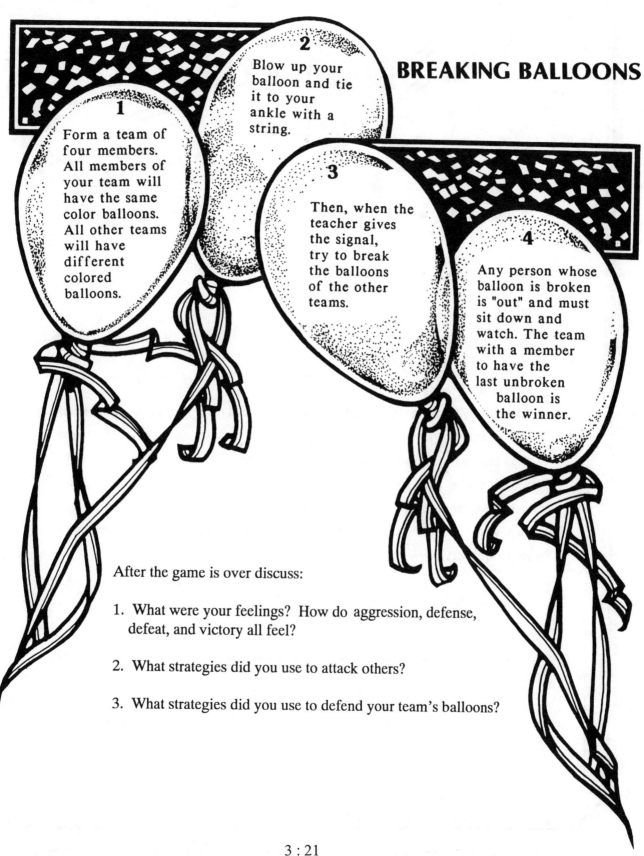

1 Form a team of four members. All members of your team will have the same color balloons. All other teams will have different colored balloons.

2 Blow up your balloon and tie it to your ankle with a string.

3 Then, when the teacher gives the signal, try to break the balloons of the other teams.

4 Any person whose balloon is broken is "out" and must sit down and watch. The team with a member to have the last unbroken balloon is the winner.

After the game is over discuss:

1. What were your feelings? How do aggression, defense, defeat, and victory all feel?

2. What strategies did you use to attack others?

3. What strategies did you use to defend your team's balloons?

Johnson, D. W., & Johnson, R. (2005). **Teaching Students To Be Peacemakers** (4th Ed.). Edina, MN: Interaction Book Company, (952)831-9500.

Blowing Off Steam

In order to accomplish this task, you must have a cooperative group!

Materials needed:

table
paper cup
grocery bag

Procedure:

Ask your classmates to kneel around the table, spacing themselves out evenly. Place the paper cup at one end of the table and tape the bag at the other end. At a given signal, join together in blowing the cup to the opposite end of the table. Everyone must work together until the cup drops into the bag. Don't touch the cup with your body. Repeat the task until you can do it more and more quickly.

Describe the activity and how it worked:

_____

_____

_____

_____

Johnson, D. W., & Johnson, R. (2005). **Teaching Students To Be Peacemakers** (4th Ed.). Edina, MN: Interaction Book Company, (952)831-9500.

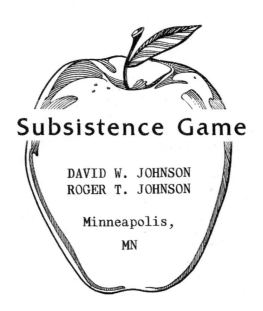

Subsistence Game

DAVID W. JOHNSON
ROGER T. JOHNSON

Minneapolis,
MN

This game simulates the effects of unequal resources in a group. It also allows for the development within the group of either cooperation or competition. It will be very important to process the group's interactions at the completion of the activity. The procedure is as follows.

1. Form groups of seven. One member should volunteer to be the recorder and another member should volunteer to be the observer. Each group should have five participants, one recorder, and one observer.

2. To play the game contained in this exercise the group needs a pack of blank food cards. The group also needs a pack of hunting and gathering cards (found at the end of the lesson).

3. The basic procedure of the game is as follows:

   a. Each participant receives three food cards.

   b. The recorder shuffles the hunting and gathering cards and places them in the center of the group.

   c. Each participant draws a card in turn (going counterclockwise), reads it to the group, and receives from or gives to the recorder the required number of food cards.

   d. The day's hunting and gathering is over when every participant has drawn one card. Participants may give any number of food cards to each other. At the end of the day they must give one food card to the recorder. Failure to do so results in death by starvation and dropping out of the game.

3 : 23

    e.   After seven rounds the week's hunting and gathering are over. Points are awarded to group members.

    f.   The game is played for a minimum of two weeks (14 rounds).

4.   The role of the observer is to record the frequency of the behaviors listed on the observation sheet. The frequencies are reported to the group during the concluding group discussion.

5.   The role of the recorder is to:

    a.   Read the Subsistence Instruction Sheet to the group.

    b.   Review the rules with participants.

    c.   Give each participant three food cards.

    d.   Shuffle the hunting and gathering cards and place them in the center of the group.

    e.   Distribute and collect food cards on the basis of the cards drawn.

    f.   At the end of each round collect one food card from each participant.

    g.   Ensure that each participant announces how many food cards s/he has at the end of each round.

    h.   Announce how many participants starved to death and who had the most food cards at the end of each week (seven rounds)

6.   When the game is over, discuss the following questions:

    a.   Who survived and who died?

    b.   How was a cooperative or a competitive strategy decided on?

    c.   How did participants feel about the impending death by starvation?

    d.   How did the dead feel when they knew others could have saved them?

    e.   How did the survivors feel when others died when they had extra food cards?

    f.   Who organized the group to create a "just" distribution of food?

    g.   What real-life situations parallel this exercise?

Johnson, D. W., & Johnson, R. (2005). **Teaching Students To Be Peacemakers** (4th Ed.). Edina, MN: Interaction Book Company, (952)831-9500.

Johnson, D. W., & Johnson, R. (2005). **Teaching Students To Be Peacemakers** (4th Ed.). Edina, MN: Interaction Book Company, (952)831-9500.

SUBSISTENCE EXERCISE: Hunting and Gathering Cards

You found no food today.	Excellent shot! You killed a deer worth two days of food. You get two food cards from the recorder.
You made a beautiful shot at what looked like a deer, but it turned out to be a strangely shaped rock. You got no food today!	You met a member of another group and fell in love. To impress your new love, you gave him/her one day's food. Give recorder one food card. If you don't have a food card, and if no one will give you one, you die of starvation!
You shot a bird. You get one food card from the recorder.	You shot a snake. You get one food card from the recorder.
Wild dogs chased you and to get away you threw them one day's food. Give the recorder one food card. If you do not have a food card, and if no one will give you one, you die of starvation.	Army ants chased you and to get away you threw them one day's food. Give the recorder one food card. If you do not have a food card, and if no one will give you one, you die of starvation.
 You fell asleep and slept all day. You got no food today.	You shot a lizard. You get one food card from the recorder.

3 : 26

Johnson, D. W., & Johnson, R. (2005). **Teaching Students To Be Peacemakers** (4th Ed.). Edina, MN: Interaction Book Company, (952)831-9500.

SUBSISTENCE EXERCISE: Hunting and Gathering Cards

Excellent shot! You aimed at a bird you thought was standing on a rock. Your arrow hit the rock, which turned out to be a pig. You get two food cards from the recorder.	 You found some wild carrots. You get one food card from the recorder.
 You found a deer, but a bear scared it away before you could shoot at it. You got no food today.	You found an apple tree. Birds had eaten almost all of them. You get one food card from the recorder.
Excellent shot! Just as you shot at a deer, a wild pig ran in the way and got killed. You receive two food cards from recorder.	Excellent shot! You killed a wild pig. You get two food cards from the recorder. 
 You shot a rabbit. You get one food card from the recorder.	While hunting, you accidently stepped on a snake and killed it. You receive one food card from the recorder.
You found no food today. Probably too hot for anything to be out and around.	On the way home you fell into a swamp. You lost two day's worth of food to a hungry crocodile. Give two food cards to the recorder. If you do not have them, and if no one will give them to you, you die of starvation.

3 : 27

Johnson, D. W., & Johnson, R. (2005). **Teaching Students To Be Peacemakers** (4th Ed.). Edina, MN: Interaction Book Company, (952)831-9500.

SUBSISTENCE EXERCISE: Hunting and Gathering Cards

While running away from a lion, you took refuge in a peach tree. You receive one food card from the recorder.	You found a nest of field mice and bopped them all on the head. You get one food card from the recorder.
You shot at a deer but missed. You got no food today! 	You found no food today.
 Lucky fluke! You shot at a deer and hit a rabbit. You get one food card from the recorder.	You shot a bird. You get one food card from the recorder.
While you were hunting, a skunk broke into your hut and ate two days' worth of food. Give two food cards to the recorder. If you do not have two food cards, and if no one will give you one, you die of starvation.	You found a berry bush. Berries are in season. You get one food card from the recorder.
While you were hunting, a lion ate you and all your food. Give all your food cards to the recorder and drop out of the game. Since you didn't starve, group's points not affected. You are reborn the next week.	 Lucky fluke! You shot at a wild pig and hit a rabbit. You get one food card from the recorder.

3 : 28

Johnson, D. W., & Johnson, R. (2005). **Teaching Students To Be Peacemakers** (4th Ed.). Edina, MN: Interaction Book Company, (952)831-9500.

SUBSISTENCE EXERCISE: Hunting and Gathering Cards

Excellent shot! You killed a deer. You get two food cards from the re-corder.	While hunting, you found a berry bush. Berries are in season. You get one food card from the recorder.
You found some wild lettuce. You get one food card from the recorder.	Best of luck! You found a deer with a broken leg. You killed it with your stone club. Two food cards!
You shot a rabbit. You get one food card from the recorder.	You looked and looked and looked and looked but found no food today!!
You shot a bird. You get one food card from the recorder.	You shot at a rabbit, but it but it zigged instead of zagged. You got no food today.
You shot an aardvark! You get one food card from the recorder.	You walked for M I L E S and found nothing to gather or shoot at. You got no food today.

3 : 29

Johnson, D. W., & Johnson, R. (2005). **Teaching Students To Be Peacemakers** (4th Ed.). Edina, MN: Interaction Book Company, (952)831-9500.

INSTRUCTION SHEET

A severe drought has devastated your world. Because food is so scarce, you have banded together into a hunting and gathering group. It is more efficient for several people to coordinate their hunting and gathering so that more territory may be covered in any one day.

There are five members of your hunting and gathering group. The food cards in your hands represent all you have left of your dwindling food supply. Since you already are weakened by hunger, you must eat at the end of each day (round) or die. At that time, you must give up one food card. When you are out of cards, you will die of starvation. A member who does not have one food card at the end of a day (round) is considered to be dead and can no longer participate in the group. Members with only one

food card may not talk. Only members with two or more food cards may discuss their situation and converse with each other. You may give food cards to each other whenever you wish to do so.

Johnson, D. W., & Johnson, R. (2005). **Teaching Students To Be Peacemakers** (4th Ed.). Edina, MN: Interaction Book Company, (952)831-9500.

DISCUSSION QUESTIONS

1. Who survived and who died?

2. How was a cooperative or a competitive strategy decided on?

3. How did participants feel about the impending death by starvation?

4. How did the dead feel when they knew others could have saved them?

5. How did the survivors feel when others died when they had extra food cards?

6. Who organized the group to create a "just" distribution of food?

7. What real life situations parallel this exercise?

Johnson, D. W., & Johnson, R. (2005). **Teaching Students To Be Peacemakers** (4th Ed.). Edina, MN: Interaction Book Company, (952)831-9500.

RULES for SUBSISTENCE

1. The game begins when the recorder gives all participants three food cards, shuffles the hunting and gathering cards, and places them in the center of the group.

2. The purpose of the game is to gain points. You receive eight points if at the end of the week of hunting and gathering (seven rounds) you have more food cards than does any other participant in your group. If no one in your group has starved at the end of the week of hunting and gathering, all participants receive five points.

3. The game is played for a minimum of two weeks. At the beginning of each week all participants begin with three food cards and with all five participants alive.

4. You draw one card during each round. You read it aloud to the group and receive from or give to the recorder the number of food cards indicated.

5. During a round you may give food cards to other particpants if you wish to.

6. All participants read the hunting and gathering cards aloud. Only those with two or more food cards, however, may discuss the game with each other. Participants with one or no food cards must be silent.

7. At the end of each round participants hold up their food cards and announce to the group how many food cards they have.

8. At the end of each round participants give one food card each to the recorder. This symbolizes the food eaten during the day to stay alive.

9. If a participant cannot give a food card to the recorder at the end of a round, the participant dies of starvation and is excluded from further rounds during that week.

10. At the end of each week of hunting and gathering (seven rounds) the recorder announces who has the most food cards and how many participants starved to death. Points are then awarded.

3 : 32

Johnson, D. W., & Johnson, R. (2005). **Teaching Students To Be Peacemakers** (4th Ed.). Edina, MN: Interaction Book Company, (952)831-9500.

RECORD SHEET

NAME	ROUND 1	ROUND 2	ROUND 3	ROUND 4	ROUND 5	ROUND 6	ROUND 7

Johnson, D. W., & Johnson, R. (2005). **Teaching Students To Be Peacemakers** (4th Ed.). Edina, MN: Interaction Book Company, (952)831-9500.

OBSERVATION SHEET

	ROUND 1	ROUND 2	ROUND 3	ROUND 4	ROUND 5	ROUND 6	ROUND 7
NUMBER OF CARDS GIVEN AWAY							
NUMBER OF CARDS TAKEN AWAY							
NUMBER OF PEOPLE STARVED							
COOPERATIVE STRATEGY SUGGESTED							
COMPETITIVE COMMENT							
OTHER							

Johnson, D. W., & Johnson, R. (2005). **Teaching Students To Be Peacemakers** (4th Ed.). Edina, MN: Interaction Book Company, (952)831-9500.

Renewable Resource Game Procedure

1. Divide class into groups of four. Place a sheet of paper labeled "Common Area" and one Record Sheet in the middle of each group. Place sixteen shares of the resource (candy, popcorn, poker chips) in the "common area" of each group.

2. The rules for the game are:

   a. A round consists of a two-minute period in which each member has an opportunity to take as many shares of the resource as he or she wants from the common area. Group members cannot put shares back in the common area. At the end of the game, each group member may keep all the shares of the resource he or she has amassed or trade them in for prizes (pencils, pens, notebook). The shares cannot be redistributed among group members after the game has ended.

   b. Each group member needs at least one share of the resource per round to be sustained. If a member does not take at least one share, he or she "dies" and no longer has the opportunity to take shares from the common area.

   c. At the end of each round, the resource will be replenished by one-half of its existing number of shares in the common area.

   d. During each round, members record on the Record Sheet how many shares each member takes from the common area and the number of shares left in the group common area. At the end of the game, the number of shares left in the common area and the number of shares each member has will be determined.

3. Round 1: Group members have the opportunity to take as many shares of the resource as they want from the common area. Members should record how many shares each member has taken and the number of shares left in the group common area. If a member takes zero shares, he or she is considered "dead" and can no longer play. At the end of the round (after every member has had the opportunity to take shares of the resource), the group will receive additional shares equaling one-half of the shares remaining in the common area.

4. Round 2: Group members have the opportunity to take as many shares of the resource as they want from the common area. Members should record how

Johnson, D. W., & Johnson, R. (2005). **Teaching Students To Be Peacemakers** (4th Ed.). Edina, MN: Interaction Book Company, (952)831-9500.

many shares each member has taken and the number of shares left in the group common area. If a member takes zero shares, he or she is considered "dead" and can no longer play. At the end of the round (after every member has had the opportunity to take shares of the resource), the group will receive additional shares equaling one-half of the shares remaining in the common area.

5. Round 3: Group members have the opportunity to take as many shares of the resource as they want from the common area. Members should record how many shares each member has taken and the number of shares left in the group common area. If a member takes zero shares, he or she is considered "dead" and can no longer play. At the end of the round (after every member has had the opportunity to take shares of the resource), the group will receive additional shares equaling one-half of the shares remaining in the common area.

6. Round 4: Group members have the opportunity to take as many shares of the resource as they want from the common area. Members should record how many shares each member has taken and the number of shares left in the group common area. If a member takes zero shares, he or she is considered "dead" and can no longer play. At the end of the round (after every member has had the opportunity to take shares of the resource), the group will receive additional shares equaling one-half of the shares remaining in the common area.

7. At the end of the game, the group determines how many total shares each member has and the total number of shares left in the common area. They then discuss the questions on the discussion sheet.

Johnson, D. W., & Johnson, R. (2005). **Teaching Students To Be Peacemakers** (4th Ed.). Edina, MN: Interaction Book Company, (952)831-9500.

Renewable Resource Game: Participant Instructions

You are about to play a game in which your group of four members has 16 shares of a renewable resource in a common area. There will be four rounds in which you have the opportunity to take shares for yourself from the common area of the resource.

During each round you may take as many shares of the resource as you like. You may choose to take no shares or you may choose to take all the shares in the common area. It is up to you. When you take shares out of the common resource area, it is forever. You can **not** put shares back into the common area or give them to other group members. In order to stay alive, each of you must take one share of the resource during each round. If you do not take a share, you will "die" and will no longer be able to play the game.

At the end of each round, the group's common shares of the resource will be renewed or replenished; your group will have one-half of the number of shares left in the common area added to the common area. If there are ten shares in the common area, for example, the group will have an additional five shares added to their common area, giving them fifteen shares to start the next round of the game. If there are nine shares in the common area, the group will receive four additional shares to be added to their common area. If there are an odd number of shares in the common area, the number received at the end of the round will be rounded down (you cannot receive one-half a share of the resource. If there are no common shares left, your group will receive no new shares of the resource.

You will have two minutes for each round.

Johnson, D. W., & Johnson, R. (2005). **Teaching Students To Be Peacemakers** (4th Ed.). Edina, MN: Interaction Book Company, (952)831-9500.

Renewable Resource Discussion Questions

1. What happened in your group? Did all members survive? Which members ended up with the most shares of the resource? How many shares were left in the common area?

2. **Sustainable yield** is the maximum rate at which people can use a renewable resources without reducing the ability of the resource to renew itself. What was the sustainable yield in this game?

3. What are the advantages and disadvantages of using a resource in a sustainable way?

Advantages	Disadvantages
It can last forever.	You need to control use of the resource.

4. What advantages and disadvantages are there to using a resource in a nonsustainable way?

Advantages	Disadvantages
People will have a large amount of the resource available when they want it and thereby make a lot of money in the short term.	People can destroy the resource base for themselves and future generations.

5. In this game, the population of each group stayed the same. In reality, however, the human population is increasing rapidly. What would have happened if one or two or three additional people would have been added to your group?

Johnson, D. W., & Johnson, R. (2005). **Teaching Students To Be Peacemakers** (4th Ed.). Edina, MN: Interaction Book Company, (952)831-9500.

6. What are three conclusions you wish to share with the entire class?

   a. _____

   b. _____

   c. _____

7. In a whole class discussion, it will be determined:

   a. Which group had the most shares of the resource left in their common area at the end of Round 4.

   b. Which groups believed that their resource could last forever? How many shares were the members of these groups taking each round?

Johnson, D. W., & Johnson, R. (2005). **Teaching Students To Be Peacemakers** (4th Ed.). Edina, MN: Interaction Book Company, (952)831-9500.

Renewable Resource Record Sheet

Round				Common Shares
1				
2				
3				
4				
Total				

Directions: Write the name of each group member above each column. After each round, write the number of shares of the resource each member took in the appropriate column. Then write the number of shares of the resource left in the common area.

Johnson, D. W., & Johnson, R. (2005). **Teaching Students To Be Peacemakers** (4th Ed.). Edina, MN: Interaction Book Company, (952)831-9500.

Chapter Four: Conflict Strategies

What Are The Two Basic Concerns

I hold it be a proof of great prudence for men to abstain from threats and insulting words toward anyone, for neither . . . diminishes the strength of the enemy; but the one makes him more cautious, and the other increases his hatred of you and makes him more persevering in his efforts to injure you.

Niccolo Machiavelli, an adviser to 16th Century Florentine princes

Dealing with a conflict of interests is like going swimming in a cold lake. Some people like to test the water, stick their foot in, and enter slowly. Such people want to get used to the cold gradually. Other people like to take a running start and leap in. They want to get the cold shock over quickly. Similarly, different people use different strategies for managing conflicts. Usually, we learn these strategies in childhood so that later they seem to function automatically on a "preconscious" level. We just do whatever seems to come naturally. But we do have a personal strategy and, because it was learned, we can always change it by learning new and more effective ways of managing conflicts.

Whether we approach conflicts cautiously or jump right in, we have to take two major concerns into account (Blake and Mouton, 1964; Johnson & F. Johnson, 2003):

- **Reaching an agreement that achieves our goals**. This is why we negotiate. We each have personal goals that we wish to achieve. We are in conflict because we have a goal or interest that conflicts with another person's goal or interest. Our goal may be placed on a continuum between being of little importance to being highly important.

- **Maintaining an appropriate relationship with the other person**. Some relationships are temporary while some are permanent. Within career, family, neighborhood, and community settings we need to maintain committed relationships so we can work together effectively to achieve mutual goals. Our relationship with the other person may be placed on a continuum between being of little importance to being highly important.

4 : 1

Johnson, D. W., & Johnson, R. (2005). **Teaching Students To Be Peacemakers** (4th Ed.). Edina, MN: Interaction Book Company, (952)831-9500.

**High
Importance**

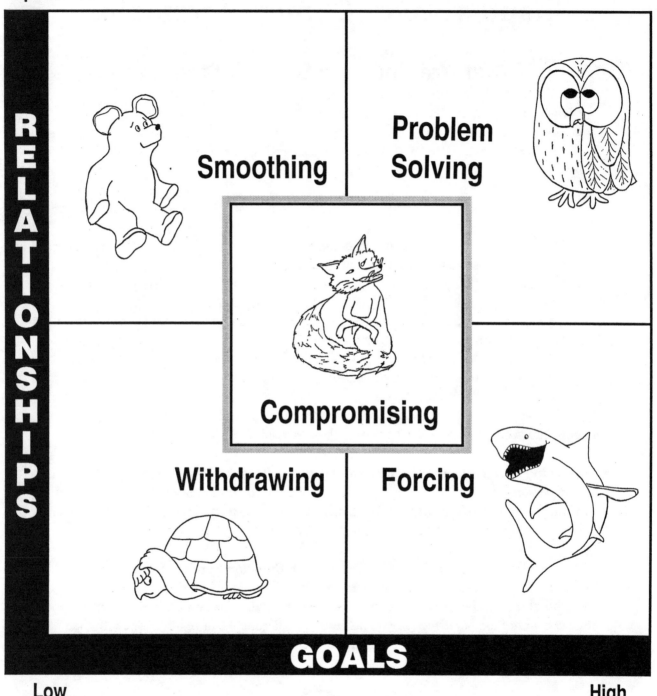

R
E
L
A
T
I
O
N
S
H
I
P
S

Smoothing

**Problem
Solving**

Compromising

Withdrawing

Forcing

GOALS

**Low
Importance**

**High
Importance**

4 : 2

Johnson, D. W., & Johnson, R. (2005). **Teaching Students To Be Peacemakers** (4th Ed.). Edina, MN: Interaction Book Company, (952)831-9500.

Importance Of Achieving One's Goals

In a conflict, disputants have to decide what they want and how important their goal is to them. The importance and commitment to the goals influences the way in which disputants manage the conflict. When disputants seek to achieve their goals, the goals may overlap or be the same as the goals of others (i.e., there may be mutual or joint goals), the goals may be opposed to the goals of others (i.e., when one achieves his or her goal, all others are prevented from achieving their goals), or your goals may be independent from the goals of others (in which case there is no conflict). When goals are perceived to be opposed, conflicts tend to be managed in destructively ways. It is primarily when goals overlap or can be reformulated as mutual goals that conflicts may be resolved constructively. At the very least, disputants have to decide how important their goal is to them and how much overlap exists among the goals of everyone involved.

Importance Of Friendships And Other Ongoing Relationships

In a conflict, disputants have to decide how important the relationship with the other disputants is to them. In resolving conflicts, disputants often focus on the nature of the agreement and whether or not they get what they want, without much consideration of whether interaction will continue with the other disputants, their ability to work together effectively will be improved or damaged, or their long-term relationship is affected positively or negatively. The specific goals disputants are striving to achieve come and go and can change overnight. The relationships among students, on the other hand, may last for years or even a life time.

The impact of conflict management on the relationships among students may be the most important outcome of the conflict. Peer relations contribute substantially to students' social and cognitive development and to the effectiveness with which individuals function as adults. The single best childhood predictor of adult functioning and psychological health, for example, is not school grades or classroom behavior; it is the quality of childhood peer relationships. Children who are generally disliked, who are aggressive and disruptive, who are unable to sustain close relationships with other children, and who cannot establish a place for themselves in the peer culture, are seriously at risk for dysfunctional behavior, psychological illness, and criminal behavior as adults. Friendships forecast good adjustment during the early weeks of kindergarten and making new friends changes children's adjustment in positive directions during the school year.

Building and maintaining constructive, positive peer relationships may be, therefore, one of the most important outcomes of schooling. The importance of friendships are that they are egalitarian (it is a relationship among equals) in which individuals spend time together, have common interests, engage in personal talks in which feelings and experiences are shared, and enjoy each other's company. Within friendships students learn about

4 : 3

Johnson, D. W., & Johnson, R. (2005). **Teaching Students To Be Peacemakers** (4th Ed.). Edina, MN: Interaction Book Company, (952)831-9500.

reciprocity, trust, loyalty, and long-term commitment to and emotional investment in another person. It is within friendships that empathy, perspective-taking, and basic social competencies are largely developed. The importance of building and maintaining long-term, positive, caring peer relationships may be seen in that friendships, provide:

1. Emotional resources, for both fun and coping with stress and adversity. Friends are the emotional foundation for providing the emotional resources to strike out into new territory, meet new people, tackle new problems, and have fun. The duration and frequency of laughing, smiling, looking, and talking are greater between friends than between acquaintances. Friendships also buffer individuals from the adverse effects of negative events (such as family conflict, terminal illness, parents' unemployment, and school failure) and contribute to positive self-regard.

2. Cognitive resources for problem solving, knowledge acquisition, and generally understanding what is going on in their lives. Friends provide models to be imitated, resulting in learning new skills and behavioral patterns. Friends tend to collaborate more successfully than do nonfriends. Friends talk more, take more time to work out differences in the understanding of the task and situation, and compromise more readily than nonfriends do. Friendships tend to be unique contexts for transmitting information from one person to another.

3. Contexts in which basic social skills are acquired or elaborated. Both cooperation and conflict occur more readily in friendships than in other contexts. Friends emphasize reciprocity, disengagement, and equity in conflict management to a greater extent than do nonfriends.

4. Templates for subsequent relationships. While new relationships are never exact copies of old ones, the organization of behavior in relationships generalizes from old ones to new ones.

It is not only friendships that are long-term relationships. There may be peers with whom students interact with or work with everyday whom they would not consider to be friends, and there may be adults (i.e., teachers, administrators, parents, grandparents) with whom students interact frequently over long periods of time. When friends are not available, other relationships may be elastic enough to serve the friendship functions. While children with friends are better off than children without friends, relationships with others (such as teachers, grandparents, pets) may have the same effects. Managing conflicts constructively with these nonfriends may have considerable influence on the quality of a person's life.

Reconciliation

When conflicts are characterized by bitterness and anger, part of the resolution has to include reconciliation among the participants so that their relationships are repaired and

Johnson, D. W., & Johnson, R. (2005). **Teaching Students To Be Peacemakers** (4th Ed.). Edina, MN: Interaction Book Company, (952)831-9500.

they can interact positively in the future. **Reconciliation** is bringing people into friendly relations after an estrangement. Reconciliation occurs during and at the end of ongoing conflict. It is difficult to do, as appeals to "put the conflict behind us" may be seen as a ploy used by the stronger party to ignore or diminish those who were damaged in the conflict. Reconciliation may be possible only after (a) a resolution to the conflict has been created that is considered "just" by all participants and/or (b) the people involved have forgiven each other. If there is a clear winner and loser in a conflict, reconciliation is difficult to achieve. If injustice exists in the situation or in the relationship, reconciliation may not be possible.

There are three types of justice that must exist for reconciliation to occur: distributive (which deals with fair outcomes), procedural (which deals with fair processes), and inclusionary (which deals with whether all relevant parties are considered to be members of the same moral community). Reconciliation depends on all parties in a conflict believing the resolution is just to everyone, the procedures used to resolve the conflict were just, and that all parties are members of the same moral community. In many middle schools and high schools, for example, any student who dresses differently from the norm, wears their hair differently, or behaves differently may be morally excluded and viewed as fair game for teasing, taunting, and being rejected. Reconciliation after such experiences is difficult. For justice to occur, parties must have moral value and worthy of considerations of fairness. If a person is excluded from the moral community, then whether the procedures for resolving the conflict were just or whether the outcomes were fair can appear irrelevant or inapplicable.

The Five Strategies For Managing Conflicts

How important your personal goals are to you and how important the relationship is to you affect how you act in a conflict. Given these two concerns, there are five basic strategies that may be used to manage conflicts:

- **Problem-Solving Negotiations**: When both the goal and the relationship are highly important to you, you initiate problem-solving negotiations to resolve the conflict. Solutions are sought that ensure both you and the other person fully achieve your goals and resolve any tensions and negative feelings between the two of you. You maintain your interests and try to find a way of reconciling them with the other's interests. This strategy requires risky moves, such as revealing your underlying interests while expecting the other to do the same.

- **Smoothing**: When the goal is of little importance to you but the relationship is of high importance, you give up your goals and facilitate the other person's goal achievement in order to maintain the relationship at the highest quality possible. When you think the other person's interests are much stronger or important than yours, you smooth and

Johnson, D. W., & Johnson, R. (2005). **Teaching Students To Be Peacemakers** (4th Ed.). Edina, MN: Interaction Book Company, (952)831-9500.

give the other person their way. When you are smoothing, do so with good humor. Be pleasant about it.

- **Forcing or Win-Lose Negotiations**: When the goal is very important but the relationship is not, you seek to achieve your goal at the expense of the other person's goal achievement by forcing or persuading the other to yield. You compete for a win. When you are buying a used car, for example, you usually concentrate on spending as little money as possible regardless of how the salesperson feels. In a tennis match, you usually try to win without regard for how the other person feels about being defeated.

- **Compromising**: When both the goal and the relationship are moderately important to you, and it appears that both you and the other person cannot get what you want, you may need to give up part of your goals and sacrifice part of the relationship in order to reach an agreement. Compromising may involve meeting in the middle so each gets half or flipping a coin to let chance decide who will get his or her way. Compromising is often used when disputants wish to engage in problem-solving negotiations but do not have the time to do so.

- **Withdrawing**: When the goal is not important and you do not need to keep a relationship with the other person, you may wish to give up both your goals and the relationship and avoid the issue and the other person. Avoiding a hostile stranger, for example, may be the best thing to do. Sometimes you may wish to withdraw from a conflict until you and the other person have calmed down and are in control of your feelings.

In using these strategies there are five important points to consider. **First, to be competent in managing conflicts, you must be able to engage competently in each strategy**. You need to practice all five strategies until they are thoroughly mastered. You do not want to be an overspecialized dinosaur who can deal with conflict in only one way. Each strategy is appropriate under a certain set of conditions and, based on the dual concerns of one's goals and the relationship with the other person, you choose the conflict strategy appropriate to the situation.

Second, some of the strategies require the participation of the other disputant and some may be enacted alone. You can give up your goals by using withdrawing and smoothing no matter what the other disputant does. When you try to achieve your goals by using forcing, compromising, and problem-solving, the other disputant has to participate in the process.

Third, the strategies tend to be somewhat incompatible in the sense that choosing one of them makes choosing the others less likely. Though sometimes used in combination (temporarily withdrawing before initiating problem-solving negotiations), withdrawing implies lack of commitment to one's goals, while negotiating implies high commitment to

Johnson, D. W., & Johnson, R. (2005). **Teaching Students To Be Peacemakers** (4th Ed.). Edina, MN: Interaction Book Company, (952)831-9500.

one's goals. Forcing implies low commitment to the relationship while smoothing implies high commitment to the relationship. Essentially, the five strategies are independent from each other and when you engage in one the likelihood of your being able to switch effectively to another is not high.

Fourth, certain strategies may deteriorate or evolve into other strategies. When you try to withdraw, and the other disputant pursues you and will not allow you to withdraw, you may respond with forcing. When you try to initiate problem-solving negotiations and the other disputant responds with forcing, you may reciprocate by engaging in win-lose tactics. When time is short, problem-solving negotiations may deteriorate into compromising.

Check Your Understanding

Demonstrate your understanding of the following concepts by matching the definitions with the appropriate concept. Check your answers with your partner and explain why you believe your answers to be correct.

Answer	Concept	Definition
	1. Withdrawing	a. Achieving your goal at the expense of the other person's goal achievement.
	2. Forcing	b. Physically or psyhcologically leaving the situation and avoiding the issue and the other person.
	3. Smoothing	c. Agreeing to a settlement that gives you and the other person only part of what each of you wanted.
	4. Compromising	d. Seeking an agreement that allow both parties to achieve their goals while maintaining a high quality relationship.
	5. Problem-Solving	e. Facilitating the other person's goal accomplishment while giving up the possibility of achieving one's own goals

Fifth, whether problem-solving or win-lose negotiations are initiated depends on your perception of the future of the relationship. When conflicts arise, the potential short-term gains must be weighed against potential long-term losses. When you perceive the relationship as being unimportant, you may go for the "win" by attempting to force the other person to capitulate or give in. The relationship may be perceived as unimportant because (a) there will be only one or a few interactions or (b) you are so angry at the other person that only the present matters. When you perceive the relationship as being

Johnson, D. W., & Johnson, R. (2005). **Teaching Students To Be Peacemakers** (4th Ed.). Edina, MN: Interaction Book Company, (952)831-9500.

important, then you will try to solve the problem in a way that achieves the other person's goals as well as your own. The relationship may be perceived to be important because it is ongoing and long-term or there are strong positive emotions (such as liking and respect) that bond you to the other person. **The shadow of the future looms largest when interactions among individuals are durable and frequent. Durability** ensures that individuals will not easily forget how they have treated, and been treated by, each other in the future. **Frequency** promotes stability by making the consequences of today's actions more salient for tomorrow's dealings. When individuals realize they will work with each other frequently and for a long period of time, they see that the long-term benefits of cooperation outweigh the short-term benefits of taking advantage of the other person. In ongoing relationships, the future outweighs the present so that the quality of the relationship is more important than the outcome of any particular negotiation. In schools, all relationships are long-term and, therefore, the shadow of the future is ever present.

Within the ongoing relationships (in a school or any other social system), **there are six basic rules to follow in resolving conflicts**.

Rule 1: Do Not Withdraw From Or Ignore Conflict

In headaches and in worry, Vaguely life leaks away.

W. H. Auden

Withdrawal is physically or psyhcologically leaving the situation and avoiding the issue and the other person, that is, giving up your personal goals and the relationship with the other person. The procedure for withdrawing is to avoid the other person and give up your needs and goals related to the conflict. You leave the presence of the other person or refuse to talk about the issue. Withdrawal is appropriate when the goal is not important and you do not need to keep a relationship with the other person. The perceived feasibility of withdrawal increases as the relationship is perceived to be ending and the other person seems irrational and unable to problem solve.

There are a number of reasons why you may wish to withdraw from a conflict (Johnson & F, Johnson, 2003). **First**, you may not know the other person and may not care about the issue. Avoiding a hostile stranger may be the best thing to do. **Second**, you may be afraid of potential social isolation, humiliation, and loss of status as friends and schoolmates become involved and choose sides. You may fear that if you express your anger or resentment you will be disliked, be rejected, be attacked, or be seen as a complainer. Facing a conflict and attempting to resolve it carries the risk of creating a residue of interpersonal antagonisms that will hurt your social status in the school. **Third**, from past experience you may believe that it is hopeless to try to resolve the conflict. When a person has continually experienced negative outcomes in conflict situations, a state of learned helplessness results in which the person believes that there is nothing he or she can do to

Johnson, D. W., & Johnson, R. (2005). **Teaching Students To Be Peacemakers** (4th Ed.). Edina, MN: Interaction Book Company, (952)831-9500.

create a positive resolution of a conflict (Seligman, 1975). Consequently, it seems easier to physically and/or psychologically withdraw from a conflict than to face it. **Fourth**, you may be inhibited to express anger, resentment, or envy toward a schoolmate because you consider it bad manners or immature to do so. **Fifth**, there may be times when strategically you temporarily withdraw from and ignore a conflict in order to confront the other person at a more advantageous time or deal with the conflict when more information is available.

In the long run, it is rarely easier to withdraw (physically and psychologically) from a conflict than to face it. When there is a long-term relationship involved, such as in a school, work, or family setting, you should almost never withdraw. Rather, you should face and resolve the conflict. It is a fallacy to believe that ignoring a conflict will make it go away. Refusing to face a conflict has personal as well as interpersonal costs. Ignoring a conflict does not make it disappear, it:

- Keeps emotional energy tied up in fear, resentment, and hostility. Repressing anger, for example, can lead eventually to emotional explosions that create new conflicts and revive old ones in destructive ways.

- Results in emotions (such as anger, resentment, fear, and dislike) being expressed indirectly. Indirect expressions of anger, for example, include sulkiness, uncooperativeness, sarcasm, or talking behind the other person's back. New conflicts are created, incurring further costs.

- Results in the conflict being dealt with in indirect ways. Indirectly dealt-with conflicts have the longest life expectancy and the most costs (often seemingly unrelated to the original conflict).

- Results in repressing irritation about many small conflicts until you inappropriately explode in anger about the latest one. This is sometimes known as "gunny sacking."

In the long run, it is almost always more wise to face your conflicts and openly negotiate constructive resolutions to them and, therefore, you should not withdraw from or ignore your conflicts.

Rule 2: Do Not Engage In Forcing

I know I am among civilized men because they are fighting so savagely.
Voltaire

Forcing is the achievement of your goal at the expense of the other person's goal achievement, that is, you strive to reach an agreement that is more favorable to you than to the other person. By achieving your goal, you deprive the

Johnson, D. W., & Johnson, R. (2005). **Teaching Students To Be Peacemakers** (4th Ed.). Edina, MN: Interaction Book Company, (952)831-9500.

other person of the possibility of their achieving his or her goal. Forcing is sometimes known as win-lose negotiations. There are times when you negotiate to win. You go for the win when your goals are important and when the relationship with the other person has no future. You seek to achieve your goals at all costs without concern for (a) the goals of others or (b) the feelings and attitudes of others toward you. Buying a used car or trying to get into a crowded restaurant are two instances where forcing may be appropriate. Forcing involves (a) assuming that conflicts are settled when one person "wins" and the other person "loses" and (b) overpowering opponents by force or persuasion. The perceived feasibility of forcing increases as the relationship is seen as temporary and the opponent's willingness to yield increases.

Helpful hints in going for the win are (a) make an extreme opening offer (if you are willing to pay $1,500, offer $500), (b) compromise slowly (try to get the other person to compromise first), (c) point out everything that is wrong and unreasonable about the other person's position, and (d) be ready to walk away with no agreement. You want to change the other's evaluation of how many concessions are required to reach an agreement through a combination of tactics for forcing the other to yield and tactics for persuading the other to yield. Tactics used to force the other to yield include making threats, imposing penalties that will be withdrawn if the other concedes, and taking preemptive actions designed to resolve the conflict without the other's consent (such as taking a book home that the other insists is his). Such tactics are aimed at overpowering, overwhelming, or intimidating others. Tactics to persuade the other to yield include presenting persuasive arguments aimed at convincing others to concede, imposing a deadline, committing oneself to an "unalterable" position, or making demands that far exceed what is actually acceptable.

One purpose of forcing may be to demonstrate dominance over another person to establish one's place in a social hierarchy. **Social dominance theory** is based on the assumption that in any situation, resources are limited and, therefore, resource acquisition compels competition among the individuals or groups involved. Each participant strives to establish a position in the social dominance hierarchy by acquiring as many of the scarce resources as possible. The participant's ability to successfully compete for limited resources defines his or her position in the social hierarchy. Acquiring the resources involves win-lose negotiations or, in other words, forcing.

Forcing can develop inadvertently. In negotiations, each person takes a position, argues for it, and makes concessions to reach a compromise or searches for a mutually beneficial solution. This involves successively taking, and then giving up, a sequence of positions. The danger in this procedure is that individuals tend to lock themselves into the positions they are taking. The more you clarify your position and defend it against attack, the more committed you become to it. The more you try to convince the other person of the impossibility of changing your position, the more difficult it becomes for you to do so. Your ego becomes identified with your position. You may become more interested in saving face than in seeking a wise agreement. In defending your position, and trying to

Johnson, D. W., & Johnson, R. (2005). **Teaching Students To Be Peacemakers** (4th Ed.). Edina, MN: Interaction Book Company, (952)831-9500.

win, less attention is devoted to meeting the underlying concerns of the other person. Agreement becomes less likely.

The decision to engage in win-lose negotiations may be based on three assumptions:

1. You will never be interdependent with the other person again. This is often mistaken, as unforeseen circumstances tend to arise where you may have to cooperate with the other person. It is only when you will never interact with the person again that win-lose negotiations are appropriate.

2. You will be able to dominate the other person in all future interactions. This is often mistaken, as in later situations the other person may (a) have resources that you need and therefore has more power than you or (b) no longer need the resources you control and be independent from you. Bullying often backfires. Even when the person works for you, circumstances can arise when you need his or her good will.

3. The conflict cannot be redefined as a mutual problem. This is often mistaken, as it is only small, one-dimensional conflicts that cannot be recast as a problem. If two or more issues are at stake, the possibility for problem-solving exists. A famous example is the dispute between Israel and Egypt. When Egypt and Israel sat down to negotiate at Camp David in October 1978, it appeared that they had before them an intractable conflict. Egypt demanded the immediate return of the entire Sinai Peninsula; Israel, which had occupied the Sinai since the 1967 Middle East war, refused to return an inch of this land. Efforts to reach agreement, including the proposal of a compromise in which each nation would retain half of the Sinai, proved completely unacceptable to both sides. As long as the dispute was defined in terms of what percentage of the land each side would control, no agreement could be reached. Once both realized that what Israel really cared about was the security that the land offered, while Egypt was primarily interested in sovereignty over it, the stalemate was broken. The two countries were then able to reach an integrative solution: Israel would return the Sinai to Egypt in exchange for assurances of a demilitarized zone and Israeli air bases in the Sinai.

There are very few times in your life when you negotiate with someone you will never interact with again. There are very few times in your life when you can dominate another person over and over again. There are very few conflicts that cannot be defined as a problem to be solved. The majority of the time, therefore, you will want to engage in problem-solving negotiations.

In addition, in long-term relationships such as among classmates or between students and faculty, engaging in win-lose negotiations is ineffective and often destructive. Unfortunately, win-lose strategies are often used in schools (DeCecco & Richards, 1974; Flanders, 1964; Gump, 1964; Rafalides & Hoy, 1971). Teachers and administrators often try to dominate students through authoritarian control by coercing them into doing what the

Johnson, D. W., & Johnson, R. (2005). **Teaching Students To Be Peacemakers** (4th Ed.). Edina, MN: Interaction Book Company, (952)831-9500.

teacher or administrator wants. The result tends to be student resistance and alienation. Coercion and threats of punishment by school personnel frequently escalated conflict and prevented resolution.

It is a fallacy to believe that you can "win" without damaging the relationship. Forcing usually has negative effects (such as creating resistance and resentment) and reduces the likelihood of working together effectively in the future. Reactance theory (Brehm, 1966) predicts that any attempt to reduce someone's perceived freedom or control will motivate that person to reassert freedom or control. In other words, the harder you push the other person to give in, the harder the other person will push back. The more you force, the more the other person resists and the angrier the other person gets. When forcing is successful, winning may result in a sense of pride and achievement. When it is unsuccessful, it may result in depression, guilt, shame, and failure. Forcing always carries a high risk of (a) alienating the other person and starting a spiral of win-lose tactics, (b) being censured by a third-party, and (c) disapproved of by interested audiences.

When you have to face the other person again and again in the future, winning can create anger and resentment that seriously damages the ability of the two of you to work together productively. The best advice is , *"Never walk away with a win; keep negotiating until the other person and you both have what you want. If you walk away with a win, you will have to watch your back every time you pass a dark doorway, and life is too short to be constantly watching your back!"* In other words, in long-term, ongoing relationships, forcing is almost always inappropriate.

Rule 3: Assess For Smoothing

A soft answer turneth away wrath.

Holy Bible

When you attach little importance to the goal, but you care about the relationship, you may wish to smooth. **Smoothing** is the facilitation of the other person's goal accomplishment while giving up the possibility of achieving one's own goals. It often involves letting the other person have his or her way. Within long-term relationships, you have considerable concern about the other person's interests and well-being. You are, after all, striving to achieve mutual long-term goals and the quality of your life depends at least partially on the quality of the relationship you maintain with the other person. The procedure for appropriate smoothing is when two people (a) share mutual long-term goals, (b) each accurately and clearly presents his or her true wants and interests, (c) each weighs the true interests of one another and determine whose interests are stronger or more important, and (d) one person gives up his or her interests to help the other achieve his or her goals. This is known as one-step negotiating. If the issue is of little importance to you, or if you determine that the other person's interests are much stronger than yours, you smooth by

4 : 12

Johnson, D. W., & Johnson, R. (2005). **Teaching Students To Be Peacemakers** (4th Ed.). Edina, MN: Interaction Book Company, (952)831-9500.

agreeing to his or her proposal or facilitating his or her goal achievement. The perceived feasibility of smoothing increases as the other person's interests seem more important than yours, the other person is perceived to be abiding by the norm of mutual responsiveness (has recently engaged in smoothing in your relationship), and time is very short.

Appropriate smoothing should be reciprocal. Ongoing relationships should be guided by the norms of (a) mutual responsiveness (both persons should be committed to fulfilling each other's goals and concerned about each other's well-being), (b) reciprocity (your concern for the other should result in the other being concerned about you), and (c) equity (over a long period of time the number of times you give up your interests for the other's benefit should be equal to the number of times the other person gave up his or her needs for your benefit). If everyone involved follows these norms, over time each will have his or her major wants and interests satisfied by the others.

Concern for the other person in a conflict may be genuine (based on friendship, love, or collegiality) or instrumental (based on perceived interdependence where the other person has some control over one's rewards and penalties). In both cases, the concern is based on a view of the future after the conflict has been resolved. The current issue is perceived to be less important than the long-term health of the relationship. The danger of smoothing is that it may be perceived as weakness and thus encourage the other person to engage in forcing in future conflicts. In conflicts, however, the opportunity to smooth is often missed because people lose awareness of the future and concentrate so hard on winning in the present that they ignore the importance of maintaining good relationships.

It is a fallacy to give up your interests and let the other person have what he or she wants out of timidity, fear, and wanting to be liked. Inappropriate smoothing is hiding your true interests from the other person and agreeing to a course of action that is detrimental to you simply because you want to be liked and accepted and you are afraid that the relationship is too fragile to survive an open conflict. You avoid the conflict in favor of superficial harmony. You may be afraid that you cannot discuss the conflict without damaging the relationship or that if the conflict continues, someone will get hurt and the relationship will be ruined.

In long-term relationships, smoothing is an important way to resolve potential conflicts in which the other person's interests are more important than one's own. Typically, everytime you smooth, you strengthen the relationship.

Rule 4: Compromise When Time Is Short

Compromising is agreeing to a settlement that gives you and the other person only part of what you wanted. You seek a compromise when (a) time is too short to engage in problem-solving negotiations and (b) both the goal and the relationship seem of moderate importance to you. Compromise is based on the premise that half a loaf is better than

4 : 13

Johnson, D. W., & Johnson, R. (2005). **Teaching Students To Be Peacemakers** (4th Ed.). Edina, MN: Interaction Book Company, (952)831-9500.

none! The procedure is to propose possible agreements and counteragreements that require each person to give up some of what he or she wants until both individuals settle on the agreement that is the best they can get under the circumstances. When you seek a compromise, you give up part of your goal and try to persuade the other person to do the same. You seek a solution in and settle on an agreement that is the middle ground between your two opening positions. You are willing to sacrifice part of your goals and part of the relationship in order to find a quick agreement. For example, when there is only twenty minutes of computer time available, and both you and your classmate want to use the computer, compromising so that each gets the computer for 10 minutes may be the best way to resolve the conflict. The perceived feasibility of compromising increases as the disputants' commitment to their interests decreases and time pressures increase. While compromising appears to be an equal distance from the four other strategies, it actually lies between problem-solving and smoothing and far away from withdrawal and forcing (van de Vliert, 1990; van de Vliert & Prein, 1989).

The problem with compromising is that any agreement that is reached may reflect a mechanical splitting of the difference between positions rather than a solution carefully crafted to meet the legitimate interests of each person. The result is frequently an agreement less satisfactory to each person than it could have been. Sometimes, though, you should be satisfied with less. Remember the story of the boy and the nuts. A boy who was very fond of nuts was told one day that he could have a handful. *"As big a handful as I like?"* he asked. *"As big a handful as you can take,"* his mother replied. The boy at once put his hand into the pitcher of nuts and grasped all his fist would hold. But when he tried to get his hand out, he found he could not because the neck of the pitcher was too narrow. He tried and tried to squeeze his hand through. At last he burst into tears. There he stood crying, yet unwilling to let a single nut go. *"The fault is not with the pitcher,"* his mother said. *"It is your greed that makes you cry. Be satisfied with half as many nuts and you will be able to get your hand out."*

In conflicts you may often have to modify your goals and settle for only part of what you originally wanted. Most often, however, compromising is not a good idea and should be done only when time is short.

Rule 5: Engage In Problem-Solving Negotiations

He that wrestles with us strengthens our nerves, and sharpens our skill. Our antagonist is our helper.

Edmund Burke, Reflection of the Revolution in France

Problem-solving negotiations is the seeking of agreements that allow both parties to achieve their goals while maintaining a high quality relationship. When both your goals and the relationship are of high importance to you, you

Johnson, D. W., & Johnson, R. (2005). **Teaching Students To Be Peacemakers** (4th Ed.). Interaction Book Company, (952)831-9500.

initiate problem-solving negotiations. To engage in problem-solving negotiations jointly with the other person you must define the conflict as a problem to be solved (this involves both persons stating what they want and how they feel), identifying the interests underlying each other positions (this involves both persons stating the reasons underlying their wants and feelings), stepping back and viewing the problem from both sides (this involves mutual perspective reversal), identifying a number of potential agreements that would maximize joint gain while improving the relationship, and jointly choosing the agreement that seems most advantageous for both sides and the future of the relationship.

It is impossible to interact day after day without conflicts arising. When individuals work together, sharing ideas, information, resources, and materials, they are bound to encounter problems. An open discussion of a conflict is not always a helpful thing to have. It is a mistake to assume that you can always openly discuss a conflict with another person. It is also a mistake to assume that you can never openly and directly discuss a conflict with another person. Whether you decide to initiate problem-solving negotiations depends on:

1. The strength of the relationship (generally, the stronger the relationship, the more direct and open your discussion can be).

2. The ability of the other person to discuss the conflict (the other person may not be able to discuss the conflict in a problem-solving way if his or her anxiety or distress level is too high, ability to change is too low, conflict-resolution skills are too low, or ego-strength or self-esteem are too low). Only initiate negotiations if you think the relationship is strong enough and the other person is able to discuss the conflict in a problem-solving, helpful way.

3. The amount of time available to discuss the conflict. Beginning a discussion of the conflict does not mean that the conflict will be quickly resolved. It is a start, not the end. Be sure you and the other person have the time to discuss the conflict. When time is short, or if the you and the other person cannot commit full attention to the conflict, the discussion of the conflict should be postponed to a later time. Make an appointment. Do not "hit and run." A hit-and-run occurs when you start a conversation about the conflict, give your definition and feelings, and then disappear before the other person has a chance to respond. Hit-and-runs tend to be harmful. They create resentment and anger rather than a constructive discussion.

Once you initiate problem-solving negotiations, you follow these general guidelines:

1. **Focus on the problem, not the person.** When negotiating it is imperative to separate the person from the problem. The conflict should be over issues, not personalities. Keep the negotiations free of personal attacks, criticisms, recriminations, and abusive language. You (a) make it clear it is the person's ideas or actions you disagree with, not the other individual as a person and (b) separate the other person's criticism of your actions and ideas from personal rejection.

4 : 15

Johnson, D. W., & Johnson, R. (2005). **Teaching Students To Be Peacemakers** (4th Ed.). Edina, MN: Interaction Book Company, (952)831-9500.

2. **Manage your emotions skillfully.** Conflicts often breed intense emotions. You cannot initiate negotiations effectively if your anger is out of control and you want to punish and hurt the other person. You cannot initiate negotiations effectively if you are afraid that the other person will lose his or her temper and harm you psychologically or physically. Only when emotions are under control can effective problem-solving negotiations take place.

3. **Take the easy conflicts first.** In initiating negotiations, take the easiest problems first. Learn to walk before you run. First use your negotiating procedures and skills on the easy problems and then use them on the harder issues. If it is not possible to identify a small issue, you may wish to choose a large one and divide it into smaller parts. A number of small agreements can then be pieced together into a sizable package. In addition, do not wait too long to initiate negotiations. Small conflicts are much easier to resolve than are large ones. Begin negotiations when issues are immediate, small, and concrete.

4. **Build trust between oneself and the other disputant.** The greater the trust among disputants, the greater the likelihood that they will engage in problem-solving negotiations. Trust tends to be high when disputants (a) expect to engage in future cooperative interaction, (b) perceive each other as belonging to the same overall group, (c) are engaged in a cooperative effort that requires the efforts of both to succeed, (d) see themselves as being able to punish the other for failing to cooperate or believe a third party will punish the other for failing to cooperate, and (e) are helpful towards the opponent (Johnson & F. Johnson, 2003).

Whenever possible, structure the conflict so that problem-solving negotiations are possible. The feasibility of problem solving negotiations increases as (a) the positive interdependence among disputants increases (the greater the positive interdependence, the more likely disputants are to engage in problem solving negotiations), (b) disputants' confidence increases that they and their opponents have the skills required to engage in problem solving, and (c) disputants' perceptions increase that the other is trustworthy (will not use the information revealed about the disputant's interests in an exploitative way).

Rule 6: Use Your Sense Of Humor

Humor is one of the most important aspects of keeping conflicts constructive. Keep your sense of humor during negotiations. Help the other person to do the same. Do not make the same mistake that Sam and Sally did. Sam and Sally both worked as copy writers for different advertising firms. Their daily job was to think up funny and humorous lines to go into commercials. One of the things they most enjoyed about each other was their sense of humor. Yet when they began to talk about a conflict, all humor was buried. They would yell, scream, demand, force, withdraw, pout, and try to hurt each other. Their creativity

Johnson, D. W., & Johnson, R. (2005). **Teaching Students To Be Peacemakers** (4th Ed.). Edina, MN: Interaction Book Company, (952)831-9500.

was locked away by their anger. Their relationship dramatically improved when they learned to stop yelling and deliberately wrote three humorous lines about the nature of the conflict to share with each other.

If laughter is not the best medicine, it is surely one of the best. Laughter can help keep you both psychologically and physically healthy. Laughter is a reflex, a series of involuntary spasms of the diaphragm. This movement forces the breathing muscles to contract and relax in quick succession, increasing the size of the chest cavity—which allows the lungs to take in more oxygen and expel more carbon dioxide than normal. As a result, laughter exercises the lungs, increases the blood's oxygen level, increases circulation and metabolism, and gently tones the entire cardiovascular system—"internal jogging." Muscles of the chest, abdomen, and face get a gentle workout and, if the joke is a real winner, so do the arms and legs. Following the laugh, these muscles relax and the pulse rate and blood pressure temporarily decline. Since muscle relaxation and anxiety cannot exist at the same time, the effect is that a good, hearty laugh may buy you up to 45 minutes of relaxation. Laughter also releases endorphins, the body's natural painkiller. **Any conflict will seem easier to resolve after disputants have laughed about it.** Whenever you are in a conflict, use your sense of humor.

Conclusions

Within any conflict you will have two concerns: to achieve your goals and to maintain effective working relationships. Those two concerns result in five possible strategies for managing conflicts: withdrawing, forcing, smoothing, comproming, and problem-solving. In deciding which of the five strategies to use within a conflict, you consider six rules:

1. Do not withdraw from or ignore conflict.	4. Compromise when time is short.
2. Do not engage in "win-lose" negotiations.	5. Initiate problem-solving negotiations.
3. Assess for smoothing.	6. Use your sense of humor.

Being able to choose how you wish to manage your conflicts empowers you considerably. You will want to learn how to use all five strategies appropriately. Reseach indicates that the most competent business executives, managers, and supervisors tend to use problem-solving negotiations and smoothing as their dominant conflict strategies. They tend to be highly relationship oriented, problem-solving when their goals are important and smoothing when they are not. Incompetent business executives, managers, and supervisors tend to use forcing and withdrawing most frequently. Within schools, teachers and administrators typically use forcing and withdrawal as their most frequent strategies. When faced with misbehaving students teachers often first try to force the student to behave and then to expel the student from the classroom or school (which is a form of

Johnson, D. W., & Johnson, R. (2005). **Teaching Students To Be Peacemakers** (4th Ed.). Edina, MN: Interaction Book Company, (952)831-9500.

withdrawal). In schools, it is especially important to replace such behavior whenever possible with problem-solving negotiations and smoothing.

In long-term, ongoing relationships, problem-solving negotiations and smoothing are the strategies that work best. When the goal is important to you, initiate problem-solving negotiations. When it is not, smooth. Because you almost always need to maintain good relationships, you will rarely want to force or withdraw.

In some ways the five strategies present a simplified view of how most conflicts are managed. The complexities of the interaction between two individuals may exceed their initial approaches to the conflict. You need, therefore, to be aware of your second most frequently used strategy, as that is the one you will tend to use when you are highly anxious and upset. Within most conflicts there are initial strategies followed by backup strategies followed by other strategies that are based on what the other person is doing. You may wish to initiate problem-solving negotiations, but when faced with a colleague who is forcing, you may have to force back. Whatever the other person does, however, keep seeking ways to begin problem-solving negotiations.

Johnson, D. W., & Johnson, R. (2005). **Teaching Students To Be Peacemakers** (4th Ed.). Edina, MN: Interaction Book Company, (952)831-9500.

CREATIVE CONFLICT CONTRACT

Write down your major learnings from reading this chapter and participating in training session one. Then write down how you plan to implement each learning. Share what you learned and your implementation plans with your base group. Listen carefully to their major learnings and implementation plans. You may modify your own plans on the basis of what you have learned from your groupmates. Volunteer one thing you can do to help each groupmate with his or her implementation plans. Utilize the help groupmates offer to you. Sign each member's plans to seal the contract.

MAJOR LEARNINGS	IMPLEMENTATION PLANS

Date: _____ Participant's Signature: _____

Signatures Of Group Members: _____

_____

Johnson, D. W., & Johnson, R. (2005). **Teaching Students To Be Peacemakers** (4th Ed.). Edina, MN: Interaction Book Company, (952)831-9500.

How I Act In Conflicts: Instructions

Different people learn different ways of managing conflicts. The strategies you use to manage conflicts may be quite different from those used by your classmates, teachers, and administrators. The following tasks give you an opportunity to increase your awareness of what conflict strategies you use and how they compare with the strategies used by others.

Task 1: Common Conflicts

1. Review the definition of conflicts of interests. List the most frequent and most difficult conflicts you have with other students, teachers, administrators, and parents. The conflicts need to be interpersonal and of some importance.

2. Meet in a group of four. Each member shares his or her conflicts. The most common conflicts of interests members have are listed.

Task 2: Your Conflict Behavior

Working individualistically, by yourself, complete the conflict strategies questionnaire, How I Act In Conflicts.

Task 3: Case Studies

1. Working individualistically, read the first case study carefully and rank order the alternative resolutions for "most effective" to "least effective" and for "most likely" to "least likely."

2. Do the same two rankings in your group of four. Work cooperatively. One group member should observe using the attached observation sheet. The other three members should do the ranking. All three active members of the group need to agree on the rankings and be able to explain the reasoning behind the two rankings. Each member of the group should:

    a. Listen carefully.

    b. Argue his or her point of view.

    c. Not change his or her mind unless he or she is logically persuaded.

    d. Express his or her feelings.

After finishing the first case study the group should go on to the second and then the third, repeating the same procedure of first ranking individually and then cooperatively as a group.

4 : 20

Johnson, D. W., & Johnson, R. (2005). **Teaching Students To Be Peacemakers** (4th Ed.). Edina, MN: Interaction Book Company, (952)831-9500.

Task 4: Understanding The Conflict Strategies

1. Divide the group into pairs. Each pair reads this chapter, using the pair-reading procedure given below, to ensure that both members understand what the five conflict strategies are and when they may be used appropriately. The pair-reading procedure is:

   a. Read all of the section headings to get an overview.

   b. Both persons silently read the first paragraph.

   c. The summarizer summarizes the content of the paragraph in his or her own words.

   d. The accuracy checker listens carefully, checks the summary for accuracy and completeness, adds anything that is left out, and relates the content of the paragraph to something learned previously.

   e. The two persons then silently read the next paragraph. The roles of summarizer and accuracy checker are rotated. The procedure is repeated. The two continue until they have read and discussed all the paragraphs in the chapter.

2. Write the name of each group member on separate slips of paper. Then write the conflict strategy that best fits the actions of the person named. Give the slips of paper to the person named. Each member should end up with three slips of paper describing how the other members perceive his or her strategy in managing conflicts.

Task 5: Processing How The Group Manages Conflicts

There are four sources of information about conflict behavior of group members:

1. The responses on the questionnaire:

   a. Score your questionnaire using the table provided. Rank the five conflict strategies from the one you use the most to the one you use the least. This will give you an indication of how you see your own conflict strategy. The second most frequently used strategy is your backup strategy, that is, the one you use if your first strategy fails.

   b. Determine the average rankings for the group on the "group summary sheet."
2. The results of the discussions of the case studies. Each of the alternatives listed in the case studies represents one of the strategies discussed in this chapter. Match the alternatives to the strategies they represent. Determine which order you would have used the strategies and which order the group would have used the strategies.

Johnson, D. W., & Johnson, R. (2005). **Teaching Students To Be Peacemakers** (4th Ed.). Edina, MN: Interaction Book Company, (952)831-9500.

3. The data collected by the observer. The observers total the rows and columns of their observation sheets. Group members analyzed the data collected by the observer. Note how you behaved during the discussion of the case studies. The categories on the observation sheet do not match the five strategies measured in the questionnaire. You can, however, make some conclusions as to whether your behavior matched the way you see yourself behaving in conflict situations.

4. Your own impressions as to how group members interacted with each other. Think carefully about the interaction among group members during the discussion of the case studies. What strategies were used when members disagreed with each other. Share your impressions as to how conflict was managed in the group discussion of the case studies.

In your group discuss:

1. What is your group's "most" likely strategies?

2. What is your group's "least" likely strategies?

3. What are 5 conclusions about managing conflicts constructively in your group?

4. What positive behaviors were demonstrated by each member of the group?

This is a cooperative task. One set of conclusions should be derived from the whole group and everyone should receive feedback on his or her behavior. All members are expected to participate, give their impressions and information about the way in which members manage conflicts, ensure that all members receive some positive feedback, and summarize the group's conclusions.

Johnson, D. W., & Johnson, R. (2005). **Teaching Students To Be Peacemakers** (4th Ed.). Edina, MN: Interaction Book Company, (952)831-9500.

How I Act In Conflicts

The proverbs listed below can be thought of as descriptions of some of the different strategies for resolving conflicts. Proverbs state traditional wisdom, and these proverbs reflect traditional wisdom for resolving conflicts. Read each of the proverbs carefully. Using the following scale, indicate how typical each proverb is of your actions in a conflict.

5 = very often the way I act in a conflict

4 = frequently the way I act in a conflict

3 = sometimes the way I act in a conflict

2 = seldom the way I act in a conflict

1 = never the way I act in a conflict

_____ 1. It is easier to refrain than to retreat from a quarrel.

_____ 2. If you cannot make a person think as you do, make him/her do as you think.

_____ 3. Soft words win hard hearts.

_____ 4. You scratch my back, I will scratch yours.

_____ 5. Come now and let us reason together.

_____ 6. When two quarrel, the person who keeps silent is the most praiseworthy.

_____ 7. Might overcomes right.

_____ 8. Smooth words make smooth ways.

_____ 9. Better half a loaf than no bread at all.

_____ 10. Not everything that is faced can be changed, but nothing can be changed until it is faced.

_____ 11. He who fights and runs away, lives to fight another day.

_____ 12. He has conquered well that has make his enemies flee.

_____ 13. Kill your enemies with kindness.

_____ 14. A fair exchange brings no quarrel.

_____ 15. No person has the final answer, but every person has part of the truth.

4 : 23

Johnson, D. W., & Johnson, R. (2005). **Teaching Students To Be Peacemakers** (4th Ed.). Edina, MN: Interaction Book Company, (952)831-9500.

_____ 16. Stay away from people who disagree with you.

_____ 17. Battles are won by those who believe in winning.

_____ 18. Kind words are worth much and cost little.

_____ 19. Tit for tat is fair play.

_____ 20. Difference of opinion leads to inquiry, and inquiry to truth.

_____ 21. Avoid quarrelsome people as they will only make your life miserable.

_____ 22. A person who will not flee will make others flee.

_____ 23. A soft answer turneth away wrath.

_____ 24. One gift for another makes good friends.

_____ 25. Only by giving up your monopoly on the truth can you profit from the truths of others.

_____ 26. The best way of handling conflicts is to avoid them.

_____ 27. Put your foot down where you mean to stand.

_____ 28. Gentleness will triumph over anger.

_____ 29. Getting part of what you want is better than not getting anything at all.

_____ 30. He that wrestles with us strengthens our nerves and sharpens our skill.

_____ 31. There is nothing so important that you have to fight for it.

_____ 32. There are two kinds of people in the world, the winners and the losers.

_____ 33. When one hits you with a stone, hit him/her with a feather.

_____ 34. When both people give in half way, a fair settlement is achieved.

_____ 35. By digging and digging, the truth is discovered.

Taken from: **Human Relations and Your Career** (1978) by David W. Johnson. Englewood Cliffs, NJ: Prentice Hall.

Johnson, D. W., & Johnson, R. (2005). **Teaching Students To Be Peacemakers** (4th Ed.). Edina, MN: Interaction Book Company, (952)831-9500.

How I Act In Conflict: Individual Scoring

Withdrawing	Forcing	Smoothing	Compromising	Problem Solving
____ 1	____ 2	____ 3	____ 4	____ 5
____ 6	____ 7	____ 8	____ 9	____ 10
____ 11	____ 12	____ 13	____ 14	____ 15
____ 16	____ 17	____ 18	____ 19	____ 20
____ 21	____ 22	____ 23	____ 24	____ 25
____ 26	____ 27	____ 28	____ 29	____ 30
____ 31	____ 32	____ 33	____ 34	____ 35
____ Total	____ Total	____ Total	____ Total	____ Total

The higher the total score for each conflict strategy, the more frequently you tend to use that strategy. The lower the total score for each conflict strategy, the less frequently you tend to use that strategy.

How I Act In Conflicts: Group Scoring

	1	2	3	4	5	Total
Problem Solving						
Smoothing						
Compromising						
Forcing						
Withdrawing						

4 : 25

Johnson, D. W., & Johnson, R. (2005). **Teaching Students To Be Peacemakers** (4th Ed.). Edina, MN: Interaction Book Company, (952)831-9500.

Individual Conflict Profile

Name:_____   Date:_____

Questionnaire	Case Study	Observations
1.	1.	
2.	2.	
3.	3.	
4.	4.	
5.	5.	

How I Would Describe My Approach To Conflict:

_____

_____

_____

_____

_____

_____

_____

_____

Johnson, D. W., & Johnson, R. (2005). **Teaching Students To Be Peacemakers** (4th Ed.). Edina, MN: Interaction Book Company, (952)831-9500.

What Should I Do?

Many people engage in conflicts without much conscious thought or planning. They just react when they should be thinking carefully about what is the most effective thing to do. When you find yourself in a conflict you have to choose a strategy that is appropriate and constructive. Given below is a table indicating what to do depending on how important the goal and the relationship are to you. Working with a partner, describe a conflict you are having with a schoolmate, friend, or family member. Then decide how important the goal is to you and how important the relationship is to you. Remember, any relationship is highly important that is ongoing (you will have to associate, interact, work, or live with the person throughout the foreseeable future).

Choosing A Strategy Table

Goal	+	Relationship	=	WITHDRAW
Goal	+	Relationship	=	FORCE
Goal	+	**Relationship**	=	SMOOTH
Goal	+	*Relationship*	=	COMPROMISE
Goal	+	**Relationship**	=	PROBLEM-SOLVE

My Conflict Is: _____

_____

_____

_____

Circle how important your goal is to you and how important the relationship is to you. Then look in the above table and decide which strategy you should use.

Goal   Relationship

Goal   *Relationship*

Goal   **Relationship**

Johnson, D. W., & Johnson, R. (2005). **Teaching Students To Be Peacemakers** (4th Ed.). Edina, MN: Interaction Book Company, (952)831-9500.

Conflict Observation Form

Name: _____ Date: _____

Group Being Observed: _____ Class: _____

Action					Total
Contributes Ideas, Opinions					
Encourages Participation					
Emphasizes Mutual Goals					
Asks For Proof, Facts, Rationale					
Summarizes, Integrates					
Criticizes Others' Ideas					
Differentiates Members' Ideas					
Integrates Members' Ideas					
Total					

Put the name of a group member above each column. Put a tally mark in the appropriate box each time a group member contributes. Make notes on the back when interesting things happen that are not captured by the categories. Write down one (or more) positive contributions make by each group member.

4 : 28

Johnson, D. W., & Johnson, R. (2005). **Teaching Students To Be Peacemakers** (4th Ed.). Edina, MN: Interaction Book Company, (952)831-9500.

Jimmy Anderson

You have a classmate, Jimmy Anderson, who is very active, easily bored, and seeks attention. He often disrupts your work and the work of your classmates by being a nuisance and by being aggressive. He often does not stay with one task long enough to finish. He seems to prefer to bother others rather than do his own work. Today, as you are reading a book, he sits down next to you and starts squirming, pokes you with a pencil, puts his hand over the page you are reading, and generally bothers you. This has happened several times before and you are fed up with Jimmy's behavior.

The conflict could be resolved several ways. Five are described below. Read them carefully and rank them from:

1. Most effective in resolving the conflict (1) to least effective (5).

2. Most likely to be used in resolving the conflict (1) to least likely (5).

Effective	Alternative Action	Likely
	I lay it on the line. I tell Jimmy that I am fed up with his actions. I state that the interrupting and annoying actions had better stop because I will not stand for it. Whether he likes it or not, he is going to stop bothering me or else.	
	I ignore what he is doing and keep my feelings to myself. I try to be extra nice to him. I want to win him over to be a friend. I engage him in friendly conversation,, find out about his interests, and smooth over any disagreements between us.	
	I ignore Jimmy and continue working. I plan to avoid any contact with him in the future. I can sit across the room from him. I hope that he will stop as he sees me less and less.	
	I turn around and try to bargain with him. If he will stop bothering me and interrupting my work I will help him with his schoolwork.	
	I turn around and confront him. I state that I want him to stop interrupting my reading. I state his actions are frustrating and making me angry at him. I ask him to describe how he sees the conflict and how he feels. I suggest that we follow the negotiation procedure to solve our problem.	

Johnson, D. W., & Johnson, R. (2005). **Teaching Students To Be Peacemakers** (4th Ed.). Edina, MN: Interaction Book Company, (952)831-9500.

Donna Jones

You have a classmate, Donna Jones, who seems to dislike you. When you work on group projects with her, you can feel the resentment. She never seems to do anything overtly, but classmates tell you that she makes faces behind your back and constantly puts you down outside of class. Today Donna is sitting next to you. Out of the corner of your eye you see her make faces and gestures at you. Several of your classmates are laughing. You decide enough is enough.

The conflict could be resolved several ways. Five are described below. Read them carefully and rank them from:

1. Most effective in resolving the conflict (1) to least effective (5).

2. Most likely to be used in resolving the conflict (1) to least likely (5).

Effective	Alternative Action	Likely
	I turn around and "nail her" in the act. I tell Donna that I am fed up with her actions. I state that the put downs, faces, and gestures had better stop because I will not stand for it. Whether she likes it or not, she is going to stop or else.	
	I ignore what she is doing and keep my feelings to myself. I try to be extra nice to her. I want to win her over to be a friend. I engage her in friendly conversation to find out what she likes and what she is interested in.	
	I ignore Donna and continue working. I plan to avoid any contact with her in the future. I can sit across the room from her. I hope that she will stop as she sees me less and less.	
	I turn around and try to bargain with her. If she will stop making faces, gestures, and put-downs, I will help her with math (which is a hard subject for her).	
	I find a time to talk to her. I tell her I want her to stop making faces and gestures, as it hurts my feelings and makes me angry. I ask her how she sees the conflict and how she feels. I suggest we negotiate to solve our problem.	

Johnson, D. W., & Johnson, R. (2005). **Teaching Students To Be Peacemakers** (4th Ed.). Edina, MN: Interaction Book Company, (952)831-9500.

The Book That Both Wanted

Form pairs. Read the case study. Answer each question as a pair. If you cannot answer the question, seek help from a nearby pair. Probe your partner's ideas by asking such questions as, "Yes, that might happen, what else do you think might happen?"

Donald and David usually have lots of fun together. One day, however, they have trouble. Donald is using a book that David wants to read. David wants the book right now. So does Donald. What can David do so he can read the book? David can think of five ways.

1. Rank the five alternatives from the best thing to do to resolve the conflict (1) to the worst thing to do (5). Why is Number 1 the best thing to do?

2. Rank the five alternatives from the one you would do first to resolve the conflict (1) to the one you would do last (5). Why would you do Number 1 first?

Best	Alternative	Me
	Force Donald to let him have the book now. David grabs the book and says "Give me the book or else you'll be sorry."	
	Give up wanting the book and give up on Donald as a friend. "I don't want the book anymore and I don't like you anymore," David says.	
	Let Donald use the book as long as he wants to keep Donald as a friend. "You can have the book. I really didn't want it," says David.	
	Make a deal by trading for it or alternating reading the book. "If you let me use the book I will let you have my turn at the computer," David says.	
	Negotiate a way that both can use the book together. "Let's negotiate and think of several ways we both can use the book," David says.	

Discuss the following three alternative endings to the story. How does each person feel in each ending and what will happen next?

First, David decides to force Donald to let him have the book. He says, "*Give me the book now or else you'll be sorry*!" Then he grabs the book and tries to keep it away from Donald, who jumps up and tries to grab it back.

How does David feel?

How does Donald feel?

What do you think will happen next?

Johnson, D. W., & Johnson, R. (2005). **Teaching Students To Be Peacemakers** (4th Ed.). Edina, MN: Interaction Book Company, (952)831-9500.

Second, David decides to make a deal. "*Is there anything else you want to do right now besides read the book?*" David asks. "*I would like to use the computer,*" Donald replies. "*If I give you my turn on the computer will you give me the book now?*" David asks.

How does David feel?

How does Donald feel?

What do you think will happen next?

Third, David decides to negotiate for the book. "*We have a problem,*" David says. "*Both of us want to read the book now. Maybe we can think of several options as to how we both could use the book.*" "*I don't see how, but I'm willing to try,*" Donald replies. "*We both want the book,*" David said. "*Let's say how we feel and give our reasons for wanting the book now. Then we can show our understanding and think of options as to how we can both get to read the book.*" "*OK,*" Donald said.

How does David feel?

How does Donald feel?

What do you think will happen next?

What are three ways for the two of them to use the book together?

1.

2.

3.

4 : 32

Johnson, D. W., & Johnson, R. (2005). **Teaching Students To Be Peacemakers** (4th Ed.). Edina, MN: Interaction Book Company, (952)831-9500.

Which Strategy Would You Use?

1. Pick a real conflict that a member of the class is involved in. Write out five different ways of managing the conflict (forcing, withdrawing, smoothing, compromising, problem solving). Number the strategies from "1" to "5" and then number five spots in the room from "1" to "5."

2. Class members think of which strategy they would use. After considering the pro's and con's of each option, students write down their choice and the reasons why it is the best option on the sheet of paper.

3. All members of the class signify their choice by going to the spot in the room that represents the option they have chosen. They pair up with another student who made the same choice, compare and combine their reasons, and make a list of three reasons why their choice is the best strategy. Each student needs a copy of the reasons.

4. Form groups of up to five members (one student for each strategy). Each student presents the reasons for using the strategy they picked. The other students listen carefully and then paraphrase the reasons. If the paraphrase is not accurate or complete, the student presenting corrects the paraphraser. Follow the rules for good paraphrasing.

5. Students decide if they wish to change their minds and choose a different strategy. The teacher asks students to go to the spot they now think would be the best strategy to use. The teacher counts how many students in each spot. The procedure may be repeated if there is time.

Rules For Paraphrasing

1. Put yourself in the other person's shoes.

2. Restate the other person's ideas and feelings in your own words. State as correctly as possible the other's reasons for believing his or her option will make the best agreement.

3. Start your remarks with, *You want...*, *You feel...*, and *You think...*

4. Show understanding and acceptance by nonverbal behaviors: tone of voice, facial expressions, gestures, eye contact, and posture.

Johnson, D. W., & Johnson, R. (2005). **Teaching Students To Be Peacemakers** (4th Ed.). Edina, MN: Interaction Book Company, (952)831-9500.

Using The Conflict Strategies

First, with a partner, write a story about two students who have a conflict. Second, write out five different endings for the story, one for each of the strategies (Forcing, Withdrawing, Smoothing, Compromising, Problem Solving). For each strategy, what would you do and what would you say?

Strategy	Actions & Behaviors	Phrases
Withdrawing		
Forcing		
Smoothing		
Compromising		
Problem Solving		

You need to be competent in applying all five strategies. The most important, however, is problem solving. Working with a partner, write out what happens in each of the instances when two individuals use different strategies:

1. Problem solver against a withdrawer	3. Compromiser against a forcer
2. Smoother against a forcer	4. Problem solver against a smoother

4 : 34

Johnson, D. W., & Johnson, R. (2005). **Teaching Students To Be Peacemakers** (4th Ed.). Edina, MN: Interaction Book Company, (952)831-9500.

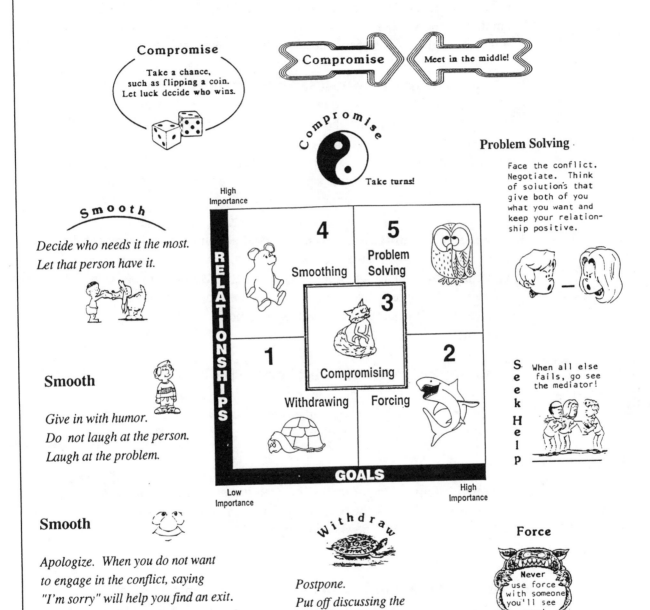

Strategy Game

Form groups of three. Each member rolls a dice to select a strategy. The member then acts the strategy out. Continue until each group member has acted out all the strategies.

Compromise

Take a chance, such as flipping a coin. Let luck decide who wins.

Compromise **Meet in the middle!**

Compromise Take turns!

Problem Solving

Face the conflict. Negotiate. Think of solution's that give both of you what you want and keep your relationship positive.

Smooth

Decide who needs it the most. Let that person have it.

High Importance

RELATIONSHIPS

| 4 Smoothing | 5 Problem Solving |
| 1 Withdrawing | 3 Compromising | 2 Forcing |

GOALS

Low Importance   **High Importance**

Smooth

Give in with humor.
Do not laugh at the person.
Laugh at the problem.

Seek Help

When all else fails, go see the mediator!

Smooth

Apologize. When you do not want to engage in the conflict, saying "I'm sorry" will help you find an exit.

Withdraw

Postpone.
Put off discussing the conflict until you both want to resolve it and are in control of your emotions.

Force

Never use force with someone you'll see soon!

4 : 35

Johnson, D. W., & Johnson, R. (2005). **Teaching Students To Be Peacemakers** (4th Ed.). Edina, MN: Interaction Book Company, (952)831-9500.

Six Conflict Rules For Ongoing Relationships

1. **Do not withdraw from or ignore conflicts.** When the goal is not important and you do not need to keep a relationship with the other person, withdrawing from the conflict may be appropriate. If the relationship is going to continue, however, ignoring a conflict keeps emotional energy tied up in resentment, hostility, or fear. In the long run, it is almost always easier to face a conflict in an ongoing relationship.

2. **Do not engage in "win-lose" negotiations.** When the goal is very important to you but the relationship is unimportant, forcing the other person to give in may be appropriate. In an ongoing relationship, however, you almost never use go for the "win" because the loser may be resentful and want revenge. In the long run, it is almost always easier to ensure that the other person is satisfied and happy with the resolution of the conflict.

3. **Assess for smoothing.** When the goal is unimportant to you (or far more important to the other person than to you) and the relationship is very important, smoothing may be appropriate. Giving up your needs for the needs of another person only works in the long run if the other person reciprocates. It is a mistake, however, to smooth if in fact the goal is very important to you.

4. **Compromise when time is short.** When the goal and the relationship are of moderate importance to you, you may wish to compromise. Usually, compromising is used only when there is not enough time to solve the problem.

5. **Initiate problem-solving negotiations.** When both the goal and the relationship are important to you, you initiate negotiations to solve the problem. You ask the other person to join with you in problem-solving negotiations if he/she is rational and able to do so.

6. **Use your sense of humor.** Humor is very helpful in keeping conflicts constructive. Laughter usually does a great deal to resolve the tension in conflicts and help disputants think more creatively about how to solve the problem.

Johnson, D. W., & Johnson, R. (2005). **Teaching Students To Be Peacemakers** (4th Ed.). Edina, MN: Interaction Book Company, (952)831-9500.

Chapter Five: Teaching Students To Negotiate

You Cannot Not Negotiate

Not everything that is faced can be changed but
Nothing can be changed until it is faced.

James Baldwin

Negotiation is woven into the daily fabric of our lives in and out of school. Many students (and faculty), however, do not know how to negotiate and those who do often negotiate very poorly. Negotiating with skill and grace is not easy. For students to resolve conflicts of interests constructively, they must learn how to negotiate. Negotiation is a process by which persons who have shared and opposed interests and want to come to an agreement try to work out a settlement (Johnson & F. Johnson, 2003). In order to resolve differences in interests and maintain good working relationships, negotiations must take place throughout the school day. Conflicts continually occur, resolutions are negotiated, and you live with the consequences of the agreements you have made. You spend a great deal of time negotiating, even when you (a) do not think of yourself as doing so and (b) are not fully aware that negotiations are taking place.

Two students, Meg Mine and Nennah Notyours have lost their pencils. Meg, in searching the floor, finds a pencil under Nennah's desk and proclaims that she has found her lost pencil. *"Hey,"* Nennah says, *"that's my pencil! I can tell by the teeth marks!"* *"Not a chance,"* replies Meg. *"See these scratch marks on the side of the pencil? I always do that with my finger nail!"* In negotiating for the pencil Meg and Nennah have a choice as to how they will negotiate with each other. They can each try to get the pencil (and see who wins) or they can try to find a mutually satisfying solution to their problem. You can negotiate in two ways. You can go for a "win" or you can try to solve the "problem." Both are appropriate under certain circumstances, but in ongoing relationships, it is problem-solving negotiations that is most appropriate.

As seen in the previous chapter, negotiations can be classified into two types: win-lose or forcing and problem-solving. The heart of conflict resolution in schools is the use of problem-solving negotiations. This chapter, therefore, will go through the procedure of engaging in problem-solving negotiations step by step. Important factors influencing the outcomes of negotiating are then noted.

Johnson, D. W., & Johnson, R. (2005). **Teaching Students To Be Peacemakers** (4th Ed.). Edina, MN: Interaction Book Company, (952)831-9500.

Figure 5.1 Negotiations

Types
- Win–Lose
- Problem Solving

Problem Solving Negotiations

1. Decide What You Want
   Jointly Define As Mutual Problem
   Jointly Define As Small and Specific

2. Describe Your Feelings

3. Describe Reasons For Your Position
   Express Cooperative Intentions
   Presenting, Listening
   Focus On Interest, Not Positions
   Differentiate Before Integrating
   Empower Other Person

4. Reverse Perspectives
   Checking Perceptions
   Paraphrasing
   Presenting Other's Position

5. Invent Options For Mutual Benefit
   Avoiding Obstacles
   Inventing Creative Options

6. Reach A Wise Agreement
   Try, Try Again

Negotiating In Good Faith

Refusal Skills

Coordinating Motivation

Johnson, D. W., & Johnson, R. (2005). **Teaching Students To Be Peacemakers** (4th Ed.). Edina, MN: Interaction Book Company, (952)831-9500.

IMPORTANT POINTS ABOUT NEGOTIATIONS

It takes two to negotiate. You cannot negotiate without the consent and participation of the other disputant. **Negotiations create two types of interdependence among disputants.** The first is participation interdependence (negotiations cannot take place without the cooperation of the other disputant) and outcome interdependence (an agreement can only be achieved with the cooperation of the other disputant). Negotiators are dependent on each other to participate in the negotiating process and to reach an agreement.

Negotiations are a mixed-motive situation in which there are both cooperation and competitive elements. Negotiators wish to reach an agreement and wish to make that agreement as favorable to themselves as possible. They face a **goal dilemma** between (a) maximizing their own outcomes and (b) reaching an agreement. The two goals can seriously interfere with each other.

Negotiators are dependent on each other for information about each other's wants, goals, and interests. **Information dependence creates two issues**. The first is trusting the other--will the other disputant tell the truth about his or her wants, goals, and interests. The second is trustworthiness--should the negotiator be honest and open in revealing his or her own wants, goals, and interests.

Negotiators strive for both primary and secondary gains. The **primary gain** is determined by the nature of the agreement. The **secondary gain** is determined by (a) the effectiveness of the working relationship with the other disputant and (b) the impact of the negotiations on interested third parties.

During negotiations contractual norms are developed. The norms become the ground rules for conducting the negotiations and managing the difficulties involved in reaching an agreement. Two common norms are the **norm of reciprocity** (a disputant should return the same benefit or harm given him or her by the other disputant) and the **norm of equity** (the benefits received or the costs accrued by the negotiators should be equal).

Negotiations have a beginning, a middle, and an end. The strategies and tactics used to initiate negotiations, exchange proposals and information, and precipitate an agreement can be quite different and sometimes contradictory.

Negotiations are an ever present factor in human life. Everyone has to negotiate every day. You cannot avoid negotiating. This does not mean it is easy. It takes years of practice to learn how to negotiate with skill, finesse, and grace.

5 : 3

Johnson, D. W., & Johnson, R. (2005). **Teaching Students To Be Peacemakers** (4th Ed.). Edina, MN: Interaction Book Company, (952)831-9500.

Problem-Solving Negotiations

By blending the breath of the sun and the shade, true harmony comes into the world.

Tao Te Ching

Imagine that you and another person are rowing a boat across the ocean and you cannot row the boat by yourself. While the two of you may have conflicts about how to row, how much to row, what direction to row, and so forth, you still seek food and water for the other person as well as for yourself. Otherwise, the boat cannot be propelled and you will perish. Your conflicts become mutual problems that must be solved to both persons' satisfaction. You negotiate to solve the problem when (a) your goals are very important to you (i.e., you want to cross the ocean and survive) and (b) you have an ongoing cooperative relationship with the other person that must be maintained in good working order (i.e., so you will row together and make progress in crossing the ocean). In problem-solving negotiations the goal is to discover an agreement that will benefit everyone involved. Such agreements are called integrative solutions, which are advantageous because they:

- Join the two parties' interests and thereby reduce resistance to reaching an agreement.

- Are likely to be highly stable because they maximize joint benefit. Compromises, coin tosses, and other mechanical agreements are often unsatisfying to one or both parties and, therefore, create a situation in which the conflict is likely to appear again later.

- Strengthen the relationship between parties. Strong relationships both help maintain agreements made and facilitate the development of integrative solutions in subsequent conflicts.

- Contribute to the welfare of the broader community of which the two parties are members. For example, a school usually benefits as a whole when its students, faculty, and staff are able to reconcile their differences creatively.

You negotiate differently with classmates, teachers, administrators, and parents than you do with strangers or acquaintances. Within ongoing relationships you are expected to show considerable concern about the other person's interests and well being. You are, after all, striving to achieve the same goals and the productivity and quality of life of both of you are affected by how the conflict is managed. You negotiate in a way that gains benefits for all (as opposed to creating winners and losers). Cooperators resolve conflicts as partners, side-by-side, not as adversaries. They are partners in a hard-headed, side-by-side search for a fair agreement advantageous to both sides.

The six basic steps in negotiating a problem solving resolution to a conflict of interests are:

Johnson, D. W., & Johnson, R. (2005). **Teaching Students To Be Peacemakers** (4th Ed.). Edina, MN: Interaction Book Company, (952)831-9500.

1. Determining what each person wants.

2. Determining how each person feels.

3. Exchanging reasons and the rationale for their positions and feelings.

4. Reversing perspectives.

5. Inventing at least three optional agreements for mutual benefit.

6. Reaching a wise agreement.

Step One: Describe What You Want

If a man does not know to which port he is sailing, no wind is favorable.

Seneca

The first step of negotiating to solve the problem is to describe what you want. In doing so, you should:

1. Be assertive.

2. Use appropriate communication skills.

3. Describe the problem in as small and specific way as possible.

4. Jointly agree on the definition of the conflict as a mutual problem.

Be Assertive

Negotiating begins when you describe what you want. Everyone has a perfect right to express what his or her wants, needs, and goals are (Alberti & Emmons, 1978). You have a perfect right to assert what you want and the other person has a perfect right to assert what he or she wants. Two of the major mistakes in defining a conflict are to be aggressive and nonassertive.   Being **aggressive** is similar to forcing, where you try to dominate the other person by trying to hurt him or her psychologically or physically to force him or her to concede. Being **nonassertive** is similar to inappropriate smoothing, where you say nothing, give up your interests, and keep your wants to yourself, letting the other person have his or her way. Being **assertive**, on the other hand, is stating your wants, needs, and

Johnson, D. W., & Johnson, R. (2005). **Teaching Students To Be Peacemakers** (4th Ed.). Edina, MN: Interaction Book Company, (952)831-9500.

goals directly to another person in an honest and appropriate way that respects both yourself and the other person. Assertiveness, is related to such positive interpersonal behavior as self-regulation, making personal choices, being expressive, being self-enhancing, and achieving desired goals (Eisenberg & Mussen, 1989). Assertiveness skills enable one to solve problems, resolve conflicts, and help prevent depression (Seligman, 1995). Children, adolescents, and young adults need to be taught to be assertive.

Just as everyone has a perfect right to assert what he or she wants, everyone has a perfect right to refuse to give you what you want. When someone wants something that is detrimental to your interests or wellbeing, you have a perfect right to say "no." No one has to act against his or her best self-interests just to please someone else. After asserting your needs and goals, therefore, do not expect the other person to do exactly as you wish. Do not confuse letting others know what you want with demanding that they act as you think they should. Providing others with information about your interests is different from trying to force others to facilitate your goal accomplishment.

Check Your Understanding

Demonstrate your understanding of the following concepts by matching the definitions with the appropriate concept. Check your answers with your partner and explain why you believe your answers to be correct.

Answer	Concept	Definition
	1. Assertive	a. You say nothing, give up your interests, and keep your wants to yourself, letting the other person have his or her way.
	2. Aggressive	b. You state your wants, needs, and goals directly to another person in an honest and appropriate way that respects both yourself and the other person.
	3. Nonassertive	c. You try to dominate the other person by trying to inflict psychological or physical harm to force him or her to concede.

Use Appropriate Communication Skills

Communicating what you want involves taking ownership by making personal statements that describe your wants and goals. To clearly communicate your wants and goals to the other person:

1. Make personal statements that refer to "I," "me," "my," or "mine."

Johnson, D. W., & Johnson, R. (2005). **Teaching Students To Be Peacemakers** (4th Ed.). Edina, MN: Interaction Book Company, (952)831-9500.

2. Be specific about your wants, needs, and goals and establish their legitimacy.

3. Acknowledge the other person's goals as part of the problem. Describe how the other person's actions are blocking what you want. In doing so, separate the behavior from the person. More specifically, a **behavior description** includes:

   a. A personal statement that refers to "I," "me," "my," or "mine."

   b. A behavioral description statement that includes the specific behaviors you have observed and does not include any judgment or evaluation or any inferences about the person's motives, personality, or attitudes.

4. Focus on the long-term cooperative relationship. During most conflicts of interests you will be discussing the current problems in your relationship. Negotiations within a long-term cooperative relationship include discussing how the relationship can be changed so the two of you can work together better. During such conversations, you will need to make relationship statements. A **relationship statement** describes some aspect of the way the two of you are interacting with each other. A good relationship statement indicates clear ownership (refers to I, me, my, or mine) and describes how you see the relationship. "*I think we need to talk about our disagreement yesterday*" is a good relationship statement.

Besides communicating clearly and descriptively what you want, you must listen carefully to what the other person wants. There is no set of skills more important for negotiating than being a good listener (see Johnson, 1991, 2003). To listen to another person you must (a) face the person, (b) stay quiet (until your turn), (c) think about what the person is saying, and (d) show you understand.

In communicating your wants and goals, you must do so in ways that define the conflict (a) as a mutual problem and (b) in as small and specific way as possible.

Jointly Define The Conflict As A Mutual Problem

A house divided against itself cannot stand.

Abraham Lincoln

Two drivers, coming from different directions, are roaring down a one-lane road. The sooner they reach their destinations, the more money they will make. Soon they will crash head-on. If the two drivers define the situation as a competition to see who will "chicken out," they will probably crash and both will die. If the two drivers define the situation as a problem to be solved, they will tend to see a solution in which they alternate giving each other the right-of-way. Even simple and small conflicts become major and difficult to resolve when they are defined in a competitive, "win-lose" way. Even major and difficult conflicts become simple and easy to resolve when they are defined in a cooperative, problem-solving way. One of the most constructive things you can do in a conflict is to define the conflict as a mutual problem to be solved. Doing so will tend to increase communication, trust, liking for each other, and cooperation.

Check Your Understanding

Demonstrate your understanding of the following concepts by matching the definitions with the appropriate concept. Check your answers with your partner and explain why you believe your answers to be correct.

Answer	Concept	Definition
	1. Personal Statement	e. Describes the specific behaviors you have observed without any judgment or evaluation or any inferences about the person's motives, personality, or attitudes
	2. Behavioral Description	b. Describes some aspect of the way the two of you are interacting with each other.
	3. Relationship Statement	d. Takes ownership by referring to "I," "me," "my," or "mine."

Jointly Define The Conflict As Being Small And Specific

Fred wants to join a baseball game on the playground. *"You can't play,"* Ralph shouts. *"We already have our teams!"* *"You are no longer my friend,"* Fred shouts back. *"You're selfish and mean! I'll never help you with your homework again!"* In defining a conflict there is an unfortunate tendency to be global and general. Fred is defining the conflict as being one of friendship and gratitude. This creates difficulty in resolving the conflict. He could just as easily have defined the conflict as being one of arriving late or finding a way to make the teams even.

In defining a conflict, the smaller and more specific it is defined, the easier it is to resolve. When involved in a conflict, think small. The more global, general, and vague the definition of the conflict, the harder the conflict is to resolve. Defining a conflict as, *"She always lies,"* makes it more difficult to resolve than defining it as, *"Her statement was not true."* When it comes to resolving conflicts, small is easy, large is hard!

5 : 8

Johnson, D. W., & Johnson, R. (2005). **Teaching Students To Be Peacemakers** (4th Ed.). Edina, MN: Interaction Book Company, (952)831-9500.

Step Two: Describe Your Feelings

Many of us in business, especially if we are very sure of our ideas, have hot tempers. My father knew he had to keep the damage from his own temper to a minimum.

Thomas Watson, Jr., Chairman Emeritus, IBM

The second step of negotiating to solve a problem is to describe how you feel. To express your feelings constructively, it helps to know what feelings are, the importance of expressing your emotions in conflict situations, the difficulties in expressing your emotions, how to express your feelings constructively, and the results of expressing your feelings. **Feelings** are internal physiological reactions to your experiences. When you experience a feeling, you may have a surge of energy, a quickening of your heart beat, or a rise in your body temperature. Although feelings are internal reactions, they do have outward signs. Sadness is inside you, but you cry or frown on the outside. Anger is inside you, but you may stare and shout at the person you are angry with. Feelings are always internal states, but you use overt behaviors to express your feelings. There are five aspects of experiencing and expression a feeling (Johnson, 2003):

1. You gather information about what is going on through your five senses (seeing, hearing, touching, tasting, smelling).

2. You decide what the information means by interpreting the meaning of the information you sense.

3. You have a feeling based on your interpretation.

4. You decide how you intend to express your feeling.

5. You express your feeling.

An example is as follows. You may see a curve to the other person's lips as he or she is talking to you (sensing). You interpret the expression as a smirk and conclude that the person is making fun of you (interpreting). You feel angry (feeling). You decide to insult the person to show him or her that you will not take being made fun of (intending). You then deliver a series of put-downs that reduces the other person to tears (expressing). Often, we sense, interpret, feel, intend, and express all so fast that it seems as though it is only one step instead of five! It takes some practice in slowing down the process so that you are aware of each of the five steps. Understanding the five aspects of experiencing and expressing a feeling gives you the basis for skillfully and appropriately communicating your feelings and for changing negative feelings (such as anger, depression, guilt, hopelessness, frustration, and fear) to positive ones. The only way other people can know

Johnson, D. W., & Johnson, R. (2005). **Teaching Students To Be Peacemakers** (4th Ed.). Edina, MN: Interaction Book Company, (952)831-9500.

for sure how you are feeling and reacting is for you to tell them. You must specifically describe your feelings when trying to define a conflict as a problem.

To express your feelings constructively, you must recognize what they are and accept them as being legitimate. Feelings that are not accepted and recognized can (a) create bias in your judgments, (b) create insecurities that make it more difficult to deal with the conflict in constructive ways, and (c) reduce your control over your behavior. In addition, many conflicts cannot be resolved unless feelings are openly recognized and expressed. If individuals hide or suppress their anger, for example, they may make an agreement but stay hostile toward the other person. Their ability to work effectively with the other person is damaged, as is their ability to resolve future conflicts constructively. And the conflict will tend to reoccur regardless of what the agreement is. Finally, it is through experiencing and sharing feelings that close relationships are built and maintained. Feelings provide the cement holding relationships together as well as the means for deepening relationships and making them more effective and personal.

Communicating your feelings clearly and unambiguously is difficult. There is a tendency in conflicts to hide feelings and reactions for fear of being rejected, laughed at, or exploited. The more personal the feelings, the greater the risk you may feel. Expressing feelings such as anger, hurt, fear, disappointment, and despair, furthermore, takes considerable skill and experience.

Hiding your feelings from other people is difficult. You may cry when you do not want to, raise your voice when it is best not to, or even laugh at a time that disturbs others. Such signals are inherently ambiguous and may confuse other people or may mislead them as to how you really feel. Since they are not a part of a direct attempt to communicate your feelings, they are known as indirect expressions. Other ways your feelings may be communicated indirectly are through **labels** ("You are rude, hostile, and self- centered.") **commands** ("Shut up!"), **questions** ("Are you always this crazy?"), **accusations** ("You do not care about me!"), **sarcasm** ("I'm glad you are early!"), **approval** ("You are wonderful!"), **disapproval** ("You are terrible!"), and **name calling** ("You are a creep!") (Johnson, 2003).

Such indirect ways of expressing feelings are common, but ineffective because they do not give a clear message to the receiver. Communicating your feelings directly and unambiguously requires direct description. There are four ways you can describe a feeling directly (Johnson, 2003).

1. Identify or name it: "I feel angry." "I feel embarrassed." "I like you."

2. Use sensory descriptions that capture how you feel: "I feel stepped on." "I feel like I'm on cloud nine." "I feel like I've just been run over by a truck." Because we do not have enough names of labels to describe all our feelings, we make up ways to describe them.

Johnson, D. W., & Johnson, R. (2005). **Teaching Students To Be Peacemakers** (4th Ed.). Edina, MN: Interaction Book Company, (952)831-9500.

3. Report what kind of action the feeling urges you to do: "I feel like giving you a hug." "I feel like slapping your face." "I feel like jumping over the moon."

4. Use figures of speech as descriptions of feelings: "I feel like a stepped-on toad." "I feel like a pebble on the beach."

A description of a feeling must include (a) a personal statement (refers to "I," "me," "my," or "mine.") and (b) a feeling name, simile, action urge, or figure of speech. A more detailed way to describe your feelings is reflected in the following format: I _____ (feeling) when you _____ (specific behavior) because _____ (how it affects me). An example is, *"I feel angry when you break in line ahead of me because I think it isn't fair and I think you ought to wait your turn like everyone else."*

If you want to communicate clearly, your verbal and your nonverbal expression of feelings must be congruent. Many of the communication difficulties experienced in relationships spring from giving contradictory messages to others by indicating one kind of feeling with words, another with actions, and still another with nonverbal expressions.

You may expect several results from describing your feelings. One is that describing your feelings to another person often helps you to become more aware of what it is you actually do feel. Many times we have feelings that seem ambiguous or unclear to us. Explaining them to another person often clarifies our feelings to ourselves as well as to the other person.

Another result is that describing your feelings often begins a dialogue that will improve your relationship. If other people are to respond appropriately to your feelings, they must know what the feelings are. Even if the feelings are negative, it is often worthwhile to express them. Negative feelings are signals that something may be going wrong in the relationship, and you and the other person need to examine what is going on in the relationship and figure out how it may be improved.

Finally, by reporting your feelings, you provide information that is necessary if you and the other person are to understand and improve your relationship. The greater the amount of information and the more accurate and complete it is, the greater the likelihood that the conflict will be resolved constructively.

Checking Your Perception Of Another Person's Feelings

Before you respond to a person's feelings, you need to check to make sure you really know what the other person actually feels. Sometimes other people will clearly describe their feelings and other times they will express them in ambiguous and confusing ways. In order to respond you will have to clarify how they really feel. When other people describe their

Johnson, D. W., & Johnson, R. (2005). **Teaching Students To Be Peacemakers** (4th Ed.). Edina, MN: Interaction Book Company, (952)831-9500.

feelings to us, we can usually accept their feelings to be what they say they are. But if other people express their feelings indirectly (such as through sarcasm) or nonverbally (such as through a frown), we often need to clarify how they actually feel.

The best way to check whether or not you accurately understand how a person is feeling is through a perception check. A **perception check** has three parts:

1. You describe what you think the other person's feelings are.

2. You ask whether or not your perception is accurate.

3. You refrain from expressing approval or disapproval of the feelings.

"*You look sad. Are you?*" is an example of a perception check. It describes how you think the person is feeling, then it asks the person to agree with or correct your perception, and it does both without making a value judgment about the feeling. A perception check communicates the message, "*I want to understand your feeling—is this the way you feel?*" It is an invitation for other people to describe their feelings more directly. And it shows you care enough about the person to want to understand how the person feels.

Check Your Understanding

Demonstrate your understanding of the following concepts by matching the definitions with the appropriate concept. Check your answers with your partner and explain why you believe your answers to be correct.

Answer	Concept	Definition
	1. Feelings	a. You describe what you think the other person's feelings are, ask whether or not your perception is accurate, and refrain from expressing approval or disapproval of the feelings.
	2. Indirect Expression Of Feelings	b. Internal physiological reactions to your experiences.
	3. Direct Expression Of Feeling	c. labels, commands, questions, accusations, sarcasm, approval, disapproval, and name calling
	4. Perception Check	d. A personal statement and a feeling name, simile, action urge, or figure of speech.

Johnson, D. W., & Johnson, R. (2005). **Teaching Students To Be Peacemakers** (4th Ed.). Edina, MN: Interaction Book Company, (952)831-9500.

Perception checking will help you avoid actions you later regret because they are based on false assumptions about what the other person is feeling. Our impressions are often biased by our own fears, expectations, and present feelings. We frequently misperceive how other people are feeling, and it is therefore essential that we check out our perceptions before taking action.

Step Three: Exchanging Reasons For Positions

To be persuasive we must be believable; to be believable we must be credible; to be credible, we must be truthful.

Edward R. Murrow, Journalist

Susan is usually a compliant student in Ms. Holubec's English class. Today, however, she comes up to Ms. Holubec's desk and states, "*I won't do this homework assignment. I don't care what you do to me, I'm not going to do it!*" Ms. Holubec, having read this book, immediately recognized that Susan is presenting a position and she did not yet know what her reasons are. She said, "*May I ask why?*" In order to negotiate successfully and reach an agreement that satisfies both people, you have to approach the other person on the basis the reasons underlying his or her wants and feelings.

The classic example of the need to separate interests from positions is that of two sisters, each of whom wanted the only orange available. "*I want the orange,*" the older sister said. "*I want the orange,*" the younger sister replied. Their positions, ("*I want the orange!*") were opposed. Their interests, however, may not be. "*I want the peel to make an orange cake,* " the older sister said. "*I want the inner pulp to make orange juice,*" the younger sister replied. Often, when conflicting parties reveal their underlying interests, it is possible to find a solution that suits them both.

The heart of problem-solving negotiations is discovering how both parties can achieve their goals while maintaining a good relationship with each other. Discovering how both parties can simultaneously achieve their goals depends on understanding the reasons underlying their wants and feelings. A common mistake is to assume that because the other person's position is opposed to yours, his or her interests are also opposed. Behind opposed positions may lie shared and compatible goals, as well as conflicting ones.

In problem-solving negotiations, to say what you want and how you feel is not enough. You must also give your reasons for wanting what you want and feeling as you do. It is not enough to say, "*I want to use the computer now and I'm angry at you for not letting me have it.*" You must also say, "*I have an important homework assignment due today and this is my only chance to get it done.*" Your reasons are aimed at (a) informing the other person and (b) persuading him or her to facilitate the achievement of your goals. In other words, you must explain your interests as well as your position:

5 : 13

Johnson, D. W., & Johnson, R. (2005). **Teaching Students To Be Peacemakers** (4th Ed.). Edina, MN: Interaction Book Company, (952)831-9500.

1. Your **position** is what you want (your goals) and how you feel.

2. Your **interests** are the benefits you hope to receive by achieving your goal in resolving the conflict. The benefits you hope for are illuminated in your reasons underlying your wants and feelings.

In listening to the wants and feelings of the other person and trying to see how you and the other person can both get what you want, you need to understand the other person's interests. You may have to ask the other person why he or she has taken a certain position. You may ask a friend to study with you. She may reply "*no.*" Until you understand the reasons for the "*no*" you will not be able to think creatively of ways for both of you to get what you want. The statement in doing so is, "*May I ask why?*" If the answer is vague, you add, "*Could you be more specific..., What do you mean when you say..., I'm not sure I understand.*" Your tone of voice and other nonverbal cues are as important as the words when you ask these questions. If you sound sarcastic your attempt to understand the other person will backfire.

Your ultimate goal in understanding the interests of the other disputant is to create an agreement in which both parties can achieve their goals. In order to do so, it is important to understand the differences between the initially stated wants of both disputants. Conflicts cannot be resolved unless you understand what you are disagreeing about. You must understand the differences between your wants and those of the other person. Only then will you be able to think of ways both sides can reach their goals. The more you differentiate between your interests and those of the other person, the better you will be able to integrate them into a mutually satisfying agreement.

General Issues

Throughout the negotiating process, you need to highlight the long-term cooperative relationship between you and the other disputant. This is known as enlarging the shadow of the future and is done in three ways. The first is to stress dealing with the conflict in a problem-solving way. You want to say such things as, "*This situation means that we will have to work together,*" "*Let's cooperate in reaching an agreement,*" "*Let's try to reach an agreement that is good for both of us.*" The second is to state that you are committed to maximizing the joint outcomes. Successful negotiation requires finding out what the other person really wants and showing him or her a way to get it while you get what you want. The third is to enlarge the shadow of the future by stating that you are committed to the continuation and success of the joint cooperative efforts. In doing so, you may wish to point out (a) the long-term mutual goals and (b) the ways the two of you will be interdependent for the foreseeable future.

Johnson, D. W., & Johnson, R. (2005). **Teaching Students To Be Peacemakers** (4th Ed.). Edina, MN: Interaction Book Company, (952)831-9500.

The clear and unambiguous expression of cooperative intentions in negotiations results in higher quality agreements being reached in a shorter amount of time (i.e., better agreements faster). The other person becomes less defensive, more willing to change his or her position, less concerned about who is right and who is wrong, and more understanding of your views and ideas (Johnson, 1971, 1974; Johnson, McCarty, & Allen, 1976). The other person tends to see you as an understanding and trustworthy person whom he or she can confide in.

A second general issue during negotiations is to empower the other disputant. You **empower** the other person when you give him or her the ability to act to influence their outcomes in the situation. It is important that you do not let the other person feel powerless. Shared power and wise agreements go hand in hand. There are two ways to empower the other person. The first is by being open to negotiations and flexible about the option you like the best. If he or she can negotiate with you then he or she has power and options. Willingness to negotiate is based on being open to the possibility that there may be a better option available than you now realize. Staying tentative and flexible means that you do not become overcommitted to any one position until an agreement is reached. The second is to provide power through choice among options. Generate a variety of possible solutions before deciding what to do. If Susan says to Ms. Holubec, *"You have to agree to let me not do my homework!"* he will feel powerless. If Susan said, *"I could hand in my homework later, I could do part of the homework now and the rest later, or I could do a substitute assignment I am more interested in, let's choose the option that seems the best!"* both she and Ms. Holubec feel powerful.

Check Your Understanding

Demonstrate your understanding of the following concepts by matching the definitions with the appropriate concept. Check your answers with your partner and explain why you believe your answers to be correct.

Answer	Concept	Definition
	1. Position	a. Communicate commitment to maximizing joint outcomes and mutual benefit
	2. Interests	b. Give the other the ability to act to influence their outcomes in the situation
	3. Cooperative Intentions	c. What you want (your goals) and how you feel.
	4. Empower	d. The benefits you hope to receive by achieving your goal in resolving the conflict

Johnson, D. W., & Johnson, R. (2005). **Teaching Students To Be Peacemakers** (4th Ed.). Edina, MN: Interaction Book Company, (952)831-9500.

The psychological costs of being helpless to resolve grievances include frustration, anxiety, and friction. When a person is powerless, the person may become hostile and resist reaching an agreement or apathetic and agree to something he or she does not really want. You do not want the other person to do either one. We all need to believe that we have been granted a fair hearing and that we should have the power and the right to gain justice when we have been wronged. If it becomes evident that we cannot gain justice, frustration, anger, depression, and anxiety may result (Deutsch, 1985).

Potential Problems

There are three problems in analyzing underlying interests. **First**, sometimes a person does not understand the interests underlying his or her position and preferences and, therefore, cannot describe them to others. **Second**, disputants may not wish to reveal their interests out of fear that the other will use this information to personal advantage. Revealing one's wants, goals, and interests always carries the risk of having one's vulnerability exploited. **Third**, a person's interests are often organized into hierarchical trees, with the initial interests discussed being the tip of the iceberg. With more and more discussion, deeper and deeper interests may be revealed.

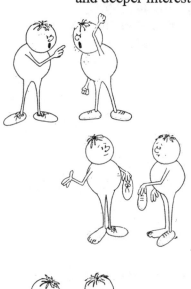

Step Four: Understanding The Other's Perspective

The test of a first-rate intelligence is the ability to hold two opposed ideas in the mind at the same time, and still retain the ability to function.

F. Scott Fitzgerald

Juanita and Betsy sit by each other in class. Juanita comes from a well-off upper-middle-class family. Betsy's parents struggle to pay the rent and provide enough food for the family. Betsy and Juanita both win $20 in a school drawing. Juanita says, "*Hey, I won $20. Imagine that.*" Then she continues eating lunch and reading a magazine. Betsy starts jumping up and down shouting, "*I won! I won! I won $20!*" She throws her arms around her friend, crying and laughing in her excitement. Why did Juanita and Betsy react so differently to the news that they had each won $20 in a school drawing?

In order to negotiate successfully with another person, you must be able to take the other person's perspective and understand how the conflict appears to the other person. **Social perspective-taking** is

5 : 16

Johnson, D. W., & Johnson, R. (2005). **Teaching Students To Be Peacemakers** (4th Ed.). Edina, MN: Interaction Book Company, (952)831-9500.

the ability to understand how a situation appears to another person and how that person is reacting cognitively and emotionally to the situation. The opposite of perspective-taking is **egocentrism** or being unaware that other perspectives exist and that one's own view of the conflict is incomplete and limited.

In order to settle a conflict, it is necessary to have a clear understanding of all sides of the issue and an accurate assessment of their validity and relative merits. Negotiation requires a realistic assessment of common and opposed interests. Often it requires the sacrifice of some of the opposed interests so that the common benefits, concerns, and advantages may be emphasized. In order to be able to propose alternative agreements that will solve the problem, you must understand how the other person sees the problem. Understanding the other person's perspective, however, is not the same as agreeing with it.

To see the situation from the other's shoes, you need to understand several aspects of perspectives. **First, each person has a unique perspective (a way of viewing the world and his or her relation to it) that is different from the perspectives of others**. As a result of their life experiences, no two people will see a problem in exactly the same way. Each person will view an event somewhat differently.

Second, a person's perspective selects and organizes what the person attends to and experiences. All experiences are interpreted and understood within the perspective in which they are viewed. People tend to see only what their perspective allows them to see. People also tend to see only what they want to see. Out of a mass of detailed information, people tend to pick out and focus on those facts that confirm their prior perceptions and to disregard or misinterpret those that call their perceptions into question. Each side in a negotiation tends to see only the merits of its case, and only the faults of the other side.

Third, each person can have different perspectives at different times. If you have been lifting 100-pound bags of cement and someone tosses you a 40- pound bag, it will seem very light. But if you have been lifting 20-pound bags, the 40-pound bag will seem very heavy. When you are hungry, you notice all the food in a room. When you are not hungry, the food does not attract your attention. As your job role, experiences, assumptions, physiological states, and values change, your perspective will change.

Fourth, the same message can mean two entirely different things from two different perspectives. If you provoke your coworker, she may laugh. But if you provoke your boss, she may get angry and fire you! Different perspectives mean the message will be given different meanings. From one perspective, the same message may be interpreted as friendly teasing or as hostile insubordination. A person's perspective determines how a message will be interpreted.

Johnson, D. W., & Johnson, R. (2005). **Teaching Students To Be Peacemakers** (4th Ed.). Edina, MN: Interaction Book Company, (952)831-9500.

Fifth, misunderstandings often occur because we assume that everyone sees things from the same perspective as we do. If we like Italian food, we assume that all our friends like Italian food.

Perspective-taking improves communication and reduces misunderstandings and distortions by influencing how messages are phrased and received. The better you understand the other person's perspective, the more able you are to phrase messages so the other person can easily understand them. If a person does not know what snow is, for example, you do not refer to "*corn snow*" or "*fresh powder*." In addition, understanding the other person's perspective helps you accurately understand the messages you are receiving from that person. If the other person says, "*That's just great*!" for example, the meaning reverses if you know the person is frustrated. You must be able to stand in the sender's shoes to understand accurately the meaning of the messages that person is sending you.

Engaging in perspective taking tends to improve the relationship with the other person. You are more liked and respected when the other person realizes that you are seeing his or her perspective accurately and using it to create potential agreements that benefit both sides equally.

Seeing a situation from a variety of points of view demonstrates membership in the broader moral community. By seeing the situation from the opponent's perspective students (a) remain moral persons who are caring and just and (b) realize that the other person is someone who is entitled to caring and justice.

Failure to understand the other's perspective increases the likelihood of the conflict being managed destructively. In their study of conflict in schools, DeCecco and Richards (1974) found that the inability to take the perspectives of others seriously impeded negotiations as a means of conflict resolution.

You ensure that you accurately see the situation from the other person's perspective by:

1. Asking for clarification or correction to make sure your understanding is accurate. This is called perception checking.

2. Stating your understanding of the other's wants and needs. This is often done by paraphrasing.

3. Presenting the other's position from his or her perspective.

5 : 18

Johnson, D. W., & Johnson, R. (2005). **Teaching Students To Be Peacemakers** (4th Ed.). Edina, MN: Interaction Book Company, (952)831-9500.

Paraphrasing

It is not enough to understand the other person's perspective. You must also let the other person know that you understand his or her perspective. One of the major ways to both clarify your understanding of the other person's perspective and communicate your understanding to him or her, is paraphrasing. The keystone to good listening is paraphrasing. **Paraphrasing** is restating, in your own words, what the person says, feels, and means. This improves communication in several ways. First, it helps you avoid judging and evaluating. When you are restating, you are not passing judgment. Second, restating gives the sender direct feedback as to how well you understand the messages. If you do not fully understand, the sender can add messages until you do. If you are interpreting the message differently from the way he intended it, the sender can clarify. Being able to clarify and elaborate are important for making sure communication is taking place. Third, paraphrasing communicates to the sender that you want to understand what he is saying. It shows that you care about him enough to listen carefully, that you are interested, that you take what he is saying seriously, and that you want to understand. Finally, paraphrasing helps you get into the sender's shoes. It helps you see the message from the sender's perspective. By restating the message as accurately and fairly as possible, you begin to see things from the sender's point of view.

Paraphrasing is often a simple restatement of what has been said. At first, it may feel dumb to restate what another person has said. It may feel awkward and unnatural until you get used to doing it. But the speaker will be grateful for a chance to clarify or add to his original statement, and he will feel grateful for being understood. Paraphrasing becomes harder when it includes feelings as well as ideas. And it is not limited to only the words the sender uses. Nonverbal cues are also important.

Often in a conflict it is helpful to follow the **paraphrasing rule**: Before you can reply to a statement, restate what the sender says, feels, and means correctly and to the sender's satisfaction. When you use paraphrasing, there is a rhythm to your statements. The rhythm is, "*You said...; I say....*" First you say what the sender said (You said). Then you reply (I say). Paraphrasing is often essential in defining a conflict so that a constructive resolution may be negotiated.

Paraphrasing helps you get into the other person's shoes and see the conflict from his or her perspective. It helps you avoid judging the other's position. It gives the other person feedback as to how well you understand his or her position. And it communicates that you want to understand the other person. The guidelines for paraphrasing are:

1. Put yourself in the other person's shoes.

2. Restate the other person's wants, feelings. And reasons in your own words.

5 : 19

Johnson, D. W., & Johnson, R. (2005). **Teaching Students To Be Peacemakers** (4th Ed.). Edina, MN: Interaction Book Company, (952)831-9500.

3. Start your remarks with, "You want…," You feel…," and "You think…"

4. Show understanding and acceptance by nonverbal behaviors: Tone of voice, facial expressions, gestures, eye contact, and posture.

The most effective way to gain insight into the other person's perspective is to role play that you are the other person and present the other person's position and reasoning as if you were he or she (this is known as **perspective-reversal**). Then have the other person do the same. The more involved the two of you get in arguing for the other's position, the more you will understand how the conflict appears from the other person's viewpoint. Such role-playing is invaluable in finding solutions that are mutually acceptable. A systematic series of studies on the impact of perspective reversal on the resolution of conflicts has been conducted (Johnson, 1971). The results indicated that skillful perspective reversal increases cooperative behavior between negotiators, clarifies misunderstanding of the other's position, increases understanding of the other's position, and aids one's ability to perceive the issue from the other's frame of reference. He also found the perspective reversal skillfully used can result not only in a reevaluation of the issue and a change of attitude toward it, but also in the perspective reverser being perceived as a person who tries to understand the other's position, as an understanding person in general, as a person willing to compromise, and as a cooperative and trustworthy person. Temporarily arguing your opponent's position does result in insight into your opponent's perspective and changes your attitudes about the issues being negotiated.

There is nothing more important in resolving conflicts constructively than understanding how the conflict appears from the other person's perspective. Once you can view the conflict both from your own perspective and the other person's perspective, you can find mutually beneficial solutions. You can also communicate to the other person that you really understand his or her thoughts, feelings, and needs. It is usually much easier to resolve a conflict when the other person feels understood. The more skilled you are in seeing things from other people's shoes, the more skilled you will be in resolving conflicts constructively.

Step Five: Inventing Options

One completely overcomes only what one assimilates.

Andre Gide

The fifth step of negotiating is to identify several possible agreements. One will rarely do. People have a tendency to "satisfy," that is, agree to the first reasonable solution that is proposed. But doing so shuts off consideration of even more advantageous agreements. Instead, negotiators should "maximize," by finding the agreement that maximizes joint benefit. The surest way to ensure that you are "maximizing" is to generate several

Johnson, D. W., & Johnson, R. (2005). **Teaching Students To Be Peacemakers** (4th Ed.). Edina, MN: Interaction Book Company, (952)831-9500.

alternative agreements before deciding on which one to adopt. To invent a number of potential agreements, you must avoid a number of obstacles and you must think creatively.

Check Your Understanding

Demonstrate your understanding of the following concepts by matching the definitions with the appropriate concept. Check your answers with your partner and explain why you believe your answers to be correct.

Answer	Concept	Definition
	1. Social Perspective Taking	a. Restating, in your own words, what the person says, feels, and means
	2. Egocentrism	b. Before you can reply to a statement, restate what the sender says, feels, and means correctly and to the sender's satisfaction.
	3. Paraphrasing	c. The ability to understand how a situation appears to another person and how that person is reacting cognitively and emotionally to the situation.
	4. Paraphrasing Rule	d. Presenting the other's wants, feelings, and reasons, as if they were your own
	4. Perspective Reversal	d. Being unaware that other perspectives exist and that one's own view of the conflict is incomplete and limited

Inventing options does not come naturally. Not inventing options is the normal state of affairs, even within the easiest negotiations. In most negotiations there are four major obstacles that inhibit the inventing of a number of options:

1. Judging prematurely. Nothing is so harmful to inventing options as a critical attitude waiting to pounce on the drawbacks of any new idea. Premature criticism is the first impediment to creative thinking.

2. Searching for the single answer. Premature closure and fixation on the first proposal formulated as the single best answer is a sure short-circuit of wise decision making.

3. Assuming a fixed pie. This inhibits creative thinking. Do not assume that the less for you, the more for me. Rarely, if ever, is this assumption true. Expanding the

Johnson, D. W., & Johnson, R. (2005). **Teaching Students To Be Peacemakers** (4th Ed.). Edina, MN: Interaction Book Company, (952)831-9500.

pie is a key to flexible problem solving. Imagine you want to see one movie and your date wants to see another movie. You also know your date likes to eat at a certain restaurant. By enlarging the pie to include which restaurant you go to for dinner before going to a movie, an integrative agreement is possible (one picks the restaurant, one picks the movie).

4. Being concerned only with your own immediate wants and goals. In a relationship, to meet your needs you also have to meet the other person's wants. Shortsighted self-concern leads to partisan positions, partisan arguments, and one-sided solutions.

5. Defensively sticking with the status quo to avoid the fear of the unknown inherent in change. Changing creates anxiety about potential new and unknown problems and guilt over ineffective or inappropriate behavior in the past. Many times people try to justify past actions by refusing to change.

Follett (1940) gives an example of a conflict between two people reading in a library room. One wants to open the window for ventilation, the other to keep it closed in order not to catch cold. To resolve their conflict they searched for creative options. They finally agreed to open a window in the next room, thereby letting in fresh air while avoiding a draft. To find potential agreements that will maximize joint outcomes often takes creative problem solving. **Creativity** means bringing something new into existence. To invent creative options, you need to:

1. Think of as many options as possible. The more the options, the greater the room for negotiations. Find ways to expand the number of options on the table rather than looking for a single answer. One of the keys to wise decision making is selecting from a great number and variety of options.

2. Separate the act of inventing options from the act of judging them. Invent first, judge later.

3. Gather as much information as possible about the problem. The more you know about the problem, the easier it is to find solutions.

4. See the problem from different perspectives and reformulate it in a way that lets new orientations to a solution emerge. Such a reformulation often produces a moment of insight by one or both participants. The insight is often accompanied by intense emotional experiences of illumination and excitement and leads to the reformulation of the problem so that solutions emerge.

5. Search for mutual gains. There always exists the possibility of joint gain. Look for solutions that will leave the other person satisfied as well. Try to maximize joint outcomes.

5 : 22

Johnson, D. W., & Johnson, R. (2005). **Teaching Students To Be Peacemakers** (4th Ed.). Edina, MN: Interaction Book Company, (952)831-9500.

6. Invent ways of making decisions easily. Give the other person choices that are as painless as possible. If you want a horse to jump a fence, do not raise the fence! Propose "yesable" agreements.

7. Test each proposed agreement against reality. What are its strengths and weaknesses? What does each person gain and lose? How does it maximize joint outcomes?

The types of agreements that help maximize joint outcomes include:

1. Expand the pie by finding ways to increase the resources available: Many conflicts arise from a perceived resource shortage. In such circumstances, integrative agreements can be devised by increasing the available resources.

2. Package deals in which parties include in one agreement several related issues. A package deal involving homework, in-class behavior, and helping another student may be easier to reach than trying to negotiate each separately.

3. Trade-offs in which two different things of comparable value are exchanged. A student may agree to do his homework if the teacher agrees to never call on him in class.

4. Tie-ins in which an issue considered extraneous by the other person is introduced and you offer to accept a certain settlement provided this extraneous issue will also be settled to one's satisfaction.

5. Carve-outs in which an issue is carved out of a larger context, leaving the related issues unsettled. This is the opposite of a tie-in.

6. Logrolling in which each party concedes on his or her low priority issues and high priority to the other person.

7. Cost cutting in which one person gets what he or she wants and the other's cost of conceding on those issues is reduced or eliminated.

8. Bridging the initial positions by creating a new option that satisfies both parties' interests that is different from each originally thought they wanted. Rubin, Pruitt, and Kim (1994), for example, discuss a married couple in conflict over whether to vacation at the seashore or in the mountains. After some discussion, they identified their interests as swimming and fishing. They then agreed to visit a lake region that was neither at the seashore or in the mountains, but offered excellent swimming and fishing.

Johnson, D. W., & Johnson, R. (2005). **Teaching Students To Be Peacemakers** (4th Ed.). Edina, MN: Interaction Book Company, (952)831-9500.

After inventing a number of options, you and the other person will have to agree on which one to try out first. Some realistic assessment of the alternatives then takes place. In trying to decide which alternative to try first it may help to remember Aesop's fable about the mice in trouble. The mice were saying, "It's terrible! Just terrible! We really must do something about it! But what?" The mice were talking about the cat. One by one they were falling into her claws. She would steal up softly, then spring suddenly, and there would be one mouse less. At last the mice held a meeting to decide what to do. After some discussion a young mouse jumped up. "I know what we should do! Tie a bell around the cat's neck! Then we would hear her coming and we could run away fast!" The mice clapped their little paws for joy. What a good idea! Why hadn't they thought of it before? And what a very clever little fellow this young mouse was! But now a very old mouse, who hadn't opened his mouth during the whole meeting, got up to speak. "Friends, I agree that the plan of the young mouse is very clever indeed. But I should like to ask one question. Which of us is going to tie the bell around the cat's neck?" The moral is that there is no use adopting an option that cannot be implemented by one or both persons.

Check Your Understanding

Demonstrate your understanding of the following concepts by matching the definitions with the appropriate concept. Check your answers with your partner and explain why you believe your answers to be correct.

Answer	Concept	Definition
	1. Satisficing	a. Finding the agreement that maximizes joint outcomes and mutual benefit
	2. Maximizing	b. Agreement that maximizes the joint outcomes of participants
	3. Integrative Agreement	c. Bringing something new into existence
	4. Creativity	d. Agree to the first reasonable solution that is proposed

In inventing alternative agreements, it often helps to describe what you are doing and neglecting to do that create and continue the conflict. Knowing how your actions help create and continue the conflict is essential for planning how to resolve it. And neglecting to do something constructive helps create and continue the conflict just as much as doing something destructive. You may want the other person to change. But the easiest thing to change is your own actions. If you wish to resolve a conflict, you must begin with deciding how to change your actions. It would be nice if everyone else changed so we would never have to. But you do not have control over the actions of others. They do. What you do

Johnson, D. W., & Johnson, R. (2005). **Teaching Students To Be Peacemakers** (4th Ed.). Edina, MN: Interaction Book Company, (952)831-9500.

have control over is your own actions. You can change your actions much more easily than you can change the other person's actions!

Once a variety of optional agreements are invented that maximizes mutual gain and fulfills the interests of all parties, one of the options is selected to be the initial agreement.

Step Six: Reaching A Wise Agreement

I never let the sun set on a disagreement with anybody who means a lot to me.

Thomas Watson Sr., Founder, IBM

Given that we are all separate individuals with our own unique wants and goals, whenever we interact with others, we will have some interests that are congruent and other interests that are in conflict. It takes wisdom to manage the combination of shared and opposed interests and reach an agreement. Wise agreements are those that meet the following criteria.

The first requirement for a wise agreement is that the agreement must meet the legitimate goals of all participants and be viewed as fair by everyone involved. In deciding on which option to adopt, keep in mind the importance of preserving mutual interests and maximizing joint benefits. Avoid having either side "win."

The second requirement is that the agreement should clearly specify the responsibilities and rights of everyone involved in implementing the agreement. This includes:

1. The ways each person will act differently in the future. These responsibilities should be stated in a specific (tells who does what when, where, and how), realistic (each can do what he or she is agreeing to do), and shared (everyone agrees to do something different) way.

2. How the agreement will be reviewed and renegotiated if it turns out to be unworkable. This includes (a) the ways in which cooperation will be restored if one person slips and acts inappropriately and (b) the times participants will meet to discuss whether the agreement is working and what further steps can be taken to improve cooperation with each other. You cannot be sure the agreement will work until you try it out. After you have tested it for a while, it is a good idea to set aside some time to talk over how things are going. You may find that you need to make some changes or even rethink the whole problem. The idea is to keep on top of the problem so that the two of you may creatively solve it.

It is important that both you and the other person understand which actions trigger anger and resentment in the other. Criticism, put downs, sarcasm, belittling, and other actions

Johnson, D. W., & Johnson, R. (2005). **Teaching Students To Be Peacemakers** (4th Ed.). Edina, MN: Interaction Book Company, (952)831-9500.

often trigger a conflict. If the two of you understand what not to do as well as what to do, the conflict will be resolved much more easily.

The third requirement is that the agreement maintains or even improves the relationship among disputants. In deciding on which option to adopt, keep in mind the importance of shared good feelings and preserving your shared history. Focus on the long-term relationship to ensure that the agreement is durable. Point out that the long-term survival and quality of the relationship should not be jeopardized by any agreement reached. The agreement and the process of reaching the agreement strengthens participants' ability to work together cooperatively in the future (the trust, respect, and liking among participants should be increased). All participants in the conflict must remain moral persons who are caring and just. They should see each other as being entitled to caring and justice.

The fourth requirement for a wise agreement is that the agreement and the process of reaching the agreement strengthen participants' ability to resolve future conflicts constructively. Conflicts of interests will reoccur frequently and each time one is faced and resolved the procedures and skills used should be strengthened and validated.

The fifth requirement for a wise agreement is that it is based on principles that can be justified on some objective criteria (Fisher & Ury, 1981). The objective criteria may be:

1. Everyone has an equal chance of benefiting (such as flipping a coin, one cuts, the other chooses, or letting a third party arbitrator decide).

2. Fairness (taking turns, sharing, equal use). One way to assess fairness is to list the gains and losses for each person if the agreement is adopted and then see if they balance.

3. Scientific merit (based on theory, tested out, evidence indicates it will work).

4. Community values (those who are most in need are taken care of first).

Evaluate each of the proposed options on the basis of these objective criteria. Think through which standards are most appropriate to evaluate the options and make a decision based on principal. The more you do so, the more likely you are to produce a final agreement that is wise and fair.

Using objective criteria to evaluate a possible agreement may result in clarifying what is "fair" and "just" from both sides of the issue. Remember King Solomon. One of the first problems the new King Solomon was presented with involved two women who both claimed the same baby. They wanted him to decide whose it was. Sitting on his throne, Solomon listened carefully. The two women lived together in the same house. Their babies had been born only three days apart. Then one of the babies died. The first woman said, "*This woman's child died in the night. She then arose and took my son from beside*

Johnson, D. W., & Johnson, R. (2005). **Teaching Students To Be Peacemakers** (4th Ed.). Edina, MN: Interaction Book Company, (952)831-9500.

me and placed the dead child next to me. When I woke to feed my baby, I found her dead child in my arms." "No!" the other woman cried frantically. *"The living child is my son!"* Solomon calmly said, *"Bring me a sword and bring me the baby. Divide the living child in two and give half to the one and half to the other."* Everyone was shocked. *"No! Please don't!"* screamed the real mother. *"She can have the child. Don't kill it!"* "No," the other woman said, *"let the child be neither mine nor yours, but divide it."* "Aha!" said Solomon. *"Now I know to whom the child belongs."* Then pointing to the woman who had asked that the baby's life be spared, he said, *"Give her the living child. She is its mother."*

Try, Try Again

Difference of opinion leads to inquiry, and inquiry to truth.

Thomas Jefferson

When you fail at negotiating an integrative agreement that is wise, the next step is to start over. To be successful at negotiating in a problem-solving way, you must remember to try, try again. No matter how far apart the two sides seem, no matter how opposed your interests seem to be, keep talking. With persistent discussion a viable and wise decision will eventually become clear.

When two students cannot agree, the teacher (or administrator) may send them to the problem-solving rug to keep negotiating until they reach agreement. The rules for the rug are:

➢ Both students must sit on the rug until the conflict is resolved.

➢ No touching. Verbal exchanges only.

➢ Be patient. It may take them a long time.

➢ When an agreement is reached, tell the teacher or administrator (who will praise them).

Negotiating In Good Faith

You can bring your credibility down in a second. It takes a million acts to build it up, but one act can bring it down...People are suspicious because for several thousand years that suspicion was warranted...we try very hard not to do things that will create distrust.

Howard K. Sperlich, President, Chrysler

Corporation

Johnson, D. W., & Johnson, R. (2005). **Teaching Students To Be Peacemakers** (4th Ed.). Edina, MN: Interaction Book Company, (952)831-9500.

Everyone has a negotiating reputation. The promises of some people are to be believed. Other people rarely keep their commitments. You want to build a reputation of being someone who is honest, truthful, and trustworthy and, therefore, fulfills your promises. You want your word to be good.

There are strategies you can use when your word has **not** been good in the past. They are:

❖ Pay your debts. Whatever you have agreed to do in the past and not yet done, do it. Once you have fulfilled past promises, your current promise will be more credible.

❖ Use collateral. The collateral should be something of value, something the other person does not expect you to give up. While being significant enough to be meaningful, the collateral should not be something so outrageous that it is not believable. Promising to give someone $1,000 if you break your word is not believable.

❖ Have a cosigner who guarantees your word. Find someone who trusts you that the other person trusts, and have them guarantee that you will keep your word.

Refusal Skills: This Issue Is Not Negotiable

Not all issues are negotiable. Students must be able to:

❑ Know when an issue is and is not negotiable.

❑ Be able to say *"no"* or *"I refuse to negotiate this issue."*

Table 5.3 Reasons For Saying "No"

Unclear	Clear
My intuition tells me "no"	Illegal
I am not sure	Inappropriate
The right option is not there	It will hurt other people
I have changed my mind	I will not be able to keep my word

There are times when students should not negotiate. Students must always have the option of saying *"no"* to negotiations. There are clear reasons for doing so, such as the issue being

5 : 28

Johnson, D. W., & Johnson, R. (2005). **Teaching Students To Be Peacemakers** (4th Ed.). Edina, MN: Interaction Book Company, (952)831-9500.

illegal, inappropriate, damaging to other people, or they do not think they can keep their word. There are also unclear reasons, such as intuition, being unsure, not seeing the right option, and having changed their mind. You will save considerable time and trouble if you do not let others persuade you to agree to something you do not wish to do.

Coordinating Motivation To Resolve The Conflict

There are often differences in motivation to resolve a conflict. You may want to resolve a conflict but the other person could care less. The other person may be very concerned about resolving a conflict with you, but you may want to avoid the whole thing. Today you may want to resolve the conflict but the other person does not, while tomorrow the situation may be reversed. Usually, a conflict cannot be resolved until both persons are motivated to resolve it at the same time.

The motivation to resolve a conflict is based on the costs and gains of continuing the conflict for each person. The costs of continuing a conflict may be the loss of a friendship, loss of enjoyment from work, the loss of job productivity, the loss of a friend, or the loss of respect from the other person. The gains for continuing the conflict may be satisfaction in expressing your anger or resentment and the protection of the status quo. By protecting the status quo, you avoid the possibility that things will get worse when the conflict is resolved. Answering the following questions may help you clarify your motivation and the motivation of the other person to resolve the conflict:

✓   What do I gain from continuing the conflict?

✓   What does the other person gain from continuing the conflict?

✓   What do I lose from continuing the conflict?

✓   What does the other person lose from continuing the conflict?

A person's motivation to resolve a conflict can be changed. By increasing the costs of continuing the conflict or by increasing the gains for resolving it, the other person's motivation to resolve it can be increased. Through changing the costs and gains, you can change both your and the other person's motivation to resolve the conflict.

When the outcomes of negotiations are presented as gains more concessions are made than when the outcomes are presented as losses. Negotiators who think in terms of losses or costs are more likely to take the risk of losing all by holding out in an attempt to force further concessions from the opponent. A negotiator should try to present information in a way that leads the opposition to see what they have to gain from a settlement.

Johnson, D. W., & Johnson, R. (2005). **Teaching Students To Be Peacemakers** (4th Ed.). Edina, MN: Interaction Book Company, (952)831-9500.

Summary

You negotiate to resolve conflicts of interests. **Conflicts of interests** exist when your actions interfere with or block another person from achieving his or her goal. A **goal** is an ideal state of affairs that we value and are working to achieve. **Interests** are the potential benefits to be gained by achieving goals. Goals are based on **wants** (a desire for something) and **needs** (a necessity for survival). On the basis of our wants and needs we set goals. When two or more people have mutual goals they are in a cooperative relationship; when the goals of two or more people are opposed they are in a competitive relationship. Resolving conflicts of interests requires negotiation. **Negotiation** is a process by which persons who have shared and opposed interests and want to come to an agreement try to work out a settlement.

Negotiations may be rarely used in most schools. DeCecco and Richards (1974) conducted a study of junior high and high schools students and found that students reported that negotiations were tried in only 17 percent of the conflicts; decisions were imposed by school authorities 55 percent of the time. Students, however, report that they prefer direct negotiations to resolve student-student and teacher-student conflicts and do want to learn how to negotiate.

Teaching students may impact their later career success. A recent survey conducted for Accountemps (a large accounting, bookkeeping, and data processing temporary personnel service that is a division of Robert Half International Inc.) of vice presidents and personnel directors of 100 of the nation's 1,000 largest corporations found that the people who manage America's leading corporations spend over four working weeks a year dealing with the problems caused by employees who cannot resolve their conflicts with each other. In answer to the question, *"What percent of management time is spent dealing with conflicts among employees,"* respondents revealed that executives spend an average of 9.2 percent of their time or, based on a 40-hour week, 4.6 weeks a year attempting to deal with employee conflicts and the difficulties and disruptions they cause. In 1976, the American Management Association sponsored a survey on conflict management (Thomas & Schmidt, 1976). The respondents included 116 chief executive officers, 76 vice-presidents, and 66 middle managers. They reported that about 24 percent of their time is spent dealing with conflict. The sources of conflicts they faced included misunderstandings, personality clashes, value and goal differences, substandard performance, disagreement over methods of work, lack of cooperation, competition, and noncompliance with rules and policies. School and hospital administrators, mayors, and city managers report that conflict resolution commands nearly 49 percent of their attention. In addition to taking up valuable management time, employee conflicts can seriously reduce any company's productivity and its ability to compete effectively in the marketplace. Knowing how to negotiate constructive resolutions to conflicts of interests is an essential skill that may significantly affect students' career success.

Johnson, D. W., & Johnson, R. (2005). **Teaching Students To Be Peacemakers** (4th Ed.). Edina, MN: Interaction Book Company, (952)831-9500.

There are two types of negotiations. Win-lose negotiations (or forcing) occur when participants want to make an agreement more favorable to themselves than to the other persons. It is appropriate primarily when the relationship with the other disputant is brief and temporary. The majority of the time, however, persons negotiate within an ongoing relationship. That requires problem-solving negotiations where the goal is to reach an agreement that benefits everyone involved. Within ongoing relationships individuals are committed to the well-being of the other person as well as to their own well-being. In order to negotiate mutually beneficial agreements participants must:

- State what they want and listen carefully to what the other person wants. Participants agree on a definition of the conflict that specifies it as a small and specific mutual problem to be solved.

- State how they feel and listen carefully to how the other person is feeling.

- State the reasons why they want what they do and feel how they do. Participants exchange reasons for their positions by expressing cooperative intentions, exchanging reasons, focusing on interests not positions, exploring how their interests are incompatible and compatible, and empowering each other by giving choices.

- Present the opposing perspective as completely and accurately as they can, summarizing the other's position and interests. Participants gain an understanding of the other person's perspective by paraphrasing and checking their perceptions of the other person's interests and reasons.

- Invent options for mutual gain by inventing creative options and avoiding the obstacles to creative problem solving.

- Reach a wise agreement that (a) meets the legitimate goals of all participants, (b) enhances their ability to work together cooperatively, (c) strengthens their ability to resolve future conflicts constructively, and (d) is based on principles that can be justified on some objective criteria,

One of the most difficult aspects of initiating problem-solving negotiations is managing emotions. Managing anger is especially problematic. If disputants try to hide it, very likely the problem will not be correctly identified and a wise agreement will not be reached. But if disputants express their anger destructively, the relationship may be severely damaged if not ruined.

Johnson, D. W., & Johnson, R. (2005). **Teaching Students To Be Peacemakers** (4th Ed.). Edina, MN: Interaction Book Company, (952)831-9500.

CREATIVE CONFLICT CONTRACT

Write down your major learnings from reading this chapter and participating in training session one. Then write down how you plan to implement each learning. Share what you learned and your implementation plans with your base group. Listen carefully to their major learnings and implementation plans. You may modify your own plans on the basis of what you have learned from your groupmates. Volunteer one thing you can do to help each groupmate with his or her implementation plans. Utilize the help groupmates offer to you. Sign each member's plans to seal the contract.

MAJOR LEARNINGS	IMPLEMENTATION PLANS

Date: _____ Participant's Signature: _____

Signatures Of Group Members: _____

_____

Johnson, D. W., & Johnson, R. (2005). **Teaching Students To Be Peacemakers** (4th Ed.). Edina, MN: Interaction Book Company, (952)831-9500.

STEPS OF PROBLEM-SOLVING NEGOTIATIONS

STEPS	RATIONALE
State What You Want	Problem solving requires that disputants are open and honest about what is wanted. Each person needs to know what he or she wants and be able to describe it as a mutual small and specific problem.
State How You Feel	Resolution of conflicts requires that feelings be openly recognized and expressed. Rejected and unrecognized feelings create bias, block positive feelings, reduce self-control, and interfere with cognitive processing.
State Reasons For Wants And Feelings	Moving beyond positions to the underlying reasons for wants and feelings helps separate interests from positions and helps differentiate interests so that integrative agreements may be identified.
Reverse Perspectives	Higher level cognitive reasoning, accurate communication, and identifying integrative agreements depend on being able to view the problem from both perspectives simultaneously.
Create Three Or More Potential Agreements That Maximize Joint Outcomes	In order to maximize joint outcomes (as opposed to reaching only a satisfying agreement), it is necessary to identify a variety of potential agreements from which to choose the one that appears to be most advantageous to all parties.
Agree On One Agreement And Shake	Each alternative agreement needs to be evaluated to determine on objective criteria that it is fair to all parties. The agreement must maximize joint outcomes and strengthen participants' future ability to (a) work together and (b) resolve conflicts constructively.

Johnson, D. W., & Johnson, R. (2005). **Teaching Students To Be Peacemakers** (4th Ed.). Edina, MN: Interaction Book Company, (952)831-9500.

Conflicts Of Interests Identification Form

WHAT ARE THE CONFLICTS OF INTERESTS I HAVE WITH:

1. Other Students

    a. _____

    b. _____

    c. _____

2. Teachers

    a. _____

    b. _____

    c. _____

3. Administrators

    a. _____

    b. _____

    c. _____

4. Parents

    a. _____

    b. _____

    c. _____

Johnson, D. W., & Johnson, R. (2005). **Teaching Students To Be Peacemakers** (4th Ed.). Edina, MN: Interaction Book Company, (952)831-9500.

Making A Profit: Instructions

1. You are about to participate in a negotiation between a buyer and a seller of three commodities (oil, gas, coal). Your group of four has been divided into two pairs. One pair will be buyers and one pair will be sellers. The exercise has three parts:
   a. Preparing for negotiations.
   b. Negotiating.
   c. Discussing what happened in negotiations.

2. Each commodity has nine possible prices, represented by the letters of the alphabet (A, B, C, D, E, F, G, H, I). There is Price "A," Price "B," Price "C," and so forth.

3. For each price, there is a profit you will make if the other negotiator agrees to that price (Agreement "A" results in "x" dollars of profit for you, agreement "B" results in "x" dollars or profit, and so forth).

4. In **preparing for negotiations**, you have two **tasks**:
   a. Understand your profit schedule so that you know which possible agreements are most and least profitable for you.
   b. Make sure your partner understands the profit schedule.

5. To help you complete these tasks, answer the following questions:

   a. **What is your most important commodity?**   _____

   b. **What is your least important commodity?**   _____

   c. **For Price C for Oil, what would your profit be?**   _____

   d. **For Price G for Coal, what would your profit be?**   _____

   e. **What agreement (three letters, one for each commodity) would maximize your profit?** _____ Oil   _____ Gas   _____ Coal

6. During negotiations, each of you will negotiate, one-on-one, with a member of the other pair. One of you is a buyer and one of you is a seller.

7. You need to reach one agreement that includes all three commodities, such as AAA, III, or BFG. In negotiations, you might say, "*I will give you 'A' for oil, 'B' for gas, and 'C' for coal.*"

8. **During negotiations you may not show your profit schedule to the other negotiator.** Only verbal communication is allowed.

5 : 35

Johnson, D. W., & Johnson, R. (2005). **Teaching Students To Be Peacemakers** (4th Ed.). Edina, MN: Interaction Book Company, (952)831-9500.

Making A Profit Exercise: Buyer Profit Sheet

Oil		Gas		Coal	
Price	*Profit*	*Price*	*Profit*	*Price*	*Profit*
A	$4,000	A	$2,000	A	$1,000
B	3,500	B	1,750	B	875
C	3,000	C	1,500	C	750
D	2,500	D	1,250	D	625
E	2,000	E	1,000	E	500
F	1,500	F	750	F	375
G	1,000	G	500	G	250
H	500	H	250	H	125
I	0	I	0	I	0

The nine prices for each commodity are presented by the letters A to I. Next to each price is the profit you would make for reselling each commodity if you bought it at that price. Reach one agreement that includes all three commodiities, such as AAA, III, or BFG.

You can say anything you wish during negotiations, but you may not show this profit sheet to the seller you are negotiating with.

Johnson, D. W., & Johnson, R. (2005). **Teaching Students To Be Peacemakers** (4th Ed.). Edina, MN: Interaction Book Company, (952)831-9500.

Making A Profit Exercise: Seller Profit Sheet

Oil		Gas		Coal	
Price	*Profit*	*Price*	*Profit*	*Price*	*Profit*
A	.0	A	0	A	0
B	125	B	250	B	500
C	250	C	500	C	1,000
D	375	D	750	D	1,500
E	500	E	1,000	E	2,000
F	625	F	1,250	F	2,500
G	750	G	1,500	G	3,000
H	875	H	1,750	H	3,500
I	$1,000	I	$2,000	I	$4,000

The nine prices for each commodity are presented by the letters A to I. Next to each price is the profit you would make for each commodity if you sold it at that price. Reach one agreement that includes all three commodiities, such as AAA, III, or BFG.

You can say anything you wish during negotiations, but you may not show this profit sheet to the buyer you are negotiating with.

Johnson, D. W., & Johnson, R. (2005). **Teaching Students To Be Peacemakers** (4th Ed.). Edina, MN: Interaction Book Company, (952)831-9500.

Making A Profit: Agreement Form

Date:_____ Name:_____ ____Male ____Female Grade:_____

1. Your **task** is to negotiate one agreement that includes a price for each of the three commodities (oil, gas, coal). The nine prices for each commodity are presented by the letters A to I. Reach one agreement that includes all three commodities, such as AAA, III, or BFG.

2. It is expected that you will make (and respond to) proposed agreements. You might say, *"I will give you 'A' for oil, 'B' for gas, and 'C' for coal."* You want to reach an agreement (any agreement is better than no agreement), but you also want the agreement to be profitable for you.

3. When an agreement is reached, write it down and sign it.

4. **You may not show your profit schedule to the other negotiator.** Only verbal communication is allowed.

We Agree On The Following Prices (Check One Letter In Each Column):

Oil	Gas	Coal
____ A	____ A	____ A
____ B	____ B	____ B
____ C	____ C	____ C
____ D	____ D	____ D
____ E	____ E	____ E
____ F	____ F	____ F
____ G	____ G	____ G
____ H	____ H	____ H
____ I	____ I	____ I

_____
Seller's Signature

_____
Buyer's Signature

_____
Print Seller's Name

_____
Print Buyer's Name

Johnson, D. W., & Johnson, R. (2005). **Teaching Students To Be Peacemakers** (4th Ed.). Edina, MN: Interaction Book Company, (952)831-9500.

Making A Profit: Discussion Guide

1. What commodity was most important to the other negotiator? _____

2. What commodity was least important to the other negotiator? _____

3. How did you and the other negotiator communicate information about your profit schedules? Was information exchange:

   a. **Direct** (buyer and seller accurately told each other their profit schedules).

   b. **Indirect** (buyer and seller deduced each other's profit schedule by comparing each other's responses to different offers).

4. Complete the following table by entering your agreement (a letter) for each commodity, your profit from that agreement, the other's profit from that agreement, and the joint profit the two of you made. **Joint profit** is the sum of the profits of the buyer and the seller.

Commodity	Agreement	Your Profit	Other's Profit	Joint Profit
Oil				
Gas				
Coal				
Total				

5. What agreement would have maximized joint profit? _____

6. Did each negotiator try to maximize own profit or try to maximize joint profit?

7. What factors helped you reach an agreement that maximized joint profit?

8. What factors hindered you reaching an agreement that maximized joint profit?

9. Did you and the other person offer package deals or did you negotiate the commodities one at a time?

10. Write down four conclusions you can make about negotiations on the basis of your experience in this simulation. You will share your conclusions with the rest of the class.

Johnson, D. W., & Johnson, R. (2005). **Teaching Students To Be Peacemakers** (4th Ed.). Edina, MN: Interaction Book Company, (952)831-9500.

WHICH BOOKS TO TAKE

Scientists have suddenly discovered that a large comet is going to strike the earth. All life, if not the earth itself, will be destroyed. You and the other member of your pair have been chosen to move from Earth to a new planet. Life on the new planet will be harsh and difficult. You will be starting life over, trying to develop a farming and technological society at the same time. Because of the limited room in the spaceship, you can only bring three books for the two of you. ***"Think carefully,"*** the captain says. ***"You will never return to Earth. You will never be able to get more books from Earth."***

1. Work by yourself. **First**, decide on two books you personally want to bring. Choose the books you think will be most (a) important to save and (b) helpful to starting a new civilization. **Second**, plan how to convince the other person that the books you have chosen are two important to leave behind.

2. Meet as a pair. Only three books can go. You have to decide which three. You cannot take half of one and half of another. You cannot choose by chance (such as flipping a coin). Come to an agreement as to which three books your pair will take to the new planet and why. **Use the negotiation procedure given below to do so**. Each member should state what books he or she wants to take, how he or she feels, and the reasons why the books are important and should not be lost forever. After an agreement is reached, each person must be able to explain the reasons why the three books were selected.

BOOK	IMPORTANCE	HELPFUL
1.		
2.		

Person One	Person Two
I want	I want
I feel	I feel
My reasons are	My reasons are
My understanding of your wants, feelings, and reasons is	My understand of your wants, feelings, and reasons is
Three plans to solve the problem are	Three plans to solve the problem are
We choose a plan and agree	We choose a plan and agree

Johnson, D. W., & Johnson, R. (2005). **Teaching Students To Be Peacemakers** (4th Ed.). Edina, MN: Interaction Book Company, (952)831-9500.

What I Want, What You Want

Conflicts begin when two people want the same thing. When one person says, "I want the ice cream bar" and another person says, "I want the ice cream bar," a conflict exists.

It is OK to want something and to say so. Every person every minute of the day wants something. **You have a perfect right to tell people what you want.** So does every other person. You are both OK to stand up for yourself and tell people what you want.

The first step in negotiating is for each person to say what he or she wants. To practice the first and last steps of negotiating, go through the procedure of:

Person One	Person Two
I want . . .	I want . . .
Meet me in the middle.	OK. Shake.

Wanting The Same Cookie

Divide into groups of four. Have one group of four sit in a row facing another group of four. Each person says to the person he or she is facing:

Person One	Person Two
I want the cookie.	I want the cookie.
Let's meet in the middle. Each of us will get half. You cut and I will choose.	O.K. Shake.

Move to the next person and say the same thing. Do not stop until you have practiced the sequence four times.

Why is dividing the cookie in half a good idea?

Where else can you use this procedure? Divide into pairs. Write down three places where you can use this procedure.

1. _____

2. _____

3. _____

Johnson, D. W., & Johnson, R. (2005). **Teaching Students To Be Peacemakers** (4th Ed.). Edina, MN: Interaction Book Company, (952)831-9500.

How I Feel, How You Feel

It is not enough to say what you want. You also need to say how you feel. Sometimes you may feel angry. Sometimes you may feel frustrated. Sometimes you may feel afraid.

In conflicts, everyone has feelings. Both sides need to say how they feel. You need to say how you feel. The other person needs to say how he or she feels. To stand up for yourself, you need to let other people know how you feel. Both you and the other person have a perfect right to your feelings and may tell others what they are.

The second step of negotiating is for each person to see how he or she feels. To practice the first, second, and last steps of negotiating, go through the procedure of:

Person One	Person Two
I want . . .	I want . . .
I feel . . .	I feel . . .
Let's take turns. Flip a coin to see who goes first.	OK. Shake.

Wanting The Same Book

Divide into groups of four. Have one group of four sit in a row facing another group of four. Each person says to the person he or she is facing:

Person One	Person Two
I want the book.	I want the book.
I feel frustrated.	I'm afraid you won't let me have the book.
Let's take turns. Flip a coin to see who goes first.	O.K. Shake.

Move to the next person and say the same thing. Do not stop until you have practiced the sequence four times.

Why is taking turns a good idea? Where else can you use this procedure? Divide into pairs. Write down three places where you can use this procedure.

1. _____

2. _____

3. _____

Johnson, D. W., & Johnson, R. (2005). **Teaching Students To Be Peacemakers** (4th Ed.). Edina, MN: Interaction Book Company, (952)831-9500.

Why I Want It, Why You Want It

It is not enough to say what you want. You must also say **why** you want it. You must have reasons for wanting something. You must share your reasons with the other person and the other person must share his or her reasons with you. The **third step** of problem-solving negotiations is to say why you want what you want and why you feel as you do. Practice these steps of negotiating.

Person One

I want . . .
I feel . . .
My reasons are . . .
We could do it together.

Person Two

I want . . .
I feel . . .
My reasons are . . .
We could do it together.

Wanting To Play The Same Game

Divide into groups of four. Form two rows of four students each. The two rows face each other. Each person says to the person he or she is facing:

Person One

I want to play chess.
I feel frustrated!
I'm frustrated because you are interfering with my daily practice to improve my chess game.
We could play chess together.

Person Two

I want to play chess.
I feel angry!
I'm angry because I've been waiting all day for my turn and now you are trying to crowd in line.
O.K. Shake.

Move to the next person and say the same thing. Do not stop until you have practiced the sequence four times.

Why is playing chess together a good idea?

Johnson, D. W., & Johnson, R. (2005). **Teaching Students To Be Peacemakers** (4th Ed.). Edina, MN: Interaction Book Company, (952)831-9500.

My Understanding Of You, Your Understanding Of Me

Resolving conflicts takes more than understanding what you want and feel and why. You must also understand what the other person wants and how the other person feels. And you must make sure the other person knows you understand him or her. The **fourth step** of problem-solving negotiations is to summarize what the other person wants and feels and why. Practice these steps of negotiating.

Person One	Person Two
I want . . .	I want . . .
I feel . . .	I feel . . .
My reasons are . . .	My reasons are . . .
My understanding of you is . . .	My understanding of you is . . .
You need it more than I do. You can have it.	Thanks. Shake.

Divide into groups of four. Form two rows of four students each. The two rows face each other. Each person says to the person he or she is facing:

Person One	Person Two
I want to use the computer now!	I want to use the computer now!
I feel upset.	I feel frustrated.
I want to use the computer to try out a new computer game.	I want to use the computer to do my homework.
My understanding of you is that you will be frustrated if you do not get to do your homework on the computer now.	My understanding of you is that you will be upset if you do not get to play your new computer game now.
You need the computer more than I do. You can use it first.	Thanks. Shake.

Rules For Paraphrasing:

1. Put yourself in the other person's shoes.

2. Restate the other person's ideas and feelings in your own words. State as correctly as possible what the other person wants, feels, and why.

3. Start your remarks with, *You want...*, *You feel...*, and *You think....*

4. Show understanding and acceptance by nonverbal behaviors--tone of voice, facial expressions, gestures, eye contact, and posture.

5 : 44

Johnson, D. W., & Johnson, R. (2005). **Teaching Students To Be Peacemakers** (4th Ed.). Edina, MN: Interaction Book Company, (952)831-9500.

Inventing Options For Mutual Gain

Resolving conflicts takes more than understanding yourself and the other person. You must also identify several possible agreements that benefit both sides. The fifth step in problem-solving negotiations is to think of at least three plans to solve the problem.

Person One	Person Two
I want . . .	I want . . .
I feel . . .	I feel . . .
My reasons are . . .	My reasons are . . .
My understanding of you is . . .	My understanding of you is . . .
Three plans to solve the problem are . . .	Three plans to solve the problem are . . .
Let's pick Plan B.	O.K. Shake.

Where Is My Book?

Face your partner. Go through the steps of negotiating a solution to the problem. Be sure to create at least three plans before you choose one. Then repeat with a new partner.

Person One	Person Two
I want you to return the book you borrowed.	I want you to stop bugging me about that book.
I'm angry.	I'm irritated.
I'm angry because you promised to return the book right away if I let you borrow it.	I'm irritated because you keep asking me to return the book when you know I can't find it.
My understanding of you is that you can't find my book and you are irritated because I keep asking you to return it to me.	My understanding of you is that you are angry because you didn't want to lend me your book but did only because I promised to return it right away.
One plan to solve the problem is . . .	Another plan to solve the problem is . . .
A third plan to solve the problem is . . .	A fourth plan to solve the problem is . . .
Let's pick plan _____ .	O.K. Shake.

Plan A: _____

Plan B: _____

Plan C: _____

Johnson, D. W., & Johnson, R. (2005). **Teaching Students To Be Peacemakers** (4th Ed.). Edina, MN: Interaction Book Company, (952)831-9500.

Negotiating: The Whole Procedure

Conflicts end when an agreement is reached. To reach an agreement, you and the other person must negotiate. The purpose of negotiating is to reach a wise agreement that is fair to everyone involved. To negotiate you must understand the procedure. The more skillful you are in using the procedure, the easier it will be to reach a wise agreement. To become skillful, practice the procedure over and over again until it becomes automatic. The steps of negotiating are as follows.

Person One	Person Two
I want	I want
I feel	I feel
My reasons are	My reasons are
My understanding of your wants, feelings, and reasons is`	My understand of your wants, feelings, and reasons is
Three plans to solve the problem are	Three plans to solve the problem are
We choose a plan and agree	We choose a plan and agree

When resolving a conflict it is important to remember:

1. **You both have the conflict**. You must work together to solve it. Solve conflicts as friends, not enemies.

2. **You both have wants**. You have a perfect right to express them. For the conflict to be resolved constructively, both of you must honestly state what you want.

3. **You both have feelings**. They must be expressed in order for the conflict to be resolved constructively. Keeping frustration, angry, hurt, fear, or sadness inside only makes the conflict more difficult to resolve.

4. **You both have reasons for wanting what you want and feeling like you do**. Ask for each other's reasons and make sure you see the conflict from both perspectives.

5. **You both have your perspective or point-of-view**. In order to resolve the conflict constructively, you must see the conflict from both perspectives.

6. **You both need to generate several alternative wise agreements that maximize the benefits to both of you**. Wise agreements make both persons happy.

7. **You both need to select the agreement that seems most wise and seal it with a handshake**. Never agree on a solution that leaves one person happy and one person unhappy.

5 : 46

Johnson, D. W., & Johnson, R. (2005). **Teaching Students To Be Peacemakers** (4th Ed.). Edina, MN: Interaction Book Company, (952)831-9500.

Stop Calling Me Names

Find a partner and role play the following situation:

Person One	Person Two
I want you to stop calling me names.	I want to keep calling you names
I feel hurt.	I feel fine when I call you names.
The reason I want you to stop calling me names is it upsets me so much I can't learn.	The reason I want to keep calling you names is that it makes me feel powerful to know I can hurt your feelings.
My understanding of you is that you want to call me names so you can feel powerful.	My understanding of you is that you want me to stop calling you names because it hurts your feelings and upsets you so much you can't do your schoolwork.
One way we could resolve our conflict is for one of us to give in. I could let you call me names. Or you could stop calling me names.	Another way we could resolve our conflict is for us to make a deal. I could stop calling you names. You could help me run for student council.
A third plan would be for us to decide on a time when you could call me names and a time you could not. We could have a half-hour a day name-calling time	Perhaps we should plan to work together on several projects so we could get to know each other better. If we got to know each other, I would not call you names.
Let's try plan four.	Agreed. Shake.

Where else can you use this procedure? Working with your partner, write down three situations in which you could use this procedure.

1. _____

2. _____

3. _____

Johnson, D. W., & Johnson, R. (2005). **Teaching Students To Be Peacemakers** (4th Ed.). Edina, MN: Interaction Book Company, (952)831-9500.

© Johnson & Johnson

Building A Bridge

To Successful Resolution

Of A Conflict

I want. . .

I feel. . .

The reason is. . .

My understanding of you is. . .

Maybe we should try. . .

Let's choose and shake!

Maybe we should try. . .

My understanding of you is. . .

The reason is. . .

I feel. . .

I want. . .

REMEMBER THAT EACH TIME YOU FIND YOURSELF IN A CONFLICT SITUATION YOU HAVE THE CHANCE TO BUILD YOUR OWN RESOLUTION BRIDGE!

5 : 48

Johnson, D. W., & Johnson, R. (2005). **Teaching Students To Be Peacemakers** (4th Ed.). Edina, MN: Interaction Book Company, (952)831-9500.

BRIDGE TO UNDERSTANDING

Mediator _____   Date _____

	PERSON 1	PERSON 2
WANT		
FEEL		
REASONS		
UNDERSTANDING OF YOU		
THREE OPTIONS		
AGREEMENT		
SIGNATURE		

5 : 49

Conflicts Of Interests

Read each conflict description and decide how you would manage the conflict if you were the teacher. Be realistic. Assume the students are in secondary school.

Form a pair with another student. Discuss each conflict and come to an agreement as to how it should be managed. Write out your plan. One member of each group will be randomly selected to share the group's solutions with the rest of the class.

Conflict Descriptions

Two students, Meg Mine and Nennah Notyours, begin to argue about who owns a pen. Both claim it. The argument leads to a small fistfight. Both students end up feeling angry and rejected.

In your class the teacher gave the assignment of making a collage on a serious social problem, such as pollution, discrimination, drugs, or crime. The idea of the project was to get the students to express themselves and their ideas in a visual manner and to increase their awareness of how art can be an impressive and persuasive tool. Sam Smartmouth raised his hand and said he did not see the importance of this sort of thing. He said he was not going to do it and asked why the teacher could not assign something more interesting and valuable.

Donna Donot and Gary Getalong are members of a cooperative group. They constantly put each other down, criticize each other, and even make fun of each other's contributions. They both want to be the group leader and spend most of their energy undermining each other's efforts to direct and control the group's activities.

Ralph Rascal rarely is prepared to take tests. One day Ms. VicTim was giving a test and Ralph tossed a lighted firecracker under her seat. After the explosion she calmly asked, "Who put that firecracker under my seat?" Several students started laughing.

Johnson, D. W., & Johnson, R. (2005). **Teaching Students To Be Peacemakers** (4th Ed.). Edina, MN: Interaction Book Company, (952)831-9500.

Role Plays

1. The school has called an assembly. You took an aisle chair. Before the assembly begins you place your books on your chair and leave to get a drink of water. When you get back, you find your books sitting in the aisle and another student in your chair. What do you do? Role play the exchange.

2. You are standing in the hallway by your locker when another student smashes into you. You are thrown against your locker and drop your books. The other student laughs. What do you do? Role play the exchange.

3. You tell a friend in confidence about someone you would like to go out with. The next day several people comment on it. You get your friend alone to talk about it. What do you do? Role play the exchange.

4. You have been sick with mono for several weeks. Your science teacher refuses to extend the deadline for your final project. Since you can not finish the project in time, this means that you will receive a low grade in the class. You believe the teacher is being very unfair. You decide to try talking to the teacher again. Role play the exchange.

5. Chris borrows your history book. The next day, when Chris returns your book, it is muddy and the cover is torn. You believe that when you borrow something, you are responsible for taking care of it. You have to spend 20 minutes cleaning the book and taping the cover back together. Chris laughs and calls you a "neatness freak." What do you do? Role play the exchange.

6. You are making a presentation to a class. Two classmates who are hostile towards you sit together in the back of the class and continually make sarcastic remarks in loud whispers that can be easily heard by the whole class. You decide to talk to the two classmates about it. Role play the exchange.

Preparing For The Role Play

You are to prepare to role play your assigned character by reading the description of the situation and your characters experiences. In doing so, write out the answers to the following questions:
1. **What do you want?**
2. **How do you feel?**
3. **What are your reasons for wanting what you want and feeling as you do?**

Johnson, D. W., & Johnson, R. (2005). **Teaching Students To Be Peacemakers** (4th Ed.). Edina, MN: Interaction Book Company, (952)831-9500.

Hamlet And His Father's Ghost

The scene is the battlements of the castle of the King of Denmark. It is midnight, the witching hour. The ghost of Hamlet's father appears and beckons Hamlet to follow the ghost for a private talk. They have a conflict that must be resolved. Find a partner. Flip a coin to see who will be Hamlet and who will be his father's ghost. Then resolve the conflict using the problem-solving negotiation procedure.

Ghost

I am your father's spirit. Listen to me. If you ever loved me you must avenge my foul, strange, and most unnatural murder. I was not bitten by a poisonous snake. The serpent that bit me now wears my crown. He is an incestuous beast. He seduced your mother, a seemingly virtuous queen. Then, when I was asleep in the garden, he poured poison into my ear. My own brother, your uncle, killed me to gain both my crown and my wife. This is horrible,! Horrible! You must kill him! You are my son and it is your duty to avenge my death. I can not rest in my grave until my murder is avenged. You must fulfill your obligation and put me to rest. Denmark will not prosper with such a man on the throne. The king must be committed to the welfare of Denmark, not himself. And besides, if he has a son you will lose your birthright.

Hamlet

I did not know you were murdered. This is surprising. I thought you died of a snake bite. The fact that my uncle murdered you is even more a surprise, as he is very friendly and nice to me. I certainly want justice, but let us not be hasty. Asking me to kill him is a serious request. First, I may be too young and inexperienced to do it right. You would do better to ask one of your generals to do it. Second, killing my uncle could seriously damage my future career options and quality of life. Don't be so blood-thirsty. Think of my future! Third, this is not the time for me to kill someone. I am a carefree youth! I am in love. I'm still in school. I have years of learning and maturing left before I will be ready to kill someone. Fourth, I might go to hell, if I killed my uncle. Finally, killing my uncle is a complex task. I have to catch him alone doing something wicked so his soul will go to hell. What use is it if I kill him when he is doing something virtuous and he goes to heaven? This is not one of the usual "walk into the room and stab him" killing. I'm not sure I want to do that much work!

5 : 52

Johnson, D. W., & Johnson, R. (2005). **Teaching Students To Be Peacemakers** (4th Ed.). Edina, MN: Interaction Book Company, (952)831-9500.

Negotiable Versus Nonnegotiable Issues

Not every issue is negotiable and you should know the difference between a negotiable and nonnegotiable issue. You must be able to say "no" when someone tries to negotiate a nonnegotiable issue. Your **tasks** are to make a list of negotiable and nonnegotiable issues and to practice saying "no" when someone brings up a nonnegotiable issue. To prepare, read the section on **Refusal Skills** in Chapter Five of **Teaching Students To Be Peacemakers**.

1. Draw two columns on a sheet of paper. Label the first column "Negotiable" and the second column "nonnegotiable." In the first column write "Eat a salad for lunch." In the second column write "shoplift." When you eat for lunch is negotiable. Breaking the law is not negotiable.

2. Working in a pair, list five issues that are negotiable and five issues that are not negotiable. Both of you need a copy.

3. Find a new partner. **Share** your list of negotiable and nonnegotiable issues. **Listen** to his or her list. **Create** a new list from the best ideas of both of you.

4. Return to your original partner. **Share** your new list. **Listen** to his or her new list. **Create** a final list from the best ideas from both of you.

5. Role play a situation in which someone is trying to get you to do something you do not want to do. Pick one of the nonnegotiable issues. Try to negotiate it with your partner. Your partner should say, to your every attempt, "*No, I won't do it. That issue is nonnegotiable.*" Then reverse roles. Your partner tries to negotiate one of the nonnegotiable issues with you. You reply to his or her every attempt, "*No, I won't do it. That issue is nonnegotiable.*"

Person 1	Person 2
Help me cheat on this test.	No, I won't. That issue is nonnegotiable.
It's only one test. No one will ever know.	No, I won't. That issue is nonnegotiable.
If you're my friend, you'll help me cheat.	No, I won't. Cheating is nonnegotiable.

Nonnegotiable!

5 : 53

Johnson, D. W., & Johnson, R. (2005). **Teaching Students To Be Peacemakers** (4th Ed.). Edina, MN: Interaction Book Company, (952)831-9500.

Who Owns This?

To negotiate effectively and communicate clearly you must speak for yourself. You are more easily understood if you take ownership for your thoughts, feelings, and needs. The purpose of this exercise is to give you practice in recognizing who owns the thoughts, feelings, or needs in a message. A message can be owned by the sender, no one, or someone other than the sender. The sender can be speaking for him- or herself, for no one, or for someone else.

Working in a pair, read each of the statements listed below. Put a:

S for each statement where the sender is speaking for him or herself.

N for statements where the sender is speaking for no one.

O for statements where the sender is speaking for someone else.

Agree on each answer. Then combine with another pair and compare answers. Discuss each statement until everyone agrees.

Statements

_____ 1. Everyone loves the teacher.

_____ 2. I like you.

_____ 3. The rumor is that you are a nice person.

_____ 4. We think this song is great!

_____ 5. No one would like math.

_____ 6. Bill thinks you are strange.

_____ 7 Most people would be mad if you did that to them.

_____ 8. I can tell by looking at your face that you feel terrible.

Johnson, D. W., & Johnson, R. (2005). **Teaching Students To Be Peacemakers** (4ᵗʰ Ed.). Edina, MN: Interaction Book Company, (952)831-9500.

Describing Others' Behavior

To negotiate effectively and communicate clearly, you need to describe other people's behavior without passing judgment. Working with a partner, put a:

D for each statement that **describes** a person's behavior.

J for each statement that **judges** a person's behavior.

Agree on each answer. Then combine with another pair and compare answers. Discuss each statement until everyone agrees.

Statements

_____ 1. Sam interrupted Sally.

_____ 2. Mark is very sincere.

_____ 3. I do not like Sally.

_____ 4. Mark is very shy.

_____ 5. Today on the way to school, I saw three butterflies.

_____ 6. Jane is trying to make me mad.

_____ 7. Sam changed the subject.

_____ 8. Sam contributed six ideas to our discussion.

5 : 55

Johnson, D. W., & Johnson, R. (2005). **Teaching Students To Be Peacemakers** (4th Ed.). Edina, MN: Interaction Book Company, (952)831-9500.

Describing, Not Evaluating

To define a conflict, you must tell the other person what you want. How you say what you want has positive or negative effects on how the conflict turns out.

Defining a conflict is like lacing your shoes. If you start out wrong, the whole thing gets messed up. If you call the other person names, insult or blame him or her, the conflict will probably turn out badly. Positive outcomes are more likely to occur is you define the conflict in terms of the other person's actions, not his or her personality or innate nature. Describing the other's person's actions needs to be caring, non-threatening, and non-judgmental. Using the person's name shows respect and caring. The words you use can make the other person angry or can make the other person want to resolve the conflict.

Working as a pair, write a "**D**" by statements that describe, and write an "**E**" by statements that evaluate:

_____ 1. You are a mean person!

_____ 2. Sam. I don't like it when you call me names. Tell me what's wrong?

_____ 3. You are a rotten bully!

_____ 4. Bob. I do not like being pushed. Please stop.

_____ 5. You are an evil witch!

_____ 6. I feel hurt when you say untrue things about me. Tell me why you are angry.

Try your skill at describing, not evaluating. Working as a pair, write your answers to each of the following:

1. A friend "snoops" into your things:

2. A classmate teases you:

3. A classmate accuses you of not working hard enough on a joint project:

Your Challenge

With your partner, create a role play using one of the above situations.

Johnson, D. W., & Johnson, R. (2005). **Teaching Students To Be Peacemakers** (4th Ed.). Edina, MN: Interaction Book Company, (952)831-9500.

"You and Me" Relationship Statements

To negotiate effectively, you must be able to make good relationship statements. Working with a partner, put a:

- **R** for each statement that describes how the speaker sees the relationship.

- **J** for a poor relationship statement that judges.

- **O** for a poor relationship statement that speaks for the other person.

- **P** for a poor relationship statement that is about a person, not a relationship.

Agree on each answer. Then combine with another pair and compare answers. Discuss each statement until everyone agrees.

Relationship Statements

_____ 1. We really enjoyed ourselves last night.

_____ 2. Our relationship is really lousy!

_____ 3. You look sick today.

_____ 4. You're angry again. You're always getting angry.

_____ 5. You have not spoken to me for two days. Is something wrong with our relationship?

_____ 6. I think we need to talk about our disagreement yesterday.

_____ 7. We are great at communicating.

_____ 8. You really make me feel appreciated and liked.

_____ 9. I think you are feeling better.

Johnson, D. W., & Johnson, R. (2005). **Teaching Students To Be Peacemakers** (4th Ed.). Edina, MN: Interaction Book Company, (952)831-9500.

● Describing Your Feelings ●

To negotiate effectively and to communicate clearly, you must describe your feelings (as opposed to expressing them indirectly). Working with a partner, put a:

- **D** before a statement that describes the sender's feelings.
- **No** before a statement that conveys feeling without directly describing what the feeling is.

Agree on each answer. Then combine with another pair and compare answers. Discuss each statement until everyone agrees.

Statements

1. _____ a. Stop driving this fast! Slow down right now!

   _____ b. Your driving this fast frightens me.

2. _____ a. Do you have to stand on my foot?

   _____ b. You are so mean and vicious you don't care if you cripple me for life!.

   _____ c. I am annoyed at you for resting your 240-pound body on my foot.

3. _____ a. I feel ecstatic about winning the Reader's Digest Sweepstakes!

   _____ b. This is a wonderful day!.

4. _____ a. You're such a helpful person.

   _____ b. I really respect your ideas; you're so well informed.

5. _____ a. Everyone here likes to dance with you.

   _____ b. When I dance with you I feel graceful and relaxed.

   _____ c. We all feel you're a great dancer.

Johnson, D. W., & Johnson, R. (2005). **Teaching Students To Be Peacemakers** (4th Ed.). Edina, MN: Interaction Book Company, (952)831-9500.

6. _____ a. If you don't start cleaning up after yourself, I'm moving out!

_____ b. Did you ever see such a messy kitchen in your life?

_____ c. I am afraid you will never do your share of housework.

7. _____ a. This is a very interesting book.

_____ b. I feel this is not a very helpful book.

_____ c. I get very excited when I read this book.

8. _____ a. I don't feel competent enough to contribute anything of worth to this group.

_____ b. I'm not competent enough to contribute anything worthwhile to this group.

▪ Answers ▪

1. a. No. Commands like these communicate strong feelings, but they do not name the feeling that underlies the commands.

   b. D. This statement both expresses and names a feeling. The person communicates the feeling by describing himself as frightened.

2. a. No. A feeling is implied through a question, but the specific feeling underlying the question is not described.

   b. No. This statement communicates considerable feeling through an accusation, but it is not clear whether the accusation is based on anger, hurt, fear, or some other feeling.

   c. D. The person describes the feeling as annoyance. Note that the speaker also "owns" the feeling by using the personal pronoun "I."

3. a. D. The speaker describes herself as feeling ecstatic.

   b. No. This statement communicates positive feelings without describing what they are. The speaker appears to be commenting on the weather when in fact the statement is

Johnson, D. W., & Johnson, R. (2005). **Teaching Students To Be Peacemakers** (4th Ed.). Edina, MN: Interaction Book Company, (952)831-9500.

an expression of how the speaker feels. We cannot tell whether the speaker is feeling proud, happy, caring, accepted, supported, or relieved.

4. a. No. The speaker makes a value judgment communicating positive feelings about the other person, but the speaker does not describe the feelings. Does the speaker admire the other person or like the other person, or is the speaker only grateful?

   b. D. The speaker describes the positive feelings as respect.

5. a. No. This statement does name a feeling (likes) but the speaker is talking for everyone and does not make clear that the feeling is personal. A description of a feeling must contain "I," "me," "my," or "mine" to make clear that the feelings are within the speaker. Does it seem more friendly for a person to say, "I like you," or "Everybody likes you?"

   b. D. The speaker communicates clearly and specifically the feeling the speaker has when dancing with the other person.

   c. No. First, the speaker does not speak for herself, but rather hides behind the phrase "we feel." Second, "You're a great dancer" is a value judgment and does not name a feeling. Note that merely placing the word feel in front of a statement does not make the statement a description of feeling. People often say feel when they mean think or believe.

6. a. No. This statement communicates general and ambiguous negative feelings about the person's behavior. It refers to the condition of the apartment or house and the speaker's future behavior, but not to the speaker's inner feelings.

   b. No. The speaker is trying to communicate a negative feeling through a rhetorical question and a value judgment. Although it is clear the feeling is negative, the specific feeling is not described.

   c. D. The speaker describes fear as the negative feeling connected with the other person's housework.

   Note: Notice that in a and b the feelings could easily have been interpreted as anger. Many times the expression of anger results from an underlying fear. Yet when the receiver tries to respond, she may understand that the other person is angry without comprehending that the basic feeling to be responded to is a feeling of fear.

Johnson, D. W., & Johnson, R. (2005). **Teaching Students To Be Peacemakers** (4th Ed.). Edina, MN: Interaction Book Company, (952)831-9500.

7. a. No. The speaker communicates a positive value judgment that conveys feelings, but the specific feelings are not described.

   b. No. The speaker uses the words "I feel" but does not then describe or name a feeling. Instead, the speaker gives a negative value judgment. What the speaker actually meant was "I believe" or "I think" the book is not very good. People commonly use the word feel when they mean think or believe. Consider the difference between, "I feel you don't like me" and "I believe (think) you don't like me."

   c. D. The speaker describes a feeling of excitement while reading this book.

   Note: Many times people who say they are unaware of what they feel--or who say they don't have any feelings about something--state value judgments without recognizing that this is the way their positive or negative feelings get expressed. Many times useless arguments can be avoided if we are careful to describe our feelings instead of expressing them through value judgments. For example, if Joe says the book is interesting and Fred says it is boring, they may argue about which it "really" is. If Joe, however, says he was excited by the book and Fred says he was frustrated by it, no argument should follow. Each person's feelings are what they are. Of course, discussing what it means for Joe and Fred to feel as they do may provide helpful information about each person and about the book.

8. a. D. Speaker communicates a feeling of incompetence.

   b. No. Warning! This statement is potentially hazardous to your health! Although it sounds much the same as the previous statement, it states that the speaker actually is incompetent. The speaker has passed a negative value judgment on himself and labeled himself as incompetent.

   Note: Many people confuse feeling with being. A person may feel incompetent yet behave very competently or a person may feel competent and perform very incompetently. A person may feel hopeless about a situation that turns out not to be hopeless once his behavior is given an appropriate focus. A sign of emotional maturity is that a person does not confuse feelings with the reality of the situation. An emotionally mature person knows he can perform competently, even though he feels incompetent. He does not let his feelings keep him from doing his best because he knows the difference between feelings and performance and knows that the two do not always match.

5 : 61

Johnson, D. W., & Johnson, R. (2005). **Teaching Students To Be Peacemakers** (4th Ed.). Edina, MN: Interaction Book Company, (952)831-9500.

Body Talk

Body langauge is another way of communicating. As you react to different situations, your body takes on certain positions.

Picture yourself at times when you feel the emotions listed below. Describe how your body looks when you feel these ways.

Embarrassment _____

_____

Nervousness _____

_____

Excitement _____

_____

Boredom _____

_____

Now draw a line from each face below to the feeling it shows.

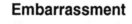

Embarrassment

Nervousness

Excitement

Boredom

Anger

Happiness

5 : 62

Johnson, D. W., & Johnson, R. (2005). **Teaching Students To Be Peacemakers** (4th Ed.). Edina, MN: Interaction Book Company, (952)831-9500.

Is This The Way You Feel?

To negotiate effectively and to communicate clearly, you need to check your perceptions of other people's feelings. Working in a pair, put a:

PC for each perception check.

J for each statement that makes a judgment about the other person.

O for each statement that speaks for the other person rather than for yourself.

Q for each question that does not include a description of your perceptions of the other person's feelings.

Agree on each answer. Then combine with another pair and compare answers. Discuss each statement until everyone agrees.

Statements

_____ 1. Are you angry with me?

_____ 2. You look as if you are upset about what Sally said. Are you?

_____ 3. Why are you mad at me?

_____ 4. You look as if you feel put down by my statement. That's stupid!

_____ 5. What is it about your teacher that makes you resent her so much?

_____ 6. Are your feelings hurt again?

_____ 7. You look unhappy. Are you?

_____ 8. Am I right that you feel irritated that nobody commented on your suggestions?

Johnson, D. W., & Johnson, R. (2005). **Teaching Students To Be Peacemakers** (4th Ed.). Edina, MN: Interaction Book Company, (952)831-9500.

Differentiating Between Positions and Interests

For each of the following situations identify and write out each person's **position** and **interests** that caused them to take that position. Then find a partner and come to agreement on the answers. One member will be chosen randomly to give the pair's answers.

Sue wants the orange so she can use the peel to make an orange cake. Jim wants the orange so he can use the insides to make orange juice.

	Sue	Jim
Position		
Interests		

Jeremy wants the book so he can read it. Andrew wants the book so he can sit on it and see better.

	Jeremy	Andrew
Position		
Interests		

Davy wants the computer so he can write his science report. Tyler wants the computer to practice keyboarding.

	Davy	Tyler
Position		
Interests		

Jim wants the pencil so he can write with it. John wants the pencil to erase mistakes.

	Jim	John
Position		
Interests		

Betsy wants the ball so she can practice catching it. Sam wants the ball so she can practice throwing it.

	Betsy	Sam
Position		
Interests		

Whenever someone takes a position, ask them "why" in order to learn their interests.

Johnson, D. W., & Johnson, R. (2005). **Teaching Students To Be Peacemakers** (4th Ed.). Edina, MN: Interaction Book Company, (952)831-9500.

Your Point OF View

Everyone has his or her own point of view. Some people like Chinese food. Some people do not. If you like Chinese food, you tend to assume that everyone does. If you like to be teased, you assume that everyone likes to be teased.

In resolving conflicts it is important to understand the other person's point of view. An example of the need to understand other's points of view is given below. Read the story with your partner.

The Wise Men And The Buffalo

Once upon a time, four blind men who were considered to be very wise wanted to know what a buffalo looked like. When a buffalo was brought to their town, they all went to touch it. The first wise man grabbed hold of the buffalo's tail. "The buffalo is like a rope," he yelled. The second wise man rubbed his hands over the buffalo's side. "No, No! The buffalo is like a big furry rug," he cried. The third wise man grabbed hold of the buffalo's horn. "The buffalo is like a spear!" he shouted. "You are all wrong," the fourth man exclaimed. "The buffalo is like a table!" He was holding two of the buffalo's legs. "Rope!" "Rug!" "Spear!" "Table!" The blind men yelled at each other for the rest of the day. They never did agree on what a buffalo looked like.

Johnson, D. W., & Johnson, R. (2005). **Teaching Students To Be Peacemakers** (4th Ed.). Edina, MN: Interaction Book Company, (952)831-9500.

Your Point Of View Exercise

Working in your pair, answer the following questions. Then join another pair and share your answers.

1. Which blind man was right? _____

   _____

2. What was their conflict based on? _____

   _____

3. Were they really "wise"? How do you tell if someone is wise? _____

   _____

4. How could the wise men have discovered what a buffalo really looks like? _____

   _____

5. What is the moral of the story? What does the story tell you about solving conflicts?

   _____

———————————————— ·•· ————————————————

In your pair, rewrite the ending of the story to make it come out with a good solution to the conflict.

_____

_____

_____

_____

_____

Johnson, D. W., & Johnson, R. (2005). **Teaching Students To Be Peacemakers** (4th Ed.). Edina, MN: Interaction Book Company, (952)831-9500.

Paraphrasing  © Johnson & Johnson

1. Pick a real conflict that a member of the class is experiencing and identify four good alternative agreements. Number the agreements from "1" to "4" and then number the four corners of the room from "1" to "4."

2. Class members think of which option would make the best agreement. After considering the pro's and con's of each option, students write down their choice and the reasons why it is the best option on the sheet of paper.

3. All members of the class signify their choice by going to the corner of the room that represents the option they have chosen. They pair up with another student who made the same choice, compare and combine their reasons, and make a list of three reasons why their option is the best agreement. Each student needs a copy of the reasons.

4. Form groups of four (one student from each corner). Divide each group into pairs (student 1 meets with student 2, student 3 meets with student 4). One student presents his or her reasons. The other student listens carefully and then paraphrases the reasons. If the paraphrase is not accurate or complete, the student presenting corrects the paraphraser. The two students then reverse roles. Follow the rules for good paraphrasing. When both partners have paraphrased accurately and fully, switch partners (1 with 3, 2 with 4) and do present/paraphrase again. Switch partners again (1 with 4, 2 with 3) so that each student paraphrases the three other positions.

5. Students then decide if they wish to change their minds and choose a different option. The teacher asks students to go to the corner they now think would be the best option to agree to. The teacher counts the number of students in each corner. The procedure may be repeated if there is time.

Rules for Paraphrasing

1. Put yourself in the other person's shoes.

2. Restate the other person's ideas and feelings in your own words. State as correctly as possible the other's reasons for believing his or her option will make the best agreement.

3. Start your remarks with, *You want...,* *You feel...,* and *You think...*

4. Show understanding and acceptance by nonverbal behaviors: tone of voice, facial expressions, gestures, eye contact, and posture.

Johnson, D. W., & Johnson, R. (2005). **Teaching Students To Be Peacemakers** (4th Ed.). Edina, MN: Interaction Book Company, (952)831-9500.

Name _____ **Date** _____

Dear Edy One

Below you will find a letter to Edy. Read the message and meet with your partner to write three plans to solve the problem. Both of you need to agree on the plans. Write them in the boxes below, using extra sheets if you need them.

Dear Edy,

One member of my group is always day-dreaming when we are supposed to be working on a group project. It really bugs me!

Disgusted

Plan A

Plan B

Plan C

Name _____ Date _____

Dear Edy Two

Here is another letter mailed to Edy. Read the message and meet with your partner to write three plans to solve the problem. Both of you need to agree on the plans. Write them in the boxes below, using extra sheets if you need them.

> *Dear Edy,*
>
> There is a person in my group who won't let me contribute. She interrupts me and refuses to listen to my ideas. How can I get her to give me a chance to talk without hurting her feelings or making her angry?
>
> "Ignored"

Plan A

Plan B

Plan C

Name _____ Date _____

Dear Edy Three

Below you will find a letter to Edy. Read the message and meet with your partner to write three plans to solve the problem. Both of you need to agree on the plans. Write them in the boxes below, using extra sheets if you need them.

Dear Edy,

There is a person in our group who is always putting everyone down and pretending it is just a joke. No one wants to be in our group anymore because of all the insults we have to put up with. They are afraid to talk because this person makes fun of what they say. What can I do to get our group back together?
"Squelched"

Plan A

Plan B

Plan C

Johnson, D. W., & Johnson, R. (2005). **Teaching Students To Be Peacemakers** (4th Ed.). Edina, MN: Interaction Book Company, (952)831-9500.

Brainstorming Optional Agreements

Brainstorming is a procedure that encourages divergent thinking and the production of many different ideas in a short period of time. In brainstorming you first generate a list of ideas and second you evaluate them. The rules for brainstorming are:

1. Think of as many different ideas as possible. Go for quantity. Write down all ideas. The longer the list, the better.

2. Do not criticize or evaluate ideas. Accept all ideas. Encourage silly, far out ideas. Piggyback on each other's ideas.

3. Set a time limit and keep the pace quick. Review the problem frequently to keep attention focused.

Form a pair. Consider the following conflict. Then brainstorm seven potential agreements to resolve the conflict.

Davy: You keep giving me false compliments. It's embarrassing to be around you because you keep telling me how wonderful I am. I'm glad you like me, but I can't bear to be overpraised and it makes me feel you are not sincere.

Virginia: I like telling people how great they are. Whenever I see you doing something well, I'm going to tell you about it. It's a habit. I just do it.

What can Davy and Virginia do to resolve their conflict so that both get what they want and like each other better than ever. Follow the above rules for brainstorming.

_____

_____

_____

_____

_____

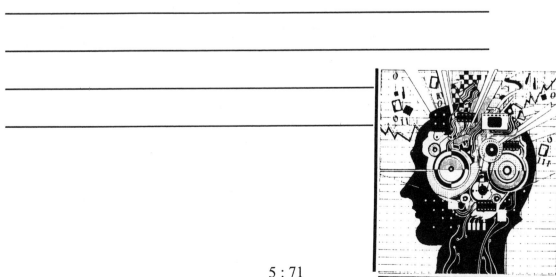

5 : 71

Johnson, D. W., & Johnson, R. (2005). **Teaching Students To Be Peacemakers** (4th Ed.). Edina, MN: Interaction Book Company, (952)831-9500.

Brainstorming Optional Agreements (continued)

_____

_____

Put a plus or a minus to indicate what you think of each option. Then check the idea you both like the best.

With your partner pick a conflict that you or one of your friends is involved in. Brainstorm potential agreements that would solve the problem. Then evaluate each one and check the one you like the best.

Ideas

How We Feel About the Idea . . .

Name   *Name*

Johnson, D. W., & Johnson, R. (2005). **Teaching Students To Be Peacemakers** (4th Ed.). Edina, MN: Interaction Book Company, (952)831-9500.

Using Balance Sheets to Make Wise Decisions

Roger was a coin collector; his wife, Ann, loved to raise and show championship rabbits. Their income did not leave enough money for both to practice their hobbies, and splitting the cash they did have would not have left enough for either. The conflict over whether to spend their extra money on coins or rabbits was so severe that they were thinking about getting a divorce. Think of three optional agreements that would allow them to stay married. Then use the balance sheet to decide what to do. Use the following procedure.

1. Evaluate the first alternative agreement on the basis of the gains and losses for:

   a. Person 1.

   b. Person 2.

   c. Others in the class, school, family, and/or community.

2. Once all the gains and losses have been listed for the first alternative agreement, rate each in terms of its importance on a five-point scale from 1 (no importance) to 5 (extremely important).

3. Evaluate whether (a) each person will feel proud or ashamed if this alternative is agreed to and (b) important other people think that you have made the right decision.

4. Repeat these steps for each of the other alternative agreements.

5. After a balance sheet has been completed for each alternative agreement, rank the alternatives from "most desirable" to "least desirable."

Table 3.3 Conflict Decision Balance Sheet

	Gains	Rating	Losses	Rating	Approval
Person 1					
Person 2					
Others					

Johnson, D. W., & Johnson, R. (2005). **Teaching Students To Be Peacemakers** (4th Ed.). Edina, MN: Interaction Book Company, (952)831-9500.

Using Balance Sheets (continued)

Repeat the process with the following two conflicts. Like the one above, they actually happened.

> Edythe and Buddy shared an office but had different work habits. Edythe liked to do her work in silence while Buddy liked to socialize in the office and have the radio on. Their conflict over noise became so severe that each went to their boss and demanded that the other be moved or even fired.

> Keith loved to spend his evenings talking to people all over the world on his ham radio set. From the time he got home from work until it was time to go to bed, he would sit with his ham radio conversing with far away people. His wife, Simone, felt cheated out of the few hours of each day they could spend together. Keith did not want to give up his radio time and Simone was not willing to forego the time they had together. The conflict became so severe that Simone was thinking about getting a divorce.

Pick a conflict you are presently involved in. Complete balance sheets for your conflict. Then negotiate with the other person some more.

Each of the three conflict examples given above actually happened. Here are the **solutions** that were negotiated with the help of a counselor.

1. Roger and Ann decided to put all the first year's money into Ann's rabbits, and then after the rabbits were grown use the income from their litters and show prizes to pay for Roger's coins.

2. Edythe and Buddy decided that on Mondays and Wednesdays Buddy would help keep silence in the office. On Tuesdays and Thursdays Edythe would work in a conference room that was free, leaving Buddy alone in the office to play the radio. On Fridays the two worked together on joint projects.

3. Keith and Simone decided that four nights a week Keith would spend the evening talking with Simone. Afterwards he would stay up late and talk to his ham radio friends. On the following mornings Simone would drive Keith to work instead of having him go with a carpool, which allowed him to sleep later.

There are few problems that can not be solved with the creative thinking of two problem-solving negotiators.

Johnson, D. W., & Johnson, R. (2005). **Teaching Students To Be Peacemakers** (4th Ed.). Edina, MN: Interaction Book Company, (952)831-9500.

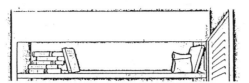

Negotiating for What You Need

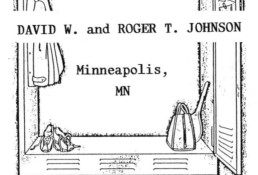

DAVID W. and ROGER T. JOHNSON

Minneapolis,
MN

Subject Area: Universal

Grade Level: Any

Lesson Summary: This lesson requires students to learn and practice negotiation skills in order to obtain the resources they need to complete the assigned task. The required resources are unequally distributed among pairs. In working on the task, students will have to (a) access the resources they need from other pairs and (b) decide how to respond to proposals from others for their pair's resources.

Instructional Objectives: Teach negotiation skills.

Time Required: Thirty to sixty minutes.

Materials:

Item	Materials Needed
Scissors, ruler, paper clips, pencils, two 4-inch squares of red paper, two 4-inch squares of white paper	One Set For Pair 1
Scissors, glue, two 8 1/2" x 11" sheets of gold paper, white paper, and blue paper	One set for Pair 2
Felt-tipped markers, two 8 1/2" x 11" sheets of green paper, white paper, and gold paper	One set for Pair 3
One 8 1/2" x 11" sheet of green, gold, blue, red, and purple paper	One set for Pair 4
Task sheet	One sheet per pair

Johnson, D. W., & Johnson, R. (2005). **Teaching Students To Be Peacemakers** (4th Ed.). Edina, MN: Interaction Book Company, (952)831-9500.

Decisions

Cluster Size:

Eight, divided into four pairs. Groups of 12 may be used with four triads if the teacher wishes.

Assignment To Groups:

Randomly assign students to groups of eight. Within the group of eight have students count off from 1 to 4. The two 1's make a pair, the two 2's make a pair, the two 3's make a pair, and the two 4's make a pair.

Materials:

Each pair is given a packet of materials (see materials table).

The Lesson

Instructional Task:

Distribute an envelope of materials and a Task Sheet to each pair. Explain that each pair has a different set of materials, but they all have to complete the same tasks. They are to negotiate with the other pairs in their group for the materials required to complete the tasks. Pairs may negotiate only with pairs from their cluster. They may **not** negotiate with pairs who are members of another cluster. More specifically, each pair is to complete the following tasks:

1. Make a 3" x 3" square of white paper.

2. Make a 4" x 2" rectangle of gold paper.

3. Make a 3" x 5" **T** in green and white paper.

Johnson, D. W., & Johnson, R. (2005). **Teaching Students To Be Peacemakers** (4th Ed.). Edina, MN: Interaction Book Company, (952)831-9500.

4. Make a four-link paper chain.

5. Make a 4" x 4" flag, in any three colors.

The first pair to complete all tasks is the winner. Pairs may negotiate with each other for the resources they need to complete the tasks.

Positive Interdependence:

One set of products from the pair, both members must agree on how to complete each task, and both must participate actively in the tasks and the negotiations with the other pairs.

Individual Accountability:

The teacher will observe each pair to ensure that both members are working on the tasks and negotiating with other pairs. Pairs in which both members are not engaging in the task work and in negotiations will be disqualified.

Monitoring And Processing

While the groups are working, observe to:

1. Verify that both members of each pair are working on the tasks and negotiating.

2. Determine what negotiation strategies are being used by each student.

Intervene to energize any lagging pairs and keep pairs aware of the time limits.

After all pairs have completed the tasks, have each cluster discuss how resources were negotiated, which pair had the most power and why, and what effects the competition had on the negotiations. Each student should receive feedback on the strategies they used in negotiations.

Johnson, D. W., & Johnson, R. (2005). **Teaching Students To Be Peacemakers** (4th Ed.). Edina, MN: Interaction Book Company, (952)831-9500.

Negotiating Task Sheet

Each group is to complete the following tasks:

1. Make a 3" x 3" square of white paper.

2. Make a 4" x 2" rectangle of gold paper.

3. Make a 3" x 5" **T** in green and white paper.

4. Make a four-link paper chain.

5. Make a 4" x 4" flag, in any three colors.

The first pair to complete all tasks is the winner. Pairs may negotiate with each other for the resources they need to complete the tasks.

The tasks are to be completed cooperatively: One set of products from the pair, both members must agree on how to complete each task, and both must participate actively in the tasks and the negotiations with the other pairs.

We'll trade you some of our red paper for some of your blue.

Johnson, D. W., & Johnson, R. (2005). **Teaching Students To Be Peacemakers** (4th Ed.). Edina, MN: Interaction Book Company, (952)831-9500.

Chapter Six: Managing Anger

The Nature And Value Of Anger

If you are patient in one moment of anger, you will escape a hundred days of sorrow.

Chinese Proverb

Jim and Sam have been in the same classes for two years. Repeatedly Sam pushes Jim, teases him, takes his pencils, and generally bothers him. Today Jim has had enough. When Sam grabs his pencil, Jim loses his temper, jumps up, and tries to grab his pencil back. The teacher quickly intercedes, but Jim keeps yelling at Sam to leave him alone.

Emotions are always involved in conflicts, and one of the most common is anger. Anger is a defensive emotional reaction that occurs when we are frustrated, thwarted, or attacked. You get angry when other people obstruct your goal accomplishment, frustrate your attempts to accomplish something, interfere with your plans, make you feel belittled and rejected, or indicate that you are of no value or importance. When you get angry at other people the results can be either destructive or constructive. Anger tends to be destructive when (a) you express anger in a way that creates dislike, hatred, frustration, and a desire for revenge on the part of the other person or (b) it is repressed and held inside (which tends to create irritability, depression, insomnia, and physiological problems such as headaches and ulcers). Anger tends to be constructive when you feel more energy, motivation, challenge, and excitement, and the other person feels friendship, gratitude, goodwill, and concern. In this chapter we shall examine the nature of anger and how it can be managed in constructive rather than destructive ways.

Anger both causes and accompanies distress. Anger can result in tight muscles, teeth grinding, piercing stares, headaches, heart attacks, loud voices, projectiles, and smashed furniture. When we are angry our blood boils, we are fit to be tied, we have reached the end of our rope, and what happened is the last straw. Anger is an emotion that occurs regularly in the life of every person, more often and with greater intensity at some times than at others. Failure to manage anger constructively can lead to alienation of loved ones, disrupted work performance, and even cardiovascular disorder. Proper recognition, understanding, acceptance, and channeling of anger can make life more comfortable, productive, and exciting. In order for anger to be managed constructively, its components must be identified, and its major functions must be understood. The useful and constructive aspects of anger must be promoted while the destructive and useless aspects of anger are quelled. Rules for constructive anger management must be followed.

Johnson, D. W., & Johnson, R. (2005). **Teaching Students To Be Peacemakers** (4th Ed.). Edina, MN: Interaction Book Company, (952)831-9500.

Figure 6.1 Managing Anger

The Nature of Anger

Rules for Managing Constructively

EXPRESSING ANGER CONSTRUCTIVELY
- **Behavioral Descriptions**
- **Describing Own Feelings**
- **Making Nonverbal Messages Congruent**
- **Listening Skills**
- **Assessing Impact on Other**

ELIMINATING ANGER IN ONE'S LIFE
- **Irrational Beliefs Underlying Anger and Blaming**
- **Managing Your Feelings**
- **Disposable Feelings**

How To Deal With Another Person's Anger

Anger And Negotiations

Johnson, D. W., & Johnson, R. (2005). **Teaching Students To Be Peacemakers** (4th Ed.). Edina, MN: Interaction Book Company, (952)831-9500.

The main components involved in most human anger are as follows:

❖ Anger is usually a defense against something

❖ Anger occurs when we are not getting something we want or would like. We get angry when we are frustrated, thwarted, or attacked.

❖ Anger has in it a sense of righteousness and a belief that one's personal rights have been violated. When we are angry, we usually believe that we are rightfully angry because the other person has acted unjustly or irrationally.

❖ There is a narrowing of perceptual focus and priorities when we are angry. All our attention is focused on the person and behavior we are angry with.

❖ There is a demand aspect of anger. It makes us demand that we get our way.

❖ There is considerable physiological arousal that demands expression in physical action. We not only are ready to "fight" or "flee," there is a demand that we actually do so.

When we plan how to manage our anger constructively, we need to keep in mind that anger is a righteous but defensive reaction to frustration and aggression based on an unidimensional perceptual focus, a physical demand to take action, and a belief that we must get our way.
There are at least eight major functions of anger. Each is described briefly below.

1. **Anger gives us energy and increases the strength with which we act.** Anger mobilizes us for action and thereby provides considerable physical energy to apply toward achieving our goals.

2. **Anger disrupts ongoing behavior by making us agitated and impulsive as well as interfering with our ability to process information and attend to what is taking place.** Anger disrupts behavior. It causes people to focus continually on the injustice that has been done to them or on the attack they are defending against. Someone who is angry has trouble attending to the tasks at hand and has difficulty comprehending new information. Anger often results in impulsive actions aimed at correcting the situation.

3. **Anger makes it easier to express negative feelings and give negative feedback, which might not be expressed if we were not angry.** Expressing negative feelings often provides information needed for accurately defining problems. Anger is a sign that something is going on that needs to be changed. Expressing anger constructively can increase trust by showing that the relationship is strong enough to handle strains. Healthy relationships depend on the ability of both partners to give accurate but negative feedback to each other, and anger helps them to do so. But the potential negative aspect of such

Johnson, D. W., & Johnson, R. (2005). **Teaching Students To Be Peacemakers** (4th Ed.). Edina, MN: Interaction Book Company, (952)831-9500.

forthrightness is that the strength of the negative feelings or feedback may be inappropriate to the provocation, may be overstated, or may be stated in such an offensive and threatening way that the conflict is escalated and the other person becomes fearful and angry.

4. **Anger is a defense against being vulnerable.** Anger changes internal anxiety to external conflict. Anger can overcome anxiety and fear and encourage us to take actions we would never take otherwise. A small child may strike out in anger against a much bigger peer. A subordinate may confront a boss she is afraid of. A very shy person when angry may introduce himself to strangers.

5. **Anger makes us more aggressive and antagonistic.** Feeling angry can be a signal that aggressive actions are called for. Many times we become aggressive through habit when faced with a provocation and strike out verbally or physically at the other people in the situation.

6. **Anger can be a signal that an event is a provocation or that something frustrating or unpleasant is taking place.** Discovering that we are angry can help clarify what is taking place within a situation.

7. **Anger helps us maintain a sense of virtue and righteousness in the face of opposition.** Anger helps us maintain a belief that we are right, justified, and superior.

8. **Anger can intimidate other people and is therefore a source of interpersonal power and influence.** When we want to overpower another person, get our way, or dominate a situation, being angry can often help us to do so.

Being angry at another person can be an unpleasant experience. We can make the other person resentful and hostile when we express anger. We can become anxious after we have expressed anger as we anticipate rejection, counter-anger, and escalation of the conflict. Yet anger can have many positive effects on our problem solving if we learn to manage it constructively.

Rules for Managing Anger Constructively

Aesop tells of a bear roaming through the woods in search of berries who happened on a fallen tree in which a swarm of bees had stored their honey. The bear began to nose around the log very carefully to find out if the bees were at home. Just then one of the swarm came home from the clover field with a load of pollen. Guessing what the bear was after, the bee flew at him, stung him sharply, and then

6 : 4

Johnson, D. W., & Johnson, R. (2005). **Teaching Students To Be Peacemakers** (4th Ed.). Edina, MN: Interaction Book Company, (952)831-9500.

disappeared into the hollow log. The bear immediately lost his temper and sprang on the log tooth and claw to destroy the nest. But this only brought out the whole swarm. The poor bear had to take to his heels, and he was able to save himself only by diving into a pool of water. Sometimes it is wiser to bear a single hurt in silence than to provoke a thousand injuries by flying into a rage.

In managing your anger constructively, there is a set of rules to follow. **The first rule in managing anger is to recognize and acknowledge the fact that you are angry.** Anger is a natural, healthy, normal human feeling. Everyone feels it. You need not fear or reject your anger. For one thing, repressed, denied anger does not vanish but often erupts suddenly in verbal and physical assaults on people and property as well as overreactions to minor provocations. In addition, repression and denial of your anger can create headaches, ulcers, muscle pains, and other physiological ailments. Remember that anger and aggression are not the same thing. You can express anger without being aggressive.

The second rule is to decide whether or not you wish to express your anger. This involves at least two steps—clarifying the intent of the other person and deciding how to respond. First, you ask for clarification to make sure the other person has done something aggressive or provocative in nature. Do not assume that aggression was intended without checking it out. It may be a misunderstanding. If it was not a misunderstanding, you proceed to the second step. Second, you decide whether to express your anger directly or keep it hidden. There are a number of considerations to keep in mind. Remember that anger makes you impulsive. Impulsive, antagonistic acts can escalate conflict and get you into trouble. Remember that your information-processing capacity will decrease as your anger increases, making your decision about how to respond somewhat suspect. Remember to beware of the righteousness of your anger. In most situations it is not a matter of punishing people you think have acted in an unjust way. It is a matter of ensuring that a constructive outcome results from the situation. Do not attempt to prove you were right or that you are morally superior. Think of how to solve the problem. Remember to face your anger and respond while the provocation is small. Do not disregard small irritations and little frustrations. Small feelings, if they are kept inside and allowed to build up, become big feelings. Finally, remember it is often helpful to delay taking action and talk the situation over with a friend before deciding how to respond. There are times when you should avoid expressing anger. When letting the other person know you are angry will be ineffective or destructive, you need to be able to switch to a more productive and suitable pattern of behavior. Whenever it is possible, however, express your anger. Keep your life clear. Deal with issues and provocations when they arise and when you feel angry, not after days or weeks of letting resentment and hostility build up.

The third rule is to express your anger directly and descriptively when it is appropriate to do so. The specific procedures and skills for expressing anger are discussed later in this chapter. To preview that discussion, five points may be mentioned. **First,** express your anger to the appropriate person and make it to the point. Do not generalize. Be specific about the provocation. Make the statement of your anger

Johnson, D. W., & Johnson, R. (2005). **Teaching Students To Be Peacemakers** (4th Ed.). Edina, MN: Interaction Book Company, (952)831-9500.

descriptive, accurate, and to the point, and express it to the appropriate person. **Second**, take responsibility for your anger (the other person did not make you become angry, your anger resulted from your interpretation of the causes of the other person's behavior). **Third**, make your anger part of a confrontation aimed at beginning negotiations. You must be willing to become more involved with the other person and the situation when you express your anger. **Fourth**, use both verbal and nonverbal messages skillfully. Nonverbal messages are more powerful in expressing feelings than are words, but they are also more difficult to understand. To communicate your anger clearly, you need to be skilled in both verbal and nonverbal communication. You need to be able to make your words and nonverbal messages congruent with each other. **Finally**, make the expression of anger cathartic. Catharsis is the release of pent-up emotion either by talking about feelings or engaging in active emotional release by crying, laughing, or shouting. Anger needs to be expressed in a way that terminates it and gets it over and done with. Anger is not a feeling to hold on to. Once you have expressed your anger constructively, let it go.

The fourth rule of managing your anger constructively is to express it indirectly or react in an alternative way when direct expression is not appropriate. If it is not appropriate to express your anger directly, free yourself from the anger before discussing the conflict with the other person. Feelings do need to be expressed. The stronger the feeling, the stronger the need for expression. In privacy you can swear at your boss, hit a punching bag, or swim hard while imagining what you would like to say to a certain acquaintance. There may be many times when you cannot express your anger directly to the people provoking you. Yet it is important to express your anger in a way that ends it. You do not want to stay angry forever. The sooner you get rid of the feelings, the happier your life will be. Expressing and terminating anger indirectly usually involves the following:

❖ Physical Exercise: There is a general maxim that when one is angry and wants to feel better tomorrow, then one should exercise today. Vigorous exercise like jogging, swimming, tennis, or volleyball provides physical release of energy that is important in releasing anger.

❖ Private Physical Expression: Strongly express the feeling in private by shouting, swearing, crying, moaning, throwing pottery, pillow fights, and even hitting a pillow against a wall while yelling. This will provide a physical release of energy and anger.

❖ Psychological Detachment: Resolve the situation in your mind or resign yourself to it. Tell yourself things that can help. Give up thoughts of revenge and getting back at other people. You want to resolve the problem. You can put up with an unfair teacher. An obnoxious peer is not really that bad. Let the negative feelings go, do not hang on to them. They will only make your life unpleasant. Another alternative is to change the way you view the provocation, thereby changing your feeling of anger. Through modifying your interpretations of what the other person's

Johnson, D. W., & Johnson, R. (2005). **Teaching Students To Be Peacemakers** (4th Ed.). Edina, MN: Interaction Book Company, (952)831-9500.

behavior means, you can control your feelings, responding with amusement or indifference rather than with anger. This skill is discussed at length later in this chapter.

❖ Relaxation: Learn to relax when you wish so that you can relax yourself when your anger has been triggered. As you learn to relax more easily, your ability to regulate your anger will improve.

By learning alternative ways of reacting to provocations and indirect ways of expressing anger, you will be able to choose the most effective response. Such freedom gives you an advantage in situations in which other people are trying to provoke you, as the best way to take charge of such a situation is not to get angry when most people would expect or even want you to do so.

The fifth rule is to stay task oriented. You can control and contain your anger and usually be far more effective in managing the situation by staying focused on the goal to be achieved, not on what the other person is saying and doing. When the other person is angry, do not get distracted into his or her anger. Rather, stay focused on the task. Do not let yourself get sidetracked or baited into a quarrel. Taking insults personally distracts you from your task and involves you in unnecessary conflict. Recognize what the other person is doing, but do not be provoked by it; rather, stay task-oriented and focused on the issue. There is evidence that anger directed toward a person will be far more destructive than will anger directed toward an issue. Viewing an incident as a personal affront is likely to result in disruptive and defensive anger, while viewing an incident as a problem to be solved is likely to result in discriminative, expressive, and energizing anger.

The sixth rule is to analyze, understand, and reflect upon your anger. Get to know yourself so that you recognize (a) the events and behaviors that trigger your anger and (b) the internal signs of arousal that signal you are becoming angry. You can control your anger. You can find your own buttons so that you know when someone else is pushing them. It is important for you to understand the regularities of your anger patterns—when, in what circumstances, and with whom you become angry. You can then plan how to avoid frustrating, anger-provoking situations. And you can explicitly decide what you want and plan in detail how to manage situations to obtain it without getting angry. As you become more and more sharply tuned to the signs of tension and upset inside you, you will achieve greater ability to short-circuit the anger process. You can train yourself to use the initial flash of irritation as a signal that anger is on the way and that you may therefore need to switch to a more productive and suitable behavior pattern. Signs of internal arousal can be alerting signals that you are becoming upset and that effective action is called for if a positive outcome is to result. Thus you can learn to stop anger before it develops.

Anger often results from your believing that things are not going the way you want them to go or that you are powerless in a situation in which you want to be able to influence other people.

6 : 7

Johnson, D. W., & Johnson, R. (2005). **Teaching Students To Be Peacemaker** Interaction Book Company, (952)831-9500.

Remember, you gain power and influence when you keep calm and refuse to get angry. Since anger is sometimes due to doubting yourself or letting yourself feel threatened by someone else, it is important to remember that you are a worthwhile person and that you have many strengths and competencies. This can keep you from feeling angry. And you should always beware of the righteousness of your anger. It can be blind.

The seventh rule is to congratulate yourself when you have succeeded in managing your anger constructively. Feel good about your success. Don't focus on your mistakes and failings or on the nastiness of other people. Focus on your ability to manage your anger constructively.

The eighth rule is to express emotions other than anger. Besides expressing negative feelings, it is important to express positive feelings while discussing a conflict. There are positive feelings, such as liking, appreciation, and respect, that strengthen your relationship with the other person. Both positive and negative feelings have to be communicated with skill in a conflict.

Expressing Anger Constructively

I was angry with my friend:
I told my wrath, my wrath did end.
I was angry with my foe:
I told it not, my wrath did grow.

William Blake

Expressing anger constructively can be one of the most difficult aspects of resolving conflicts. There is a risk in expressing feelings such as anger. When you express anger, you have to worry about alienating the other person. Expressing anger could lead to losing the relationship or even losing your job. And you have to worry whether the other person will also get angry at you. Being exposed to the anger of others is painful. To express anger constructively you must first be aware that you are angry, accept anger as natural and normal, and decide to express it.

Keeping anger buried is usually harmful, causing a number of problems. First, it adds to your frustrations. This is not sensible. Getting angry over a frustration does not usually remove the frustration and always adds to your discomfort. **Second**, anger prevents you from solving problems. Being hateful simply fills your thoughts with delicious ways of getting even with others, not with how to get others to behave differently toward you. The net result is that things get worse and worse as you become angrier and angrier. **Third**, concealed anger is often displaced onto other persons. Not expressing anger at a student or colleague can lead to displacing anger at your friends, family, or some stranger. Hidden anger does not vanish, but often suddenly erupts in physical violence and assaults

Johnson, D. W., & Johnson, R. (2005). **Teaching Students To Be Peacemakers** (4th Ed.). Edina, MN: Interaction Book Company, (952)831-9500.

on both people and property. **Fourth**, anger can make you physically sick. Headaches, high blood pressure, and physical pains are not helpful when you are trying to resolve a conflict. **Fifth**, repeated failure to express anger in words sometimes produces the appearance of apathy. If you repeatedly fail to express anger in words, you may give the impression that you don't care. In the long run, keeping anger to yourself will only hurt you and your relationships.

There are several advantages to expressing anger directly in a conflict. Anger conveys to other people what your commitments are and which commitments must be respected or changed. Expressing anger can clear the air so that positive feelings can once again be felt and expressed. Problems that are being ignored are brought to the surface and highlighted through the expression of anger. Anger can override fear and feelings of vulnerability and lead you to act more competently in troublesome situations.

Directly Expressing Anger

I never let the sun set on a disagreement with anybody who means a lot to me.

   Thomas Watson, Sr., Founder, IBM

Many of us in business, especially if we are very sure of our ideas, have hot tempers. My father knew he had to keep the damage from his own temper to a minimum.

   Thomas Watson, Jr., Chairman Emeritus, IBM

Ralph has been caught taking other students' things all year. Today Jim brought a special rock he found on his vacation to Canada last summer to school and suddenly it was missing. The teacher finds it in Ralph's desk, but Ralph denies all knowledge of how it got there and claims he did not take it. Jim is fed up. He believes Ralph is dishonest. Jim accuses Ralph of stealing his rock. Ralph stubbornly claims he is innocent, Jim gets more and more angry.

To express your anger constructively, you describe the other person's behavior, you describe your feelings, and you make your nonverbal messages congruent with your words. The purpose of asserting your anger is to create a shared understanding of the relationship so it may be improved or so you may be more effective in achieving your goals. You want the other person to know how you perceive and feel about his or her actions, and you wish to end up knowing how the other person perceives and feels about your actions. You want to discuss the situation until you and the other person have a common perspective or frame of reference in viewing the relationship and your interactions with each other.

Johnson, D. W., & Johnson, R. (2005). **Teaching Students To Be Peacemakers** (4th Ed.). Edina, MN: Interaction Book Company, (952)831-9500.

Behavioral Descriptions

A behavioral description is a combination of describing the other person's actions and a personal statement to take ownership of your observations. In describing the other person's provocative actions, you need to be skillful in observing what actually occurred and in letting the other person know what behavior you are responding to by describing it clearly and specifically. To do this, you must describe visible evidence, behavior that is open to anyone's observation. Restrict yourself to talking about the actions of the other person. Using personal statements is also a good idea so that it is clear that you are taking ownership for your observations. An example of a good behavior description is, "*Jim, by my count, you have just interrupted me for the third time.*" (Not, "*Jim, you are really being rude,*" which is negative labeling or, "*Jim, you always want to be the center of attention,*" which imputes an unworthy motive.)

Descriptions of Your Own Feelings

You describe your feelings by using personal statements (referring to "I," "me," or "my") and specifying the feeling by name or by action-urge, simile, or some other figure of speech. Your description will be more helpful and effective if it is specific rather than general ("You bumped my arm" rather than "You never watch where you are going"), tentative rather than absolute ("You seem unconcerned about completing our project" rather than "You don't care about the project and you never will"), and informing rather than demanding ("I haven't finished yet" rather than "*Stop interrupting me*"). This latter point needs reemphasizing because of its importance; the description of your anger should be noncoercive and should not be a demand that the other person change. Avoid judgments of the other person ("You are egocentric"), name calling or trait labeling ("You're a phony"), accusations and imputing undesirable motives to the other person ("You always have to be the center of attention"), commands, demands, and orders ("Stop talking and listen!"), and sarcasm ("You're really considerate, aren't you?" when the opposite is meant). By describing your feelings about the other person's actions, your feelings are seen as temporary and capable of change rather than as permanent. It is better to say, "At this point, I am very annoyed with you" than "I dislike you and I always will."

Making Nonverbal Messages Congruent

In describing your feelings you need to make your nonverbal messages similar to your verbal ones. When you express anger verbally, your facial expression should be serious, your tone of voice neutral to cold, your eye contact direct, and your posture rather stiff. Contradictory verbal and nonverbal messages may indicate to the other person that you are untrustworthy and often make the other person anxious.

Johnson, D. W., & Johnson, R. (2005). **Teaching Students To Be Peacemakers** (4th Ed.). Edina, MN: Interaction Book Company, (952)831-9500.

Listening Skills

While discussing your anger with another person it is important to use good listening skills. Use perception checks to make sure that you are not making false assumptions about the other person's feelings and intentions ("My impression is that you are not interested in trying to understand my ideas. Am I wrong?" "Did my last statement bother you?"). And when negotiating the meaning of the other person's actions and in clarifying both your feelings and the feelings of the other person, use paraphrasing to make sure you accurately understand the other person and that the other person feels understood and listened to.

Assess Impact On Other

Take into account the impact your anger will have on the other person. While you will usually feel better after expressing anger constructively and directly to another person, the other person may feel alienated and resentful. After expressing anger directly, it is important to make sure that the other person has a chance to respond and clarify his or her feelings before the interaction is ended.

Summary

To express anger constructively, first describe the other person's provocative behavior and then describe your anger verbally while making your nonverbal messages congruent with your words. An example would be, "Jim, by my count you have just interrupted me for the third time in the past half hour, and I am both frustrated and angry as a result" (while maintaining a serious facial expression, a neutral to cold tone of voice, direct eye contact, and a rather stiff posture). You should then be ready to negotiate on the meaning of Jim's actions and on whether or not anger is the appropriate feeling to have.

In expressing anger your attitude should not be, "Who's right and who's wrong?" but rather, "What can each of us learn from this discussion that will make our relationship more productive and satisfying?" As a result of the discussion, each of you will act with fuller awareness of the effect of your actions on the other person as well as with more understanding of the other person's intentions. One, both, or neither of you may act differently in the future because of this increased awareness. Any change in future behavior needs to be self-chosen rather than compelled by a desire to please or a need to submit to the other person.

Finally, make sure the timing of the expression of your anger is appropriate. Generally, express your anger when there is time enough to discuss the situation and the provocation.

6 : 11

Johnson, D. W., & Johnson, R. (2005). **Teaching Students To Be Peacemakers** (4th Ed.). Edina, MN: Interaction Book Company, (952)831-9500.

The closer in time your reaction is expressed to the provocation, the more constructive the discussion will be.

Assertiveness and Aggressiveness

All people have a perfect right to express their thoughts, feelings, opinions, and preferences and to expect that other people will treat them with respect and dignity. In interpersonal situations involving stress and anger, you may behave nonassertively, aggressively, or assertively. When you behave nonassertively, you say nothing in response to a provocation, keeping your feelings to yourself, hiding feelings from others, and perhaps even hiding your feelings from yourself. Nonassertive behavior is often dishonest and involves letting other people violate your personal right to be treated with respect and dignity.

Aggressive behavior is an attempt to hurt someone or destroy something. It infringes on the rights of others and involves expressing your feelings indirectly through insults, sarcasm, labels, put-downs, and hostile statements and actions. Aggressive behavior involves expressing thoughts, feelings, and opinions in a way that violates others' rights to be treated with respect and dignity.

Assertive behavior involves describing your feelings, thoughts, opinions, and preferences directly to another person in an honest and appropriate way that respects both yourself and the other person. It enables you to act in your own best interests, to stand up for yourself without undue anxiety, to express honest feelings comfortably, and to exercise personal rights without denying the rights of others. Assertive behavior is direct, honest, self-enhancing self-expression that is not hurtful to others and is appropriate for the receiver and the situation.

In general, it is a good idea to raise your restraints and inhibitions against aggressive and nonassertive behavior and to lower any inhibitions, restraints, or anxieties you have about being assertive.

Irrational Beliefs Underlying Anger And Blaming

Long-term anger is based on two irrational beliefs. The first is that you must have your way and that it is awful not to get everything you want. This is known as catastrophizing. The second is that people are bad and should be severely dealt with if they have behaved wrongly. If you see the cause of your frustration as being wicked people who deserve to be punished for their evil acts, you are stuck in a blame orientation. A blame orientation distracts you from finding a solution to your frustration.

Johnson, D. W., & Johnson, R. (2005). **Teaching Students To Be Peacemakers** (4th Ed.). Edina, MN: Interaction Book Company, (952)831-9500.

A blame orientation is especially destructive when it is applied to yourself. Self-blame exists when you say "bad me" to yourself or when you judge your basic self-worth on the basis of your inadequate or rotten behavior. Self-blame is in effect being angry at yourself. Self-blame involves a double attack: one against your actions and the other against yourself as a person. If you spill coffee on your desk you can see your behavior as being uncoordinated, or you can see your behavior as clumsy and yourself as rotten and no good. Self-blame is similar to giving yourself a grade on the basis of a behavior you do not like. When you blame yourself you believe it is catastrophic that you are not getting what you want, that it is your fault, and therefore you are a bad person who should be severely punished. When you blame yourself (or others) you have to carry the anger around inside you, subjecting yourself to a great deal of stress and even making yourself sick. Perhaps most important, blaming yourself distracts you from finding a solution to your problems. All the punishment in the world does not promote creative insight into how a situation may be more constructively managed.

You should never blame yourself (or others) for:

❖ Not having the intelligence to do as well as you would like. If the intellectual ability is not there, you cannot blame yourself. Either it is in your genes or it is not.

❖ Being ignorant. Ignorance means that you have not yet learned a skill. You cannot blame yourself if you did not know better.

❖ Having behaved badly. You should separate your behavior and your self-worth. You are not your actions. Engaging in a bad behavior does not make you a bad person.

❖ Not being perfect. In perfectionism, you attempt to be all things rather than who you are. A perfectionist never has developed an internal sense of how much is good enough. Only when you can stop trying to be perfect do you ever become free to be who you are.

❖ Being psychologically disturbed at the time. Everyone at times enters psychological states such as anger, depression, grief, fear, and even extreme tiredness that result in behaving in ways destructive to the best interests of ourselves or others. Psychological problems do not result from being possessed by demons. Being psychologically disturbed does not make you an evil person.

To combat a blame orientation you must first change your basic assumptions that (a) it is a catastrophe when you do not get what you want and (b) whoever is the blame must be severely punished. Second, you must engage in an internal debate to replace your old assumptions with the new, more constructive, ones. Never blame anyone (including yourself). Always separate the person from his actions. Third, you must forgive yourself (and others) for everything. The sooner you forgive yourself the better. Sooner or later

Johnson, D. W., & Johnson, R. (2005). **Teaching Students To Be Peacemakers** (4th Ed.). Edina, MN: Interaction Book Company, (952)831-9500.

you forgive yourself and those you disagree with. Since you will eventually forgive, the sooner you do so the better for you. Finally, you must be problem oriented. Focus on the problem to be solved, not on the failure of you or others to live up to your expectations. Remember that when you blame others they become much more hostile and angry with you, escalating the conflict into destructive directions.

Managing Your Feelings

I have known a great many troubles, but most of them never happened .

Mark Twain

There are times when your relationships may result in great happiness, satisfaction, growth, and joy. There are other times when your relationships may result in depression, sadness, anger, worry, frustration, or guilt. You will be depressed occasionally about a relationship or angry at the way in which other people are treating you. If the feelings are dealt with constructively, they will not last very long. But if you have destructive patterns of interpreting what is happening in your life, you can be depressed and upset all the time. You can turn small events into tragedies. You could, for example, react as if a colleague's not liking you were as serious as finding out you have incurable cancer. There are people who are talented at taking an occasional small event and creating major feelings of depression or anger that stay with them for several days or weeks. Don't be one of them.

How you feel is important for your enjoyment of life and for your ability to relate effectively to other people. If you are depressed, angry, worried, and anxious about your relationships, then you need to take some sort of action. You need to get rid of negative feelings and to promote positive feelings, such as happiness, contentment, pride, and satisfaction.

To change negative or destructive feelings, you have two choices. You can choose to try to change things outside of yourself. You can change jobs, friends, location, and careers. Or you could choose to change things within yourself. You can change your interpretations of what is happening in your life. Changing your interpretations will change your feelings. In choosing whether to try to change something outside of yourself or inside yourself, it is important to remember: The easiest thing to change in your life is yourself.

Let's take an example. Sam believes his boss is always picking on him. He thinks that his boss gives him the dirtiest jobs to do. Sam thinks that his colleagues are not made to work as hard as he is. The principal always seems to be criticizing Sam but not his colleagues. All this makes Sam angry, depressed, worried, and frustrated. Sam also feels that the situation is hopeless. "What can I do?" asks Sam. "My boss has all the power. He can fire me, but I can't do anything to him."

Johnson, D. W., & Johnson, R. (2005). **Teaching Students To Be Peacemakers** (4th Ed.). Edina, MN: Interaction Book Company, (952)831-9500.

Sam has two choices. He can try to change his boss. Or he can try to change his feelings. Psychologists would tell Sam it is easier to change his feelings than to change his boss. What do you think?

Disposable Feelings: Like It or Dump It

Habits can not be thrown out the upstairs window. They have to be coaxed down the stairs one step at a time.

Mark Twain

The five aspects of expressing feelings discussed are:

1. Gather information through your five senses.

2. Interpret the information.

3. Experience the feelings appropriate to your interpretations.

4. Decide how you intend to express your feelings.

5. Express your feelings.

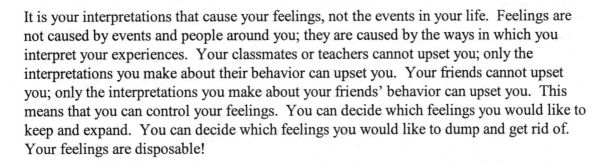

It is your interpretations that cause your feelings, not the events in your life. Feelings are not caused by events and people around you; they are caused by the ways in which you interpret your experiences. Your classmates or teachers cannot upset you; only the interpretations you make about their behavior can upset you. Your friends cannot upset you; only the interpretations you make about your friends' behavior can upset you. This means that you can control your feelings. You can decide which feelings you would like to keep and expand. You can decide which feelings you would like to dump and get rid of. Your feelings are disposable!

Depending on your interpretations, you can feel satisfaction, pride, enjoyment, fun, contentment, and challenge about your relationships. Or you can feel depressed, anxious, worried, angry, sad, hopeless, and helpless about your relationships. When your interpretations result in feelings that contribute to a painful and troubled life, you are managing your feelings destructively. When you have feelings of depression and anxiety, your work suffers, the people around you suffer, and you are just no fun to be around. Maintaining relationships means that you are able to manage your interpretations so that you are not overly depressed, anxious, angry, or upset.

Your interpretations are heavily influenced by the assumptions you make about what is good or bad, what you do or do not need, and what causes what in the world. Sometimes

Johnson, D. W., & Johnson, R. (2005). **Teaching Students To Be Peacemakers** (4th Ed.). Edina, MN: Interaction Book Company, (952)831-9500.

people have assumptions that cause them to be depressed or upset most of the time. You can assume, for example, that your teachers have to like you more than any other student. Since there is always somebody your teachers will like better than you, such an assumption will keep you unhappy. You will be depressed because your teachers do not like you best! Assumptions such as this one are irrational. An irrational assumption is a belief that makes you depressed, anxious, or upset most of the time. The belief (such as, the teacher has to like me best or else my life is ruined) is accepted as true without any proof. If you believe that you have to be perfect or else you are absolutely worthless, you have an irrational assumption. If you believe that everyone in the world has to think you are absolutely marvelous or else you will be miserable, you have an irrational assumption. If you think you are unemployable because you can't immediately find a job, you have an irrational assumption. Irrational assumptions can only make you feel miserable because they lead to depressing interpretations. All you have to do to ruin your life is to make a few irrational assumptions and refuse to change them no matter how much pain they cause!

It takes energy to have destructive feelings. It takes energy to hold on to irrational assumptions. It takes energy to make interpretations that lead to miserable feelings. It takes energy to try to ignore, deny, and hide these miserable feelings. The fewer irrational assumptions you have the more energy you will have for enjoying yourself and your relationships! The more quickly you get rid of your irrational assumptions and the destructive feelings they cause, the more energy you have for enjoying yourself and your relationships!

To maintain constructive relationships you need to:

- ❖ Be aware of your assumptions.

- ❖ Know how they affect your interpretation of the information gathered by your senses.

- ❖ Be able to tell how rational or irrational your assumptions are.

- ❖ Dump your irrational assumptions by replacing them with rational ones.

You can change your irrational assumptions. The easiest way is to: (1) become highly aware of when you are making an irrational assumption; (2) think of a rational assumption that is much more constructive; and (3) argue with yourself until you have replaced your irrational assumption with a rational one.

Irrational assumptions are learned. Usually they are learned in early childhood. They were taught to you by people in your past. Irrational assumptions are bad habits just like smoking or alcoholism. What was learned as a child can be unlearned as an adult. If you keep arguing against your irrational assumptions, you will soon develop rational ones! Do not let yourself feel bad just because you have developed bad thinking habits in the past!

Johnson, D. W., & Johnson, R. (2005). **Teaching Students To Be Peacemakers** (4th Ed.). Edina, MN: Interaction Book Company, (952)831-9500.

How To Deal With Another Person's Anger

David is a senior who never does his homework. The teacher assigned a major project that counts for a major part of your grade. If all members do their part of the project, each group member will receive 10 bonus points. You were assigned to a cooperative learning group that included David. Today the first efforts of all group members were due and David has done nothing. You calmly tell him that you need the bonus points to ensure an "A" in the course and that he should do his part of the project. David becomes furious at you. The intensity of his anger is frightening, even though normally he is not a particularly aggressive person.

Everybody gets angry. You do, and so do your classmates and teachers. But figuring out what to do when another person is angry at you is tough. Letting your anger or another student's anger get out of hand is disastrous. But so is hiding it. Hidden anger only smolders until it explodes later "for no good reason." Here are some suggestions for dealing with an angry classmate.

1. **Give others the "right" to feel angry.** Remember that anger is a natural human feeling. Other students have a "right" to feel and express anger as well as happiness, joy, sadness, grief, and pain. So do you. Remember that anger is different from aggression. Aggression is an attempt to hurt someone or destroy something. It infringes on the rights of others. Anger is a feeling indicating that the person feels frustrated or thwarted. This distinction may help you to react appropriately to the many kinds of upsetting things an angry classmate may do. Also, remember that it is better for the anger to be expressed and dealt with than hidden. When feelings are repressed, denied, or ignored, they will come out later in one way or another, usually in ways that are more difficult to deal with.

2. **Do not get angry back.** When another student gets angry at you, the first step is for you to control your own feelings. Losing your temper will only escalate the conflict and make things worse.

3. **Recognize the temptation to use aggression is a sign that the person is feeling weak and helpless.** The other person is probably at his or her wit's end and does not know what to do. Help him or her back off, cool down, and try something else. Remind them that being hurtful escalates the situation.

4. **Focus attention on the task, not on the other person's anger.** Focus both your and the other person's attention on the task to be completed. Losing your temper will not help to identify and solve the problem. Do not let yourself get sidetracked or baited into a quarrel when the other person is angry. Recognize what the other person is doing, but do not be provoked by it. Rather, stay focused on the task. Keep refocusing the other person's attention on the task.

Johnson, D. W., & Johnson, R. (2005). **Teaching Students To Be Peacemakers** (4th Ed.). Edina, MN: Interaction Book Company, (952)831-9500.

5. **Explain the situation.** Understanding a situation can help the other person understand the cause of his or her anger, and begin to calm down. Your explanation can include telling how you feel, and asking for consideration. An example is, "Your yelling usually does not bother me, but today I have a headache; could you please keep your voice volume down?"

6. **Talk to yourself.** Prepare yourself for the experience by saying such things to yourself as, "I'm good at managing other peoples' anger," ignore the anger by saying such things to yourself as, "His anger is a minor annoyance, not a major catastrophe," cope with your arousal and agitation by saying such things to yourself as, "Breath deep, relax, slow your pulse down," and reward yourself for coping successfully by saying such things to yourself as, "You were terrific; you were calm during the whole conversation!"

7. **Use affection.** Sometimes a sudden show of affection will help an angry classmate regain control.

8. **Teach the person to express anger in words.** Talking is an acceptable steam valve, and helps the student to avoid "blowing up." Teach your fellow students to put angry feelings into words instead of fists.

9. **Be a good model.** Model expressing anger constructively.

10. **When you can not handle a situation, seek help. Do not hesitate to seek help from others when you need to.** The help could be to physically restrain a violent person. Or it could be a person to talk through a situation with in order to think more creatively about how to handle a person who is emotionally upset at the time.

Anger And Negotiations

Negotiating is an ever present activity. Negotiations within ongoing relationships are different from negotiations between strangers and adversaries. If you must live, work, and interact with each other after an agreement is reached, the long-term relationship becomes more important than the settlement of any one issue. This means that negotiations are aimed at solving a problem, not at "winning." Most negotiations occur informally. When negotiating must be done in a more careful and complete way, they are initiated through confrontation.

In confronting another person and beginning negotiations, individuals must express their feelings constructively and respond to the emotional expressions of the other in a constructive way. Perhaps the most difficult emotion to manage constructively within conflict situations is anger. Individuals may refuse to negotiate out of anger, they may engage in forcing out of anger, and they may avoid smoothing out of anger. At any time in negotiations participants may become angry at each other and express it. Both your own

Johnson, D. W., & Johnson, R. (2005). **Teaching Students To Be Peacemakers** (4th Ed.). Edina, MN: Interaction Book Company, (952)831-9500.

anger towards the other person and the other person's anger toward you must be managed constructively. If you perfect your skills in managing your anger and in responding to the anger of others constructively, you will tend to be a highly competent negotiator even under the most difficult conditions.

Summary

Emotions are always involved in conflicts, and one of the most common is anger. Anger is a defensive emotion reaction that occurs when you are frustrated, thwarted, or attacked. You get angry when other people obstruct your goal accomplishment, frustrate your attempts to accomplish something, interfere with your plans, make you feel belittled and rejected, or indicate that you are of no value or importance. When you get angry at other people the results can be either destructive or constructive. Anger tends to be destructive when (a) you express anger in a way that creates dislike, hatred, frustration, and a desire for revenge on the part of the other person or (b) it is repressed and held inside (which tends to create irritability, depression, insomnia, and physiological problems such as headaches and ulcers). Anger tends to be constructive when you feel more energy, motivation, challenge, and excitement, and the other person feels friendship, gratitude, goodwill, and concern.

To manage anger constructively you should recognize and acknowledge that you are angry. Then decide whether or not you wish to express your anger. You express your anger directly and descriptively when it is appropriate to do so. You express it indirectly or react in an alternative way when direct expression of anger is not appropriate. During it all, you stay task oriented. You analyze, understand, and reflect on your anger. You congratulate yourself on managing your anger constructively and you express any other emotions (such as respect or appreciation) you are feeling directly and descriptively. To express anger constructively you describe the other's actions and you describe your angry feelings verbally while making your nonverbal messages congruent with your words. You listen carefully to what the other person is saying, and you assess the impact of the anger on the other person. And you let your anger go.

Long-term anger is based on two irrational beliefs—that you must get your way and the other person must be punished. To ensure that you do not keep anger long-term, you must manage your feelings in ways that let you dispose of anger. You begin by deciding to change yourself (rather than the other person) because you can control yourself while you cannot control external events. You dispose of your anger through controlling how you interpret the information you receive through your senses. Your interpretations are based on the assumptions you make about what is good or bad, what you do or do not need, and what causes what in the world. Finally, in a conflict you must control your reactions to other people's anger toward you as well as your anger toward them. You give them the "right" to feel angry, you try not to get angry back, you focus your attention on the task. You describe the situation, and talk to yourself to keep yourself calm.

Johnson, D. W., & Johnson, R. (2005). **Teaching Students To Be Peacemakers** (4th Ed.). Edina, MN: Interaction Book Company, (952)831-9500.

CREATIVE CONFLICT CONTRACT

Write down your major learnings from reading this chapter and participating in training session one. Then write down how you plan to implement each learning. Share what you learned and your implementation plans with your base group. Listen carefully to their major learnings and implementation plans. You may modify your own plans on the basis of what you have learned from your groupmates. Volunteer one thing you can do to help each groupmate with his or her implementation plans. Utilize the help groupmates offer to you. Sign each member's plans to seal the contract.

MAJOR LEARNINGS	IMPLEMENTATION PLANS

Date: _____ Participant's Signature: _____

Signatures Of Group Members: _____

_____

Johnson, D. W., & Johnson, R. (2005). **Teaching Students To Be Peacemakers** (4th Ed.). Edina, MN: Interaction Book Company, (952)831-9500.

Managing Anger Constructively: A Checklist

1. Anger occurs when we are not getting something we want or would like (when we feel frustrated, thwarted, attacked, belittled, devalued).

2. Anger can:

   a. Add to your frustrations. This is not sensible. Getting angry over a frustration does not usually remove the frustration and always adds to your discomfort.

   b. Prevents you from solving problems. Being hateful simply fills your thoughts with delicious ways of getting even with others, not with how to get others to behave differently toward you. The net result is that things get worse and worse as you become angrier and angrier.

   c. Make you physically sick.

3. Beware of its:

   a. Narrowing of perceptual focus and priorities.

   b. Righteousness, blame orientation, and desire to punish.

   c. Demand that you get your way.

   d. Physiological arousal.

4. Rules:

   a. Recognize and acknowledge your anger.

   b. Decide whether you wish to express it. Know how to detach and let it go if you decide not to.

   c. When it is appropriate to do so, express anger directly and descriptively. Once you have expressed your anger constructively, let it go.

   d. Express it indirectly or react in an alternative way when direct expression is not appropriate.

      1. Physical exercise.

      2. Private physical expression.

6 : 21

Johnson, D. W., & Johnson, R. (2005). **Teaching Students To Be Peacemakers** (4th Ed.). Edina, MN: Interaction Book Company, (952)831-9500.

      3. Psychological detachment.

      4. Relaxation.

  e. When the other person is angry, stay focused on the task/issue. Do not get distracted into his or her anger.

  f. Analyze, understand, and reflect upon your anger.

5. Anger is based on two irrational beliefs:

  a. You must have your way. It is awful not to get everything you want.

  b. People are bad and should be severely dealt with if they have behaved wrongly. They are wicked for frustrating you and deserve to be punished.

6. Express your anger constructively by:

  a. Describing the other person's behavior.

  b. Describing your anger.

  c. Making your verbal and nonverbal messages congruent.

  d. Checking your perceptions of the other person's behavior and the assumptions you are making about the meaning of the behavior.

  e. Paraphrasing the other person's replies.

7. Respond to other people's anger constructively by:

  a. Giving others the "right" to feel angry.

  b. Not getting angry back.

  c. Recognize the temptation to use aggression is a sign that the person is feeling weak and helpless.

  d. Focus attention on the task, not on the other person's anger.

  e. Exjplain the situation.

  f. Talk to yourself to manage provocations.

Johnson, D. W., & Johnson, R. (2005). **Teaching Students To Be Peacemakers** (4th Ed.). Edina, MN: Interaction Book Company, (952)831-9500.

Understanding My Anger EXERCISE

Being aware of our feelings is an important and somewhat difficult task. Many of us were taught to hide our feelings. We learned to pretend we did not have them. This is especially true of feelings we consider negative, such as anger. We often keep our anger inside and act as if it were not there. We deny to ourselves that we are angry. In order to be aware of our anger and express it appropriately, we must understand what makes us angry.

Working by yourself, complete the following statements. Be specific. Try to think of times when you were angry or someone was angry at you.

1. I feel angry when my friends...

2. When I'm angry at my friends, I usually...

3. After expressing my anger, I feel...

4. The way I express anger usually makes my friends...

5. When my friends express anger toward me, I feel...

6. When I feel that way, I usually...

7. After reacting to my friends' anger, I feel...

8. My reaction to my friends' anger usually results in...

9. I feel angry when my teacher...

10. When I'm angry at my teacher, I usually...

11. The way I act when I'm angry at my teacher makes me feel...

12. The way I act when I'm angry at my teacher usually results in my teacher...

13. When my teacher expresses anger at me, I feel...

14. When I feel that way I usually...

6 : 23

Johnson, D. W., & Johnson, R. (2005). **Teaching Students To Be Peacemakers** (4th Ed.). Edina, MN: Interaction Book Company, (952)831-9500.

15. After reacting to my teacher's anger, I feel...

16. My reactions to my teacher's anger usually result in my teacher...

In a group of two share your answers and listen carefully to your partner's answers. Write down:

a. Five major things that make you and your partner angry.

b. Five major ways in which you and your partner express anger.

c. Five major conclusions you and your partner have come to about what happens when anger is expressed.

Find a new partner. **Share** answers, **listen** to his or her's, and utilize the best ideas of both to **create** a new list of conclusions about what happens when anger is expressed.

Johnson, D. W., & Johnson, R. (2005). **Teaching Students To Be Peacemakers** (4th Ed.). Edina, MN: Interaction Book Company, (952)831-9500.

How Would You Feel If . . .?

Different people feel differently about the same thing. Some people get angry when they are teased, others do not. You are going to play a game about feelings. For each of the situations given below, write down how you would feel. Then meet with a partner and share your answers. If the two of you would feel differently, discuss why until you both understand each other's reactions. How would you feel if:

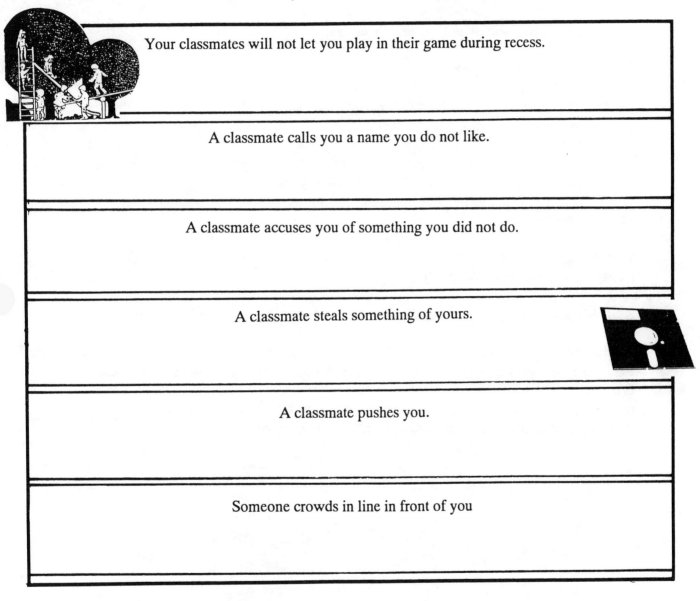

Your classmates will not let you play in their game during recess.

A classmate calls you a name you do not like.

A classmate accuses you of something you did not do.

A classmate steals something of yours.

A classmate pushes you.

Someone crowds in line in front of you

Does your partner feel differently than you in these situations? Explain why different people feel differently about the same experiénce. Explain why you may feel differently at two different times about the same experience.

6 : 25

Johnson, D. W., & Johnson, R. (2005). **Teaching Students To Be Peacemakers** (4th Ed.). Edina, MN: Interaction Book Company, (952)831-9500.

Talking To Yourself To Manage Provocations

Any meeting to discuss a conflict can be divided into four stages:

1. Preparing emotionally for the meeting.

2. Listening to the other person's angry statements.

3. Coping with the arousal and agitation resulting.

4. Congratulating yourself for coping successfully.

For each stage, there are a number of statements you should make to yourself to help you manage the provocation successfully. The assumption is that through controlling what you say to yourself before, during, and following a provocation, you can change your conflict behavior and instruct yourself in more constructive behavioral patterns. The purpose of this exercise is to give you some practice in differentiating among the self- statements for each stage and applying them to a conflict situation you have recently been involved in. The procedure is:

1. Form into triads and classify the self-statements below according to the four stages of managing a provocation constructively.

2. Read the two case studies. Identify the statements you would make for each stage.

3. Identify a conflict situation that usually creates anger and distress in you. Working as a triad, take the conflict situation of each member and work out a series of self-statements that can be used during each stage of managing the provocation constructively. Each member of the triad should develop a set self-statements that will help him or her manage the conflict situation more constructively next time it appears.

Johnson, D. W., & Johnson, R. (2005). **Teaching Students To Be Peacemakers** (4th Ed.). Edina, MN: Interaction Book Company, (952)831-9500.

Managing Provocations By Talking To Yourself

Given below are statements you could say to yourself to help yourself manage a conflict situation constructively. Working as a triad, classify each statement given below as belonging in one of the four stages of managing a provocation constructively.

Stage What I Say To Myself

1. _____ Dealing with her anger is only a minor annoyance.

2. _____ Listen carefully for the issue, not the feelings.

3. _____ Getting upset will not work. Stay relaxed.

4. _____ I did that well!

5. _____ I got through that without getting angry. Way to go!

6. _____ What does she want?

7. _____ It is not worth getting upset over.

8. _____ Listening to her anger will be easy.

9. _____ I will be able to manage the situation.

10. _____ He is trying to get me angry. I am not going to.

11. _____ I did not take anything personally. Good job!

12. _____ What is the issue? Do not get distracted into a quarrel.

13. _____ I am excellent at managing provocations.

14. _____ So he is insulting me. So what? The issue is more important.

15. _____ Calm down. I can't expect people to act the way I want them to.

16. _____ Take a few deep breaths and relax before we start.

17. _____ Good for me!

18. _____ It will be easy.

19. _____ What does she want?

20. _____ Relax.

6 : 27

Johnson, D. W., & Johnson, R. (2005). **Teaching Students To Be Peacemakers** (4th Ed.). Edina, MN: Interaction Book Company, (952)831-9500.

Were You Talking About Me?

One of your classmates, John, has asked to talk with you after school. He has heard that you were talking about him in the cafeteria during lunch. He is hurt, angry, and upset. You did mention several good points and a couple of bad points about John in a general discussion of who were the most and least popular students. Although you mention far more positive than negative points about John, he has heard only that you were criticizing him behind his back. In preparing for the meeting, what are the statements you can make to yourself to:

1. Prepare emotionally for the meeting.

2. Prepare to listen to the John's angry statements.

3. Cope with your arousal and agitation during the meeting.

4. Congratulate yourself for coping successfully with his anger.

I Didn't Do It!

Sally is a student in your class who continually bothers everyone. She pushes, nudges, hits, and trips people regularly. Jane came to you crying with a cut lip and a bruised knee, complaining that Sally hit her and then pushed her down. You ask Sally if the two of you can talk about it during your joint study hall. Sally is extremely angry, saying that she did not touch Jane and Jane is lying. Sally sees you as being very unfair. You know that once study hall starts and you start to talk to Sally, she will start yelling and calling you names. In preparing for the meeting, what are statements you can make to yourself to:

1. Prepare emotionally for the meeting.

2. Prepare to listen to the Sally's angry statements.

3. Cope with your arousal and agitation during the meeting.

4. Congratulate yourself for coping successfully with her anger.

Johnson, D. W., & Johnson, R. (2005). **Teaching Students To Be Peacemakers** (4th Ed.). Edina, MN: Interaction Book Company, (952)831-9500.

Assumptions, Assumptions, What Are My Assumptions?

What are common irrational assumptions? How do you know if your assumptions are rational or irrational? One way is to compare them with the following list of rational and irrational assumptions taken from the writings of Albert Ellis (1962). Do you make any of these assumptions? Do you have any of the irrational assumptions listed below? Do you make any of the rational assumptions listed below? Can you tell the difference between the rational and the irrational ones?

Read each of the statements listed below. Write *yes* for any assumption that describes how you think. Write *no* for any assumption that does not describe how you think. Then reread each statement. Write *R* for the rational assumptions. Write *I* for the irrational assumptions. Keep your answers. You will use them in a later lesson.

Common Assumptions

_____ 1. I must be loved, liked, and approved of by everyone all the time or I will be absolutely miserable and will feel totally worthless.

_____ 2. It would be nice if I were liked by everyone, but I can survive very well without the approval of most people. It is only the liking and approval of close friends and people with actual power over me (such as my boss) that I have to be concerned with.

_____ 3. I have to be absolutely 100 percent perfect and competent in all respects if I am to consider myself worthwhile.

_____ 4. My personal value does not rest on how perfect or competent I am. Although I'm trying to be as competent as I can, I am a valuable person regardless of how well I do things.

_____ 5. People who are bad, including myself, must be blamed and punished to prevent them from being wicked in the future.

_____ 6. What is important is not making the same mistakes in the future. I do not have to blame and punish myself or other people for what has happened in the past.

Taken from: Reaching Out: Interpersonal Effectiveness and Self-Actualization (4th ed.) by David W. Johnson. Englewood Cliffs, NJ: Prentice Hall, 1990.

6 : 29

Johnson, D. W., & Johnson, R. (2005). **Teaching Students To Be Peacemakers** (4th Ed.). Edina, MN: Interaction Book Company, (952)831-9500.

Assumptions (continued)

_____ 7. It is a total catastrophe and so terrible that I can't stand it if things are not the way I would like them to be.

_____ 8. There is no reason the world should be the way I want it to be. What is important is dealing with what is. I do not have to bemoan the fact that things are not fair or just the way I think they should be.

_____ 9. If something terrible could happen, I will keep thinking about it *as if* it is actually going to take place.

_____10. I will try my best to avoid future unpleasantness. Then I will not worry about it. I refuse to go around keeping myself afraid by saying, "What if this happened?" "What if that happened?"

_____11. It is easier to avoid difficulties and responsibilities than to face them.

_____12. Facing difficulties and meeting responsibilities is easier in the long run than avoiding them.

_____13. I need someone stronger than myself to rely on.

_____14. I am strong enough to rely on myself.

_____15. Since I was this way when I was a child, I will be this way all my life.

_____16. I can change myself at any time in my life, whenever I decide it is helpful for me to do so.

_____17. I must become upset and depressed about other people's problems.

_____18. Having empathy with other people's problems and trying to help them does not mean getting upset and depressed about their problems. Overconcern does not lead to problem solving. How can I be of help if I am as depressed as others are?

_____19. It is terrible and unbearable to have to do things I don't want and don't like to do.

_____20. What I can't change I won't let upset me.

6 : 30

Johnson, D. W., & Johnson, R. (2005). **Teaching Students To Be Peacemakers** (4th Ed.). Edina, MN: Interaction Book Company, (952)831-9500.

INTERPRETATIONS

The assumptions we make greatly influence our interpretations of the meaning of events in our life. These interpretations determine our feelings. The same event can be depressing or amusing, depending on the assumptions and interpretations we make. The purpose of this exercise is to focus a group discussion on the ways in which assumptions affect our interpretations and how we feel.

1. Form groups of four. Take the ten episodes below and discuss the following questions:
   a. What irrational assumption is the person making?
   b. How does this assumption cause the person to feel the way she does?
   c. What rational assumption does the person need in order to change her feelings into more positive feelings?
2. In your group, discuss assumptions each of you have that influence your feelings of depression, anger, frustration, distress, and worry. When you are experiencing each of these feelings, what assumptions are causing you to feel that way? How can you change these assumptions to make your life happier?

Episodes

1. Sally likes to have her coworkers place their work neatly in a pile on her desk so that she can add her work to the pile, staple it all together, and give it to their supervisor. Her coworkers, however, throw their work into the supervisor's basket in a very disorderly and messy fashion. Sally then becomes very worried and upset. "I can't stand it," Sally says to herself. "It's terrible what they are doing. And it isn't fair to me or our supervisor!"

2. Jill has been given responsibility for planning next year's budget for her department. This amount of responsibility scares her. For several weeks she has done nothing on the budget. "I'll do it next week," she keeps thinking.

3. John went to the office one morning and passed a person he had never met in the hallway. He said, "Hello," and the person just looked at him and then walked on without saying a word. John became depressed. "I'm really not a very attractive person," he thought to himself. "No one seems to like me."

Taken from: Reaching Out: Interpersonal Effectiveness and Self-Actualization (4th ed.) by David W. Johnson. Englewood Cliffs, NJ: Prentice Hall, 1990.

Johnson, D. W., & Johnson, R. (2005). **Teaching Students To Be Peacemakers** (4th Ed.). Edina, MN: Interaction Book Company, (952)831-9500.

Interpretations (continued)

4. Dan is an intensive-care paramedic technician and is constantly depressed and worried about whether he can do his job competently. For every decision that has to be made, he asks his supervisor what he should do. One day he came into work and found that his supervisor had quit. "What will I do now?" he thought. "I can't handle this job without her."

5. Jane went to her desk and found a note from her supervisor that she had made an error in the report she worked on the day before. The note told her to correct the error and continue working on the report. Jane became depressed. "Why am I so dumb and stupid?" she thought to herself. "I can't seem to do anything right. That supervisor must think I'm terrible at my job."

6. Heidi has a knack for insulting people. She insults her coworkers, her boss, customers, and even passersby who ask for directions. Her boss has repeatedly told Heidi that if she doesn't change she will be fired. This depresses Heidi and makes her very angry at her boss. "How can I change?" Heidi says. "I've been this way ever since I could talk. It's too late for me to change now."

7. Tim was checking the repairs another technician had made on a television set. He found a mistake and became very angry. "I have to punish him," he thought. "He made a mistake and he has to suffer the consequences for it."

8. Bonnie doesn't like to fill out forms. She gets furious every day because her job as legal secretary requires her to fill out form after form after form. "Every time I see a form my stomach ties itself into knots," she says. "I hate forms! I know they have to be done in order for the work to be filed with the courts, but I still hate them!"

9. Bob is very anxious about keeping his job. "What if the company goes out of business?" he thinks. "What if my boss gets angry at me?" "What if the secretary I yelled at is the boss's daughter?" All day he worries about whether he will have a job tomorrow.

10. Jack is a very friendly person who listens quite well. All his coworkers tell their problems to Jack. He listens sympathetically. Then he goes home deeply depressed. "Life is so terrible for the people I work with," he thinks. "They have such severe problems and such sad lives."

6 : 32

Johnson, D. W., & Johnson, R. (2005). **Teaching Students To Be Peacemakers** (4th Ed.). Edina, MN: Interaction Book Company, (952)831-9500.

CHANGING YOUR FEELINGS

Now that you have discussed how people can make their assumptions more constructive, you may want to apply your own advice to yourself. The purpose of this exercise is to give you a chance to discuss your own negative feelings and see what assumptions are causing them. The procedure is:

1. Form groups of four. Draw straws to see who goes first in your group. Then go around the group in a clockwise direction. Each member completes the following statements:
   a. What depresses me about school or work is . . .
   b. When I get depressed about school or work I . . .
   c. The assumptions I am making that cause me to be depressed are . . .
   d. Constructive assumptions I can adopt to change my depression to more positive feelings are . . .

   Listen carefully to what each group member says. If he is not sure of his assumptions, help him clarify them. Give support for making his assumptions more constructive.

2. Now go around the group again and discuss how each member completes these statements:
   a. The things I worry about are . . .
   b. What I do when I get worried is . . .
   c. The assumptions I am making that cause me to be worried are . . .
   d. Constructive assumptions I can adopt to change my worry to more positive feelings are . . .

3. Now try anger:
   a. The things I get angry about are . . .
   b. What I do when I get angry is . . .
   c. The assumptions I am making that cause me to be angry are . . .
   d. Constructive assumptions I can adopt to change my anger to more positive feelings are . . .

4. Let's see how you feel about your career!
   a. The negative feelings I have when I think about my career are . . .
   b. The things I do when I have those feelings are . . .
   c. The assumptions I am making that cause the feelings are . . .
   d. Constructive attitudes I can adopt to change these feelings to more positive ones are . . .

5. Discuss in your group what the members learned about themselves and the ways in which they manage their feelings.

- - - - -

Taken from: <u>Reaching Out: Interpersonal Effectiveness and Self-Actualization</u>
(4th ed.) by David W. Johnson. Englewood Cliffs, NJ: Prentice Hall,
1990.

Johnson, D. W., & Johnson, R. (2005). **Teaching Students To Be Peacemakers** (4th Ed.). Edina, MN: Interaction Book Company, (952)831-9500.

HOW DO I MANAGE MY FEELINGS ?

There are five questions below. Each question has two parts. Check *a* if your way of managing feelings is best described by the *a* part of the question. Check a *b* if your way of managing feelings is best described by the *b* part of the question. Think about each question carefully. Be honest. No one will see your answers. The results are simply for your own self-awareness.

1. ____ **a.** I am fully aware of what I am sensing in a given situation.
    ____ **b.** I ignore what I am sensing by thinking about the past or the future.

2. ____ **a.** I understand the interpretations I usually make about other people's actions. I investigate my feeling by asking what interpretation is causing it. I work to be aware of interpretations I am making.
    ____ **b.** I deny that I make any interpretations about what I sense. I ignore my interpretations. I insist that I do not interpret someone's behavior as being mean. The person *is* mean.

3. ____ **a.** I accept my feeling as being part of me. I turn my full awareness on it. I try to feel it fully. I take a good look at it so I can identify it and tell how strong it is. I keep asking myself, "What am I feeling now?"
    ____ **b.** I reject my feeling. I ignore it by telling myself I'm not angry, upset, sad, or even happy. I deny my feeling by telling myself and others, "But I'm not feeling anything at all." I avoid people and situations that might make me more aware of my feelings. I pretend I'm not really feeling the way I am.

4. ____ **a.** I decide how I want to express my feeling. I think of what I want to result from the expression of my feeling. I think of what is an appropriate way to express the feeling in the current situation. In my mind, I review the sending skills.
    ____ **b.** Since I've never admitted to having a feeling, I don't need to decide how to express it! I don't think through what might happen after I express my feelings. I never think about what is appropriate in a situation. When my feelings burst I am too emotional to remember good sending skills.

- - - - - - - -

Taken from: Reaching Out: Interpersonal Effectiveness and Self-Actualization (4th ed.) by David W. Johnson. Englewood Cliffs, NJ: Prentice Hall, 1990.

Johnson, D. W., & Johnson, R. (2005). **Teaching Students To Be Peacemakers** (4th Ed.). Edina, MN: Interaction Book Company, (952)831-9500.

How Do I Manage My Feelings? (continued)

5. _____ **a.** I express my feelings appropriately and clearly. Usually, this means describing my feeling directly. It also means using nonverbal messages to back up my words. My words and my nonverbal messages communicate the same feeling.

   _____ **b.** I express my feelings inappropriately and in confusing ways. Usually, this means I express them indirectly through commands, accusations, put-downs, and evaluations. I may express feelings physically in destructive ways. My nonverbal messages express my feelings. I shout at people, push or hit them, avoid people, refuse to look at them, or don't speak to them. I may hug them, put my arm around them, give them gifts, or try to do favors for them. My words and my nonverbal messages often contradict each other. I sometimes smile and act friendly toward people I'm angry at. Or I may avoid people I care a great deal for.

6 : 35

Johnson, D. W., & Johnson, R. (2005). **Teaching Students To Be Peacemakers** (4th Ed.). Edina, MN: Interaction Book Company, (952)831-9500.

Being Positive About Yourself While Trying Again

Critical Thoughts	Encouraging Thoughts
Circle the self put-down that you might use when you make a mistake.	**Circle the comments you like best for handling a mistake.**
You stupid idiot. Why can't you do something right!	That didn't work. What shall I try next?
I'll never get it.	Everyone makes mistakes. Just try it again.
I really blew it this time.	I'll see if I can do better next time.
I hate myself.	I only did one thing poorly. Look at everything I did right!
Why am I such a loser?	I'm learning from my mistakes and that makes me a winner!

1. Form a group of three.

2. Each member writes out a failure or two they have experienced recently. The failures are placed in a hat (or bag).

3. Each member draws a failure out of the hat. The member then:

   a. Makes a series of negative self-statements about the failure.

   b. Makes a series of positive self-statements about the failure.

4. This procedure is repeated until every member has gone through the sequence at least twice.

5. List three reasons why it is hard to change negative self-statements to positive ones. Then list three reasons why it is important to learn how to change negative self- statements to positive ones.

6 : 36

Johnson, D. W., & Johnson, R. (2005). **Teaching Students To Be Peacemakers** (4th Ed.). Edina, MN: Interaction Book Company, (952)831-9500.

Predicting:
Short-Term and Long-Range Thinking

Form a group of three. Discuss and agree on the meaning of short-term and long-range. Then discuss the following situations.

1. Roger took something of yours. What could you do?

   a. What might be the short-term effect of your action?

   b. What might be the long-range effect of your action?

2. Edythe pushed you in the hallway and you fell down. What could you do?

   a. What might be the short-term effect of your action?

   b. What might be the long-range effect of your action?

3. Helen is telling lies about you. What could you do?

   a. What might be the short-term effect of your action?

   b. What might be the long-range effect of your action?

4. Frank is calling you names. What could you do?

   a. What might be the short-term effect of your action?

   b. What might be the long-range effect of your action?

5. Sally and Jane have asked Rosita not to play with you. What could you do?

   a. What might be the short-term effect of your action?

   b. What might be the long-range effect of your action?

Johnson, D. W., & Johnson, R. (2005). **Teaching Students To Be Peacemakers** (4th Ed.). Edina, MN: Interaction Book Company, (952)831-9500.

Childhood Messages

Usually we act out of habit, automatically, without conscious decision-making and planning. Habitual ways of responding to a conflict situation are based on messages we learned about conflict as we were growing up.

1. Your **task** is to identify key messages about conflict that you have learned while you were growing up from parents, teachers, peers, religious leaders, and so forth.

2. Work **cooperatively** in a pair. List six messages the two of you were taught. Each member must make a copy of the list.

3. Form a new pair. **Share** your list with your new partner. **Listen** carefully to his or her list. **Create** a new list out of the best ideas from the two of you.

4. Return to your original partner. **Share** your modified list. **Listen** to his or her modified list. **Create** a final list based on the best thinking of the two of you. Be ready to share your list with the whole class.

5. With your partner write down three conclusions about how these messages affect your actions in conflict situations today. Pick one of the people who taught you the messages and role play a scene in which the message is being taught to you.

Examples Of Childhood Messages About Conflict

Don't hit below the belt.	Fighting never solved anything.
Girls don't fight.	Don't pick a fight, but if you're in one, win!
Turn the other cheek.	Never hit a girl.
Bite your tongue.	An eye for an eye, a tooth for a tooth.
If you haven't anything nice to say, don't say anything at all.	If you finish second, no one will know your name.

6 : 38

Johnson, D. W., & Johnson, R. (2005). **Teaching Students To Be Peacemakers** (4th Ed.). Edina, MN: Interaction Book Company, (952)831-9500.

Handling Put-Downs

Everyone gets put down. Often put-downs are presented as humor and sometimes they are funny. Other times they just hurt. Everyone needs to learn how to manage put-downs so that your self-esteem is not damaged and the attacker is not encouraged to do it again. First, you determine whether the put-down is a valid or invalid accusation. If it is invalid, then it is the other person's mistake. If the put-down is valid, then there is no reason to feel hurt because valid feedback helps (not hurts) you. Besides, no one is perfect. Second, to discourage the attacker from putting you down in the future, you could do the following:

1. **The very best thing to do when you are put-down is to ignore it and the person making it**. Most times people make put-downs to get attention. Being ignored is the thing that attackers dislike most.

2. **But, if you must say something to the person who put you down, do not respond with a put-down**. Insulting back only escalates the situation and results in more put-downs.

3. **It is better to cut the person off by giving a quick comeback that is not nasty and shows that you are unaffected by the put-down**.

   "I don't agree."   "Really? I didn't know that."

   "Big deal."   "So what?"   "Who cares?"

4. **You could also agree with the person**:

   "How did you know?"   "You know, you're right."

   "Who told you?"   "I never noticed that before."

5. Finally, **you could make a joke of it**:

   "Would you put that in writing?"   "That was supposed to be a secret."

   "Watch it or I'll call my lawyer."   "Are you talking to the right person?"

Johnson, D. W., & Johnson, R. (2005). **Teaching Students To Be Peacemakers** (4th Ed.). Edina, MN: Interaction Book Company, (952)831-9500.

Protecting Yourself From Put-Downs

When you are "put down" you can (a) feel hurt, rejected, and ashamed, (b) become angry at the other person, and/or (c) avoid both through the images you think of and the things you say to yourself. Practice the following:

1. Imagine yourself protected from put downs by:

   a. A suit of armor.

   b. An invisible cape.

   c. A bullet-proof vest.

2. Imagine the put down is something you can side step:

   a. A breeze that sails by without touching you.

   b. An arrow or bullet that speeds by and misses you.

3. Ignore what the other person says and say things to yourself that are true:

   a. About the other person:

      1. "Something must be bugging him(her)."

      2. "Someone who puts others down usually feels bad about himself (herself)."

      3. "Poor person. He(she) must not like herself."

      4. "He(she) is trying to impress others. He(she) must need friends."

   b. About yourself:

      1. "No matter what they say, I'm still an O.K. person."

      2. "I know it isn't true."

      3. "I won't let this bother me. I know I'm a good person."

      4. "Sticks and stones will break my bones, but words will never hurt me."

      5. "If they really knew me, they wouldn't say that."

6 : 40

Johnson, D. W., & Johnson, R. (2005). **Teaching Students To Be Peacemakers** (4th Ed.). Edina, MN: Interaction Book Company, (952)831-9500.

Anger Arousers

In discussing conflicts there are certain actions that can make other people angry. Given below is a list of statements. Each represents one type of anger arouser. Working with a partner, match the statement with the type of anger arouser it represents.

Statement	Anger Arouser
Juan: *"Don't worry, I'll pay you back!"* **Miguel**: *"You never, ever pay back money you owe someone!"*	**Sarcasm** is a harsh form of put-down or ridicule. In a conflict, sarcasm almost always makes the other person angry.
Nancy: *"Sorry your jacket got dirty."* **Megan**: *"You are such a jerk!"*	**Negative Judgments** is stating that the other person is wrong or bad.
Bill: *"I think..."* **Sam**: *"What you think doesn't matter, it's what you did that counts."*	**Interrupting** is cutting the other person off before he or she has finished speaking.
Jane: *"This would be fair."* **Jan**: *"Oh yes, that's fair all right. That's really fair! The whole world will stand up and shout that's fair!"*	**Ignoring** is doing something else while someone is talking to you or brushing off what another person is saying as unimportant.
Jeff: *"I'm sorry."* **Julie**: *"I know you and you are a liar."*	**Globalizing** is attaching a negative label to a person by saying, *"You always do this"* or *"You never do that."*
Chris: *"You should apologize to me!"* **Jean**: *"You are so wrong, so very, very wrong!"*	**Blaming/Accusing** is stating the problem is someone's fault and that person needs to be punished.
Pam: *"I'm really worried I hurt Karl's feelings."* **Judy**: *"So what. Can you loan me $5.00?"*	**Insulting/Name-Calling** is attaching a negative label to the person as part of a personal attack.
Gene: *"I don't know what you're talking about!"* **Raymond**: *"It's all your fault and you should be penalized!"*	**Stating Opinion As Fact** is stating your opinion as if it were the absolute truth, leaving no room for discussion.

6 : 41

Johnson, D. W., & Johnson, R. (2005). **Teaching Students To Be Peacemakers** (4th Ed.). Edina, MN: Interaction Book Company, (952)831-9500.

Just Joking

Sometimes we say things that hurt other people's feelings. Put- downs are common in most schools. Making cutting remarks that attack schoolmates self-esteem may be seen as "cool."

   1. With a partner, write out how each person feels in the following situations.

   2. Rewrite each of the situations, changing the rejecting behavior to accepting behavior.

Just Joking!

Sam, a new student, is assigned to a coooperative learning group. Jim says, "Does he have to be in our group?"

Sam:

——————————————
——————————————
——————————————

Jim:

——————————————
——————————————
——————————————

Jane walks by a group in the hallway. Sally says, "She is having a bad hair day."

Jane:

——————————————
——————————————
——————————————

Sally:

——————————————
——————————————
——————————————

Just Joking!

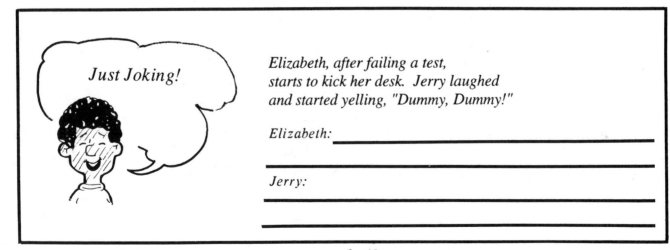

Just Joking!

Elizabeth, after failing a test, starts to kick her desk. Jerry laughed and started yelling, "Dummy, Dummy!"

Elizabeth: ——————————————

——————————————

Jerry: ——————————————

——————————————

Johnson, D. W., & Johnson, R. (2005). **Teaching Students To Be Peacemakers** (4th Ed.). Edina, MN: Interaction Book Company, (952)831-9500.

Chapter Seven: Teaching Students To Mediate

Nature Of Mediation

William Ury often tells a tale of an old gentleman who in his will requests that his estate be divided among his three sons in the following manner: One-half to his eldest son, one-third to his middle son, and one-ninth to his youngest son. When the loving father died his estate consisted of seventeen camels. The three sons attempted to divide up the estate according to their father's wishes but quickly found that they could not do so without cutting some of the camels into pieces. They argued and argued without agreeing on how to divide the camels. Eventually, a village elder rode up on her own dusty camel and inquired about their problem. The three brothers explained the situation. The elder then offered to make her own camel available if that might help. It did. With eighteen camels, the brothers could solve the problem. The oldest soon took nine camels (one-half of eighteen), the middle son choose six more (one-third of eighteen), and the youngest son extracted two camels (one-ninth of eighteen). Nine plus six plus two equals seventeen. Almost before the three brothers knew what had happened, the wise woman climbed back onto her own camel and rode off into the setting desert sun.

This story illustrates what a clever and creative mediator can do. A **mediator** is a neutral person who helps two or more people resolve their conflict by assisting them through the steps of problem-solving negotiations so that an agreement is reached that both believe is fair, just, and workable. A mediator does not tell disputants what to do, decide who is right and who is wrong, or talk about what he or she would do in such a situation. The mediator is simply a facilitator with no formal power over either disputant. Mediation exists, therefore, when a neutral and impartial third party assists two or more people in negotiating a constructive resolution to their conflict. The participants in the conflict who seek mediation are called disputants. Mediation is an extension of the negotiation process and is a collection of strategies to promote more efficient and effective negotiations. When mediation has been successful:

❖ The conflict will be resolved so that all disputants have benefited.

❖ The relationship between the students will be as good as or even better than ever.

❖ Students' ability to engage in problem-solving negotiating and self-confidence in doing so will be increased. An important purpose of the mediator is to increase disputants' ability to manage their conflicts on their own in the future.

Johnson, D. W., & Johnson, R. (2005). **Teaching Students To Be Peacemakers** (4th Ed.). Edina, MN: Interaction Book Company, (952)831-9500.

Figure 7.1 Mediating

End Hostilities
- Stop Hostilities
- Cool Down Disputants
- Conflict Forms

Ensure Commitment To Mediation
- Arrange Mediation Area
- Introduce Mediation Process And Rules

Facilitate Negotiations
- Highlight Cooperative Context
- Help Disputants Present Wants
- Help Disputants Present Feelings
    Resist Pressure To Take Sides
    Paraphrase

Help Disputants Present Reasons
- Present
- Separate Interests From Positions
- Keep Focus On Problem
- Reframe Issues

Help Disputants Reverse Perspectives

Help Disputants Invent Options
- Invent Options That Maximize Mutual Gain
    Complete Balance Sheet
- Help Disputants Reach Wise Agreements

Formalize Agreement

When Mediation Fails
- Teacher Mediates
- Teacher Prevents Future Conflicts

Training Disputants
- Story Telling
- Problem Puppets
- Role Playing
- Role Reversal

Johnson, D. W., & Johnson, R. (2005). **Teaching Students To Be Peacemakers** (4th Ed.). Edina, MN: Interaction Book Company, (952)831-9500.

Students can be trained to be peer mediators. A **peer mediator** is a student who has been trained to be a neutral and impartial third party who assists two or more schoolmates negotiate a constructive resolution to their conflicts. The mediator's job is to assist classmates to negotiate agreements about what they will and will not do in order to resolve their conflict. Peer mediators have two responsibilities: (a) help disputants resolve their conflict constructively and (b) teach disputants how to negotiate more effectively.

How To Mediate

Many students would rather have a student mediator handle their disputes than a teacher, counselor, or principal. Many faculty members like peer mediation because it works, thereby saving them considerable time and aggravation. Being a mediator is very satisfying as it involves helping schoolmates and learning something new about others and oneself. Helping schoolmates resolve their conflicts, however, does not mean that the mediator will never need similar help. Students are not mediators because they are better persons than their classmates. They are mediators because they have been trained in the procedures and skills required and it is their turn to fulfill the mediator role. At any time they too may need help in resolving a conflict.

It is not enough for a student to want to help classmates solve their problems. Students must be skilled in using mediation procedures. Being an effective mediator takes hard work and considerable practice. Mediation is not magic and it is far more than using "common sense." Mediators must know exactly what they are doing and why they are doing it. The procedure for mediation consists of a series of steps:

1. End hostilities: Break up fights and cool down students.

2. Ensure both people are committed to the mediation process and are ready to negotiate in good faith: The mediator introduces the process of mediation, sets the ground rules, and introduces him- or herself.

3. Help the disputants engage in problem-solving negotiations successfully: This includes taking the two persons through the negotiation sequence of:

   a. Describing to each other what they want.

   b. Describing to each other how they feel.

   c. Exchanging reasons why they want what they want and feel as they do.

   d. Reversing perspectives so that each person is able to present the other's position and feelings to the other's satisfaction.

7 : 3

Johnson, D. W., & Johnson, R. (2005). **Teaching Students To Be Peacemakers** (4th Ed.). Edina, MN: Interaction Book Company, (952)831-9500.

    e. Inventing at least three options for mutual benefit.

    f. Reaching a wise agreement and shaking hands.

4. Formalize the agreement: The agreement is solidified into a contract. Disputants must agree to abide by their final decision. The mediator becomes "the keeper of the contract," checking back with the disputants periodically to ensure the agreement is working and both sides are abiding by their commitments.

Step 1: End Hostilities

Mediation begins with ending the hostilities among students and cooling them down enough so that constructive negotiating may take place.

Breaking Up Hostilities

There are three ways to break up hostilities. **The first and foremost is for student mediators to find a teacher or staff member to end the hostilities.** Peer mediators are helpers, not police officers. If there is physical fighting, peer mediators should not get involved. They find a faculty or staff member to separate the fighters. The mere presence of a teacher is enough to stop many hostilities. Ideally, two teachers would work together to end hostilities. If a teacher (or pair of teachers) is going to separate two students who are physically fighting, the teacher(s) should have a clear, practiced procedure to do so. Possible procedures include firmly ordering the students to stop or restraining the fighters (never restrain one student without restraining the other because restraining one may open him or her to the attack of the other, which will not win the teacher any points as a peacemaker). Restraining fighters should be used only in a real emergency as taking violent action against a student opens the teacher(s) to counter-violence.

Second, classes can be trained to end hostilities as spectators. Teachers can and should train their classes in procedures to stop fights (and other hostilities) and then have the class practice the procedures in "fight drills" the same way they are trained in "fire drills." Some of the procedures classes could practice are everyone leaving (taking away the audience), surrounding the disputants and chanting, "*Stop fighting, stop fighting,*" or surrounding the disputants and singing some happy song such as "*Ring around the Rosy*" to create a situation in which fighting is incongruous.

A third procedure for ending hostilities is to use distraction to divert disputants' attention and physical and emotional energy. Sometimes only a small distraction is needed (breaking the eye contact between disputants will often stop a fight). The teacher or peer mediator can get very close and shout loudly. A more powerful distraction is to pretend to find a ten dollar bill (which you had in your hand), and loudly say, "*Hey, who dropped this ten*

Johnson, D. W., & Johnson, R. (2005). **Teaching Students To Be Peacemakers** (4th Ed.). Edina, MN: Interaction Book Company, (952)831-9500.

dollar bill?" If disputants look to see if it is their ten dollars, then the fight is interrupted and can be ended.

Cooling Off Hostile Persons

It is often helpful to help students dissipate their emotions by separating them for a period of time. The teacher may have the class practice cool down procedures. Some procedures for cooling disputants down are:

❖   Cool-off corners where hostile individuals are sent not to be punished but to calm down. When they have cooled off, they can leave their corners.

❖   Deep breathing to relax disputants (this is called counter-conditioning because it conditions students to respond in a way that is counter to being angry and hostile):

  a. Take slow, deep breaths while you count to ten and then back to one again.

  b. Tense all your muscles and breathe in. Keep your muscles tense and hold your breath for five seconds. Then slowly exhale and relax your muscles for five seconds. Repeat this process several times.

  c. When you become skilled in breathing deep and relaxing your muscles, imagine your anger leaking out of toes as you relax. Let your anger and tension drain away through your feet. Then walk away from it.

❖   Exhausting physical activities such as jogging (or walking) several miles, multiple pushups, or hitting a punching bag until exhausted to rid disputants of their anger.

❖   Conflict Report Forms for each participant to complete. They are described in the next section.

Cooling off disputants de-escalates and postpones a conflict; it does not resolve it. Sometimes after two students have cooled off they want to skip mediation. If no hard feelings remain, let them do so. Most of the time, however, cooling off the disputants is a preliminary step to mediating the conflict.

7 : 5

Johnson, D. W., & Johnson, R. (2005). **Teaching Students To Be Peacemakers** (4th Ed.). Edina, MN: Interaction Book Company, (952)831-9500.

Conflict Report Form

Date:_____ Name:_____ ____Male ____Female

Grade:_____ Teacher:_____ Subject Area:_____

1. Who was your conflict with:_____

2. What did you want?_____

    a. How did the other's actions stop you from getting what you want?_____

    _____

    b. How did you feel?_____

3. What did the other person want?_____

    a. How did your actions stop him or her from getting what he or she wanted?

    _____

    b. How did the other person feel?_____

4. What are three potential agreements that might resolve the conflict and

    reestablish a good relationship between the two of you?_____

    a._____

    b._____

    c._____

5. What are three things you might try if this happens again? _____

    a._____

    b._____

    c._____

6. Is there anything you would like to say to the person you had the conflict

    with?_____

    _____

7 : 6

Johnson, D. W., & Johnson, R. (2005). **Teaching Students To Be Peacemakers** (4th Ed.). Edina, MN: Interaction Book Company, (952)831-9500.

Conflict Report Forms

The process of mediation is often helped if students reflect on the conflict, define it, and think of alternative ways of resolving the conflict before the mediation process begins. One procedure for doing so is the Conflict Report Form. First, the mediator gives each disputant a Conflict Report Form to fill out. If a student cannot read or write well, the mediator provides a partner to help fill out the conflict form. Second, when each disputant finishes the form, the mediator reads over the answers with the student and helps the student with any answers he or she is unsure of. Third, the mediator (a) begins mediation, using the conflict form to help disputants communicate their views of the conflict to each other (this may be done orally or the students can exchange conflict forms and write their reactions to each other's accounts) or (b) discusses what the students will do in a future situation similar to the conflict situation (for each alternative suggested, ask, "*Will this action solve the problem better than open hostilities such as fighting?*").

The conflict forms will give the mediator (and often the disputants) a clear idea of how to proceed in helping resolve the conflict. The conflict form should highlight the cooperation and negotiation procedures and skills the students need to learn to get along better with classmates. A sample conflict form is given at the end of the chapter.

Step 2: Ensure Commitment To Mediation

Once the hostilities are stopped and the students have cooled down emotionally, the mediation session can begin. Having their conflict mediated is the disputants' choice. If they decide to accept help from the mediator, they must commit themselves to the mediation process and agree to work hard to solve the problem.

Arranging The Mediation Area

Sometimes there is a special area or office for mediation to occur. How the area is arranged gives a message as to whether or not the mediation will be fair. Before mediation begins the mediator makes sure the area is neat and clean, arranges the chairs so he or she sits at the end of the table and the disputants should sit across from one another, and places a pad of paper and a pencil on the table for each person. When the mediator is ready, he or she brings the disputants into the area or room.

Introducing Oneself And The Process Of Mediation

When a mediator begins a session, he or she must confirm that the disputants understand the process of mediation and have committed themselves to making it succeed. The mediator

Johnson, D. W., & Johnson, R. (2005). **Teaching Students To Be Peacemakers** (4th Ed.). Edina, MN: Interaction Book Company, (952)831-9500.

does so by giving a memorized introduction. The following points must be covered, but different mediators may use different phrases and words to do so and younger students may need a simpler explanation of the procedures and rules than do older students. Mediators will need to develop their personal version of the introductory statement, so that they are comfortable and confident in saying it. In making the introductory statement, the mediator:

1. Introduces him- or herself and confirms the names of the disputants, making sure their names are spelled correctly on the Mediation Agreement Form.

2. Explains that as the mediator, he or she will not take sides or attempt to decide who is right or wrong. The mediator does not tell the disputants what to do. The disputants themselves must decide on the solution by negotiating a wise agreement with each other. The mediator is neutral, an objective person who has no biases regarding the dispute, who will be fair to all sides. The mediator's role is to hear both sides of the dispute, facilitate the six steps of negotiation, help disputants overcome any blocks to a settlement, and help them find a solution to their conflict that satisfies both parties.

3. Explains the ground rules for mediation and elicits disputants' promise to abide by the rules:

   a. Agree to solve the problem. The mediator asks the students if they wish to solve their problem with the help of a mediator. Mediation does not proceed until both students say "*yes*," acknowledging publicly there is a conflict and they will participate in mediation. Disputants must know that mediation is voluntary and no one can force them to participate.

   b. No name-calling. Disputants must treat each other with respect and consideration. Good manners is a necessity for successful mediation.

   c. No interrupting. The mediator explains that each person will have an opportunity to state his or her views of the conflict without interruption. While one student is talking, the other disputant cannot interrupt or comment.

   d. Be as honest as you can. Problem-solving negotiations depend on disputants being accurate and honest in their statements about what they want, how they feel, and what their underlying interests are.

   e. Agree to abide by the agreement. When you reach an agreement, you must abide by it. You must do what you have agreed to do.

4. Keep confidential everything that is said during the mediation session(s). The mediator explains that everything said during mediation sessions is confidential except for instances in which the mediator believes that a student is in danger and is committing illegal acts (i.e., drugs, weapons, or alcohol on school property or at school events). In these cases the

Johnson, D. W., & Johnson, R. (2005). **Teaching Students To Be Peacemakers** (4th Ed.). Edina, MN: Interaction Book Company, (952)831-9500.

mediator is required to report it to school authorities. Because student disputes often involve private information, peer mediators must be trusted not to tell other students what has been heard during mediation sessions.

Quiz 7:1 Check Your Understanding

Demonstrate your understanding of the following concepts by matching the definitions with the appropriate concept. Check your answers with your partner and explain why you believe your answers to be correct.

Answer	Concept	Definition
	1. Mediator	a. Form disputants sign to indicate agreement with the nature of the agreement and the responsibilities of each disputant in implementing the agreement.
	2. Ending Hostilities	b. Guide disputants through steps of problem-solving negotiations.
	3. Ensuring Commitment	c. Form disputants complete to ensure they reflect on the conflict, define it, and think of alternative ways of resolving the conflict before the mediation process begins.
	4. Facilitating Negotiations	d. Neutral person who helps two or more people resolve their conflict by assisting them through the steps of problem-solving negotiations so that an agreement is reached that both believe is fair, just, and workable.
	5. Formalizing Agreement	e. Break up fights and cool down disputants until both are rational enough to problem solve.
	6. Conflict Report Form	f. Solidify agreement into contract and checking with disputants periodically to ensure the agreement is working.
	7. Mediation Agreement Form	g. Explain nature of mediation, procedure, and rules and obtain disputants' agreement that they will participate.

5. Serves as the keeper of the contract. Whatever the disputants agree to, the mediator formalizes it into a contract and checks with the disputants periodically to ensure that the agreement is working and both are doing what they have agreed to do. If not, then mediation is reopened.

Johnson, D. W., & Johnson, R. (2005). **Teaching Students To Be Peacemakers** (4th Ed.). Edina, MN: Interaction Book Company, (952)831-9500.

Mediation Agreement Form

Date:_____ Mediators:_____

Grade:_____ Teacher:_____ Subject Area:_____

People Involved In Conflict:

_____ ____Grade ____Male ____Female

_____ ____Grade ____Male ____Female

_____ ____Grade ____Male ____Female

_____ ____Grade ____Male ____Female

What Was The Conflict:_____

_____

_____

Where Did The Conflict Take Place:_____

Was An Agreement Reached? _____Yes _____No

Person 1 Agrees To: _____ Person Two Agrees To:_____

_____ | _____

_____ | _____

_____ | _____

_____ | _____

Signature:_____ | Signature:_____

Follow-Up:_____

_____

_____

_____

Johnson, D. W., & Johnson, R. (2005). **Teaching Students To Be Peacemakers** (4th Ed.). Edina, MN: Interaction Book Company, (952)831-9500.

The mediator asks each disputant to agree to the rules. The mediator also asks if disputants have any questions about mediation. A mediation session is considered successful when both students sign an agreement containing the elements of their settlement.

Step 3: Facilitate Negotiations

After the hostilities have been cooled and the students have committed themselves to the mediation process, negotiations begin with the mediator's help. The mediator takes disputants across the "bridge to understanding" by moderating the six steps of problem-solving negotiations. Each disputant is asked in turn to:

1. Describe what happened and what he or she wants.

2. Describe how he or she feels.

3. Give the reasons and rationale for his or her wants and feelings.

4. Present his or her understanding of the other's perspective, wants, feelings, and rationale.

5. Develop three or more optional agreements that maximize joint outcomes.

6. Select one of the options and reach an agreement.

Helping Disputants State What Happened, What They Want, And How They Feel

Mediators help disputants state what happened, communicate their wants and goals (that is, position) in ways that do not escalate the conflict, and describe how they feel. The mediator helps both disputants. In order to determine the facts and events that created the conflict and kept it going, the mediator decides who will talk first and then:

➢ Highlights the cooperative context and enlarges the shadow of the future. The mediator helps the disputants see their common interests and the need to maintain a constructive long-term relationship with each other.

➢ Asks Disputant A what happened, what he or she wants, and how he or she feels.

➢ Paraphrases what Disputant A said.

➢ Asks Disputant B what happened, what he or she wants, and how he or she feels.

Johnson, D. W., & Johnson, R. (2005). **Teaching Students To Be Peacemakers** (4th Ed.). Edina, MN: Interaction Book Company, (952)831-9500.

> ➢ Paraphrases what Disputant B said.

In other words, four of the more important skills for mediators are highlighting the common interest in maintaining a constructive long-term relationship, helping students give a factual and calm account of the conflict, helping disputants describe what they want and how they feel, and paraphrasing or reflective listening to ensure that disputants are correctly understood and feel accepted and listened to.

Highlighting Cooperative Context (Enlarging Shadow Of The Future)

For disputants to engage in problem-solving negotiations they must believe that the future of the relationship is more important than is any short-term advantage from winning. The mediator reminds disputants that in the long run, they are going to sink or swim together. The cooperative interests are:

❖ We need each other to reach an agreement. If we do not cooperate and solve this problem, neither one of us will get what we want.

❖ We will work together in the future. If our relationship is damaged we will have future difficulties that will be far more damaging than not getting what we want today. In the long run, we will benefit far more from continually maximizing joint gains rather than trying to gain at the other's expense on this one issue.

The more apparent and salient the positive interdependence uniting the disputants, the clearer will be their perceptions of each other's positions and motivations, the more accurate and complete the communication, the more positive and trusting the attitudes toward the other, and the greater the likelihood the conflict will be defined as a mutual problem (Deutsch, 1973). Positive interdependence may be made salient by:

1. Highlighting any common and compatible interests shared by the disputants and describing any opposing interests as a mutual problem to be solved rather than a "win-lose" situation.

2. Pointing out the ways in which disputants:

   a. Share a mutual fate.

   b. Depend on each other for resources and assistance.

   c. Need to value the long-term relationship over short-term gain.

   d. Will lose if they become enemies.

Johnson, D. W., & Johnson, R. (2005). **Teaching Students To Be Peacemakers** (4th Ed.). Edina, MN: Interaction Book Company, (952)831-9500.

3. Pointing out that one of the potential costs of not resolving the conflict is teacher arbitration. This is known as "outside enemy interdependence." If students do not resolve the conflict, then the teacher or the principal will decide in a "winner take all" fashion. Since mediation is aimed at helping others negotiate constructive resolutions of conflict, there is a greater likelihood of having an outcome favorable to oneself through mediation than through arbitration.

The major barrier to enlarging the shadow of the future is competitiveness. The competitive interests aimed at maximizing one's own gain at the expense of the other person is based on short-term self-interest and a desire to be better off than the other individuals involved in the situation. Such motivations always interfere with problem-solving negotiations.

Helping Students Describe What Happened And What They Want

Students may refuse to talk calmly to each other. They may yell or accuse instead. The mediator's role at this point is to ask each disputant to describe:

1. What happened. The mediator says, "*Tell me what happened.*" Each student is expected to state the facts as calmly as possible and to refer primarily to the present, not the past or future. If the nature of the conflict and the events that triggered it are not clear, the mediator helps students figure out what happened by asking questions about anything he or she does not understand:

   a. "Tell me more about..."

   b. "How long has this been going on?"

   c. "When did this happen?"

   d. "What would you like to see happen now?"

2. What he or she wants. The mediator says, "*Tell the other person what you want.*" By describing what they want and what their goals are, students define their positions. Many times students will not fully understand what the problem is. Having them fill out the Conflict Report Form before mediation begins will help, but further clarification may be necessary after mediation has begun. Sometimes it is helpful to determine what each person wants to keep the other from getting as well as what each one wants for him- or herself.

Some helpful hints for mediators are as follows:

1. The mediator helps disputants describe what they want without making the other person angry, defensive, or upset. If they make evaluative or disrespectful statements, they will

7 : 13

Johnson, D. W., & Johnson, R. (2005). **Teaching Students To Be Peacemakers** (4th Ed.). Edina, MN: Interaction Book Company, (952)831-9500.

alienate others and guarantee that the other disputant will closed-mindedly reject the legitimacy of what they want, thereby sabotaging their chances for agreement.

2. The mediator enforces the no-interruptions rule so that students can state their views and wants without being distracted.

3. While disputants explain what happened and what they want, the mediator's body language should show that he or she is interested in what each student is saying. Mediators make eye contact and sit attentively. Mediators listen very carefully to gain an understanding of what issues have to be resolved in order for an agreement to be reached.

4. If students cannot give a factual and calm account of the conflict, the mediator may ask them to describe it as a neutral, third-party observer. This may provide just enough distance for the students to analyze the situation and their behavior without feeling threatened.

5. The mediator makes sure the conflict is defined as a small and specific mutual problem that can be solved.

Helping Disputants Describe How They Feel

Disputants need to state accurately and honestly how they feel if conflicts are to be resolved constructively. Frequently, however, disputants do not know how they feel. The mediator may need to help disputants understand how they feel as part of helping them describe their feelings without making evaluative remarks about the other person involved. The mediator may wish to remind students to take ownership of their feelings (use "I" messages) and describe how they feel by naming it or using sensory descriptions ("I feel stepped on"), actions urges ("I want to bury my head in the sand and play ostrich"), or figures of speech ("I feel squelched"). Often the disputants are angry at each other and frustrated because negotiating has already failed. This means that in their description of the conflict a number of angry statements may be included. The mediator may have to remind them that no name calling is allowed.

Avoiding The Pressure To Take Sides

Mediators are often pressured to take sides. Disputants frequently demand that the mediator agree that they are right and the other person is wrong. An important skill for a mediator is to remain neutral. The mediator may need to remind disputants he or she is neutral and will not indicate whether he or she agrees or disagrees with a person. The mediator does so by using words and phrases that are impartial and nonjudgmental. The mediator has to identify and refer to all of the issues in a neutral way. Do not say, "*She is angry because you stole her purse.*" Do say, "*She is angry because you had her purse.*" Do not say, "*The two of you were*

Johnson, D. W., & Johnson, R. (2005). **Teaching Students To Be Peacemakers** (4ᵗʰ Ed.). Edina, MN: Interaction Book Company, (952)831-9500.

yelling at each other about the $15." Do say, "*You talk to each other in unhelpful ways when the topic of the money comes up.*"

Paraphrasing What Each Student Says

Mediators help students clarify their views of the problem and their feelings about it. An essential skill for such clarification is paraphrasing. Mediators need to be expert listeners who can listen attentively to the content and feelings of students' statements and summarize them accurately. **Paraphrasing** consists of (Johnson, 2003):

1. Restating the facts and summarizing the events. The mediator should follow the rules for paraphrasing:

   ❖ Put yourself in the other person's shoes.

   ❖ Restate the other person's statements and feelings in your own words. State as correctly and accurately as possible the other person's statements and feelings.

   ❖ Start your remarks with , "*You want...,*" "*You feel...,*" and "*You think...*" If these above phrases sound stilted and unnatural, do not worry. If you use them frequently while mediating, you will soon adapt them to your natural speech patterns.

   ❖ Show understanding and acceptance by nonverbal behaviors: tone of voice, facial expressions, gestures, eye contact, and posture.

2. Reflecting feelings. Pay attention to the emotional aspects of each person's position. A phrase that will help you do so is, "You feel...because...." When you paraphrase, try to reflect the emotional as well as the cognitive content.

3. Remaining neutral. Do not take sides. Use words and phrases that are impartial and nonjudgmental. Identify and refer to all of the issues in a neutral way. Do not say, "She is angry because you were spreading rumors about her behind her back." Do say, "She is angry because she believes you were saying untrue things about her."

4. Refusing to give advice or suggestions. Mediators often think they know what two disputants need to do to resolve the conflict. Disputants will often ask mediators for advice, saying "What do you think we should do?" There is a great temptation to give disputants advice and tell them what to do. This temptation needs to be resisted. Generally, disputants resist agreements that are imposed on them and support agreements that they themselves develop.

5. Avoiding bringing up similar feelings and problems from your own experience. Many times mediators have faced conflicts similar to those being faced by the disputants.

Johnson, D. W., & Johnson, R. (2005). **Teaching Students To Be Peacemakers** (4th Ed.). Edina, MN: Interaction Book Company, (952)831-9500.

Mediators may wish to say, *"Here is what I did when I faced this problem,"* or *"Here is how I felt when that happened to me."* Such statements are not helpful. The mediator is there to help disputants clarify their own goals and feelings, not share his or her own experiences in similar situations.

In the following example a mediator is helping two students, Jeremy and Mark, resolve a conflict about working jointly on a report. Each student states his view of the conflict and the mediator uses paraphrasing to help them accurately identify each other's position.

Jeremy: I went to the library to get a book I need to do the assignment. Mark jumped in front of me and grabbed the book just as I was about to take it off the shelf! It really makes me mad!

Mediator: You are angry and frustrated because Mark took the book you needed just as you were reaching for it.

Jeremy: Right. The only reason he knew about the book was because I told him about it.

Mediator: You want Mark to give you the book.

Jeremy: Yeah.

Mark: I knew about the book long before Jeremy found out about it. I've used it before; that's how I knew where it was. I knew that once Jeremy got it, he would never share, so I had to get it first. He can use it after I'm done.

Mediator: You are feeling hurt. You believe you knew about the book first. You are afraid that if Jeremy checked the book out, you would never get to use it.

Mark: Yeah. Jeremy keeps things at home and does not share them.

Mediator: I'm beginning to understand. Both of you need to use the book. Mark wants to use the book right now. Jeremy wants to take the book home and use it over the weekend. Jeremy is frustrated and angry. Mark, you are hurt and anxious. Right now you are trying to use the book in ways that keeps the other person from using it. So far, you have not discussed how to use the book together or share it. Does that sound right?

Jeremy & Mark: Yes.

Mediator: We can start thinking of optional solutions now.

There are a number of reasons why paraphrasing is one of the most essential skills for a mediator (Johnson, 1971, 2003).

Johnson, D. W., & Johnson, R. (2005). **Teaching Students To Be Peacemakers** (4th Ed.). Edina, MN: Interaction Book Company, (952)831-9500.

First, through paraphrasing the mediator helps make each disputant feel understood and supported. As the disputant feels understood and accepted, his or her defensiveness will be decreased, allowing the disputant to think of new ways to resolve the conflict. Or it may simply help the disputant state the problem and his or her position more clearly.

Second, through paraphrasing the mediator helps disputants clarify their goals and needs and their feelings about the conflict. By reflecting back what the disputant has said, the mediator provides the disputant with the opportunity to reconsider and either affirm or correct the mediator's understanding of the disputant's interests and feelings. Doing so clarifies the disputant's goals, needs, and feelings not only for the mediator, but also for the disputant him- or herself.

Third, through paraphrasing the mediator helps disputants listen to each other in a more neutral and objective way.

Fourth, paraphrasing each disputant's position helps the mediator organize the issues so that he or she knows in what order they should be discussed. Usually the mediator will wish to focus attention first on the issues seemingly easiest for the disputants to resolve. If they agree on some things quickly, they will develop a momentum for resolving all their issues. In addition, it will provide an opportunity to separate the person from the problem. This may help the other disputant to think more rationally about the conflict.

Fifth, through paraphrasing the mediator slows down the interaction between the disputants and, therefore, allows a continual cooling off process.

Helping Disputants Exchange Reasons For Their Positions

After helping disputants clarify and communicate their wants and feelings, the next step in mediation is to help disputants exchange the reasons why they want what they want and feel the way they do. This is done by:

❖ Helping disputants present their reasons and the rationale for their positions.

❖ Helping disputants understand the differences between their position (what they want) and interests (why they want it).

❖ Avoiding tangents by keeping disputants focused on the issue, not on their anger toward each other.

❖ Equalizing power. It is hard for a low power person to negotiate with a high power person and vice versa.

Johnson, D. W., & Johnson, R. (2005). **Teaching Students To Be Peacemakers** (4th Ed.). Edina, MN: Interaction Book Company, (952)831-9500.

❖ Recognizing constructive behaviors during negotiations. Compliment when the students are behaving skillfully and shape their behavior by reinforcing "successive approximations" of skillful negotiating.

❖ Reframing the issue by helping disputants change perspectives.

Helping Disputants Present Their Reasons

In sharing their reasons for their wants and feelings, disputants must communicate effectively without confusing the other individuals involved and without sabotaging their chances of reaching an agreement later. Presenting reasons in a way that promotes open-minded consideration rather than closed-minded defensiveness is a skill that often requires the help of a mediator. Engaging in problem solving negotiations entails risks. The mediator provides the support and help disputants need to:

❖ Express cooperative intentions.

❖ Present their reasons and listen to the other's reasons.

❖ Focus on wants and goals, not on positions.

❖ Clarify differences between own and other's interests before trying to integrate them into an agreement.

❖ Empower the other person.

Many people are not aware of what their interests are or why they are engaging in a conflict. They are so focused on what they want that they have not thought about their reasons for wanting what they do. The mediator helps disputants clarify their reasons for engaging in the conflict and thus to understand what is motivating them to do so. The disputants can then negotiate an agreement that maximizes their interests while maintaining a good relationship with the other person.

Separating Interests From Positions

As a mediator you need to be skilled in separating each student's interests from his or her position. To do so the mediator has to define each person's position and each person's interests and not confuse the two. One example is that of Meg and Jim who both wanted the baseball. Meg wanted the ball to practice catching. Jim wanted the ball to practice throwing. Their positions ("*I want the baseball*") were opposed, but their interests were not. Often when conflicting students reveal their underlying interests, it is possible to find a solution that suits them both.

Johnson, D. W., & Johnson, R. (2005). **Teaching Students To Be Peacemakers** (4th Ed.). Edina, MN: Interaction Book Company, (952)831-9500.

Keeping Disputants Focused On The Problem

The mediator helps disputants avoid tangents by keeping them focused on the problem, not on their anger toward each other. A common occurrence within conflicts is that one person will make an angry remark, the other person will object, and soon the two are fighting over each other's insults rather than over the issue that began the conflict in the first place. *"Did you hear what he said? He always tries to hurt me!"* is a statement by one student that can change the topic of conversation to the tangent of whether the remark was really meant to hurt or not. A key mediation skill is keeping students focused on the issue to be resolved, not on emotional hurt, rejection, and anger. Mediators redirect the disputants' energies toward solving the problem rather than on emotional tangents.

Mediator's Role In Reframing Students' Definitions Of The Conflict

An example of reframing may be found in the book, *The Adventures Of Tom Sawyer*. Tom was ordered by his aunt to whitewash their fence. Tom began to think of all the fun he had planned for this day, of how everyone else would have a great time while he was stuck whitewashing the fence, and of how they would tease him about it. Tom went tranquilly to work and soon one of his friends, Ben Rogers, came along. Ben began to tease Tom about getting stuck whitewashing the fence and Tom said nothing while critically surveying his work. Ben finally got Tom's attention and said, *"Say—I'm going in a-swimming, I am. Don't you wish you could? But of course you'd druther work, wouldn't you? Course you would!"* Tom contemplated Ben a little, and said, *"What do you call work?" "Why, ain't that work?" "Well maybe it is and maybe it ain't. All I know is, it suits Tom Sawyer." "Oh, come now, you don't mean to let on that you like it?" "Like it? Well I don't see why I oughtn't to like it. Does a boy get a chance to whitewash a fence every day*?" That put things in a new light. Tom went on working but soon Ben interrupted and said, *"Say, Tom, let me whitewash a little." "No-no-I reckon it wouldn't hardly do, Ben. You see, Aunt Polly's awful particular about this fence right here on the street, you know-but if it was a back fence I wouldn't mind and she wouldn't. Yes, she's awful particular about this fence; it's got to be done very carefully; I reckon there ain't one boy in a thousand, that can do it the way it's got to be done."* Ben said, *"No-is that so? Oh, come, now-lemme just try. Only just a little-I'd let you, if you was me, Tom."* By the time he was finished Tom Sawyer had done no more white washing and had sold the opportunity to his friends for an apple, a kite, a dead rat on a string to swing it with, twelve marbles, a piece of blue bottle-glass to look through, a spool cannon, a fragment of chalk, a glass stopper, a tin soldier, two tadpoles, six firecrackers, a kitten with one eye, a brass doorknob, a dog collar, the handle of a knife, four pieces of orange peel, and a dilapidated old window sash. The fence had three coats of whitewash on it and if he hadn't run out of whitewash, he would have bankrupted every boy in town. The moral of this story is that the resolution of any conflict is possible if you can get the participants to look at it from the proper perspective.

Johnson, D. W., & Johnson, R. (2005). **Teaching Students To Be Peacemakers** (4th Ed.). Edina, MN: Interaction Book Company, (952)831-9500.

One of the major tasks of a mediator is to get the two persons to "reframe" their perception of the conflict, that is, view the conflict from a different perspective. Ways to help disputants reframe their perception of the conflict and the other person's actions are:

❖ Framing as a mutual problem to be jointly solved. The first reframing the mediator works towards is for students to view the conflict as a mutual problem to be solved rather than as a "win-lose" situation.

❖ Changing perspectives.

❖ Distinguishing between intention and behavior. Students need to distinguish between what was intended and the actual result of a person's actions.

❖ Continuing to differentiate the interests and reasoning of the disputants until a new frame is achieved. If additional information about the other person's reasoning is sought, sooner or later a new "frame" will emerge. Differentiating goals and needs as well as reasoning, leads to the reframing necessary for integration and synthesis.

❖ Exploring the multiple meanings of any one behavior. When students seem stuck ask, *"What else might that behavior mean?"* The more different answers a student can think of to that question the more likely the student is to perceive a way to resolve the conflict. When students are complaining about each other's behavior, *"He's too mean,"* *"She's too picky,"* it helps to ask, *"Think of situations in which the other's behavior would be positive."* Once a positive context is thought of, the meaning of the behavior changes.

Another example of reframing is from the tale of Brer Rabbit. Brer Rabbit had got himself caught by Brer Fox and was well on his way to becoming evening dinner. Brer Rabbit was in a great deal of deep trouble. And all because he tried to win a fight with a tar baby. There did not seem much he could do about the situation but he did not seem concerned at all at being Brer Fox's dinner. He just said, "Brer Fox, I don't mind if you eat me. But oh, whatever you do, don't throw me in that briar patch." Now Brer Fox was surely looking forward to eating his old enemy but he was curiouser and curiouser about Brer Rabbit's sweating and crying about being thrown into the briar patch. And the more he questioned Brer Rabbit the more Brer Rabbit wailed about how much he feared that briar patch. Pretty soon Brer Fox became convinced that Brer Rabbit would rather be eaten than be set among those briars. So Brer Fox threw Brer Rabbit right into the briar patch. You know the rest.

Once disputants have fully explained the reasons why they want what they want and feel the way they do, the mediator helps them see the problem from both perspectives simultaneously. The path to doing so lies in each disputant being able to present the opponent's wants, feelings, and reasons to the opponent's satisfaction.

Johnson, D. W., & Johnson, R. (2005). **Teaching Students To Be Peacemakers** (4th Ed.). Edina, MN: Interaction Book Company, (952)831-9500.

Helping Disputants To Reverse Perspectives

Perhaps the most important aspect of mediation is getting disputants to understand each other's perspective on the conflict. Reaching an agreement that is fair to both sides requires that they do so. There are also times when one person may not understand why another person is upset. They may say that an issue that the other cares about is *"no big deal."* Joan claims that Ron *"bugs her"* by calling her on the phone all the time. Joan and Ron have dated a few times and Ron wants to *"go steady."* Joan wants to date other boys. She is very angry that Ron keeps calling her every night. Ron says, *"What's the big deal. So I call her. That's no crime. She's just looking for a fight."* Ron needs to put himself in Joan's shoes and see the conflict from her perspective and understand why she believes the problem is important.

Perspective taking has been thoroughly discussed in previous chapters, so little will be said about it here. The mediator's role includes helping students take each other's perspectives accurately and fully by asking:

1. Student A to present Student B's wants, feelings, and reasoning.

2. Student B to state whether Student A was accurate and clarify inaccuracies.

3. Student B to present Student A's wants, feelings, and reasoning.

4. Student A to state whether Student B was accurate and clarify inaccuracies.

In essence, disputants are asked to reverse perspectives and see the problem from the viewpoint of the other person. **Perspective reversal** is having two disputants reverse perspectives and present the opposing wants, feelings, and reasons as if they were the opposing disputant. It can be a dramatic way to help solve stubborn conflicts. There are two ways to facilitate the perspective reversal. The first is to have:

❖ Disputants change chairs or hats to symbolize the taking of each other's perspective.

❖ Disputant A presents Disputant B's wants, feelings, and reasons. Disputant B listens carefully and clarifies anything not understood, corrects any errors in the presentation, and adds anything left out.

❖ Disputant B presents Disputant A's wants, feelings, and reasons. Disputant A listens carefully and clarifies anything not understood, corrects any errors in the presentation, and adds anything left out.

❖ Disputants change back to their original chair or hat and wait for the mediator to take them to the next step of negotiating.

Johnson, D. W., & Johnson, R. (2005). **Teaching Students To Be Peacemakers** (4th Ed.). Edina, MN: Interaction Book Company, (952)831-9500.

The second is a more elaborate role-playing sequence.

❖ Have disputants role play the events leading up to and causing their conflict. If it will be helpful, other students may be brought in to role play their parts in the original conflict.

❖ Freeze the role play at the point after which the conflict has begun.

❖ Have the disputants switch roles and replay it, so that they are taking the role of their opponent and, in effect, arguing against themselves.

❖ Stop the role play after the players have gotten the feel of their opponent's point of view. Discuss the role play and see if any new alternative solutions have occurred to the students engaged in the conflict.

Helping Disputants Invent Options For Mutual Benefit

The mediator is not supposed to solve problems for disputants. The mediator is supposed to help disputants think of ways to solve problems for themselves. As student mediators have said, *"The only right solution is their solution. We're not there to suggest the answer. We're there to listen." "Check your ego at the door. You're in it for two people. You have to put your own feelings aside."*

The mediator's role at this point is to help disputants:

❖ Avoid the obstacles to creative problem solving. The obstacles include being concerned only with your own immediate needs and goals, judging prematurely, searching for the single answer, assuming a fixed pie, and defensively sticking with the status quo to avoid the fear of the unknown inherent in change.

❖ Invent creative options that are in everyone's best interests.

❖ Assess realistically the advantages and disadvantages of each optional agreement.

Inventing Options To Maximize Mutual Benefit

Disputants need to develop at least three solutions to their conflict they can accept and that will maximize mutual benefit. The mediator asks Disputant A and then Disputant B what they can do to resolve the conflict. *"We've talked about what's already happened. Where do we go from here?"* Mediators never tell disputants that they are being unreasonable or what the agreement should be. In generating options, the disputants seek to create ideal outcomes that allow all disputants to achieve their goals. Each proposed option should be:

Johnson, D. W., & Johnson, R. (2005). **Teaching Students To Be Peacemakers** (4th Ed.). Edina, MN: Interaction Book Company, (952)831-9500.

❖ Specific? Does it tell when, where, who, and how?

❖ Realistic? Can each disputant do what they say they will? For example, Davy and Terry got into a fight over which group would use the basketball court on the playground. Terry states, *"The only sure way to avoid future fights is for Davy to transfer to another school."* The mediator may wish to point out how unrealistic that proposed alternative is.

❖ Specify shared responsibilities? Are both students agreeing to do something? Say, *"Is this solution acceptable to you?"* The mediator would never say, *"That's a fair solution, isn't it?"* Do you know why?

In helping disputants develop three or more optional agreements, the mediator may wish to help disputants:

1. Break fixation: Sometimes students become fixated on one possible agreement and are unable to think of alternatives. Such fixation is one of the enemies of effective negotiating.

2. Engage in divergent thinking: **Divergent thinking** involves generating a variety of diverse ideas about how to solve a problem. Mediators have disputants think divergently before they converge on an agreement. Mediators sometimes suggest possible alternative agreements disputants overlooked to stimulate disputants' divergent thinking.

3. See their common ground: *"I hear you both agreeing that..."* Sometimes disputants are so focused on their disagreements that they are blind to the interests they share in common. It is often helpful to point out their overlap in interests and get disputants to recognize that they do share common ground.

4. Focus on the future, not on the past. Jose claims that Bobby stole his lunch tickets. Bobbie denies it. There are no witnesses. So who does the mediator believe? Often, the mediator will never know what "really" happened in the past. No one will ever know. So how will Jose and Bobbie resolve their conflict if they disagree about what happened in the past? The answer is: They must focus on the future. A future-oriented agreement will not force any one to admit he or she was wrong. It will only specify what they are to do from now on.

5. Increase their motivation to resolve the conflict by highlighting what each will gain by resolving the conflict and what each will lose if the conflict is unresolved:

❖ The mediator helps disputants analyze carefully what each has to gain by reaching an agreement. *"Ron, you may not want to apologize to Joan, but you do want to date her. If she is angry at you, she won't date you. Her friends won't invite you*

Johnson, D. W., & Johnson, R. (2005). **Teaching Students To Be Peacemakers** (4th Ed.). Edina, MN: Interaction Book Company, (952)831-9500.

> *to their parties, which means that you won't see her very often. What would you be willing to do to have Joan and her friends happy with you?"*

❖ The mediator helps disputants analyze carefully what each has to lose by not reaching an agreement. The price of not agreeing may be to have the teacher arbitrate the conflict or, in some cases, to be suspended from school. Another cost is having the strain of dealing with an enemy at school.

6. Consider possible agreements based on package deals and trade-offs. **Package deals** involve resolving several issues at the same time. A **trade-off** is the exchange of two different things of comparable value. If Ron proposes a trade-off where he will not call Joan every night if she will date no one but him, would this be acceptable? The answer is no. Not dating anyone but Ron is "worth" much more than limiting the number of phone calls. The mediator helps disputants be certain that the proposed items to be traded are of comparable value.

7. Agree on a principle about how the conflict should be managed or how future conflicts should be managed. Sometimes if disputants will not agree to resolve an issue, the mediator can get them to agree to a principle. While two disputants may not agree on whether one should replace a lost book, they may be willing to agree to the principle that it is wrong to solve problems by fighting. Once they agree on a principle, then perhaps they can agree not to fight each other in the future when they have a conflict.

8. Repair the damage caused by disputants' actions by providing restitution. Sometimes agreements are not possible unless one student agrees to repair the damage caused by his or her actions. **Restitution** is making amends for injury, mistreatment, or insult. If a student borrows a classmate's book and loses it, restitution is made by replacing the book. When a person has been insulted, restitution may be made through an apology. Many times disputes will revolve around damages that require some restitution by one of the disputants. Getting the disputants to agree on how restitution may be made is an important aspect of mediation.

9. Develop a compromise that both can live with if time runs out. Compromises tend to be unstable because neither disputant gets all of what he or she wants, and the relationship is not fully repaired. The conflict, therefore, may appear again in the future. Sometimes, however, when time runs out a stable compromise can be agreed on.

10 If disputants cannot identify possible agreements that would maximize mutual benefit, the mediator may:

❖ Return to considering disputants' goals and the reasons underlying their wants and feelings. *"What did you do that made A so upset with you?" Why are you upset at A?"* Often understanding disputants' interests is like pealing an onion. Disputants discuss one layer at a time and the discussion reveals another layer underneath.

Johnson, D. W., & Johnson, R. (2005). **Teaching Students To Be Peacemakers** (4ᵗʰ Ed.). Edina, MN: Interaction Book Company, (952)831-9500.

Eventually, disputants' interests are defined in a way that allows integrative agreements to be identified.

❖ Have disputants role play the events leading up to the conflict and the initial stages of the conflict. This is one of the most helpful procedures for encouraging students to think of optional agreements.

Completing A Balance Sheet On Each Alternative Agreement

Once three or more optional agreements have been identified that maximize joint outcomes, then disputants need to complete a balance sheet on each option to determine which would make the best agreement. A balance sheet consists of writing down:

❖ The gains and losses for each disputant if that alternative agreement was adopted.

❖ The gains and losses for interested third parties (such as mutual friends) if that alternative agreement was adopted.

❖ The agreement that is most beneficial for both disputants.

As part of the evaluation of each alternative agreement, the mediator asks each disputant what he or she could do differently in the future if the same problem arises again. The more specific the answers, the better.

Helping Disputants Reach A Wise Agreement

The goal of mediation is to arrive at a wise agreement. A **wise agreement** is one that maximizes joint outcomes, strengthens disputants' abilities to work together cooperatively, improves disputants' ability to resolve future conflicts constructively, and has an underlying logic that makes sense to disputants and relevant third parties (such as being based on commonly accepted principles or norms). The agreement should include the ways each disputant will act differently in the future and how the agreement will be reviewed and renegotiated if it turns out to be unworkable.

During the agreement process, as well as during all the steps of mediating, the mediator should use humor. Laughter is a cure for conflict.

If the disputants cannot reach an agreement, the mediator has the last word. It is important to end on a positive note. Mediators tell disputants they (a) appreciated that the disputants tried to reach an agreement, (b) are sorry disputants did not resolve the conflict, and (c) are hopeful that disputants will be able to resolve the conflict constructively in the future.

Johnson, D. W., & Johnson, R. (2005). **Teaching Students To Be Peacemakers** (4th Ed.). Edina, MN: Interaction Book Company, (952)831-9500.

Quiz 7:2 Check Your Understanding

Demonstrate your understanding of the following concepts by matching the definitions with the appropriate concept. Check your answers with your partner and explain why you believe your answers to be correct.

Answer	Concept	Definition
	1. Shadow of the Future	a. The exchange of two different things of comparable value.
	2. Neutrality	b. Form on which the gains and costs are listed for each disputant and interested third parties.
	3. Paraphrasing	c. Resolving several issues at the same time.
	4. Reframing	d. Making amends for injury, mistreatment, or insult.
	5. Perspective reversal	e. Being impartial and nonjudgmental towards each disputant.
	6. Package deal	f. Viewing the conflict from a different perspective.
	7. Trade-off	g. Restating another person's statements and feelings in your own words in a neutral, nonjudgmental way.
	8. Restitution	h. When two disputants reverse perspectives and present the opposing disputant's wants, feelings, and reasons as if they were the opposing disputant.
	9. Balance Sheet	i. Long-term positive interdependence that binds disputants together in future situations.

Step 4: Formalize The Agreement

When an agreement is reached, the mediator completes a Mediation Agreement Form and has both students sign it. The mediator ensures the agreement is written out clearly and concisely so that:

❖ Disputants' names are spelled correctly and all dates are written out completely.

❖ What disputants have agreed to do to resolve the conflict is specified. A separate paragraph should be used for each issue. Only the present tense is used. The agreement should be as specific as possible.

❖ The agreement includes the commitments each person has made to the other. Each paragraph should begin, *"Joan Johnson agrees to..."* The agreement should not include phrases that contain an implication of wrongdoing, such as *"Ron agrees never to harass Sally again."* If only part of the issues are resolved, the mediator may wish to list the issues that still need resolution.

❖ Each disputant signs the agreement and then the mediator signs as a witness. Signing the Mediation Report Form formalizes the agreement between disputants and signifies that they will abide by it.

❖ Each disputant receives a copy of the agreement. The mediator also keeps a copy.

After the agreement is signed the mediator congratulates both disputants. The mediator then rips up any notes he or she has made in front of disputants. To prevent rumors, disputants are asked to tell their friends that the conflict is ended.

The mediator becomes the keeper of the contract who verifies that disputants are doing what they have agreed to do. If the agreement breaks down, the mediator reconvenes the mediation session and helps the disputants negotiate again.

Finally, the mediator congratulates him- or herself after the disputants leave. Mediators should take satisfaction from helping others. *"We're all like hidden gold mines."*

When Peer Mediation Fails

Teacher As Mediator

When a student mediator is not successful in helping the disputants resolve the conflict, then the conflict is referred to the teacher. The teacher then mediates the conflict, using the same procedures that the peer mediator used. If that fails, the teacher arbitrates. If that fails, the conflict is referred to the appropriate administrator who first mediates and then arbitrates if it is necessary.

Preventing Future Conflicts

It is a mistake to assume that students can always openly negotiate the resolution of a conflict. There are times when conflicts are better avoided. When two students repeatedly engage in destructively managed conflicts, and mediation and arbitration do not help, the mediator can take steps to prevent the occurrence of future conflicts. To prevent a conflict from occurring,

Johnson, D. W., & Johnson, R. (2005). **Teaching Students To Be Peacemakers** (4th Ed.). Edina, MN: Interaction Book Company, (952)831-9500.

the mediator needs to understand the circumstances that brought about the conflict and the entry state of the participants. The circumstances that surround the conflict include:

1. The barriers to the occurrence of the conflict (Walton, 1987). Internal barriers to the expression of the conflict include habitual patterns of avoiding conflict, negative attitudes toward conflict, values antithetical to the engagement in conflict, and fears and anxieties about potential negative outcomes. External barriers to the expression of the conflict may include task requirements that control the interaction among students, group norms for avoiding conflict, pressure to maintain a congenial public image, and faulty perceptions of one's vulnerability and others' strength. Physical separation is a frequently used barrier to the expression of conflicts of interest. Placing members in different locations, avoiding being in the same room with certain other members, and removing a member from the group, can all suppress a conflict of interest.

Quiz 7:3 Check Your Understanding

Demonstrate your understanding of the following concepts by matching the definitions with the appropriate concept. Check your answers with your partner and explain why you believe your answers to be correct.

Answer	Concept	Definition
	1. Wise Agreement	a. Events that highlight the conflict and ensure it is ignited.
	2. Barriers To Conflict	b. A person's psychological and physical ability to deal constructively with the conflict.
	3. Triggering Events	c. Agreement that maximizes joint outcomes, strengthens disputants' abilities to work together cooperatively, improves disputants' ability to resolve future conflicts constructively, and has an underlying logic that makes sense to disputants and relevant third parties
	4. Entry State	d. Focus on one potential agreement without being able to conceive of other alternative agreements.
	5. Fixation	e. Generating a variety of diverse ideas about how to solve a problem.
	6. Divergent Thinking	f. Internal, external, and physical factors that prevent the conflict from being expressed.

2. The events that trigger the conflict (Walton, 1987). A triggering event may be as simple as two group members being physically near each other or as complex as two members being in competition. Negative remarks, sarcasm, and criticism on sensitive points are common

triggering events, as is the feeling of being deprived, neglected, or ignored. Some events may trigger a destructive cycle of conflict and others may trigger problem solving; group members will want to maximize the latter type of triggering event.

3. The entry state of the disputants. A disputant's entry state is that person's psychological and physical ability to deal constructively with the conflict. Entry level is affected by a person's level of self-awareness, ability to control his or her behavior, interpersonal effectiveness (skills in self-disclosure, trust-building, communication, and conflict resolution [Johnson, 2003]), and ability to cope with stress and adversity. If a disputant is too angry, anxious, defensive, psychologically unstable, or stuck in the status quo to negotiate effectively, then negotiations should be delayed or avoided.

The mediator analyzes the events that surround or precede a conflict. He or she determines (a) what are the internal and external barriers to problem-solving negotiations (b) what are the events that trigger open expression of the conflict, and (c) what is the entry state of each disputant. From such knowledge the mediator can choose the time and place for negotiations. To avoid the conflict, the mediator removes the triggering events, builds up the barriers to negotiations, and ignores the entry state of disputants. To initiate negotiations, the mediator increases the frequency of the triggering events, decreases the barriers to negotiations, and provides the support and help needed to ensure a constructive entry state for each disputant.

Summary

A mediator is a neutral person who helps two or more people (called disputants) resolve their conflict. There is considerable value in having students serve as peer mediators. Conflicts become resolved, discipline problems decrease, school climate improves, and conflict resolution skills are transferred to a number of settings. Mediating teaches students both interpersonal and academic skills, improves cooperative work, increases students' commitment to education, and prepares students to be citizens in a complex and conflict-filled world.

To establish a peer mediation program, teachers (a) build a cooperative classroom context by using cooperative learning the majority of the time, (b) frequently use structured academic controversies, (c) instruct students in how to negotiate, (d) teach all students mediation procedures and skills, and (e) implement the peer mediation process within the classroom and school.

To implement a peer mediation process the teacher selects each day two students to be the class mediators. Any conflicts that students can not negotiate resolutions to are referred to class mediators. The role of class mediator is rotated throughout the class so that each student serves as class mediator an equal amount of time. Students need to know how to arrange for a mediator when they need one.

Johnson, D. W., & Johnson, R. (2005). **Teaching Students To Be Peacemakers** (4th Ed.). Edina, MN: Interaction Book Company, (952)831-9500.

The procedure for mediation consists of a series of steps. First, the mediator orchestrates the ending of hostilities. Fights are broken up and students are cooled down. Second, the mediator ensures both disputants are committed to the mediation process. To ensure that both persons are committed to the mediation process and are ready to negotiate in good faith, the mediator introduces the process of mediation, sets the ground rules, and introduces him- or herself. Third, the mediator helps the two people negotiate with each other successfully. This includes taking the two persons through the negotiation sequence of (a) stating what they want, (b) stating how they feel, (c) exchanging reasons for their wants and feelings, (d) reversing perspectives so that each person is able to present the other's position and feelings to the other's satisfaction, (e) inventing at least three options for mutual benefit, and (f) reaching a wise agreement and shaking hands. Fourth, the mediator formalizes the agreement. The agreement is solidified into a contract. Disputants must agree to abide by their final decision and the mediator becomes "the keeper of the contract."

Peer mediation gives students an opportunity to resolve their dispute themselves, in mutually satisfactory ways, without having to engage the attention of a teacher. This empowers the students and reduces the demands on the teacher. The teacher can then devote less time to arbitration and discipline in general, and more time to teaching.

7 : 30

Johnson, D. W., & Johnson, R. (2005). **Teaching Students To Be Peacemakers** (4th Ed.). Edina, MN: Interaction Book Company, (952)831-9500.

CREATIVE CONFLICT CONTRACT

Write down your major learnings from reading this chapter and participating in training session one. Then write down how you plan to implement each learning. Share what you learned and your implementation plans with your base group. Listen carefully to their major learnings and implementation plans. You may modify your own plans on the basis of what you have learned from your groupmates. Volunteer one thing you can do to help each groupmate with his or her implementation plans. Utilize the help groupmates offer to you. Sign each member's plans to seal the contract.

MAJOR LEARNINGS	IMPLEMENTATION PLANS

Date: _____ Participant's Signature: _____

Signatures Of Group Members: _____

_____

Johnson, D. W., & Johnson, R. (2005). **Teaching Students To Be Peacemakers** (4th Ed.). Edina, MN: Interaction Book Company, (952)831-9500.

Warm Up:

A Difficult Situation

Form triads. Read the following case study. Assume that you are Ms. or Mr. Fair. Make a plan for mediating the conflict between Brightness and Foggy. This is a cooperative task, everyone in the group should agree on the plan and be able to describe and explain it to the class as a whole.

Brightness was always an A student. She seemed to be able to remember and understand new things very easily and, therefore, never had to study very hard. Her best friend, Foggy, was not as smart and found school work difficult. They were both in the Ms. Fair's English class. Ms. Fair announced that there was a very important test coming up and, to reward the best students, anyone who got over 90 percent correct on the test would be given a part in a short play to be presented to the entire school. Everyone in the class seemed to want to be in the play and, therefore, there was considerable discussion as to who would score 90 percent or better on the test.

Foggy asked Brightness to help her study. Since Brightness never put much effort into preparing for a test, she was not very helpful. Foggy went to another friend, Bugoff. Bugoff told her to get lost because he was too busy. Foggy was close to tears. Brightness offered to try to give more help, but Foggy told her to bug off. Brightness felt terrible.

During the test Innocence passed a note from Foggy to Brightness. In the note Foggy asked Brightness for several answers. Brightness debated whether or not to respond, but finally decided she had to or risk losing Foggy as her best friend. She wrote the answers on the note. Ms. Fair caught her, and tore up her test and declared her ineligible for the play. Foggy said nothing.

Much to everyone's amazement, Foggy scored 91 percent on the test. She accepted a major role in the play. Brightness decides she is never going to speak to Foggy again.

Johnson, D. W., & Johnson, R. (2005). **Teaching Students To Be Peacemakers** (4th Ed.). Edina, MN: Interaction Book Company, (952)831-9500.

Name_____ Date_____

Crack the Conflict Code!

Using the key at the bottom of the page, see if you and your partner can solve the puzzle to define one of your conflict terms. Above each of the numbers, place the letter which it represents and your work will be done for you.

‾6‾ ‾15‾‾20‾‾8‾‾11‾‾6‾‾17‾‾19‾‾1‾ ‾11‾‾13‾ ‾6‾

‾13‾‾17‾‾12‾‾8‾‾20‾‾7‾‾17‾ ‾3‾‾16‾‾19‾ ‾16‾‾20‾‾10‾‾9‾‾13‾

‾17‾‾3‾‾19‾ ‾2‾‾10‾‾6‾‾13‾‾13‾‾15‾‾6‾‾17‾‾20‾‾13‾

‾1‾‾20‾‾13‾‾19‾‾10‾‾24‾‾20‾ ‾17‾‾16‾‾20‾‾11‾‾1‾

‾2‾‾19‾‾7‾‾26‾‾10‾‾11‾‾2‾‾17‾ ‾3‾‾16‾‾20‾‾7‾ ‾22‾‾19‾‾12‾

‾6‾‾1‾‾20‾ ‾6‾ ‾15‾‾20‾‾8‾‾11‾‾6‾‾17‾‾19‾‾1‾ ' ‾22‾‾19‾‾12‾

‾6‾‾1‾‾20‾ ‾7‾‾20‾‾12‾‾17‾‾1‾‾6‾‾10‾ ‾6‾‾7‾‾8‾

‾22‾‾19‾‾12‾ ‾25‾‾20‾‾20‾‾9‾ ‾20‾‾24‾‾20‾‾1‾‾22‾‾17‾‾16‾‾11‾‾7‾‾5‾

‾26‾‾6‾‾11‾‾1‾ .

R	C	W	X	G	A	N	D	P	L	I	U	S
1	2	3	4	5	6	7	8	9	10	11	12	13
Z	M	H	T	B	O	E	Q	Y	J	V	K	F
14	15	16	17	18	19	20	21	22	23	24	25	26

Referral to Mediation

Your Name:_____ Date:_____

Your Relation To People Involved:_____

People Involved In Conflict: Agreed To Mediation :
                                                Yes   No   Unknown

_____   __   __   __

_____   __   __   __

_____   __   __   __

_____   __   __   __

What Is The Conflict About?_____

_____

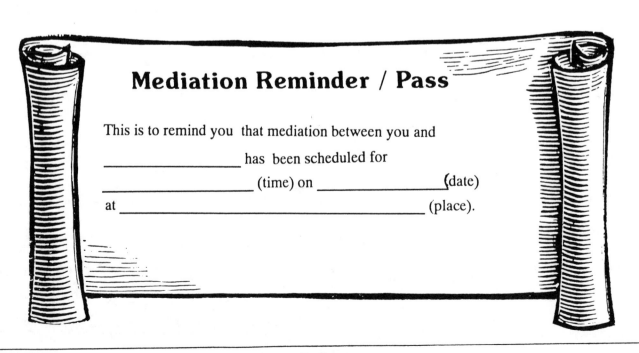

Mediation Reminder / Pass

This is to remind you that mediation between you and
_____ has been scheduled for
_____ (time) on _____ (date)
at _____ (place).

Johnson, D. W., & Johnson, R. (2005). **Teaching Students To Be Peacemakers** (4th Ed.). Edina, MN: Interaction Book Company, (952)831-9500.

MEDIATION RECORD

Name _____ Date _____

School _____ Grade Level _____

NATURE OF CONFLICT	WITH WHOM		TIME SPENT	AGREEMENT REACHED		COMMENTS
	Person I	Person II		Yes	No	

7 : 35

© Johnson & Johnson

Johnson, D. W., & Johnson, R. (2005). **Teaching Students To Be Peacemakers** (4th Ed.). Edina, MN: Interaction Book Company, (952)831-9500.

MEDIATION MENU

As a **mediator** you help two classmates resolve their conflict. You are neutral. You keep everything fair. You stand in the middle and help them go through each step of negotiating.

You Say:

My name is _____. I am a mediator. Would you like help in solving your problem (make sure both answer "yes")? Mediation is voluntary. I cannot make you do anything. I will not take sides or attempt to decide who is right or wrong. You will have to decide for yourselves how best to resolve your conflict. Our goal is to reach an agreement that is acceptable to each of you.

Each of you will have a chance to state your view of the conflict. In order for us to resolve your conflict we must agree on a set of **rules**:

1. You must agree to solve the problem.

2. No name calling.

3. Do not interrupt.

4. Be as honest as you can.

If we are successful, we will reach an agreement. You must live up to your side of the agreement. You must do what you have agreed to do.

Anything you say in mediation is confidential. I will not tell anyone.

We will now proceed across the bridge:

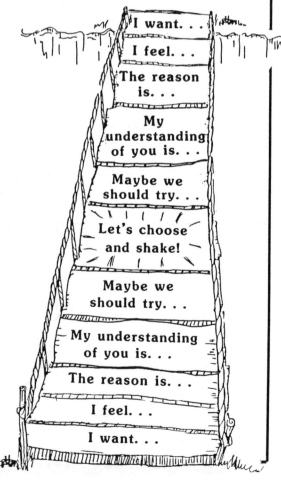

7 : 36

Johnson, D. W., & Johnson, R. (2005). **Teaching Students To Be Peacemakers** (4th Ed.). Edina, MN: Interaction Book Company, (952)831-9500.

The agreement is good if:

1. It tells when, where, who, and how.

2. Each student can do what he or she has agreed to.

3. Both students agree to do something.

Fill out the **Mediator Report Form** and have both students sign it.

You Say:

"We now have a signed agreement. Shake!"

"I am the keeper of the contract."
"I will check back with you tomorrow to see if the agreement is working."

7 : 37

Johnson, D. W., & Johnson, R. (2005). **Teaching Students To Be Peacemakers** (4th Ed.). Edina, MN: Interaction Book Company, (952)831-9500.

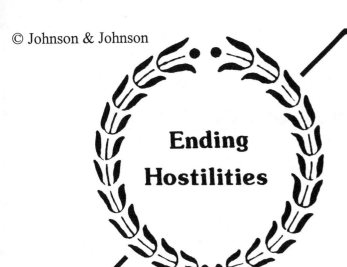

Ending Hostilities

Mediation begins with the ending of hostilities among students and cooling students down enough so that constructive negotiations may take place. There are no magic formula's for breaking up hostilities, but a few suggestions are given below.

Working with your partner, rank order the suggestions given below from the one you think will work best (1), second best (2)...to the one you think will be least effective in ending hostilities (6). Both of you must be prepared to tell the class **why** you ranked each suggestion the way you did.

_____ Get a teacher to tell the hostile students to stop.

_____ Get several students to help you separate and restrain the hostile students.

_____ Distract their attention.

_____ Take away the audience (all students leave).

_____ Get several students to chant, "Stop fighting, stop fighting."

_____ Get several students to sing a happy song such as "Ring Around The Rosy"

As a pair, lead the class in a practice role play of implementing your choice for the most effective strategy. Your purpose is to train classmates to break up hostilities on the playground and in the lunchroom.

Johnson, D. W., & Johnson, R. (2005). **Teaching Students To Be Peacemakers** (4th Ed.). Edina, MN: Interaction Book Company, (952)831-9500.

COOLING DOWN

Before you can successfully negotiate with another person you must first cool down. Anger usually interferes with problem solving. Sometimes you must wait until you are not so angry so that you can think clearly and talk calmly.

Your **task** is to read the following story and to answer the questions. Work **cooperatively** with a partner in doing so. One of you is to read the story and the other listen carefully and then summarize it in your own words. Flip a coin to choose who is the reader. Once the story is finished, answer the questions--one set of answers for the two of you, both of you have to agree, and both of you have to be able to explain.

Story

Keith asked Dale to lend him his new sport coat for a big date. Dale said "no," but Keith was so persistent that finally Dale agreed that Keith could wear the coat if he took absolutely great care of it. The next day Dale found his coat. It had mud all over it and one of the sleeves was ripped. He was furious. He wanted to find Keith and physically demolish him. He looked at the clock, however, and noted it was time for track practice. He went to track practice and ran for an hour. Later, physically exhausted, he found Keith. "What happened to my coat?" he calmly asked.

1. How did Dale feel when he found Keith? Why?

2. What happened to Dale's feelings while he was running?

3. What do you think would have happened if Dale had tried to solve the problem before he cooled off?

4. Why is cooling off important before you start negotiating? Give three reasons.

5. What are five ways to cool down before you start negotiating?

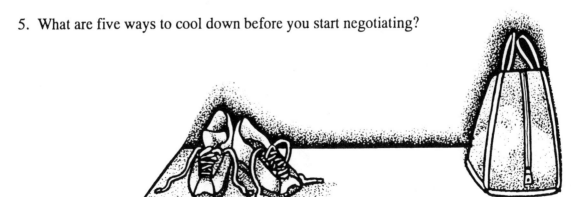

Johnson, D. W., & Johnson, R. (2005). **Teaching Students To Be Peacemakers** (4th Ed.). Edina, MN: Interaction Book Company, (952)831-9500.

Planning Your Opening Statement

1. Divide into pairs. Your **task** is to write out your opening statement in mediating a conflict among classmates. Work **cooperatively** to produce one statement from the two of you that each of you can give. Both of you need a written copy of the opening statement. Include:

   a. An introduction of yourself.

   b. A description of the process of mediation.

   c. A description of the role of the mediator.

   d. The questions of whether both students wish to solve their problem and will abide by the mediation rules.

   e. A statement of the confidentiality inherent in mediations.

   f. A statement of the goal of finding an agreement that meets both persons' needs.

2. Divide into new pairs. Give your opening statement to the other. Listen to his or her opening statement. Discuss how the statement can be given better next time.

3. Find a new partner. Give your opening statement. Listen to his or her's. Discuss how the statements could be given better next time.

4. Form groups of four. Write out at least four pieces of advice on how to make an effective opening mediation statement.

5. Participate in a whole class discussion on how to make an effective opening mediation statement.

Johnson, D. W., & Johnson, R. (2005). **Teaching Students To Be Peacemakers** (4th Ed.). Edina, MN: Interaction Book Company, (952)831-9500.

Remaining Neutral,
Not Taking Sides

An important skill for a mediator is to remain neutral and not take sides. You do so by using words and phrases that are impartial and nonjudgmental. You have to identify and refer to all of the issues in a neutral way.

Do not say, "She is angry because you stole her purse." Do say, "She is angry because you had her purse." Do not say, "The two of you were yelling at each other about the $15." Do say, "You talk to each other in unhelpful ways when the topic of the money comes up."

Jose claims that Bobby stole his lunch tickets. Bobby denies it. The mediator asks Jose if he knows anything about "the missing lunch tickets," but would never ask him about "the stolen lunch tickets." Do you know why?

Roger claims that Terry stole his social studies report. Terry says he didn't. The mediator asks Roger to describe in more detail why he believes that Terry stole his report, but Roger states, "You are not a judge and this is not a courtroom. I don't have to prove anything. I said he took it and that's that. Your job is to make him confess." What should you say?

When paraphrasing or reflective listening is used, it is important that the mediator does not impose his or her own opinion or bias on what the students say. The mediator must be able to state each student's position and feelings to that student's satisfaction.

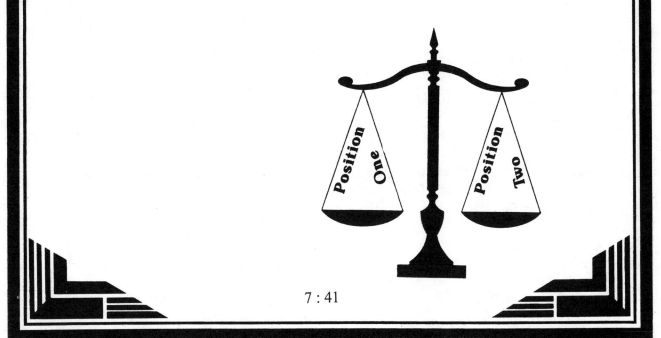

7 : 41

Johnson, D. W., & Johnson, R. (2005). **Teaching Students To Be Peacemakers** (4th Ed.). Edina, MN: Interaction Book Company, (952)831-9500.

Being An Umpire: Calling Fouls

While disputants may wish to fight fair, when they are frustrated and angry, they may try to "foul" each other. A mediator's responsibilities include being an umpire. An **umpire** makes sure that disputants' statements and actions are in the "fair" zone. Mediators must recognize and call fouls.

Task 1: With a partner, make a list of what is **fair** and what is **foul** in a conflict. An example of a list is given below. Share your list with the entire class. When other pairs are giving their lists, write down any good ideas that you did not already have on your list. When you finalize your list, use it to make a table similar to the one below.

Task 2: With your partner, for each foul on your list write out:
1. How a person would feel if they were fouled in this way?
2. How you recognize when the foul is occurring, that is, what a person says or does to foul someone in that way.

Foul	Feelings	Actions
Name Calling		
Blaming		
Put-Downs		
Making Excuses For Own Actions		
Bringing Up The Past		
Threats		
Pushing, Hitting, Shoving		
Bringing Others Into The Conflict		

Task 3: Pick a conflict you have recently seen between two class members. Plan a role play of the conflict that **first** includes several fouls and **second** shows how to resolve the conflict fairly.

Johnson, D. W., & Johnson, R. (2005). **Teaching Students To Be Peacemakers** (4th Ed.). Edina, MN: Interaction Book Company, (952)831-9500.

 **Practicing Mediation**

1. Divide into triads. These are called **role-playing triads**. Assign the roles of "the Giant," "Jack," and "mediator."

2. Combine with another triad. Then form pairs. These pairs are known as **preparation pairs**. The two Jacks get together, the two Giants get together, and the two mediators get together. They are to prepare each other to play their role. They read their instructions carefully, and plan how to present their wants, feelings, and reasons. They should make a visual to help them present their best case.

2. Return to your role-playing triad. The mediator gives the opening statement to ensure commitment to the mediation process. Both Jack and the Giant state what they want and how they feel. Each position is defined using the rules listed in Chapter 5.

3. Both Jack and the Giant present the reasons why they want and feel as they do. The mediator helps them separate their interests from their positions.

4. The Giant and Jack reverse perspectives and present each other's wants, feelings, and supporting facts and experiences. The mediator helps them reframe their views of the conflict.

5. Jack and the Giant invent at least five optional agreements that would give both what they want and build a better relationship between them. They star the three they like the best.

6. Jack and the Giant reach an agreement. The mediator gives the closing statement. The triad writes an ending to the story.

7. As a triad, write out at least three advice statements for peer mediators based on what you have learned about mediation from the role play.

8. Meet in your preparation pair. **Share** your list of advice. **Listen** carefully to your partner's advice. **Create** a new list that integrates the best ideas from both of you.

9. Return to your role-playing triad. Share your new list.

   Tell each member one thing

   you enjoyed about working with them.

Johnson, D. W., & Johnson, R. (2005). **Teaching Students To Be Peacemakers** (4th Ed.). Edina, MN: Interaction Book Company, (952)831-9500.

Jack's Position:

I'M A HERO!

My name is Jack. I lived with my mother on the edge of town. My father is dead and my mother and I were very poor. All we had was our cow Bertha. Finally, in order to eat, we had to sell Bertha. I felt so proud that my mother would trust me with such a responsibility. I lead Bertha to the market where I met an old man who convinced me to sell him Bertha for five magic bean seeds that would grow so tall that we would have enough beans to last us forever. I was so excited. Lots and lots of food forever! We would never be hungry again! But when I took the seeds home my mother told me I had been cheated and now we would starve. She threw the beans out the window and sent me to bed. I felt so bad. Somehow I had to find the money to support my mother. I cried myself to sleep. The next morning, when I woke up, I saw the beanstalk growing up into the clouds. I started climbing to find beanpods. But what I found instead was a magical land where there was a huge giant. Giants are evil, rotten creatures who like to eat boys like me, so I hid until he was asleep. Then I took his hen and ran to the beanstalk and came home. It turned out so wonderful. The hen lays golden eggs and my mother and I now have lots of food and clothes. My mother is so proud of me and so happy! She thinks I'm a hero. Several of my friends, however, think it was just luck. I keep thinking about the giant's golden harp. I would really be a hero if I could get that harp! And if I could kill the giant in the process, I might even marry a princess!

Johnson, D. W., & Johnson, R. (2005). **Teaching Students To Be Peacemakers** (4th Ed.). Edina, MN: Interaction Book Company, (952)831-9500.

Giant's Position:
I WAS ROBBED!

My name is Ralph. I've always tried to be friendly and helpful to everyone, but no one likes me. They think I'm a freak and make fun of me because I'm so big. My eyesight is poor, but I have a good sense of smell. When I smell something, I often say, "Fe, Fi, Fo, Fum." One of my problems is that I suffer from insomnia. I love music. It's my only source of happiness. The only way I can get to sleep is to listen to my golden harp play its music. It's an old family treasure. The only thing my father left me. I have no human friends. Whenever I try to make friends people are either frightened of my size or make fun of me. Because my feelings are so easily hurt, I try to avoid people. I live in a magical land in the clouds that humans can not reach and, thanks to my hen and my harp I am fairly happy. My hen lays golden eggs and my golden harp plays the most beautiful music. Without my hen and harp I would have nothing.

Recently a boy named Jack found a way into my magical land. He hid in my house and stole my hen. I'm devastated. How could he be so cruel and dishonest! I never did anything to him! I've never taken anything from him. He seems to think that because I'm big, clumsy, and ugly he can do anything he wants to me and my things. That is not right. All I have left is my golden harp and I'm afraid Jack means to come back and steal it too. What am I to do? I hate violence but I have to defend my possessions and I have to stick up for my rights.

Johnson, D. W., & Johnson, R. (2005). **Teaching Students To Be Peacemakers** (4th Ed.). Edina, MN: Interaction Book Company, (952)831-9500.

Mediation Training Role-Play Round Robin

1. Divide into new role-playing triads. Decide who is Person A, B, or C. Person C becomes the mediator. There are six role plays. For each role play, the roles within the group will rotate so that each student will get a chance to practice mediation.

2. Combine with another triad. Then form pairs ("A's," "B's." and "C's). These pairs are known as **preparation pairs**. Pair members work together to prepare each other to play their role. They read their instructions carefully, and plan how to present their wants, feelings, and reasons. They should make a visual to help them present their best case. The mediators prepare by reviewing the mediation steps.

3. Return to your role-playing triad. Students have 10 minutes for each role play. The intent of the role play is to provide students practice in mediating conflict. The mediator gives the opening statement to ensure commitment to the mediation process. Both A and B state what they want and how they feel. Each position is defined using the rules listed in Chapter 5 and each person gives his or her reasons. The two reverse perspectives, invent options, and reach an agreement.

4. The members of the triad rotate roles and follow the above procedure for the second role play. The same preparation pair is used every time. After the second role play has been finished, the members rotate roles once more and engage in the third role play. The rotation continues until all six role plays have been conducted. Each member will now have experienced being a mediator twice.

5. After the role plays are completed, the triad, working cooperatively:

   a. Discusses the issues that arose in practicing the mediation procedure.

   b. Discusses the way in which each mediator managed the resolution of the conflict.

   c. Writes out three conclusions about how mediation needs to be managed.

6. Meet in your preparation pair. **Share** your advice. **Listen** carefully to your partner's advice. **Create** a new list that integrates the best ideas from both of you.

7. Return to your role-playing triad. Share your new list. Tell each member one thing you enjoyed about working with them.

Johnson, D. W., & Johnson, R. (2005). **Teaching Students To Be Peacemakers** (4th Ed.). Edina, MN: Interaction Book Company, (952)831-9500.

Role Play 1

WHY DIDN'T YOU KEEP YOUR HANDS OFF?

Megan and Penny are in the same class. Megan worked hard on a tooth-pick sculpture. Penny, without asking, picked it up to look at it, dropped it, and it broke. Ask Megan to speak first.

Megan Says: "I'm so mad! I'm going to find something Penny made and smash it. She broke my sculpture. I **told** everyone not to touch it! I hate it when other people 'trash' my things!"

Penny Says: "It was an accident. I didn't mean to break it. I liked it and wanted to see how she did it. And now she's mad! It was just a bunch of toothpicks. She can put it back together. But if she thinks she's going to break something of mine she is mistaken. I'm mad at her just thinking about what she might try to do!"

Role Play 2

CAN'T YOU STAY ON TOPIC?

Dan and Sam are working on a report together. Ask Dan to speak first.

Dan Says: "Sam's always interrupting and trying to change the subject so we can never get anything done! It's so frustrating! Whenever we're discussing how to organize the report he starts talking about completely unrelated things! I can't get him to pay attention and think about the report!"

Sam Says: "I try to think creatively. I get new ideas about the report by trying to make new associations. I want to use my fantasy and spontaneous ideas to make our report different from those the rest of the class are doing. But I never get a chance to explain what I'm doing. Dan is so power hungry!"

7 : 47

Johnson, D. W., & Johnson, R. (2005). **Teaching Students To Be Peacemakers** (4th Ed.). Edina, MN: Interaction Book Company, (952)831-9500.

Role Play 3

WHERE'S THE BOOK?

Fred and Ralph: Although the two are friends, they got into a fight about lost library books. Ask Fred to speak first.

Fred Says: "Ralph and I were doing reports on the same topic. He wanted to borrow a book from me that I took out of the library. He promised to return it, so I lent it to him. Then I got a notice that the book is overdue and I'm being fined. If the book isn't returned, I will have to pay for it. He didn't even tell me that he lost the book!"

Ralph Says: "I meant to return the stupid book. I always do what I say. Someone broke into my locker last week and took a bunch of my things. The book must have been one of them. I forgot all about it. Now he's calling me a liar. Some friend. He didn't ask for an explanation."

Role Play 4

YOU SHOULDN'T HAVE SAID THAT!

Todd and Tim: The two are classmates who have been friendly but don't spend much time together. They were caught fighting in the hall. Ask Todd to speak first.

Todd Says: "I was just standing around in the hall talking to Chris when Tim came up and pushed me and starting yelling about how he's not on drugs. He was yelling that he's going to kill me for telling people he's doing drugs. I thought he was! I heard someone say he saw Tim doing drugs. I thought we should figure out a way to help him!"

Tim Says: "I have never taken drugs. I hate people who do drugs! I have an ear infection, have been dizzy and nauseous much of the time, and have been taking medicine. Suddenly people started spreading rumors I was on drugs. Todd is supposed to be my friend but he just went along with everyone else. So I punched him out."

Johnson, D. W., & Johnson, R. (2005). **Teaching Students To Be Peacemakers** (4th Ed.). Edina, MN: Interaction Book Company, (952)831-9500.

Role Play 5

DON'T HURT THAT DOG!

Meggy and Ensley: Meggy was walking home from school. She saw Ensley and one of her friends throwing rocks at a puppy that was tied up in a yard. Meggy wanted to help the puppy. She told Ensley to stop and Ensley began to call her names and chased her home.

Meggy Says: "That poor little puppy was all tied up and couldn't run and hide. Ensley was trying to hurt it! It was so sad. It makes me mad every time I think of it. Ensley should have tried to pet the puppy and make friends with it, not try to hurt it."

Ensley Says: "I don't like dogs. I'm scared of them. That puppy was barking at me. If it wasn't tied up, who knows what it might have done to me. I was trying to teach it not to bark or try to bite me. Meggy had no right to tell me to stop. She acted like I was a nasty person for trying to defend myself. I'm really mad at Meggy and I'm going to make her sorry she stuck her nose in my business."

Role Play 6

WATCH OUT FOR MY CHAIR!

Joan and Jane: Jane is confined to a motorized wheelchair. She is being mainstreamed into a regular fourth-grade class. She often bumps other students with her chair and frequently runs over their feet and then laughs. Today she ran over Joan's foot. Joan got angry and kicked Jane's chair several times.

Joan Says: "Jane is always running over someone's foot and laughing about it. It's not funny for the person whose foot just got crushed. She always wants us to move rather than going around. I know we're all supposed to like Joan, but I don't. She seems mean to me. If she thinks she can run over my foot and get away with it, she has another think coming!"

Jane Says: "It's hard to steer my chair. The classroom is crowded with desks and chairs, and all the students sit around on the floor and in the aisles. No one moves when I have to get by. I could complain, but I don't want to seem like a nag. So I try to make a game of it, and occasionally run over someone's foot to give them the message to move out of the way when I have to get by. My chair isn't heavy. It doesn't hurt them. I'm really mad at Joan for being so inconsiderate and using my running over her foot as an excuse to get everyone to not like me."

Johnson, D. W., & Johnson, R. (2005). **Teaching Students To Be Peacemakers** (4th Ed.). Edina, MN: Interaction Book Company, (952)831-9500.

Role Play 7
❧ RETURN MY THINGS! ❧

Jill and Jack: Jill and Jack are seniors in high school. For the past two years they went steady with each other. Jill broke up with Jack two months ago but wanted to remain friends. For several weeks Jack followed Jill around asking her to go out with him again. She refused. One day she lost her temper and told him to "get out of her life."

Jill Says: Jack calls me at home all the time insisting that I return some of "his" things. He gave me a gold necklace and four rock albums. He lent me two other rock albums. I will gladly return the albums he lent me. I am not, however, going to return the things he gave me. They were presents. While we were dating I gave him two sweaters and three books. I am not asking him to return those to me. He should stop hounding me.

Jack Says: After Jill told me to get out of her life I have stayed away from her. I did phone her a few times so I can get some albums and a gold necklace back from her. I have a new girlfriend now (although Jill does not know it) and I would like to give the necklace to her. In addition, I worked hard to get the money to buy those albums and it is not fair that Jill keeps them. It is true that Jill gave me two sweaters and three books, but that is different because she has no use for them and, therefore, does not want them back. Furthermore, I need them. She should give me my things.

Role Play 8
❧ I'LL GET YOU! ❧

Tyler and Chris: This morning Chris walked into first hour class, slammed the door, then slammed his book down on his desk. The science teacher told him to sit down and be quiet. Chris loudly stated that he was quiet. Tyler, who sits next to Chris, said, "Hey, stupid. Shut up so the rest of us can learn something and pass this course." Chris called Tyler a nerd and said, "I'll get you after school." During the class Chris poked Tyler with his pencil and kicked his chair several times. Tyler ignored it. During lunch Chris started pushing and shoving Tyler.

Tyler: I do not want to be around a jerk like Chris. He takes his problems out on everyone around him. I should not have to put up with his harassment and threats. He's much bigger than I am. I'm not going to fight him. But I'm not going to let him push me around either. I have to get an "A" in science if I'm going to get a scholarship for college. Chris keeps causing me trouble in class. That's not right.

Chris: Two weeks ago the science teacher accused me of cheating on a test. He said I was copying from Tyler. The teacher asked Tyler about it and Tyler said he thought I was looking at his paper. The teacher gave me an "F." I may now get a "D" in science. If I do, I'll be kicked off the basketball team. And it's all Tyler's fault. He should have kept his mouth shut.

Johnson, D. W., & Johnson, R. (2005). **Teaching Students To Be Peacemakers** (4th Ed.). Edina, MN: Interaction Book Company, (952)831-9500.

Practicing Mediation Through Role Playing

The purpose of the role playing is to give each participant practice in mediating a conflict. Within each situation participants should authentically portray the conflict and use all the steps of mediation to resolve it.

1. Divide into triads.

2. Working cooperatively, brainstorm a list of conflicts that occur among the students in your school:

   a. Think of seven to ten conflicts that commonly occur among students. Include actual conflicts you have seen in your classroom and school.

   b. Take three that seem either the most common or the most troublesome for you as a teacher. Script each of the three by:

      1. Writing a three to four sentence description of the situation. Include the time, place, and background needed to understand the conflict and the students' positions.

      2. Writing a three to four sentence description of each student's position, feelings, and needs. The descriptions will orient the persons' role playing each student. Designate which student should be asked to speak first.

3. Within your triad decide who is Participant A, B, or C. Participant A and B become students while participant C becomes the mediator. The roles within the group rotate, so that in Role Play 2, participants B and C become the students and participant A becomes the mediator, and in Role Play 3, participants C and A become the students and participant B becomes the mediator.

4. Participants prepare for the role play by reviewing the position and feelings of the student they are to represent. The mediator prepares by reviewing the steps in mediation and planning how to manage each stage.

5. Participants have 15 minutes for each role play. The intent of the role plays is to provide each participant with the opportunity to practice the entire mediation procedure.

6. After the three role plays have been completed, working cooperatively, the triad:

   a. Discusses the issues that arose in practicing the mediation procedure.

   b. Discusses the way in which each mediator managed the resolution of the conflict.

   c. Writes out three conclusions about how mediation needs to be managed.

Johnson, D. W., & Johnson, R. (2005). **Teaching Students To Be Peacemakers** (4th Ed.). Edina, MN: Interaction Book Company, (952)831-9500.

Facilitate Negotiations

1. Help Disputants Define The Conflict:

a. Ask each disputant: *"What happened, what do you want, how do you feel?"*

b. Paraphrase what each disputant says when it is necessary to demonstrate you are listening and understand what they are saying and when you believe the other disputant do not clearly understand what the person is saying. Paraphrasing is restating and summarizing what a person says and how they feel in an accurate, complete, and neutral way.

c. Enlarge the shadow of the future by highlighting the ways they will have to work cooperatively with each other in the future.

2. Help Disputants Exchange Reasons For Their Positions By:

a. Helping disputants present their reasons and the rationale for their positions.

b. Helping disputants understand the differences between their positions.

c. Keeping disputants focused on the issue, not on tangents such as their anger toward each other.

d. Equalizing power.

e. Recognizing constructive behaviors during negotiations.

f. Reframing the issue by helping disputants change perspectives.

3. Help Disputants Reverse Perspectives.

a. Having each disputant present the other's wants, feelings, and reasons to the other's satisfaction.

b. Role play the conflict and switch roles at critical points.

4. Help Disputants Invent Options For Mutual Gain:

a. Encourage creative thinking.

b. Complete a balance sheet on each alternative suggested.

5. Formalize The Agreement:

a. Complete **Mediation Report Form**.

b. Have disputants sign it and commit themselves to implementing agreement.

Johnson, D. W., & Johnson, R. (2005). **Teaching Students To Be Peacemakers** (4th Ed.). Edina, MN: Interaction Book Company, (952)831-9500.

One-Text Procedure

The **one-text procedure** is conducted in the following way (Fisher & Ury, 1981).

1. Listen to each student's views and ask:

   a. What does the student want?

   b. How does the student feel?

   c. What are the student's reasons?

2. Develop a rough draft of an agreement that achieves the goals of each person.

3. Ask each student to review the draft agreement. Incorporate their corrections until you believe that the proposed agreement cannot be improved further.

4. Formally present the final draft as the agreement and recommend that they accept it.

The Problem-Solving Rug

When students cannot agree, the teacher (or administrator) can send them to the problem solving rug to keep negotiating until they reach agreement. The rules for the rug are:

1. Both students must sit on the rug until the conflict is resolved.

2. No touching. Verbal exchanges only.

3. Be patient. It may take them a long time.

4. When they resolve the conflict, praise them and ask what the resolution is.

Johnson, D. W., & Johnson, R. (2005). **Teaching Students To Be Peacemakers** (4th Ed.). Edina, MN: Interaction Book Company, (952)831-9500.

Mediation Review Games

Mediation Catch

Form groups of five members. Each group stands in a circle and is given a tennis ball. Display the steps of mediating (ending hostilities, ensuring commitment to mediation, facilitating negotiations, formalizing the agreement). Throw a tennis ball into the group. Whoever catches it has to give a statement they would use to end hostilities (see the table below for an example). He or she throws the ball to another member, and that member has to give a statement he or she would use to ensure commitment to mediation. Each person who catches the ball has to give a statement they would use for the next step of mediating. Keep the ball moving until each member has covered the mediation steps several times. The faster the ball moves the better.

Mediation Baseball

Form teams of four members. Divide each group into two pairs (Twins and Yankees). They will be competing against each other. Write out a deck of cards listing the four steps of mediation (ending hostilities, ensuring commitment to mediation, facilitating negotiations, formalizing the agreement). Make at least four copies of each step. Shuffle the cards and place them in the center of the group. A member of the Twins draws a card and give a mediator statement that reflects the step on the card (see the below table for an example). If he or she makes a correct statement, he or she advances to first base. Then a member of the Yankees draws a card and gives an appropriate mediator statement. On the second round a member advances to second base. At the end of ten or fifteen minutes the game is stopped. The pair with the most "runs" wins.

Steps Of Mediation	Possible Statements
Ending Hostilities	*"Would you like a mediator?"*
Ensuring Commitment To Mediation	*"There are four rules you must follow."*
Facilitating Negotiations	*"How do you feel?"*
Formalizing The Agreement	*"Are you willing to sign the agreement?"*

Johnson, D. W., & Johnson, R. (2005). **Teaching Students To Be Peacemakers** (4th Ed.). Edina, MN: Interaction Book Company, (952)831-9500.

Chapter Eight: Implementing And Institutionalizing The Peer Mediation Program

An Overview

To teach students how to manage conflicts constructively teachers:

1. Build a cooperative context within which conflicts may be resolved constructively. This involves using cooperative learning the majority of the time.

2. Structure academic controversies so that students challenge each other's reasoning (see Johnson & Johnson, 1995).

3. Train all students how to engage in problem-solving negotiations. By teaching the negotiation procedure to all students, teachers ensure that everyone in the school is co-oriented and uses the same procedures for resolving conflicts of interests.

4. Train all students how to mediate. By teaching all students to mediate, teachers ensure that all students are capable of helping classmates work through the negotiation sequence and gain negotiation skills. Knowing that they will take their turn at being class mediators tends to make students receptive to the process of mediation and the suggestions of a mediator.

5. Implement the peer mediation program. Each day two students are selected to be the class mediators. They help classmates negotiate resolutions to their conflicts. The role of class mediator is rotated throughout the class so that each student serves as class mediator an equal amount of time. Students need to know how to arrange for a mediator when they need one.

6. Conduct practice sessions to refine students' skills in using the negotiation and mediation procedures. These practice sessions may be integrated into academic units.

7. Mediate conflicts among students when the peer mediator is unable to do so. Teachers arbitrate a conflict among students when mediation fails.

9. Refer students to the an administrator when both teacher mediation and arbitration fail. The administrator first tries to mediate the conflict and, if that fails, arbitrates.

Johnson, D. W., & Johnson, R. (2005). **Teaching Students To Be Peacemakers** (4th Ed.). Edina, MN: Interaction Book Company, (952)831-9500.

Figure 8.1 Implementing Peer Mediation Program

Build Cooperative Context

Use Academic Controversies Frequently

Teach All Students To Negotiate

Teach All Students To Mediate

Implement Program
- Each Day Select Two Class Mediators
- Mediators Are Available
- Responsibility Is Rotated So All Students Mediate
- Training Is Continued Throughout School Year To Refine And Upgrade Skills
    Direct Skill Training And Practice Sessions
    Integrated Into Subject Areas

Teacher Mediates When Student Mediation Fails

Teacher Arbitrates When Teacher Mediation Fails
- Traditional Arbitration
- Final Offer Arbitration

Administrator Mediates When Teacher Arbitration Fails

Administrator Arbitrates When Administrator Mediation Fails

8 : 2

Johnson, D. W., & Johnson, R. (2005). **Teaching Students To Be Peacemakers** (4th Ed.). Edina, MN: Interaction Book Company, (952)831-9500.

Implementing The Peacemaker Program

If civilization is to survive, we must cultivate the science of human relationships—the ability of all peoples, of all kinds, to live together, in the same world, at peace.

Franklin Delano Roosevelt

Once students understand how to negotiate and mediate, the teacher implements the peacemaker program. There are two versions of the program—elementary and secondary. The elementary version is as follows:

1. Each day the teacher selects two class members to serve as official mediators. The teacher may randomly choose students to be mediators, or the teacher may carefully match students into pairs so that introverted students are paired with extroverts, students with low academic skills are paired with high-achieving students, and so forth. Initially, mediators work in pairs. When all students are experienced enough to be comfortable with being a mediator, then they may mediate individually.

2. The mediators wear official T-shirts, hats, or armbands so that they are easily recognized. They patrol the playground and lunchroom. Generally, the mediators are available to mediate any conflicts that occur in the classroom or school.

3. Any conflicts students cannot resolve themselves are referred to the class mediators. The mediators end hostilities, ensure disputants are committed to the process of mediation, facilitate problem-solving negotiations, and formalize the agreement.

4. The role of class mediator is rotated throughout the class so that all students serve as class mediator an equal amount of time. Mediating classmates' conflicts is perhaps the most effective and dramatic way of teaching students the need for the skillful use of each step of the negotiation procedure.

5. Refresher lessons are frequently taught throughout the school year to refine students' negotiation and mediation skills.

The secondary program is very similar, except that a certain number of school mediators are chosen from each grade level (two mediators for every thirty students or so) and the role of mediator is rotated throughout the school so that all students serve as school mediator an equal amount of time.

8 : 3

Johnson, D. W., & Johnson, R. (2005). **Teaching Students To Be Peacemakers** (4th Ed.). Edina, MN: Interaction Book Company, (952)831-9500.

When All Else Fails, Arbitrate

Aesop tells of the bees, the wasps, and the hornet. A store of honey was found in a hollow tree, and the wasps declared positively that it belonged to them. The bees were just as sure that the treasure was theirs. The argument grew very heated, and it looked as if the conflict could not be settled without a battle, when at last, with much good sense, they agreed to let an arbitrator decide the matter. So they brought the conflict before the hornet, who was a judge in that part of the woods. Witnesses were called, who testified that striped, yellow and black winged creatures (like bees) had been seen near the tree. The wasps declared that the description fitted them exactly. With some thought the hornet stated that if a decision was not made soon, the honey would not be fit for anything. He, therefore, instructed the bees and the wasps both to build a honey comb. *"Whoever makes the best honey comb obviously is the owner of the honey,"* the hornet declared. The wasps protested loudly. The hornet quickly understood why they did so—they could not build a honey comb and fill it with honey. *"It is clear,"* said the hornet, *"who can make the comb and who can not. The honey belongs to the bees."*

When the peer mediator fails, the teacher may try mediation. If the teacher cannot mediate the conflict, then the teacher arbitrates. **Arbitration** is the submission of a dispute to a disinterested third party who makes a final and binding judgment as to how the conflict will be resolved. While the teacher is not always a disinterested third party, the teacher does have the authority and power to arbitrate any dispute he or she wishes to. If teacher arbitration does not end the conflict, then it is referred to an administrator. The administrator tries to mediate the conflict. If that fails, the administrator arbitrates. Arbitration is needed when the disputants are so hostile or have such opposed interests that they are incapable of reaching agreement. The adults in the school have the final responsibility to resolve such conflicts and, therefore, they will need to arbitrate when negotiation and mediation have failed. It is important to remember, however, that arbitration is the method of last resort when all negotiation and mediation attempts have failed.

Technically, arbitration may be voluntary (when it is requested by the persons in conflict) or compulsory (as in the case where a judge may order arbitration). In the classroom, arbitration will be voluntary when two students ask the teacher to decide how a conflict should be resolved and all other methods of conflict resolution have been tried and have failed. Or arbitration may be compulsory when a conflict between two students (or groups of students) becomes so severe that the teacher has to step in and arbitrate it. While mediation is an extension of negotiating, and the mediator assists the two persons in negotiating a constructive resolution to their conflict, arbitration is a judgment made by an outside person and, therefore, does not assist the students in improving their conflict skills. In arbitration the students leave the decision to the arbitrator, who hears both sides and then makes a judgment.

Johnson, D. W., & Johnson, R. (2005). **Teaching Students To Be Peacemakers** (4th Ed.). Edina, MN: Interaction Book Company, (952)831-9500.

The process of arbitration consists of:

1. Both disputants agree to abide by the arbitrator's decision. Most people agree to abide by the arbitrator's decision on the assumptions that they will have the opportunity to fully present their side of the conflict and the arbitrator will make a fair decision.

2. Each disputant submits his or her desired goal to the arbitrator. At the beginning, each side has to define what he or she wants and tell the arbitrator what he or she would like to see happen.

3. Each disputant defines the problem as he or she sees it. Both disputants get the opportunity to tell their side of the conflict.

4. Each disputant presents his or her case with documented evidence to support it. Both disputants are given an equal opportunity to present their views. The rules of mediation apply (i.e., no name calling, no interrupting, and so forth).

5. After each disputant has made a presentation of his or her case, the other disputant is given an opportunity to refute the disputant's contentions. Both disputants have the opportunity to give the arbitrator a different perspective on the issues.

6. The arbitrator makes a decision. Each disputant makes a closing statement. When both disputants have nothing more to add to the presentation of their case and the refutation of the other's case, the arbitrator has to decide. The decision most often is one wherein one disputant wins and the other disputant loses. Whether a disputant wins or loses is assumed to be secondary to having had a fair opportunity to be heard. In essence, they have had their day in court.

Arbitrators should be disinterested parties, who are extremely familiar with the particular subject matter of the case, and who are allowed to examine all the available documents and evidence.

Following Mediation With Arbitration

Arbitration tends to result in solutions to conflicts that are less stable and less effective than solutions derived by negotiation and mediation for several reasons. First, disputants tend to know their own interests better than any third party can. Second, disputants tend to commit themselves more to agreements of their own devising than to agreements imposed by the third party. Third, arbitrators are more likely to dictate compromise solutions to the conflict as opposed to integrative solutions that fulfill the goals of both parties. Another shortcoming is the **chilling effect**. When disputants anticipate that the arbitrator will "split the difference," they may adopt a tough and extreme position so that the half-way between positions is favorable to them.

Johnson, D. W., & Johnson, R. (2005). **Teaching Students To Be Peacemakers** (4th Ed.). Edina, MN: Interaction Book Company, (952)831-9500.

Teachers and administrators may engage in a combination of mediation and arbitration. Mediation is used first to try to achieve an agreement. If that fails, then arbitration is imposed. This offers several advantages over mediation or arbitration alone:

1. The threat of arbitration may motivate disputants to reach agreement during mediation, as they have more control over the agreement in mediation.

2. Students and faculty know that they will not have to deal with the same dispute again; a final settlement, whether negotiated or imposed, will surely be achieved.

3. Another third party need not be informed of the dispute all over again.

4. It enhances the mediator's power, as it tends to make disputants more attentive to the mediator's recommendations.

A danger of using a combination of mediation and arbitration is that in mediation the disputants may believe they are forced to reach an agreement because arbitration will result if they do not. Another danger is that the mediator may become too forceful during the mediation session and prematurely shift to arbitration.

Integrating Peacemaker Training In The Curriculum

It takes a lifetime to gain competence in resolving conflicts constructively. A few hours of training is not enough. Throughout the school year, therefore, teachers have to conduct follow-up lessons that upgrade and refine students' skills in using the problem-solving negotiation and mediation procedures. There are two types of follow-up lessons:

1. Specific skill lessons on communication skills, controlling anger, appropriate assertiveness, problem-solving skills, perspective-taking, creative thinking, and a wide variety of other related interpersonal and small group skills (Johnson, 1991, 2003; Johnson & F. Johnson, 2003). These have been discussed in previous chapters.

2. Lessons integrated into the ongoing academic curriculum.

The procedure for integrating the Peacemaker Training is as follows (Stevahn, 2003):

1. Choose an existing instructional unit that contains conflicts. Integrating Peacemaker Training into academic lessons does not require the purchase of new student materials or instructional resources or the development of new courses or units of study. Rather, the teacher may take almost any lesson in literature, language arts, humanities, or social studies and integrate the training into how the lesson is currently taught. In literature,

Johnson, D. W., & Johnson, R. (2005). **Teaching Students To Be Peacemakers** (4th Ed.). Edina, MN: Interaction Book Company, (952)831-9500.

for example, any Shakespeare play is filled with conflicts and books such as "Charlottes Web" and "Green Eggs and Ham" are based on conflicts. In social studies (history, civics, government, economics, and so on) conflicts over free trade, allocating resources, sources and use of energy, land use, foreign policy, and health care, and many other issues all provide opportunities for understanding the value of constructively managed conflicts and practicing negotiation and mediation procedures.

2. Create a cooperative classroom environment. This is most easily done by structuring the lesson cooperatively. A cooperative context is necessary for teaching and practicing negotiation and mediation skills. This is discussed in Chapter 2.

3. Use concrete examples from the curriculum to teach about the nature of conflict. Literary works may be used to teach about the nature of conflict by requiring students to identify conflicts in the stories they are reading. As Stevahn (2003) notes, (a) in *Old Henry* by Joan W. Blos, students may see that by not fixing up his rundown house, Henry blocks his neighbors from achieving their goal of keeping the entire community neat and tidy, (b) in *The War with Grandpa* by Robert Kimmel Smith, students may see that the fifth grade student Peter's wish to have his own room may be blocked by his grandfather coming to live with Peter's family, and (c) in *The Gold Cadillac* by Mildred D. Taylor, students may see that when Wilbert uses all of the family's savings to purchase a shiny new gold Cadillac, his wife Dee is upset because it prevents the family from buying a new house. In analyzing these conflicts students can classify the strategies used as being forcing, withdrawal, smoothing, compromise, or problem-solving negotiations (see Chapter 3).

4. Teach students the problem-solving negotiation and mediation procedures by having them role-play the characters in the curricular-embedded conflicts. Having Hamlet use the negotiation procedure with his father's ghost (see Chapter 4) or mediating between Jack and the Giant (see Chapter 6) are examples. Students are assigned to pairs or triads, given a specific character from the literary work to role play, prepare their basic statements of what they want, how they feel, and their reasons for both, and then role play the conflict using the negotiation and mediation procedures. Students' agreements can be compared with what actually happens in the play, story, or novel. Practicing the negotiation and mediation procedures through role playing in academic lessons increases the academic achievement of the students and their long-term retention of what they are learning (see Appendix A).

5. Process each role play to refine students' skills in using the problem-solving negotiation and mediation procedures. Having students discuss how well they engaged in the procedures and what they can do to improve ensures that they continually improve their skills and understanding of each step of the two procedures. Besides in engaging in guided self-assessments, students can receive feedback from the teacher and the other students involved in role plays. Students should focus on both verbal phrasing and nonverbal cues used to engage in each step of the procedures. Body posture, facial

Johnson, D. W., & Johnson, R. (2005). **Teaching Students To Be Peacemakers** (4th Ed.). Edina, MN: Interaction Book Company, (952)831-9500.

expressions, eye contact, tone of voice, hand gestures, and so on are important in both negotiations and mediation. Students learn what tends to work in creating agreements that allow all parties involved to achieve their goals.

6. Have a class discussion on how the problem-solving and mediation procedures may be used to resolve actual conflicts that occur in classrooms and schools. The primary purpose of integrating the Peacemaker Training into academic lessons is to teach students how to manage their own conflicts more constructively. Specific discussions of how the procedures may be used in students' actual conflicts help students transfer what they have learned in class to the playground and other settings. In addition, the use of the procedures in a wide variety of conflicts involving lots of different situations and circumstances, increases the likelihood that the use of the procedures will be transferred to actual conflicts in students' lives.

Reasons For Integration

Teaching students how to resolve conflicts constructively can be integrated into academic lessons in ways that enhance academic achievement as well as teach students the value of conflict and the problem-solving negotiation and mediation procedures. Teachers do not have to make an "either/or" choice. Accomplishing both simultaneously is not only possible, it is desirable for several reasons (Stevahn, 2003).

The first is time pressures. While most teachers recognize the need to teach students how to resolve conflicts constructively, many believe they do not have the time to do so. Integrating the Peacemaker training into academic lessons saves time.

Second, the history of innovations in education indicates that innovative practices tend to be ignored or discontinued unless they are effective in increasing student achievement (Fullan, 2001). There is considerable empirical evidence that integrating the Peacemaker Program into the curriculum-increases academic achievement and long-term retention (see Appendix A). Role playing increases involvement, creates insight into the character's wants, feelings, and reasoning, and creates more positive attitudes toward learning (Johnson & F. Johnson, 2003). The cognitive framework of the problem-solving negotiation procedure (want, feel, reasons, perspective reversal, three options, integrative agreement) organizes thinking about academic material and facilitates processing of the information students are learning (Stevahn, 2003). The negotiation step-by-step framework helps students more thoroughly and effectively analyze, synthesize, evaluate, and remember academic material. Finally, the integration of the Peacemaker Program into academic units requires students to learn how to present positions, express feelings, explain underlying interests and reasoning, listen effectively, take other's perspectives, engage in creative problem solving, and reach agreement on the best solution. These competencies may be used to enhance academic learning as well as resolve conflicts.

Johnson, D. W., & Johnson, R. (2005). **Teaching Students To Be Peacemakers** (4th Ed.). Edina, MN: Interaction Book Company, (952)831-9500.

Third, using the problem-solving negotiation and mediation procedures in a wide variety of conflicts involving literature, history, science, and other contexts increases the ability of students to transfer the procedures to conflicts within their own lives.

Fourth, there are numerous interpersonal benefits from learning how to resolve conflicts constructively. Relationships improve and are maintained over time. Individuals who managed conflicts constructively tend to be better liked.

Fifth, there are broad generalized positive effects on classroom learning and the school as a whole when students are taught how to manage their conflicts constructively. The school environment becomes safer and more orderly as students learn the procedures and attitudes they need to manage conflicts constructively, practice them enough to develop skills in using them, and the school provides support for engaging in the procedures (such as a school wide peer mediation program). Curriculum-integrated Peacemaker training ensures all students (a) receive the Peacemaker training, (b) engage in frequent, sustained, and meaningful practice of the procedures, and (c) participate in school discipline and classroom management systems. One high school student who participated in the curriculum-integrated *Peacemakers* training wrote:

> *We have been studying conflict managing and negotiating along with World Civilization. Now at first, I was a little skeptical about the whole thing, but after all kinds of practice and studying and applying to real-life historical situations, I came to the conclusion that these steps could really work in real life. The only problems are that not many other people know them or even care enough to use them. To put yourself in the other's shoes can be a great way to solve conflict. I really think that these steps should be taught to all kids. I really believe that they could be used to stop even wars. (Stevahn, Johnson, Johnson, & Schultz, 2002, pp. 326-327)*

Sixth, curriculum-integrated training is a key to institutionalizing the Peacemaker Program. Once it becomes a regular part of academic units, it will tend to be taught year after year.

Integrating Peacemaker Training In Co-Curricular and Extra-Curricular Programs

In most schools there are extra-curricular programs such as athletics, after-school programs and co-curricular programs such as Spanish Club, Speech Club, Odyssey of the Mind, Math League, Knowledge Bowl, Key Club, and Habitat for Humanity. In many of these programs the Peacemaker Training could be integrated as part of the program's activities. Doing so will enhance the activities of the program as well as reinforce and enhance the Peacemaker Program in the school.

Johnson, D. W., & Johnson, R. (2005). **Teaching Students To Be Peacemakers** (4th Ed.). Edina, MN: Interaction Book Company, (952)831-9500.

Multi-Year Spiral Training

Once students have been taught the basic negotiation and mediation procedures, the peer mediation program is implemented. This does not end the training. Students do not gain competence in resolving conflicts in one year. Many years of training, practice, and application are necessary. Each year the problem-solving and mediation procedures may be taught in a more complex and sophisticated way. The result is twelve years of training in how to negotiate to solve problems and mediate peer conflicts. This is a classic spiral training in which the Peacemaker Training each year builds on the training students received in prior years.

Methods For Teaching Students To Negotiate And Mediate

The success of both peer and teacher mediation depends on how skillfully students can negotiate and mediate. For younger students the teacher may use the story-telling and problem puppet procedures. For older students role playing may be used.

Story-Telling Procedure

For younger students, the storytelling procedure is effective for (a) teaching students how to resolve conflicts and (b) whole-class mediation. The procedure is:

❖ Tell the story of a conflict a using a "once upon a time" format.

❖ When the story reaches the point of conflict, stop and ask the class for suggestions for resolving it. Make sure students give specific (rather than general) suggestions. Requiring specificity helps prevent the "give-the-teacher-what-she-wants-to-hear" response.

❖ Incorporate one of the suggestions into the story, and then bring it to a conclusion.

❖ Ask the disputants if this would in fact meet their needs and if it is something they might try the next time they have a problem.

An example is the following kindergarten class:

T: *Once upon a time, Jack and Jill were playing with the toy train. Jill was playing with the engine and Jack decided he wanted the engine. Jill refused to give it to him, so Jack yelled at her and gave her a push. She pushed him back. What could they do?*

Johnson, D. W., & Johnson, R. (2005). **Teaching Students To Be Peacemakers** (4th Ed.). Edina, MN: Interaction Book Company, (952)831-9500.

1: *Say they were sorry?*

T: *That does not solve the problem with the engine. They both want to play with the engine.*

2: *You could take the engine away from both of them.*

T: *The teacher is too busy. They have to solve this by themselves.*

3: *They each could try to grab the train cars.*

T: *They tried that. It didn't work.*

4: *Why don't they share and play with the engine together?*

T: *Actually, that is just what they did. Jill asked Jack if they could play with the engine together. Jack said yes, and then they both pushed the engine together. Do you think that would work with the real Jack and Jill?*

1, 2, 3, 4: *Yes.*

T: *Well, from that day on they played happily ever after.*

Problem Puppets

Margaret and Sarah were arguing over a set of blocks. Each believed that it was their turn to get the blocks. The teacher intervened, called the class together, and showed students two puppets. *"These are the problem puppets, and they will help us solve the problem Margaret and Sarah are having,"* the teacher says. With young students, negotiation and mediation procedures may be taught with problem puppets. Puppets can provide young children enough distance from a conflict to discuss their behavior without feeling threatened.

First, use the puppets to reenact the conflict.

Second, freeze the puppet role play at a critical point in the conflict. Ask the class for suggestions on ways to resolve the conflict. Incorporate one of these suggestions, and finish the puppet play.

Third, repeat the puppet play until several different suggestions for solving the conflict have been suggested. Discuss whether or not each one will work. This helps children learn to think through the consequences of their suggestions.

Johnson, D. W., & Johnson, R. (2005). **Teaching Students To Be Peacemakers** (4th Ed.). Edina, MN: Interaction Book Company, (952)831-9500.

Fourth, ask the children to pick the suggestion they think will work best. The problem puppets can then be retired.

Role Playing To Master Negotiation And Mediation Procedures

Role playing is a helpful tool for teaching students conflict skills. Role playing can simulate real-life situations, making it possible for students to try new ways of managing conflicts without suffering any serious consequences if the methods fail. Role playing is a tool for:

1. Allowing students to experience concretely the conflict situation.

2. Identifying effective and ineffective behavior.

3. Gaining insight into their behavior in conflict situations.

4. Practicing the procedures and skills required to manage the conflict constructively.

Within role playing an imaginary situation is set up so students act and react in terms of the assumptions they are asked to adopt, the beliefs they are asked to hold, and the characters they are asked to play. The outcome of a role-playing situation is not determined in advance, and the situation is not rehearsed. Initial instructions are given and the actors determine what happens.

Role playing is especially useful in teaching students to think metacognitively about the conflicts they are involved in. Sometimes students in a conflict cannot "unlock" from their perspective sufficiently to see the conflict from all points-of-view or generate a number of possible integrative agreements that will be acceptable to both parties. A role play often will help. Before using the procedure with a real conflict, have your students practice it with hypothetical situations. Be sensitive to the fact that not all students like to participate in role plays. The procedure for using role playing is as follows.

First, describe the conflict situation, giving time, place, and background and any other information that will help the students "*get in role*." Define the roles to be played. Ask the students who are involved in the conflict to play the roles, or use volunteers. Help the students get into the situation and their roles by introducing it in such a way that the players are emotionally involved.

Second, have the players act out the conflict. If they do not know what to say or do, asking them some leading questions may help them get unstuck. Keep the role play short.

Johnson, D. W., & Johnson, R. (2005). **Teaching Students To Be Peacemakers** (4th Ed.). Edina, MN: Interaction Book Company, (952)831-9500.

Third, freeze the role play at critical points in the conflict. Ask the class for suggestions as to what could be done next. The players then incorporate one of the suggestions into the role play and finish it.

Fourth, always discuss the role play when it is finished:

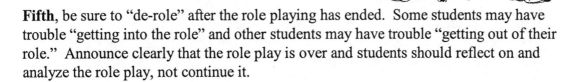

❖   How could the conflict have been prevented?

❖   How did the characters feel in the situation?

❖   Was it a satisfactory solution?

❖   What other solutions might have worked?

Fifth, be sure to "de-role" after the role playing has ended. Some students may have trouble "getting into the role" and other students may have trouble "getting out of their role." Announce clearly that the role play is over and students should reflect on and analyze the role play, not continue it.

Instructions To Students

When participating in a role playing exercise, remain yourself and act as you would in the situation described. You do not have to be a good actor to play a role. You only need to accept the initial assumptions, beliefs, background, or assigned behaviors and then let your feelings, attitudes, and behavior change as circumstances seem to require. The role play instructions describe the point of departure and the beginning frame of reference. You and the situation then take over.

Your experiences in participating in the role play may lead you to change your attitudes and future behavior. You may have emotional experiences that were not expected when the role playing began. The more real the role playing and the more effective the exercise, the more emotional involvement you will feel and the more you will learn.

In role playing, questions may be raised that are not answered in your briefing sheet. When this happens, you are free to make up facts or experiences that accord with the circumstances. Do not make up experiences or facts that do not fit the role.

In participating in role playing, you should not consult or look at your role instructions. Once they are used to start the action, you should be yourself. A role player should not act the way she feels a person described in the instructions should behave. The role player should act as naturally as possible, given the initial instructions of the role.

Johnson, D. W., & Johnson, R. (2005). **Teaching Students To Be Peacemakers** (4th Ed.). Edina, MN: Interaction Book Company, (952)831-9500.

Perspective Reversal

A more sophisticated and powerful procedure is the addition of role reversal to the role play. **Perspective reversal** is having two participants in the conflict reverse roles and play each other during the role play. It can be a dramatic way to help solve stubborn conflicts.

- ❖ Establish the role play as above. Try to use the participants in the original conflict as players.

- ❖ Freeze the role play at the point after which the conflict has begun.

- ❖ Have the participants switch roles and replay it, so that they are taking the role of their opponent and, in effect, arguing against themselves.

- ❖ Stop the role play after the players have gotten the feel of their opponent's point of view. Discuss the role play and see if any new alternative solutions have occurred to the students engaged in the conflict.

Summary

Once students have been taught the basic negotiation and mediation procedures, the Peacemaker (peer mediation) program may be implemented. All students take their turn in serving as a mediator to help their schoolmates resolve their conflicts. Follow-up lessons are then taught to upgrade and refine students' skills in using the negotiation and mediation procedures. Each year the procedures are taught in a more complex and sophisticated way The follow-up lessons focus on social skills or on practicing the negotiation and mediation procedures as part of academic lessons. The result is twelve years of training in how to negotiate to solve problems and mediate to help peers resolve their conflicts constructively.

When negotiation and mediation fail, faculty and administrators must arbitrate. Arbitration tends to be less effective than mediation. Arbitration tends to be more effective when it is conducted by the same person who mediated.

Methods for teaching mediation skills include the story telling and problem puppets for young children and role playing and perspective reversal for older students.

8 : 14

Johnson, D. W., & Johnson, R. (2005). **Teaching Students To Be Peacemakers** (4th Ed.). Edina, MN: Interaction Book Company, (952)831-9500.

CREATIVE CONFLICT CONTRACT

Write down your major learnings from reading this chapter and participating in training session one. Then write down how you plan to implement each learning. Share what you learned and your implementation plans with your base group. Listen carefully to their major learnings and implementation plans. You may modify your own plans on the basis of what you have learned from your groupmates. Volunteer one thing you can do to help each groupmate with his or her implementation plans. Utilize the help groupmates offer to you. Sign each member's plans to seal the contract.

MAJOR LEARNINGS	IMPLEMENTATION PLANS

Date: _____ Participant's Signature: _____

Signatures Of Group Members: _____

_____

8 : 15

Johnson, D. W., & Johnson, R. (2005). **Teaching Students To Be Peacemakers** (4th Ed.). Edina, MN: Interaction Book Company, (952)831-9500.

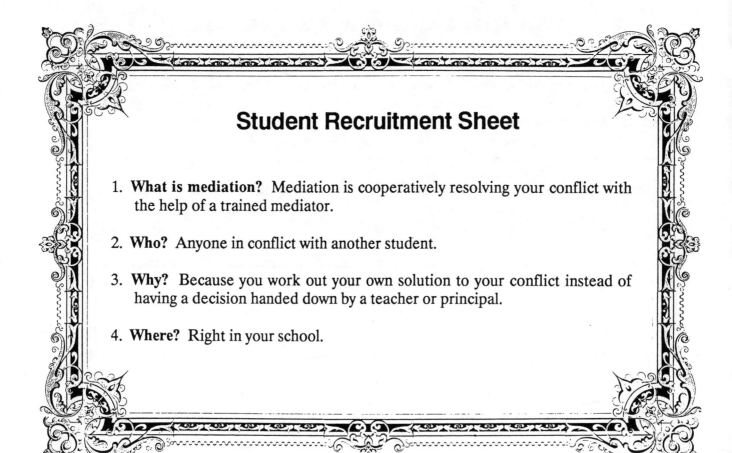

Student Recruitment Sheet

1. **What is mediation?** Mediation is cooperatively resolving your conflict with the help of a trained mediator.

2. **Who?** Anyone in conflict with another student.

3. **Why?** Because you work out your own solution to your conflict instead of having a decision handed down by a teacher or principal.

4. **Where?** Right in your school.

If you like to try new things, help others with their conflicts, be in the middle of things, or gain valuable skills, volunteer to be trained as a mediator. Before the end of the year every student in the class may take their turn being a mediator. You will be asked to:

1. Take part in 15 hours of training.

2. Attend regular meetings with the teacher and the other mediators.

3. Be available for one mediation a week during lunch or study hall.

Volunteer to Learn To Mediate

8 : 16

Johnson, D. W., & Johnson, R. (2005). **Teaching Students To Be Peacemakers** (4th Ed.). Edina, MN: Interaction Book Company, (952)831-9500.

Conflict Reporting Form

Date: _____ Reporter: _____

Others Taking Part:

_____

_____

What It Was All About: _____

_____

_____

How Did You Feel About the Way the Conflict Was Resolved?

(Circle one number)

1	2	3	4	5
Very Unhappy	*Unhappy*	*OK*	*Happy*	*Very Happy*

Drill and Review Game

1. **Mediation Catch:** Form groups of five members each. Each group stands in a circle and is given a tennis ball. Display the steps of mediating (ending hostilities, ensuring commitment to mediation, facilitating negotiations, formalizing the agreement). Throw a tennis ball. Whoever catches it has to give a statement from some aspect of the next step of mediating. Keep the game up until the mediation procedure has been covered several times.

8 : 17

Johnson, D. W., & Johnson, R. (2005). **Teaching Students To Be Peacemakers** (4th Ed.). Edina, MN: Interaction Book Company, (952)831-9500.

MEDIATOR

has learned new ways to mediate conflicts between people

at _____

School in _____

and shall from this day be accorded the title and responsibilities of

OFFICIAL MEDIATOR

_____
Teacher

_____
Special Mediation Advisor

_____
Date

Johnson, D. W., & Johnson, R. (2005). **Teaching Students To Be Peacemakers** (4th Ed.). Edina, MN: Interaction Book Company, (952)831-9500.

ASSESSING STUDENTS' UNDERSTANDING

You will benefit from assessing your understanding of each chapter and then reviewing the parts you do not fully understand. Your **tasks** are to:

1. Review the first seven chapters and write out three questions for your classmates to answer that will test their understanding of the content of the chapter. Write each question on a 3x5 index card. You will write out twenty-one questions in all.

2. Place the questions for each chapter in a bowl. There will be seven bowls (one for each chapter). Randomly draw three questions from each bowl. Write out answers to the questions you have drawn.

Work **cooperatively**. Form a pair. Agree on the questions you write for each chapter. Agree on one answer to each question you answer. One member of your pair will be randomly selected to present your answers to the class as a whole.

8 : 19

Johnson, D. W., & Johnson, R. (2005). **Teaching Students To Be Peacemakers** (4th Ed.). Edina, MN: Interaction Book Company, (952)831-9500.

Steps in Mediating

Read each of the statements given below. Number the stage of mediation each statement belongs to (1 = End Hostilities, 2 = Ensure Commitment, 3 = Facilitate Negotiations, 4 = Formalize Agreement). Work **cooperatively** in a pair. Agree on each answer. Each must be able to explain why you answered the question as you did.

_____ Will you describe your view of the conflict?

_____ Do you agree to follow these rules?

_____ Hello. My name is xx. I'm your mediator.

_____ What are three ways this problem could be solved?

_____ What happened?

_____ Tell me what xx wants, how xx feels, and the reasons why xx wants and feels as he/she does.

_____ Stop fighting! Stop fighting!

_____ Can you repeat back what xx has said?

_____ What do you want? How do you feel?

_____ Go to opposite corners in the room. Fill out the Conflict Form. Then we will talk.

_____ Do you agree to solve the problem?

_____ I have written your agreement down. Sign here. I will check back with you in two days to see if the agreement is working.

8 : 20

Johnson, D. W., & Johnson, R. (2005). **Teaching Students To Be Peacemakers** (4th Ed.). Edina, MN: Interaction Book Company, (952)831-9500.

© Johnson & Johnson

TRUE or FALSE ?

Answer each question "true" or "false." Work **cooperatively** in a pair. Agree on each answer. Each must be able to explain why you answered the question as you did.

_____ Mediators do not say who is right and who is wrong.

_____ There are at least two sides in every conflict.

_____ Once the two students feel better about each other, the conflict is over.

_____ Most students cannot say what they want.

_____ Conflict is a natural part of life.

_____ All conflicts end in violence.

_____ Feelings are irrational and confuse negotiations.

_____ It is important to learn not to get angry.

_____ Letting students interrupt and correct each other helps clarify what the conflict is.

_____ A wise agreement is one that allows both students to achieve their goals.

_____ When you are angry it is OK to embarrass or humiliate the other person.

_____ Decide who is right and have the other person apologize.

_____ Once an agreement has been reached, the job of the mediator is over.

_____ We should eliminate all conflict in our classroom.

_____ Reasons do not matter. Just focus on what each person wants.

_____ Only conflicts where physical fighting is involved need to be mediated.

_____ Humor often helps students resolve their conflict.

8 : 21

Johnson, D. W., & Johnson, R. (2005). **Teaching Students To Be Peacemakers** (4th Ed.). Edina, MN: Interaction Book Company, (952)831-9500.

TRUE or FALSE? (continued)

_____ Mediation works best when students are really angry, because then they will tell the truth.

_____ Conflicts can escalate or de-escalate, depending on what is said or done.

_____ Once a mediator has both students tell what happened, then his or her job is done.

_____ In conflicts people are so upset that it is a waste of time trying to get them to understand each other's point of view.

_____ Mediators help students think of several possible optional agreements before they decide on how best to resolve their conflict.

_____ Fighting fair shows respect for oneself and for others.

_____ Part of the final agreement is that the students should avoid contact with each other in the future.

MEDIATION RULES

List the four rules students must agree on:

1.

2.

3.

4.

8 : 22.

Johnson, D. W., & Johnson, R. (2005). **Teaching Students To Be Peacemakers** (4th Ed.). Edina, MN: Interaction Book Company, (952)831-9500.

Assessing Students' Understanding of Mediation

Qualities Of Good Mediation

Make two columns on the blackboard, one labeled "Is" and the other "Is Not." Ask students what they think a student mediator is and is not. Write their responses in the appropriate column. Add any they do not mention.

What Is Good Mediation?

Place a "yes" for each quality of good mediation and a "no" for each quality of poor mediation.

_____ A good listener.

_____ A police officer.

_____ A good teamworker.

_____ A person who interrupts or focuses attention on him- or herself.

_____ A fair person who does not take sides.

_____ A judge.

_____ A helper.

_____ A person who gives orders or advice.

_____ A dependable person.

_____ A person who talks about other students' conflicts.

_____ A person you can trust.

Johnson, D. W., & Johnson, R. (2005). **Teaching Students To Be Peacemakers** (4th Ed.). Edina, MN: Interaction Book Company, (952)831-9500.

Evaluation of Mediation Programs

You may wish to evaluate the effectiveness of your peer mediation program. There are two things you will wish to find out:

1. Was the peer mediation training conducted effectively?

2. Is the peer mediation program achieving its goals?

To answer these questions you need to collect information systematically. Included in this chapter are a several instruments to help you do so.

1. **Conflict Report Form:**

   a. Pick a time that the form can be given regularly.

   b. Have students work in pairs to fill out the form.

   c. Classify conflicts into categories.

   d. Weekly record the frequency of each type of conflict on a class chart.

   e. Make sure that students understand it is not the frequency of conflicts that matters, it is how they are managed. Conflicts should occur frequently and be managed skillfully.

2. **What do you do when you negotiate a problem?** Ask students to list the steps.

3. **What Would You Do?** Tell students that here is a conflict that two of your classrooms had. They are to think about what is happening in the conflict and, as a mediator, write what they would do to help these two classmates resolve their problem.

4. **Conflict Essay:** Ask students to write an essay (create a skit or puppet show) about what they have learned about managing conflicts.

5. **Favorite Story:** Ask students to analyze a conflict in one of their favorite stories.

Johnson, D. W., & Johnson, R. (2005). **Teaching Students To Be Peacemakers** (4th Ed.). Edina, MN: Interaction Book Company, (952)831-9500.

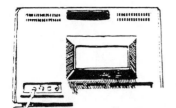

What Would YOU Do?

Here is a conflict that two of your classrooms had. Think about what is happening in the conflict. As a mediator, what would you do to help these two classmates resolve their problem? Write your answer below.

Today in school each student is given a chance to work at the computer. When your turn comes you go over to the computer and one of your classmates is still using it. You tell the person working at the computer that it is your turn, but they tell you that they have not finished yet and keep working. It is important that you use the computer during your assigned time to get your work done. What should you do?

As a mediator, I would help these two classmates resolve their conflicts by:

My Favorite Story

Choose one of your favorite books, movies, or short stories. Analyze it:

1. What is the conflict the book or movie revolves around?

2. Who is involved, when does it happen, where does it happen, and how is it managed?

3. What strategies do the characters use to manage or resolve the conflict? How successful are those strategies?

4. How would you manage the conflict? Describe your procedures, strategies, and skills in detail.

8 : 25

Johnson, D. W., & Johnson, R. (2005). **Teaching Students To Be Peacemakers** (4th Ed.). Edina, MN: Interaction Book Company, (952)831-9500.

Mediation Review Games

Mediation Catch

Form groups of five members. Each group stands in a circle and is given a tennis ball. Display the steps of mediating (ending hostilities, ensuring commitment to mediation, facilitating negotiations, formalizing the agreement). Throw a tennis ball into the group. Whoever catches it has to give a statement they would use to end hostilities (see the table below for an example). He or she throws the ball to another member, and that member has to give a statement he or she would use to ensure commitment to mediation. Each person who catches the ball has to give a statement they would use for the next step of mediating. Keep the ball moving until each member has covered the mediation steps several times. The faster the ball moves the better.

Mediation Baseball

Form teams of four members. Divide each group into two pairs (Twins and Yankees). They will be competing against each other. Write out a deck of cards listing the four steps of mediation (ending hostilities, ensuring commitment to mediation, facilitating negotiations, formalizing the agreement). Make at least four copies of each step. Shuffle the cards and place them in the center of the group. A member of the Twins draws a card and give a mediator statement that reflects the step on the card (see the below table for an example). If he or she makes a correct statement, he or she advances to first base. Then a member of the Yankees draws a card and gives an appropriate mediator statement. On the second round a member advances to second base. At the end of ten or fifteen minutes the game is stopped. The pair with the most "runs" wins.

Steps Of Mediation	Possible Statements
Ending Hostilities	*"Would you like a mediator?"*
Ensuring Commitment To Mediation	*"There are four rules you must follow."*
Facilitating Negotiations	*"How do you feel?"*
Formalizing The Agreement	*"Are you willing to sign the agreement?"*

8 : 26

Johnson, D. W., & Johnson, R. (2005). **Teaching Students To Be Peacemakers** (4th Ed.). Edina, MN: Interaction Book Company, (952)831-9500.

Chapter Nine: The Twelve Steps Of Peacemaking

The Lure Of Going For The "Win"

No logic or wisdom or will-power could prevail to stop the sailors. Buffeted by the hardships of life at sea, the voices came out of the mist to the ancient Greek sailors like a mystical, ethereal love song with tempting and seductive promises of ecstasy and delight. The voices and the song were irresistible. The mariners helplessly turned their ships to follow the Sirens' call with scarcely a second thought. Lured to their destruction, the sailors crashed their ships on the waiting rocks and drowned in the tossing waves, struggling with their last breath to reach the source of that beckoning song.

Centuries later, the Sirens still call. Educators seem drawn to competitive learning, crashing their teaching on the rocks due to the seductive and tempting attractions of trying to find out which student is "best." Students are also captured by the seduction of wanting to build their successes on the failures of their classmates. And when conflicts occur, going for the "win" has an irresistible call to many. Striving to solve the problem so both sides benefit may seem idealistic but undoable. Cooperative learning provides a far more effective alternative to competition and creates the foundation within which conflicts may be managed constructively. Problem-solving negotiations provide an alternative to the "win-lose" approach to resolving conflicts and teach students the procedures and skills required to work effectively with classmates and faculty to maximize their education and cognitive and social development.

Peer Mediation

Suzzane, who is a new student from another country, sits down to eat lunch with several classmates. Pam says, *"This is 'invitation only.' No foreigners allowed."* Suzzane, her feelings obviously hurt, says, "Sorry" and walks away. *"That's terrible,"* Mary says to Pam. *"You shouldn't have done that."* *"You're such a 'goody-goody',"* Pam replies. *"We don't want you here either!"* Mary and Pam get more and more angry and begin yelling at each other. Things come to a head when Pam pushes Mary.

9 : 1

Johnson, D. W., & Johnson, R. (2005). **Teaching Students To Be Peacemakers** (4th Ed.). Edina, MN: Interaction Book Company, (952)831-9500.

Figure 9.1 Managing Developmental Conflicts

Types
- Dependence–Independence
- Security–Anxiety
- Impulsiveness–Delay Of Gratification

Developmental Process
- Overassimilation
- Social Constraints
- Accommodation
- Identification And Internalization
- Move Toward Other End Of Continuum

Resolving Constructively
- Expect Repetition
- Face Conflict
- Be Consistent
- Provide Constructive Models
- Support Growth And Risk–Taking
- Teach Negotiation And Mediation Procedures
- Emphasize Perspective–Taking
- Do Not Make The Impersonal Personal

9 : 2

Johnson, D. W., & Johnson, R. (2005). **Teaching Students To Be Peacemakers** (4th Ed.). Edina, MN: Interaction Book Company, (952)831-9500.

Conflicts occur all the time in school. They are a natural, inevitable, potentially constructive, and normal part of school life. While in extreme cases conflicts erupt into violence, most conflicts among students are far milder, involving disagreements over rumors, name calling, boyfriends/girlfriends, and the like. Some of the conflicts are resolved. Many, if not most, are not. In most cases, students either escalate conflicts in destructive ways or disengage harboring anger and resentments that continue to simmer underneath the surface. Covert conflicts then exist in which students sit in classrooms and "fester" about their perceived grievances. Until covert conflicts are made overt and resolved, students cannot focus their attention on learning.

Several factors contribute to students' failures to resolve their conflicts constructively. Students often are from different cultural, ethnic, social class, and language backgrounds. Different students often have quite different ideas about how conflicts should be managed. The procedures and strategies students use to manage their conflicts are quite often inadequate and destructive, making things worse rather than better. Students may get angry, fight, hurl verbal abuse at each other, verbally harass each other, ignore the conflict, take their anger out on someone/something else, play head-games, or fantasize how to get revenge. These methods generally provide little chance of resolving any problems and often result in alienating students from their peers and the school staff. Most students simply do not know how to manage their conflicts constructively.

Under these circumstances, conflict can produce chaos. Teachers can respond by being police officers, arbitrators, or mediators. Ideally, however, teachers will co-orient students by teaching them the procedures and skills required to manage conflicts constructively. Conflicts, no matter what, occur all the time in school and only students themselves can restore order and peace. What is needed is a training program that creates a shared set of procedures and strategies for negotiating solutions to joint problems and mediating conflicts among classmates.

In the above example, Mary and Pam need a peer mediator to help them resolve their conflict (so do Pam and Suzzane). Roger is a class mediator for that day. He approaches Mary and Pam, separates them, helps them cool down. He then meets with them and ensures that they are committed to mediating their conflict. He asks if they want to solve the problem and does not proceed until both answer "yes." Since the role of mediator is rotated through the class, both Pam and Mary have themselves been mediators and will be again. This increases their willingness to participate in the process. Then Roger explains:

❖ *"Mediation is voluntary. My role is to help you find a solution to your conflict that is acceptable to both of you."*

❖ *"I am neutral. I will not take sides or attempt to decide who is right or wrong. I will help you decide how to solve the conflict."*

9 : 3

Johnson, D. W., & Johnson, R. (2005). **Teaching Students To Be Peacemakers** (4th Ed.). Edina, MN: Interaction Book Company, (952)831-9500.

❖ *"Each person will have the chance to state his or her view of the conflict without interruption."*

❖ *"The rules you must agree to are (a) agree to solve the problem, (b) no name calling, (c) do not interrupt, and (d) be as honest as you can."*

❖ *"If you agree to a solution, you must abide by it. You must do what you have agreed to do."*

❖ *"Anything said in mediation is confidential. I will not tell anyone what is said."*

Roger reminds Mary and Pam that they are friends, are in many of the same classes, and participate in many of the same activities. He then leads them through the negotiation procedure. Each states what she wants. Each states how she feels. Each states the reasons for her wants and feelings. Each summarizes her understanding of what the other wants, how the other feels, and the reasons underlying both. Roger helps Mary and Pam invent three optional plans to resolve their conflict. They then choose the one they like the best and shake hands. Finally, Roger closes the mediation session by formalizing the agreement and stating he would check in with them in a few days to see if the agreement was working.

Conflict management procedures and skills are too important to leave to chance. Children and adolescents need to be directly taught in school the negotiation procedures and skills and given the mediation experiences that will help them live happy and successful lives. When students are taught how to manage conflicts constructively, they become peacemakers. Part of every student's responsibilities is to manage his or her conflicts constructively and help schoolmates do likewise.

The Twelve-Steps Of Peacemaking

Providing students with an orderly environment in which to learn and even guaranteeing students' safety is becoming more and more difficult in many schools. An increasing number of public and private teachers and administrators face situations involving destructive conflicts among students and between students and faculty. Despite the widespread concern, however, very little information exists as to how to help students resolve their conflicts constructively. In response to the problems arising from frequent and destructive conflicts, schools are adopting various violence prevention and conflict resolution programs. There are three reasons for teaching all students in all schools how to manage conflicts constructively. The first is to make schools orderly and peaceful places in which high quality education can take place. The second is to utilize for instructional purposes the powerful potential of conflict to gain and hold attention, increase motivation to learn, arouse intellectual curiosity, and improve the quality and creativeness of reasoning. The third is to ensure that future generations are prepared to manage conflicts constructively in career, family, community, national, and international settings.

Johnson, D. W., & Johnson, R. (2005). **Teaching Students To Be Peacemakers** (4th Ed.). Edina, MN: Interaction Book Company, (952)831-9500.

To eliminate violence and reduce discipline problems, schools need to engage in a twelve step process.

Step One: Face Reality Of Destructive Conflicts

The first step is for schools to admit that destructive conflicts (reflected in the academic dishonesty, verbal and physical violence, and incivility) occur. In order to make the school a safe and orderly place in which to learn, the problems of student violence and increasing frequency and seriousness of discipline problems have to be faced. Even in wealthiest school districts, student incivility and disrespect for faculty and for each other is a problem that needs to be corrected.

Step Two: Implement A Violence Prevention Program

Step Two is for schools to implement a violence prevention program. Actions may be taken to reduce the number of weapons in school, suppress violent behavior, train faculty to recognize potentially violent situations and intervene, target students who repeatedly engage in violence for special attention, lead discussions of how to avoid violence, teach students how to cognitively control and manage their anger, create a district violence plan, adopt a threat-management policy, provide aftermath debriefing for victims and bystanders, and install a weapons hotline. Trying to suppress violent behaviors without replacing them with more constructive actions is a short-term strategy.

Step Three: Make The School A Conflict Positive Organization

The third step is for faculty, staff, and students to recognize that conflicts are inevitable, healthy, and potentially valuable. Conflicts, therefore, should be encouraged, not avoided or suppressed. Constructive conflict resolution, however, depends on faculty and students understanding the nature of conflict and knowing how to engage in problem-solving negotiations and mediation.

One reason to encourage conflicts is that students face a developmental imperative to engage in conflicts with adults and peers. Developmental conflicts reoccur over and over again and cycle in and out of peak intensity as students mature physically, socially, and cognitively. Students work to establish and understand their dependence versus independence, security in the status quo versus demand for growth and change, and impulsive satisfaction of needs versus delay of gratification.

Johnson, D. W., & Johnson, R. (2005). **Teaching Students To Be Peacemakers** (4th Ed.). Edina, MN: Interaction Book Company, (952)831-9500.

Step Four: Establish A Comprehensive Conflict Resolution Training Program

Step Four is for schools to establish a comprehensive conflict resolution training program. Every member of the school, student and faculty alike, need to learn the same set of procedures for managing conflicts constructively. The program should be clearly based on conflict resolution theory and research. To ensure it becomes institutionalized (i.e., a permanent and traditional aspect of school life), the program has to be linked with academic achievement. Bridges need to be built with extra-curricular and co-curricular programs.

Step Five: Create A Cooperative Context For Conflict

The fifth step is to create a cooperative context. There are two possible contexts for conflict: cooperative and competitive (in individualistic situations, people do not interact and, therefore, no conflict occurs) (Deutsch, 1973; Johnson & Johnson, 1989). It makes little sense to attempt to teach students to manage conflicts constructively if the school is structured so that students are pitted against each other in competition for scarce rewards (like teacher attention and grades of "A") and students have to defeat each other to get what they want. In competition, rewards are restricted to the few who perform the best (Deutsch, 1973; Johnson & Johnson, 1989). The research indicates that competitors typically have a short-term time orientation and focus all their energies on winning. They tend to pay little or no attention to the long-term interest in maintaining good relationships. Competitors tend to avoid communicating with each other, misperceive each other's position and motivations, be suspicious of each other, deny the legitimacy of others' needs and feelings, and see the situation only from their own perspective. Conflicts almost always are managed destructively in a competitive context.

In order for conflicts to be resolved constructively, a cooperative context must be established (Deutsch, 1973; Johnson & Johnson, 1998). The research indicates that in a cooperative context there are mutual goals that all participants are committed to achieving. Cooperators tend to seek outcomes that are beneficial to everyone involved. They typically have a long-term time orientation and focus their energies both on achieving goals and on maintaining good working relationships with others. Communication tends to be frequent, complete, and accurate with each person interested in informing the other as well as being informed. Cooperators tend to perceive accurately other participants' positions and motivations. Since they tend to trust and like each other, they are usually willing to respond helpfully to each other's wants, needs, and requests. Cooperators tend to recognize the legitimacy of each other's interests and search for a solution accommodating the needs of both sides. Conflicts tend to be defined as mutual problems to be solved in ways that benefit everyone involved. A cooperative context is most easily established by structuring the majority of learning situations cooperatively (Johnson & Johnson, 1989;

Johnson, D. W., & Johnson, R. (2005). **Teaching Students To Be Peacemakers** (4th Ed.). Edina, MN: Interaction Book Company, (952)831-9500.

Johnson, Johnson, & Holubec, 1998). Because of the substantial research indicating that cooperative learning has a wide variety of positive effects on student learning and cognitive and social development, it is being implemented widely (Deutsch, 1973; Johnson & Johnson, 1989). To create a cooperative school, (a) teachers use cooperative learning the majority of the time to promote student achievement, positive relationships among students, and psychological health, (b) faculty are organized into collegial teaching teams, and (c) cooperative procedures are used when faculty make schoolwide decisions. Such a cooperative context gives disputants a stake in each other's present and future success and well-being and, therefore, motivates them to resolve conflicts constructively.

Step Six: Train Students To Focus On Both Goals And Relationships

The sixth step is to train students to keep two concerns in mind when resolving conflicts: (a) the importance of the goals they are trying to achieve and (b) the importance of their relationship with the other person. In dealing with conflicts disputants can withdraw (giving up both the relationship and their goals), force (negotiate in a win-lose manner), smooth (giving up one's goals to maintain relationship at a high level), compromise (giving up part of their goals and part of the relationship), or solve the problem in a way that all parties get what they want. In long-term, ongoing relationships, maintaining a high quality relationship is more important than is achieving one's goals on any one issue. In ongoing relationships disputants (a) do not withdraw from or ignore the conflict, (b) do not engage in win-lose negotiations, (c) do assess for smoothing, (d) do compromise when time is short, (e) do initiate problem-solving negotiations, and (f) do use sense of humor.

Step Seven: Train All Students To Negotiate To Solve The Problem

Step Seven is to train all school members to engage in problem solving negotiations. To do so they must describe what they want and how they feel, describe the reasons underlying their position, communicate that they understand the opposing perspective, generate at least three optional agreements that maximize the mutual gain of all disputants, and choose one option and agree. Students memorize the six steps of problem solving negotiations, practice them with their classmates, and use them in real conflicts until the procedure is overlearned. Students may have to engage in the procedure dozens and dozens of times before it becomes automatic.

One of the most difficult aspects of initiating problem-solving negotiations is managing emotions. Managing anger is especially problematic. Anger tends to be destructive when (a) students express anger in a way that creates dislike, hatred, frustration, and a desire for revenge on the part of the other person or (b) anger is repressed and held inside (which

Johnson, D. W., & Johnson, R. (2005). **Teaching Students To Be Peacemakers** (4th Ed.). Edina, MN: Interaction Book Company, (952)831-9500.

tends to create irritability, depression, insomnia, and physiological problems such as headaches and ulcers). Anger tends to be constructive when its expression results in students feeling energized, motivated, challenged, and excited, and the recipient feeling friendship, gratitude, goodwill, and concern. To manage anger constructively students need to recognize and acknowledge that they are angry. They decide whether or not to express the anger. The anger can be expressed directly and descriptively when it is appropriate to do so. The anger could also be expressed indirectly or students could move to an alternative feeling when direct expression of anger is not appropriate. Students should congratulate themselves on managing anger constructively and express any other emotions (such as respect or appreciation) directly and descriptively.

Step Eight: Train All Students To Mediate

Step Eight is to train all school members in how to mediate conflicts. Mediation consists of ending hostilities, ensuring disputants are committed to the mediation process, facilitating problem-solving negotiations, and finalizing the agreement. Students memorize the four-step procedure, practice it over and over again, and use it until it is overlearned and automatic. It is the experience of mediating schoolmates' conflicts that may best teach students the importance of each step of the negotiation procedure.

Step Nine: Arbitrate As Last Resort

Step Nine is for teachers (or administrators) to arbitrate as a last resort when mediation by a peer and mediation by the teacher has failed. Arbitration consists of listening carefully to disputants, allowing them to present their best case, and making a binding decision as to how the conflict may best be resolved. In essence, teachers (and administrators) are a mediator/arbitrator. They first mediate any conflicts that cannot be mediated by a student, then arbitrate if their mediation efforts fail. The shortcomings of arbitration are such that it is to be used as a last resort only.

Step Ten: Implement Peer Mediation Program

Step Ten is to implement the peer mediation program so that all students gain experience in mediating their schoolmates' conflicts. Each day mediators are chosen and make themselves available to help resolve student conflicts. The responsibility is rotated so that every student in the school serves as mediator an equal amount of time.

Step Eleven: Continuously Train Students For Twelve Years

Step Eleven is to provide continuous negotiation and mediation training throughout the school year. Training may be given throughout the school year by conducting skill-

Johnson, D. W., & Johnson, R. (2005). **Teaching Students To Be Peacemakers** (4th Ed.). Edina, MN: Interaction Book Company, (952)831-9500.

building lessons and by integrating the problem-solving negotiation and mediation procedures into academic lessons. Teachers may weave constructive conflict resolution procedures and skills into the fabric of school life by teaching the procedures in many classes, discussing them in the school newspaper, modeling them in faculty meetings, and posting the negotiation steps throughout the school. The norms, values, and culture of the school need to promote and support the use of the negotiation and mediation procedures. The full negotiation and mediation training should be repeated every year at a higher level of complexity and sophistication.

Step Twelve: Frequently Use Academic Controversies

Step Twelve is to have teachers use academic controversy to increase student achievement, higher-level reasoning, motivation to learn, and conflict skills (Johnson & Johnson, 1979, 1989, 1995, 2003). **Academic controversy** exists when one student's ideas, information, conclusions, theories, and opinions are incompatible with those of another, and the two seek to reach an agreement. We (with colleagues such as Dean Tjosvold and Karl Smith) have developed a theory of controversy, tested it with over 20 experimental and field-experimental studies, developed curriculum units on energy and environmental issues, and trained teachers to use academic controversies in schools and colleges throughout North America, and a number of other countries. The procedure for structuring academic controversies is to have students (a) prepare scholarly positions on an academic issue, (b) advocate them, (c) refute the opposing positions while rebutting criticisms of their position, (d) view the issue from both perspectives, and (e) come to a consensus about their "best reasoned judgment" based on a synthesis of the two positions. Participating in academic controversies teaches students how to engage in social skills such as "criticizing ideas without criticizing people." The skills learned in controversy support and reinforce the skills used in negotiation and mediation.

Looking Forward

Following these twelve steps will result in a more peaceful school and eventually a more peaceful world.

A better life within the school and a more peaceful classroom begins with each individual student being better able to face conflicts and find ways to ensure that all participants benefit by the solution of underlying problems. There are few things more important for future quality of life and career success than teaching students how to manage conflicts constructively. Negotiation procedures and skills are carried with the student wherever he or she goes and, once acquired, cannot be taken away. They are a gift of incalculable value.

Johnson, D. W., & Johnson, R. (2005). **Teaching Students To Be Peacemakers** (4th Ed.). Edina, MN: Interaction Book Company, (952)831-9500.

Now that you have reached the end of this book you are at a new beginning. Years of experience in using the negotiation and mediation procedures and skills are needed to gain real expertise in managing conflicts constructively. The more you negotiate, the more you mediate, the more you will learn. Your understanding of how to build a cooperative context, choose a strategy to implement (withdrawal, smooth, force, compromise, negotiate to solve the problem), how to engage in problem-solving negotiations, how to manage anger constructively, and how to mediate will deepen as you carefully apply each in new conflict situations. In the end you may find that conflicts are opportunities to view a problem more clearly, create new positions, achieve new perspectives, and make better friends. It is through conflict that we grow, develop, learn, progress, and achieve. You will find that conflicts enrich rather than disrupt your life.

Johnson, D. W., & Johnson, R. (2005). **Teaching Students To Be Peacemakers** (4th Ed.). Edina, MN: Interaction Book Company, (952)831-9500.

How To Mediate

A **mediator** is a neutral person who helps two or more people (called disputants) resolve their conflict. The mediator has no formal power over either disputant. A mediator does **not** tell disputants what to do or decide who is right and who is wrong. When you mediate you stand in the middle and assist disputants to go through each step of problem-solving negotiations so that they reach an agreement that is fair, just, and workable.

1. **End hostilities and cool down disputants**: Usually disputants ask the mediator for help. In some cases the mediator may see a dispute taking place and ask if he or she can be of service. In rare instances, the mediator may need to get a teacher or administrator to break up a fight. The mediator must make sure that all disputants are emotionally capable of problem solving and conflict resolution. If disputants are too angry to problem solve, then they must be cooled down before mediation begins.

2. **Ensure both people are committed to the mediation process**: To ensure that both persons are committed to the mediation process and are ready to negotiate in good faith, , the mediator introduces the process of mediation, sets the ground rules, and introduces him- or herself. The mediator must make sure that disputants understand the process of mediation and have committed themselves to making it succeed.

3. **Help the disputants negotiate with each other successfully**: This includes taking the two disputants through the problem-solving negotiation sequence of:

   a. Describing what they want.

   b. Describing how they feel.

   c. Describing their reasons for wanting what they want and feeling as they do.

   d. Reversing perspectives so that each disputant is able to present the other's wants, feelings, and reasons to the other's satisfaction.

   e. Inventing at least three options for mutual benefit.

   f. Reaching a wise agreement and sealing it with a handshake.

   The mediator moderates the negotiations, making sure that all steps are engaged in, that each disputant feels listened to and understood, and that the disputants understand each other's wants, feelings, and reasons.

4. **Formalize the agreement**: The agreement is solidified into a contract. The mediator completes a **Mediation Report Form** that disputants sign, signifying their agreement to abide by the final decision and the mediator becomes "*the keeper of the contract.*"

9 : 11

Johnson, D. W., & Johnson, R. (2005). **Teaching Students To Be Peacemakers** (4th Ed.). Edina, MN: Interaction Book Company, (952)831-9500.

Implementing The Peer Mediation Program

Once students understand how to negotiate and mediate, the teacher implements the peacemaker program. There are two versions of the program--elementary and secondary. The **elementary version** is as follows:

Each day the teacher selects two class members to serve as official mediators. The teacher may randomly choose students to be mediators, or the teacher may carefully match students into pairs so that introverted students may be paired with extroverts, students with low academic skills may be paired with high-achieving students, and so forth. Initially, mediators work in pairs. When all students are experienced enough to be comfortable with being a mediator, then they may mediate individually.

The mediators wear official T-shirts, hats, or armbands so that they are easily recognized. They patrol the playground and lunchroom. Generally, the mediators are available to mediate any conflicts that occur in the classroom or school.

Any conflicts students cannot resolve themselves are referred to the class mediators. The mediators end hostilities, ensure disputants are committed to the process of mediation, facilitate negotiations, and formalize the agreement.

Any conflicts the students cannot resolve with the help of a peer mediator are referred to the teacher, who first mediates and then, if necessary, arbitrates.

The role of class mediator is rotated throughout the class so that all students serve as class mediator an equal amount of time. Mediating classmates' conflicts is perhaps the most effective and dramatic way of teaching students the need for the skillful use of each step of the negotiation procedure.

Refresher lessons are taught twice a week throughout the school year to refine students' negotiation and mediation skills.

The **secondary program** is very similar, except that a certain number of school mediators are chosen from each grade level (two mediators for every thirty students or so) and the role of mediator is rotated throughout the school so that all students serve as school mediator an equal amount of time.

9 : 12

Johnson, D. W., & Johnson, R. (2005). **Teaching Students To Be Peacemakers** (4th Ed.). Edina, MN: Interaction Book Company, (952)831-9500.

Chapter Ten: Summary And Conclusions

The Lure Of Going For The "Win"

No logic or wisdom or will-power could prevail to stop the sailors. Buffeted by the hardships of life at sea, the voices came out of the mist to the ancient Greek sailors like a mystical, ethereal love song with tempting and seductive promises of ecstasy and delight. The voices and the song were irresistible. The mariners helplessly turned their ships to follow the Sirens' call with scarcely a second thought. Lured to their destruction, the sailors crashed their ships on the waiting rocks and drowned in the tossing waves, struggling with their last breath to reach the source of that beckoning song.

Centuries later, the Sirens still call. Educators seem drawn to competitive learning, crashing their teaching on the rocks due to the seductive and tempting attractions of trying to find out which student is "best." Students are also captured by the seduction of wanting to build their successes on the failures of their classmates. And when conflicts occur, going for the "win" has an irresistible call to many. Striving to solve the problem so both sides benefit may seem idealistic but undoable. Cooperative learning provides a far more effective alternative to competition and creates the foundation within which conflicts may be managed constructively. Problem-solving negotiations provide an alternative to the "win-lose" approach to resolving conflicts and teach students the procedures and skills required to work effectively with classmates and faculty to maximize their education and cognitive and social development.

Peer Mediation

Suzzane, who is a new student from another country, sits down to eat lunch with several classmates. Pam says, *"This is 'invitation only.' No foreigners allowed."* Suzzane, her feelings obviously hurt, says, "Sorry" and walks away. *"That's terrible,"* Mary says to Pam. *"You shouldn't have done that."* *"You're such a 'goody-goody',"* Pam replies. *"We don't want you here either!"* Mary and Pam get more and more angry and begin yelling at each other. Things come to a head when Pam pushes Mary.

Conflicts occur all the time in school. They are a natural, inevitable, potentially constructive, and normal part of school life. While in extreme cases conflicts erupt into violence, most conflicts among students are far milder, involving disagreements over rumors, name calling, boyfriends/girlfriends, and the like. Some of the conflicts are resolved. Many, if not most, are not. In most cases, students either escalate conflicts in destructive ways or disengage harboring anger and resentments that continue to simmer underneath the surface. Covert conflicts then exist in which students sit in classrooms and "fester" about their

Figure 10.1 The Twelve Steps

Step One:	Face Reality of Destructive Conflicts
Step Two:	Implement A Violence Prevention Program
Step Three:	Make The School A Conflict Positive Organization
Step Four:	Establish A Comprehensive Conflict Resolution Training Program
Step Five:	Create A Cooperative Context For Conflict
Step Six:	Train Students To Focus On Both Goals And Relationships
Step Seven:	Train All Students To Negotiate To Solve The Problem
Step Eight:	Train All Students To Mediate
Step Nine:	Arbitrate As Last Resort
Step Ten:	Implement Peer Mediation Program
Step Eleven:	Continuously Train Students For Twelve Years
Step Twelve:	Frequently Use Academic Controversies

perceived grievances. Until covert conflicts are made overt and resolved, students cannot focus their attention on learning.

Several factors contribute to students' failures to resolve their conflicts constructively. Students often are from different cultural, ethnic, social class, and language backgrounds. Different students often have quite different ideas about how conflicts should be managed. The procedures and strategies students use to manage their conflicts are quite often inadequate and destructive, making things worse rather than better. Students may get angry, fight, hurl verbal abuse at each other, verbally harass each other, ignore the conflict, take their anger out on someone/something else, play head-games, or fantasize how to get revenge. These methods generally provide little chance of resolving any problems and often result in alienating students from their peers and the school staff. Most students simply do not know how to manage their conflicts constructively.

Under these circumstances, conflict can produce chaos. Teachers can respond by being police officers, arbitrators, or mediators. Ideally, however, teachers will co-orient students by teaching them the procedures and skills required to manage conflicts constructively. Conflicts, no matter what, occur all the time in school and only students themselves can restore order and peace. What is needed is a training program that creates a shared set of procedures and strategies for negotiating solutions to joint problems and mediating conflicts among classmates.

In the above example, Mary and Pam need a peer mediator to help them resolve their conflict (so do Pam and Suzzane). Roger is a class mediator for that day. He approaches Mary and Pam, separates them, helps them cool down. He then meets with them and ensures that they are committed to mediating their conflict. He asks if they want to solve the problem and does not proceed until both answer "yes." Since the role of mediator is rotated through the class, both Pam and Mary have themselves been mediators and will be again. This increases their willingness to participate in the process. Then Roger explains:

- *"Mediation is voluntary. My role is to help you find a solution to your conflict that is acceptable to both of you."*

- *"I am neutral. I will not take sides or attempt to decide who is right or wrong. I will help you decide how to solve the conflict."*

- *"Each person will have the chance to state his or her view of the conflict without interruption."*

- *"The rules you must agree to are (a) agree to solve the problem, (b) no name calling, (c) do not interrupt, and (d) be as honest as you can."*

- *"If you agree to a solution, you must abide by it. You must do what you have agreed to do."*

- *"Anything said in mediation is confidential. I will not tell anyone what is said."*

Roger reminds Mary and Pam that they are friends, are in many of the same classes, and participate in many of the same activities. He then leads them through the negotiation procedure. Each states what she wants. Each states how she feels. Each states the reasons for her wants and feelings. Each summarizes her understanding of what the other wants, how the other feels, and the reasons underlying both. Roger helps Mary and Pam invent three optional plans to resolve their conflict. They then choose the one they like the best and shake hands. Finally, Roger closes the mediation session by formalizing the agreement and stating he would check in with them in a few days to see if the agreement was working.

Conflict management procedures and skills are too important to leave to chance. Children and adolescents need to be directly taught in school the negotiation procedures and skills and given the mediation experiences that will help them live happy and successful lives. When students are taught how to manage conflicts constructively, they become peacemakers. Part of every student's responsibilities is to manage his or her conflicts constructively and help schoolmates do likewise.

The Twelve Step Program

Providing students with an orderly environment in which to learn and even guaranteeing students' safety is becoming more and more difficult in many schools. An increasing number of public and private teachers and administrators face situations involving serious conflicts among students and between students and faculty. Despite the widespread concern, however, very little information exists as to how to help students resolve their conflicts constructively. In response to the problems arising from frequent and destructive conflicts, schools are adopting various violence prevention and conflict resolution programs. There are three reasons for teaching all students in all schools how to manage conflicts constructively. The **first** is to make schools orderly and peaceful places in which high quality education can take place. The **second** is to utilize for instructional purposes the powerful potential of conflict to gain and hold attention, increase motivation to learn, arouse intellectual curiosity, and improve the quality and creativeness of problem solving. The **third** is to ensure that future generations are prepared to manage future conflicts constructively in career, family, community, national, and international settings.

To eliminate violence and reduce discipline problems, schools need to engage in a twelve step process.

Step One: Face Reality Of Destructive Conflicts

The first step is for schools to admit that destructive conflicts (reflected in the verbal and physical violence, discipline problems, and incivility) are out of control and it is not *"just a few trouble-makers"* or *"just a passing phase."* In order to make the school a safe and orderly place in which to learn, the problems of student violence and increasing frequency and seriousness of discipline problems have to be faced. Even in wealthiest school districts, student incivility and disrespect for faculty and for each other is a problem that needs to be corrected.

Step Two: Implement A Violence Prevention Program

Step Two is for schools to implement a violence prevention program. Actions may be taken to reduce the number of weapons in school, suppress violent behavior, train faculty to recognize potentially violent situations and intervene, target students who repeatedly engage in violence for special attention, lead discussions of how to avoid violence, teach students how to cognitively control and manage their anger, create a district violence plan, adopt a threat-management policy, provide aftermath debriefing for victims and bystanders, and install a weapons hotline. Such violence prevention procedures are a good idea but do not go far enough. Trying to eliminate violent behaviors without placing them with more constructive actions will have little effect. Students must be taught conflict resolution procedures and have peer mediators available to facilitate integrative negotiations.

Step Three: Make The School A Conflict Positive Organization

The third step is for schools to implement the changes they need to become a conflict positive organization. Faculty and students must recognize that conflicts are inevitable, healthy, and potentially valuable. Given that all students, faculty, and staff are skilled in resolving conflicts constructively, conflicts should be encouraged not avoided or suppressed. Faculty and students must understand what conflicts are, differentiate among types of conflicts, know how to make conflicts constructive rather than destructive, know the positive outcomes that can result from conflict, and ensure that faculty and students use the same constructive procedures for resolving conflicts.

One reason to encourage conflicts is that students face a developmental imperative to engage in conflicts with adults and peers. Developmental conflicts reoccur over and over again and cycle in and out of peak intensity as students mature physically, socially, and cognitively. Students work to establish and understand their dependence versus independence, security in the status quo versus demand for growth and change, and impulsive satisfaction of needs versus delay of gratification. Students overassimilate and push their demands to the extreme. Adults such as teachers and/or peers are forced into placing social constraints on the student and clarifying what is and is not appropriate behavior. Ideally, students accommodate the social constraints and move to the next level of social and cognitive development.

Step Four: Establish A Comprehensive Conflict Resolution Training Program

Step Four is for schools to establish a comprehensive conflict resolution training program. The program should be clearly based on the theory and research on conflict resolution. An ongoing assessment of the effectiveness of the program should be built into its implementation. To ensure it lasts long enough to become a permanent and traditional aspect of school life, the program has to be linked with academic achievement. Bridges need to be built with nonacademic programs. A comprehensive conflict resolution program has three major components: creating a cooperative context, implementing a conflict resolution / peer mediation program, and using academic controversies for instructional purposes. Every member of the school, student and faculty alike, need to learn the same set of procedures for managing conflicts constructively.

Step Five: Create A Cooperative Context For Conflict

The fifth step is to create a cooperative context for conflict by making the school a learning community in which students work together cooperatively to ensure that all learn. There are two possible contexts for conflict: cooperative and competitive (in individualistic situations, people do not interact and, therefore, no conflict occurs) (Deutsch, 1973; Johnson & Johnson, 1989). It makes little sense to attempt to teach students to manage conflicts constructively if the school is structured so that students are pitted against each other in competition for scarce rewards (like teacher attention and grades of "A") and students have to defeat each other to get what they want. In competition, rewards are restricted to the few who perform the best (Deutsch, 1973; Johnson & Johnson, 1989). The research indicates that competitors typically have a short-term time orientation and focus all their energies on winning. They tend to pay little or no attention to the long-term interest in maintaining good relationships. Competitors tend to avoid communicating with each other, misperceive each other's position and motivations, be suspicious of each other, deny the legitimacy of others' needs and feelings, and see the situation only from their own perspective. Conflicts almost always are managed destructively in a competitive context.

In order for conflicts to be resolved constructively, a cooperative context must be established (Deutsch, 1973; Johnson & Johnson, 1993). The research indicates that in a cooperative context there are mutual goals that all participants are committed to achieving. Cooperators tend to seek outcomes that are beneficial to everyone involved. They typically have a long-term time orientation and focus their energies both on achieving goals and on maintaining good working relationships with others. Communication tends to be frequent, complete, and accurate with each person interested in informing the other as well as being informed. Cooperators tend to perceive accurately other participants' positions and motivations. Since they tend to trust and like each other, they are usually willing to respond helpfully to each other's wants, needs, and requests. Cooperators tend to recognize the legitimacy of each other's interests and search for a solution accommodating the needs of both sides. Conflicts tend to be defined as mutual problems to be solved in ways that benefit everyone involved. A cooperative context is most easily established by structuring the majority of learning situations cooperatively (Johnson & Johnson, 1989; Johnson, Johnson, & Holubec, 1993). Because of the substantial research indicating that cooperative learning has a wide variety of positive effects on student learning and cognitive and social development, it is being implemented widely (Deutsch, 1973; Johnson & Johnson, 1989). To create a cooperative school, (a) teachers use cooperative learning the majority of the time to promote student achievement, positive relationships among students, and psychological health, (b) faculty are organized into colleagial teaching teams, and (c) cooperative procedures are used when faculty make schoolwide decisions. Such a cooperative context gives disputants a stake in each other's present and future success and well-being and, therefore, motive them to resolve conflicts constructively.

Step Six: Train Students To Focus On Both Goals And Relationships

The sixth step is to train students to keep two concerns in mind when resolving conflicts: (a) the importance of the goals they are trying to achieve and (b) the importance of their relationship with the other person. In dealing with conflicts disputants can withdraw, force (negotiate in a win-lose manner), smooth, compromise, or solve the problem in a way that all parties get what they want. In long-term, ongoing relationships, maintaining a high quality relationship is more importance than is achieving one's goals on any one issue. There are six rules to follow in doing so. In ongoing relationships disputants (a) do not withdraw from or ignore the conflict, (b) do not engage in win-lose negotiations, (c) assess for smoothing, (d) compromise when time is short, (e) initiate problem-solving negotiations, and (f) use their sense of humor. Engaging in problem-solving negotiations, however, takes considerable skill.

Step Seven: Train All Students To Negotiate To Solve The Problem

Step Seven is to train all school members to engage in problem solving negotiations. To do so they must describe what they want and how they feel, describe the reasons underlying their position, communicate that they understand the opposing perspective, generate at least three optional agreements that maximize the mutual gain of all disputants, and choose one option and agree. Students memorize the six steps of problem solving negotiations, practice them with their classmates, and use them in real conflicts until the procedure is overlearned and automatic. Teachers, therefore, must have students practice the steps daily.

One of the most difficult aspects of initiating problem-solving negotiations is managing emotions. Managing anger is especially problematic. Anger tends to be destructive when (a) students express anger in a way that creates dislike, hatred, frustration, and a desire for revenge on the part of the other person or (b) anger is repressed and held inside (which tends to create irritability, depression, insomnia, and physiological problems such as headaches and ulcers). Anger tends to be

constructive when students feel energized, motivated, challenged, and excited, and the other person feels friendship, gratitude, goodwill, and concern. To manage anger constructively students need to recognize and acknowledge that they are angry. They decide whether or not to express the anger. The anger can be expressed directly and descriptively when it is appropriate to do so. The anger could also be expressed indirectly or students could move to an alternative feeling when direct expression of anger is not appropriate. During it all, students should stay task oriented. They analyze, understand, and reflect on their anger. They congratulate themselves on managing anger constructively and express any other emotions (such as respect or appreciation) directly and descriptively.

Step Eight: Train All Students To Mediate

Step Eight is to train all school members in how to mediate conflicts. Mediation consists of ending hostilities, ensuring disputants are committed to the mediation process, facilitating problem-solving negotiations, and finalizing the agreement. Students memorize the four-step procedure, practice it over and over again, and use it until it is overlearned and automatic. It is the experience of mediating schoolmates' conflicts that may best teach students the importance of each step of the negotiation procedure.

Step Nine: Arbitrate As Last Resort

Step Nine is for teachers (or administrators) to arbitrate as a last resort when mediation by a peer and mediation by the teacher has failed. Arbitration consists of listening carefully to disputants, allowing them to present their best case, and making a binding decision as to how the conflict may best be resolved. In essence, teachers (and administrators) are a mediator/arbitrator. They first mediate any conflicts that cannot be mediated by a student, then arbitrate if their mediation efforts fail. The shortcomings of arbitration are such that it is to be used as a last resort only.

Step Ten: Implement Peer Mediation Program

Step Ten is to implement the peer mediation program so that all students gain experience in mediating their schoolmates' conflicts. Each day mediators are chosen and make themselves available to help resolve student conflicts. The responsibility is rotated so that every student in the school serves as mediator an equal amount of time. If not enough conflicts need mediation and, therefore, students do not get much experience mediating, teachers may have students mediate conflicts derived from literature, history, and even fairy tales.

Step Eleven: Continuously Train Students For Twelve Years

Step Eleven is to provide continuous negotiation and mediation training for twelve years. Gaining expertise in negotiation and mediation is a life-long process. It cannot be done in a three hour or even three day workshop. Students (and faculty) integrate the negotiation and mediation procedures into their behavioral repertoire by using the procedures daily. Training may be given throughout the school year by integrating the problem-solving negotiation and mediation procedures into academic lessons. Teachers weave constructive conflict resolution procedures and skills into the fabric of school life by teaching the procedures in many classes, discussing them in the school newspaper, modeling them in faculty meetings, and posting the negotiation steps throughout the school. The norms, values, and culture of the school need to promote and support the use of the negotiation and mediation procedures. The full negotiation and mediation training should be repeated every year at a higher level of complexity and sophistication.

Step Twelve: Frequently Use Academic Controversies

Step Twelve is to have teachers use academic controversy to increase student achievement, higher-level reasoning, motivation to learn, and conflict skills. **Academic controversy** exists when one student's ideas, information, conclusions, theories, and opinions are incompatible with those of another, and the two seek to reach an agreement. Over the past 25 years, we (with such colleagues as Dean Tjosvold and Karl Smith) have developed a theory of controversy, tested it by conducting over 20 experimental and field-experimental studies, developed a series of curriculum units on energy and environmental issues structured for academic controversies, and trained teachers to use academic controversies in schools and colleges throughout the United States, Canada, and a number of other countries (Johnson & Johnson, 1979, 1989, 1992). Structuring academic controversy into learning situations results in students learning that conflicts are potentially constructive and even enjoyable. The procedure for structuring academic controversies is to have students (a) prepare scholarly positions on an academic issue, (b) advocate them, (c) refute the opposing positions while rebutting criticisms of their position, (d) view the issue from both perspectives, and (e) come to a consensus about their "best reasoned judgment" based on a synthesis of the two positions. Participating in academic controversies teaches students how to (a) prepare, present, and defend a position, (b) take an opposing perspective, (c) make creative, high-quality decisions that integrate the best information and reasoning from both sides, and (d) engage in a set of social skills such as "criticizing ideas without criticizing people." Similar to cooperative learning, the use of academic controversy may be welcomed by educators because it results in increased student achievement, critical thinking, higher-level reasoning, intrinsic motivation to learn, and a number of other important educational outcomes (Johnson & Johnson, 1979, 1989, 1992). Engaging in academic controversies demonstrates the value of conflict and promotes positive attitudes toward engaging in conflict. The skills learned in controversy support and reinforce the skills used in negotiation and mediation. A detailed program to train teachers in how to structure academic controversies to ensure that all students are intellectually challenged within the classroom is presented in **Creative Controversy: Intellectual Challenge In The Classroom** (Johnson & Johnson, 1987/1992).

Final Word

Following these twelve steps will result in a more peaceful school and eventually a more peaceful world.

Teaching students how to manage conflicts constructively has many benefits for the school. When students learn how to manage their conflicts constructively the learning climate of the classroom and school change dramatically. Discipline problems are reduced as students resolve their problems without needing help and assistance from faculty and staff. Teachers have more time to teach. Time-on-task increases. A better life within the school and a more peaceful classroom begins with each individual student being better able to face conflicts and find ways to ensure that all participants benefit by the solution of underlying problems.

Knowing how to negotiate and how to mediate has far ranging effects on students. Without the ability to negotiate solutions to joint problems it is difficult to maintain caring and committed relationships over a long period of time. Resolving many of the developmental imperatives requires negotiating with parents and other adults. Conflicts with others, when managed constructively, help clarify one's values, attitudes, and identity and how one needs to change. Knowing how to negotiate and mediate teaches students both interpersonal and academic skills, improves cooperative work, increases students' commitment to education, and prepares students to be citizens in a complex and conflict-filled world. The more students learn how to take a cooperative approach to managing conflicts through joint problem-solving, the healthier psychologically they tend to be and the better able they are to deal with stress and adversity and cope with life's challenges and unforeseen adversity. There are few things more important for future quality of life and career success than teaching students how to manage conflicts constructively. Negotiation procedures and skills are carried with the student wherever he or she goes and, once acquired, cannot be taken away. They are a gift of incalculable value.

Looking Forward

Now that you have reached the end of this book you are at a new beginning. Years of experience in using the negotiation and mediation procedures and skills are needed to gain real expertise in managing conflicts constructively. The more you negotiate, the more you mediate, the more you will learn. Your understanding of how to build a cooperative context, how to negotiate, how to initiate negotiations, how to manage anger constructively, and how to mediate will deepen as you carefully apply each to new conflict situations. In the end you may find that conflicts offer the chance to see a problem more clearly, get new ideas, achieve new perspectives, and make better friends. It is through conflict that we grow, develop, learn, progress, and achieve. In the end you may find that conflicts enrich rather than disrupt your life.

Appendix A: Research On The Teaching Students To Be Peacemakers Program

The **Teaching Students To Be Peacemakers Program** (TSP) was developed in the mid-1960s as an application of social interdependence theory (Deutsch, 1962; Johnson & Johnson, 1989) and two of its subtheories, Two-Concerns Theory and Integrative Negotiation Theory. It is the most validated conflict resolution program currently being implemented in schools. The procedures reflect the authors' research on creating a cooperative context, establishing joint goals, expressing cooperative intentions, perspective-taking, expressing emotions in negotiations, equalizing power, and integrative negotiations. The Peacemaker Program has been implemented in schools throughout North America, and in several countries in Central and South America, Europe, the Middle East, Africa, Asia, and the Pacific Rim. The materials in this book have been translated into several different languages.

A meta-analysis has been reported on sixteen studies conducted on the effectiveness of the Peacemaker Program in eight different schools in two different countries (Johnson & Johnson, 2002). The studies included students from kindergarten through tenth grade and were conducted in rural, suburban, and urban settings in the United States and Canada. In most of the studies, students were randomly assigned to conditions and teachers were rotated across conditions. These carefully controlled field-experimental studies addressed a series of questions.

1. How often and what types of conflicts occur among students?"

2. What strategies did students use to manage their conflicts before training?

3. Was the training successful in teaching students the conflict procedures?

4. Can trained students engage in the integrative negotiation and mediation procedures in actual conflicts?

5. Will students use the negotiation and mediation procedures in actual conflicts?

6. Do students transfer the negotiation and mediation procedures to nonclassroom and nonschool situations?

7. When given a choice, do students engage in win-lose or problem-solving negotiations?

8. What is the quality of the resolutions?

Johnson, D. W., & Johnson, R. (2005). **Teaching Students To Be Peacemakers** (4th Ed.). Edina, MN: Interaction Book Company, (952)831-9500.

9. Does the Peacemaker training result in more positive attitudes toward conflict?

10. Does integrating the training into academic lessons increase achievement?

11. Does the TSP training result in fewer discipline problems that have to be managed by the teacher and the administration?

12. Do faculty, administrators, and parents perceive the conflict resolution positively?

13. What is the impact of the training on students' values?

Frequency And Types Of Conflicts

"How often do conflicts among students occur and what are the most commonly occurring conflicts?" The research indicates that students engage in conflicts several times a day. While in the suburban schools studied, the majority of conflicts reported were over the possession and access to resources, preferences about what to do, playground issues, and turn-taking, in the urban elementary school studied, the vast majority of conflicts referred to mediation involved physical and verbal aggression. Students described more different types of conflicts at school than at home. The conflicts at home tended to be over preferences, possessions, and access; few conflicts were reported over beliefs and relationships or involved physical fights and verbal insults. Very few conflicts occurred over academic work or basic values in either setting.

Strategies Before Training

"What strategies did students use to manage their conflicts before training?" Before training, students tended to manage their conflicts through trying to win by (a) forcing the other to concede (either by overpowering the other disputant or by asking the teacher to force the other to give in) or (b) withdrawing from the conflict and the other person. The possibility of problem-solving, integrative negotiations seemed to never to occur to most students. One of the teachers stated in her log, "*Before training, students viewed conflict as fights that always resulted in a winner and a loser. To avoid such an unpleasant situation, they usually placed the responsibility for resolving conflicts on me, the teacher.*"

Learning Problem-Solving Negotiation And Mediation Procedures

"Was the Peacemaker training successful in teaching students the negotiation and mediation procedures?" Following training, students were given a test requiring them to write from memory the steps of negotiation and the procedures for mediation. Across the studies, over 90 percent of the students accurately recalled 100 percent of the negotiation steps and the mediation procedure. Up to a year after the training had ended, on average over 75 percent of students were still able to write out all the negotiation and mediation

Johnson, D. W., & Johnson, R. (2005). **Teaching Students To Be Peacemakers** (4th Ed.). Edina, MN: Interaction Book Company, (952)831-9500.

steps. The average effect size for the studies was 2.25 for the immediate post-test and 3.34 for the retention measures (see Table 2). The training was quite effective.

Engaging In The Negotiation And Mediation Procedures

"Can trained students engage in the integrative negotiation and mediation procedures in actual conflicts?" Learning the negotiation and mediation procedures does not necessarily mean that students will use them in actual conflict situations. We used both paper-and-pencil and observation measures to determine whether students could use the procedures in actual conflicts. Students wrote out descriptions of conflicts they were involved in or were observed in actual conflicts with their classmates. The results indicate that students were quite good at applying the six-step integrative negotiation and the four step mediation procedures (see Table 2). Immediately after training, students engaged in the procedures almost perfectly (effect size = 2.16) and were still quite good in engaging in the procedures months after the training was over (effect size = 0.46).

Post-Training Strategies Used To Resolve Conflicts

"Will students use the negotiation and mediation procedures in conflicts?" Learning the negotiation and mediation procedures does not necessarily mean that students will use them in actual conflict situations. The extent to which trained students used the procedures was measured in five ways:

1. Conflict Report Forms on which students periodically recorded the conflicts they were involved in.

2. Written responses to conflict scenarios: Students were given descriptions of conflict situations (such as a conflict over access to a computer or a personal insult through name calling) and asked to write out how they would resolve the conflict.

3. Oral responses to conflict scenarios given in an interview: Students were individually interviewed. A description of a conflict was read to them, and they were asked to explain how they would resolve it.

4. Role playing responses to conflict scenarios that were videotaped: Students were randomly assigned to pairs, each assigned a role in a common conflict, and asked to role play how they would resolve it. They were videotaped doing so.

5. Actual conflicts created with a classmate: Students (a) ranked several alternative ways of completing an assignment, (b) were paired with another student who ranked the alternatives differently, (c) resolved the conflict by deciding which alternative to adopt, and (d) wrote out the actions they took (step by step).

A : 3

Johnson, D. W., & Johnson, R. (2005). **Teaching Students To Be Peacemakers** (4th Ed.). Edina, MN: Interaction Book Company, (952)831-9500.

© Johnson & Johnson

Table A:1 Summary Of Conflict Resolution And Peer Mediation Studies

Study	Year	Setting	School	Grades	Training Length	Sample Size	Control	Random -ization	Teacher Rotation
Johnson, Johnson, & Dudley	88 - 89	Suburban	Cornelia Elementary, Edina, MN	1 - 6	15 Hours, 30 Days	138 (WC)	Yes	Control Classes Randomly Selected	Yes
Johnson, Johnson, Dudley, Acikgoz	90 - 91	Suburban	Highlands Elementary, Edina, MN	1 - 6	15 Hours, 30 Days	92 (WC)	No	Classes Randomly Selected	Yes
Johnson, Johnson, Dudley, Magnuson	91 - 92	Suburban	Creek Valley Elementary, Edina, MN	2 - 5	9 Hours, 15 Days	227 (WC)	Yes	Classes Randomly Selected	No
Johnson, Johnson, Dudley, Ward, Magnuson	91 - 92	Suburban	Creek Valley Elementary, Edina, MN	2 - 5	9 Hours, 15 Days	227 (WC)	Yes	Classes Randomly Selected	No
Johnson, Johnson, Mitchell, Cotten, Harris, Louison	91 - 92	Urban	Miller Park Elementary Omaha, NE	3 - 4	10 Hours, 1.5 Days	47 (Cadre)	No	None	NA
Johnson, Johnson, Cotten, Harris, Louison	92 - 93	Urban	Miller Park Elementary, Omaha, NE	3 - 4	10 Hours, 1.5 Days	39 (Cadre)	No	None	NA
Johnson & Johnson	93-94	Urban	Miller Park Elementary, Omaha, NE	3-4	10 Hours, 1.5 Days	34 (Cadre)	No	None	NA

A : 4

Johnson, D. W., & Johnson, R. (2005). **Teaching Students To Be Peacemakers** (4th Ed.). Edina, MN: Interaction Book Company, (952)831-9500.

© Johnson & Johnson

Study	Year	Setting	School	Grades	Training Length	Sample Size	Control	Random-ization	Teacher Rotation
Johnson, Johnson, Dudley, Mitchell, Fredrickson	93 - 94	Suburban	Valley View Middle School, Edina MN	6 - 9	14 Hours, 12 Weeks	235 (WC)	Yes	Control Classes Randomly Selected	Yes
Dudley, Johnson, Johnson	93 - 94	Suburban	Valley View Middle School, Edina, MN	6 - 9	14 Hours, 12 Weeks	235 (WC)	Yes	Control Classes Randomly Selected	Yes
Stevahn, Johnson, Johnson, Green, Laginski	93 - 94	Rural, Suburban, Canada	Durham High School, Ontario	9	9.5 Hours, 2 Weeks	40 (WC)	Yes	Students Assigned To Conditions	Yes
Stevahn, Johnson, Johnson, Real	94 - 95	Rural, Suburban, Canada	Durham Region K - 8, Ontario	7 - 8	23 Hours, 4 Weeks	111 (WC)	Yes	Students Assigned To Conditions	Yes
Stevahn, Johnson, Johnson, Laginski, O'Coin	94 - 95	Rural, Suburban, Canada	Durham High School Ontario	9	10 Hours, 4 Weeks	42 (WC)	Yes	Students Assigned To Conditions	Yes
Stevahn, Johnson, Johnson, Schultz	95-96	Suburban	Mount Diablo, HS Concord, CA	9	17 ½ Hours, 3 Weeks	92	Yes	Classes Assigned To Conditions	No (Same)
Stevahn, Johnson, Johnson, Oberle, Wahl	96-97	Suburban	Highlands Elementary, Edina, MN	Kinder-garten	9 Hours, 4 Weeks	80	Yes	Students Assigned To Conditions	Yes
Stevahn, Munger, Kealey	97-98	Suburban	Dorval, Quebec	K – 6	6 Months	302	No	None	No
Stevahn, Oberle, Johnson, & Johnson	99-00	Suburban	Highlands Elementary, Edina, MN	Kinder-garten	6 ½ Hours, 2 Weeks	38	Yes	Students Assigned To Conditions	Yes

A : 5

Johnson, D. W., & Johnson, R. (2005). **Teaching Students To Be Peacemakers** (4th Ed.). Edina, MN: Interaction Book Company, (952)831-9500.

Table A:2: Mean Weighted Effect Sizes For Peacemaker Studies

Dependent Variable	Mean	Standard Deviation	Number Of Effects
Learned Procedure	2.25	1.98	13
Learned Procedure – Retention	3.34	4.16	9
Applied Procedure	2.16	1.31	4
Application – Retention	0.46	0.16	3
Strategy Constructiveness	1.60	1.70	21
Constructiveness – Retention	1.10	0.53	10
Strategy Two-Concerns	1.10	0.46	5
Two-Concerns – Retention	0.45	0.20	2
Integrative Negotiation	0.98	0.36	5
Quality of Solutions	0.73	0	1
Positive Attitude	1.07	0.25	5
Negative Attitude	-0.61	0.37	2
Academic Achievement	0.88	0.09	5
Academic Retention	0.70	0.31	4

The results from the different measures were consistent. The diversity of these measures adds validity and generalizability to the results. Responses were categorized in two ways. A content analysis was conducted that resulted in a 12-point continuum from destructive (physical and verbal aggression and avoidance) to constructive (invoking norms for appropriate behavior, proposing alternatives, and using the problem-solving negotiation procedure) actions. The data were also classified according to the Two-Concerns Conflict Strategies Theory (Johnson & F. Johnson, 2003) which proposes that disputants have two concerns: achieving their goals and maintaining a good relationship with the other person. When these two dimensions are combined, the five strategies of withdrawing, forcing, smoothing, compromising, and negotiating to solve the problem

Johnson, D. W., & Johnson, R. (2005). **Teaching Students To Be Peacemakers** (4th Ed.). Edina, MN: Interaction Book Company, (952)831-9500.

result. Overall, from Table 2 it may be seen that for the Strategy Constructiveness Scale, the average effect size was 1.60 on the post test and 1.10 for the retention tests. For the Two-Concerns Scale, the post-test effect-size was 1.10 and the retention effect size was 0.45. Trained students tended to use the integrative negotiation and mediation procedures in resolving the conflicts. There were no significant differences between males and females in the strategies used to manage conflicts. Although the training took place in school, and focused on school conflicts, there were no significant differences between the strategies used in school and in the home. Students used the strategies learned in school just as frequently in the home as they did in the school.

Transfer Of Training To Nonclassroom And Nonschool Settings

"Do students transfer the integrative negotiation and mediation procedures to nonclassroom and nonschool situations?" An important issue in conflict training is whether the procedures and skills learned will transfer to nonclassroom and nonschool settings. Three types of measures were used to determine the extent of transfer:

1. The spontaneous use of the negotiation and mediation procedures in settings other than the classroom.

2. Written descriptions of conflicts students were involved in outside of the classroom.

3. Systematic observation of students in nonclassroom settings.

The integrative negotiation and mediation procedures students learned in the classroom did generalize to nonclassroom and nonschool situations. The use of the procedures was reported on the playground, in the lunchroom, in the hallways, on school buses, and in the home. Students spontaneously wrote stories about using the negotiation and mediation procedures, students spontaneously presented skits in the school variety show involving the negotiation and mediation procedures, and parents reported that students used the negotiation and mediation procedures and skills with their brothers and sisters, their neighborhood friends, and even their pets.

In a number of studies, students regularly filled out Conflict Report Forms detailing the conflicts they were involved in and how they were resolved. Over half of these conflicts occurred in the home. An example from a fourth-grade student is, "*My conflict was when me and my brother were fighting about who would get the dry baseball and who would get the wet one. So me and my brother did conflict resolution and it ended up that I first got the wet ball and my brother got the dry ball, then I got the dry ball and my brother got the wet ball.*"

Finally, students were directly observed on the playground and other nonclassroom settings in the school (Johnson, Johnson, Dudley, Acikgoz, 1994; Stevahn, Johnson,

Johnson, D. W., & Johnson, R. (2005). **Teaching Students To Be Peacemakers** (4th Ed.). Edina, MN: Interaction Book Company, (952)831-9500.

Johnson, Oberle, & Wahl, 2000). The conflicts were classified as either low-investment or high-investment. **Low-investment conflicts** were usually light-hearted and usually lasted thirty seconds or one minute. An example of a low-investment conflict is a girl who wanted to give a picture to somebody and asked, "*Who wants this*?" More than one student wanted it and a conflict started. When one of the students got the picture, the others stopped and began to laugh, one of them said, "*Do you see what you gave up*?" The entire conflict lasted about one minute and did not consume any of the classes emotional or academic energy. Formal negotiation and mediation procedures were not used, even by trained students. **High-investment conflicts** affected the students emotionally by detracting from the students' ability to work academically, or interact with classmates in a positive manner. Often times these conflicts would last for days or longer. Once trained, students involved in high-investment conflicts did enter into integrative negotiations and seek out mediation. A group of sixth grade girls, for example, engaged in a prolonged conflict over who were "best friends" and who were no longer "best friends." In a fifth-grade class Bill and his friends believed Doug and his friends were passing notes saying nasty things about Bill. Doug denied it. But Bill responded, "*since you are doing it to us we are going to do it to you*." So Bill and his friends started passing nasty notes about Doug. The resulting conflict took several days to resolve and required mediation. Another example occurred when two girls became very angry at each other because both wanted the same part in a play. Mediation was finally required. Trained students were observed to exert very high effort to resolve the conflict, listen attentively to each other, demonstrate emotional seriousness about the conflict and its resolution, be committed to the negotiation and mediation procedures, and express personal respect for the other individuals involved.

Distributive Versus Integrative Negotiations

"When given the option, would students engage in "win-lose" or problem-solving negotiations?" A number of studies examined the impact of the Peacemaker training on the students' approach to negotiating. Students were placed in a negotiation simulation involving the buying and selling of commodities in which they could adopt a "win-lose" (maximize own outcomes) or an integrative (maximize joint outcomes) negotiation approach. Students who had received the Peacemaker training used the integrative approach significantly more frequently than did the untrained students. No untrained student adopted an integrative approach to negotiations while almost all students in the experimental condition did so. From Table 2 it may be seen that the average effect size was 0.98. Trained students were more likely to engage in integrative negotiations than were untrained students.

Resolutions

"What is the quality of the resolutions?" On the Conflict Report Form students were asked to report the nature of the resolution of the conflict. Very few of the conflicts were reported to be arbitrated by adults or resolved through forgiveness in either the control or

Johnson, D. W., & Johnson, R. (2005). **Teaching Students To Be Peacemakers** (4th Ed.). Edina, MN: Interaction Book Company, (952)831-9500.

experimental groups. The number of integrative solutions which resulted in both sides achieving their goals was much higher in conflicts among trained (rather than untrained) students. Untrained students left many conflicts unresolved. There was no significant difference between the solutions arrived at for conflicts in school or at home. Only one study had the necessary analyzes to determine an effect size (ES = 0.73). This indicates that trained students tend to find more constructive resolutions than do untrained students.

Attitudes Toward Conflict

"Does the Peacemaker training result in more positive attitudes toward conflict?" Attitudes toward conflict were measured by a word association task. One of the goals of conflict resolution and peer mediation training is to create positive attitudes toward conflict. Before training, overwhelmingly the students held negative attitudes toward conflict seeing almost no potential positive outcomes. While still perceiving conflict more negatively than positively, the attitudes of trained students became markedly more positive and less negative while the attitudes of untrained students stayed essentially the same (highly negative). The average effect size was positive attitudes toward conflict was 1.07 and for negative attitudes was -0.61.

Academic Achievement

"Does the Peacemaker training increase students' academic achievement when it is integrated into academic lessons?" The Peacemaker Training has been integrated into both English literature and history academic units to determine its impact on academic achievement. The basic design for these studies was to randomly assign students to classes in which the Peacemaker training was integrated into the academic unit studied or to classes in which the academic unit was studied without any conflict training. Students in the experimental classes both studied the academic material and learned the negotiation and mediation procedures. Students in the control classes spent all their time studying the novel. Students who received the Peacemaker training as part of the academic unit tended to score significantly higher on achievement and retention tests than did students who studied the academic unit only. Students not only learned the factual information contained in the academic unit better, they were better able to interpret the information in insightful ways. The higher achievement is all the more notable as students in the control classes spent all their time studying the academic material, while students in the experimental classes had to learn both the novel and the negotiation and mediation procedures in the same amount of time. From Table 2 it may be seen that the average post-test effect size was 0.88 and the average retention effect size was 0.70.

Linking conflict resolution training with academic learning is important, as the history of innovations in schools indicates that new programs are not widely adopted and maintained over a number of years unless they increase students' academic achievement.

Johnson, D. W., & Johnson, R. (2005). **Teaching Students To Be Peacemakers** (4th Ed.). Edina, MN: Interaction Book Company, (952)831-9500.

Academic units can then provide an arena in which frequent and continued practice of the conflict resolution procedures can take place.

Discipline Problems

"Does the TSP training result in fewer discipline problems that have to be managed by the teacher and the administration?" Students tended to resolve their conflicts without the involvement of faculty and administrators, reducing the number of discipline problems teachers had to deal by about 60 percent and referrals to administrators by about 90 percent. A teacher commented, *"Classroom management problems are nil as far as I'm concerned. We don't do a lot of disciplining per se. A lot of times, when a conflict occurs on the playground, they resolve it there and do not bring it back to the classroom. So there is a lot less I have to deal with in the classroom."*

Interviews Of Teachers, Principals, And Parents

"Do faculty, administrators, and parents perceive the conflict resolution in positive ways?" A number of participating teachers and principals were interviewed. All endorsed the program. The teachers reported that the training resulted in conflicts among students becoming less severe and destructive and, therefore, the classroom climate became more positive and the teachers (and principals) spent much less time resolving conflicts among students. The teachers and principals interviewed said that without qualification they would become involved in the training in the future. One teacher commented, *"The negotiation and mediation skills we are teaching our students will have a definite positive impact on the way our students interact with each other...these skills go beyond the scope of the classroom, and contribute to the betterment of our community, and our world."* Parents reported that students mediated conflicts at home and in other contexts from the school. Many parents whose children were not part of the project requested that their children receive the training next year. A number of parents of trained children requested that they themselves receive the training so that they could use the negotiation and mediation procedures to manage conflict management in the family.

Values Taught By The Peacemaker Program

"What is the impact of the training on values?" By participating in the TIP Program, students are implicitly taught a set of values. First, they learn that they have a right to express honestly and openly what they want and how they feel, and should listen carefully to others' wants and how feelings. Second, they learn that wants and feelings should be supported by reasoning and an understanding of one's own and others' interests. Third, they learn that it is important to view situations from all perspectives. Fourth, they learn to value the well-being of others. Fifth, they learn that successful agreements depend on joint efforts and the effort others make should be valued.

Johnson, D. W., & Johnson, R. (2005). **Teaching Students To Be Peacemakers** (4th Ed.). Edina, MN: Interaction Book Company, (952)831-9500.

Glossary

Accommodation: Adjusting behavior to conform to social constraints.

Aggression: Attempt to hurt someone or destroy somthing.

Aggressive-Passive Mentality: Students believing that either they (a) must dominate through force or (b) are passive victims unable to defend themselves or act in their own best interests. The resulting resentment powers resistance to learning.

Anger: A defensive emotional reaction that occurs when we are frustrated, thwarted, or attacked. Anger is a righteous but defensive reaction to frustration and aggression based on a unidimensional perceptual focus, a physical demand to take action, and a belief that we must get our way.

Assertiveness: Describing feelings, thoughts, opinions, and preferences directly to another person in an honest and appropriate way that respects both oneself and the other person.

Arbitration: The submission of a dispute to a disinterested third party who makes a final and binding judgment as to how the conflict will be resolved.

Behavioral Description: A statement that includes a personal statement (referring to "I," "me," or "my") and a description of the specific behaviors observed.

Blame: Believing that the cause of frustration is wicked people (including yourself) who deserve to be punished for their evil acts.

Carve-Outs: Carving an issue out of a larger context, leaving the related issues unsettled. This is the opposite of a tie-in.

Catharsis: The release of pent-up emotion experienced either by talking about feelings or by engaging in very active emotional release such as crying, laughing, or shouting.

Catastrophizing: Believing that one must have his or her way and that it is awful not to get everything wanted.

Common Fate: When one cannot succeed unless the other person succeeds and the other person cannot succeed unless one succeeds. You sink or swim together.

Competitive Learning: Students working against each other to achieve a goal that only one or a few can attain. You can attain your goal if and only if the other students involved cannot attain their goals.

Compromising: Giving up part of your goal while the other person does the same in order to reach an agreement. You seek a solution in which both sides gain something and settle on an agreement that is the middle ground between your two opening positions.

Conceptual Conflict: Conflict that exists when incompatible ideas exist simultaneously in a person's mind or when information being received does not seem to fit with what one already knows.

Conciliation: People involved in a conflict are brought together to discuss the problem. The Latin root "conciliare" means "to call or bring together, to win over" and is derived from "conilium" which is "a meeting or assembly."

Conflict: The occurrence of incompatible activities. An activity that is incompatible with another activity is one that prevents, blocks, or interferes with the occurrence or effectiveness of the second activity. Incompatible activities may originate in one person, between two or more people, or between two or more groups.

Conflict of Interests: When the actions of one person attempting to reach his or her goals prevent, block, or interfere with the actions of another person attempting to reach his or her goals.

Confronting: Directly expressing your view of the conflict and your feelings about it while at the same time inviting the other person to do the same so that negotiations may be begun. The negotiations are aimed at ensuring that you and the other person both fully meet your goals and maintain the relationship at the highest level possible.

Controversy: Conflict that exists when one person's ideas, information, conclusions, theories, and opinions are incompatible with those of another and the two seek to reach an agreement.

Cooperative Base Groups: Cooperative learning groups used to provide long-term support and assistance for academic progress.

Cooperative Learning: Students working together to accomplish shared goals. Students perceiving that they can succeed if and only if the other persons with whom they are cooperatively linked achieve their goals.

Co-Orientation: Operating under the same norms and adhering to the same procedures.

Counter-Conditioning: Conditioning students to respond in a way that is counter to destructive actions such as being hostile.

Developmental Conflict: A recurrent conflict that cycles in and out of peak intensity as the person develops socially. When recurrent incompatible activities between adult and child

based on the opposing forces of stability and change within the child cycle in and out of peak intensity as the child develops cognitively, socially, and physically.

Disputant: Person involved in a conflict of interests.

Dissociation: The internalization of social constraints and adult values but rejecting them by seeing them as alien to one's own value structure. There is outward compliance to the social constraints while inner resistance continues. Direct or "real" solutions to the conflicts are abandoned for fantasy, pretend, or imaginary solutions.

Divergent Thinking: Generating a variety of ideas about how to solve a problem.

Egocentrism: The embeddedness in one's own viewpoint to the extent that one is unaware of other points of view and of the limitation of one's perspective. Being unaware that other perspectives exist and that one's own view of the conflict is incomplete and limited.

Expand the Pie: Adding new resources so that increased options for agreement are available.

Feelings: Internal physiological reactions to your experiences.

Feeling Description: A combination of a personal statement (referring to "I," "me," or "my") and specifying the feeling by name or by action-urge simile or some other figure of speech.

Fight Form: A form disputants fill out before mediation that requires them to reflect on the conflict, define it, and think of alternative ways of resolving the conflict.

Fixation: A mind set fixed on one thing so that the person is unable to think of or see alternatives.

Forcing: Overpowering opponents by requiring them to accept your solution to the conflict. You seek to achieve your goals at all costs and without concern with the needs of others.

Formal Cooperative Learning Groups: Cooperative learning groups used to teach specific academic content and social skills.

Fundamental Attribution Error: Belief that other people's behavior is caused by their personalities and nature while one's own behavior is caused by circumstances and situational factors.

Goal: An ideal and desired state of affairs that people value and are working to achieve.

Goal structure: The type of social interdependence specified among individuals as they strive to achieve their goals.

Groups Processing: Discussion of how well group members are achieving their goals and maintaining effective working relationships among members.

Hit-And-Run: You start a conversation about the conflict, give your definition and feelings, and then disappear before the other person has a chance to respond.

Identification: When a person tries to be like someone he or she loves, admires, or fears by incorporating their qualities and attributes into him- or herself.

Individual Accountability: When the performance of each individual student is assessed and the results given back to the group and the individual.

Individualistic Learning: Students work by themselves to accomplish learning goals unrelated to those of their classmates.

Informal Cooperative Learning Groups: Cooperative learning groups used to ensure active cognitive processing of information during a lecture or direct teaching.

Interests: The potential benefits to be gained by achieving goals. An individual's wants, needs, values, and goals.

Integration: The internalization of social constraints and adult values and accepting them into one's own value structure.

Irrational Assumption: A belief that makes you depressed, anxious, or upset most of the time.

Joint Outcome: Sum of benefits for everyone involved.

Manipulation: It is influencing others in ways they do not fully understand with consequences that are undesirable for them but highly desirable for oneself.

Mediation: When a neutral and impartial third party actively assists two or more people (called disputants) to negotiate a constructive resolution to their conflict. The Latin root "mediare" means "to divide in the middle."

Mote-Beam Mechanism: Students see small misbehaviors of opponents while ignoring one's own large misbehaviors.

Mutual Causation: When whether you succeed or fail depends both on your own efforts and the efforts of the other person. You must depend on the other person to help you succeed and he or she must depend on you to help him or her succeed.

Negotiation: A process by which persons who have shared and opposed interests and want to come to an agreement try to work out a settlement.

Nonnegotiable Norms: Norms individuals are expected to follow without exception, such as those outlawing physical violence against oneself or another person, public humiliation and shaming, and lying and deceit.

Nonassertiveness: You say nothing in response to a provocation, keeping your feelings to yourself, hiding feeling from others, and perhaps even hiding your feelings from yourself.

Norm of Mutual Responsiveness: Rule that you should be committed to fulfilling each other's goals and concerned about each other's interests.

Norms: Shared expectations about the behavior that is appropriate within the situation.

One-Step Negotiations: Each person (a) assesses the strength of his or her interests, (b) assesses the strength of the other person's interests, and (c) agrees that whoever has the greatest need is given his or her way.

Oppositional Interaction: Students discouraging and obstructing each other's efforts to achieve. Students focus both on increasing their own achievement **and** on preventing any classmate from achieving higher than they do.

Overassimilation: Pushing new skills and opportunities to beyond socially defined limits.

Package Deals: When several issues that are considered part of the agreement are settled.

Paraphrasing: Restating, in one's own words, what the person says, feels, and means.

Perception-Checking: Asking for clarification or correction to make sure your understanding is accurate. It involves describing what you think the other person's feelings are, asking whether or not your perception is accurate, and refraining from expressing approval or disapproval of the feelings.

Personal Statements: Statements that refer to "I," "me," "my," or "mine."

Perspective: A person's way of viewing the world and his or her relation to it.

Positive Interdependence: Students perceive that they are linked with others in a way that one cannot succeed unless the other members of the group succeed (and vice versa) and/or that they must coordinate their efforts with the efforts of their groupmates to complete a task. They perceive that they "sink or swim together."

Problem-Solving Negotiations: When each negotiator has as his or her goal the reaching of an agreement that benefits everyone involved. You negotiate to solve the problem when you have an ongoing cooperative relationship with the other person, must negotiate an agreement to resolve the current conflict, and then will continue the cooperative efforts and the relationship.

Promotive Interaction: Students helping, assisting, encouraging, facilitating, and supporting each other's efforts to learn, achieve, complete tasks, and produce in order to reach the group's goals.

Relationship Statements: Personal statements that describe some aspect of the way the two of you are interacting with each other.

Restitution: Making amends for injury, mistreatment, or insult.

Role Reversal: Having two participants in a conflict reverse roles and play each other during a role play.

Self-Blame: When you judge your basic self-worth on the basis of your inadequate or rotten behavior.

Self-Fulfilling Prophecy: Perceiving another person as being immoral and hostile and behaving accordingly, thus evoking hostility and deceit from the other person.

Single Step Solution: When you, after assessing how important your goals are to you and how important the other person's goals are to him or her, decide to give up your goals and help the other person achieve his or her goals. In a relationship it is important that each person gives in to the other about 50 percent of the time.

Smoothing: Giving up your goals and letting the other person have his or her way in order to maintain the relationship at the highest level possible. When the goal is of no importance to you but the relationship is of high importance, you smooth.

Social Constraints: Limits placed on a person's behavior by other people that define what is realistic and unrealistic behavior within the relationship and setting.

Social Perspective Taking: The ability to understand how a situation appears to another person and how that person is reacting cognitively and emotionally to the situation.

Tie-Ins: When an issue considered extraneous by the other person is introduced and you offer to accept a certain settlement provided this extraneous issue will also be settled to one's satisfaction.

Trade-Offs: The exchange of two different things of comparable value.

Win-Lose Negotiations: When each negotiator has as his or her goal making an agreement more favorable to oneself than to the other negotiator.

Wise Agreements: An agreement fair to all participants, based on principles, that strengthens participants' abilities to work together cooperatively, and improves participants' ability to resolve future conflicts constructively.

References

Blake, R., & Mouton, J. (1962). The intergroup dynamics of win-lose conflict and problem-solving collaboration in union-management relations. In M. Sherif (Ed.), Intergroup relations and leadership, (5, pp. 94-140). New York: John Wiley.

Blake, R., & Mouton, J. (1964). The managerial grid. Houston, TX: Gulf.

Coleman, J. (1961). The adolescent society. New York: Free Press.

Collins, W., & Laursen, B. (1992). Conflict and relationships during adolescence. In C. Shantz & W. Hartup (Eds.), Conflict in child and adolescent development (pp. 216-240). Cambridge: Cambridge University Press.

DeCecco, J., & Richards, A. (1974). Growing pains: Uses of school conflict. New York: Aberdeen Press.

Deutsch, M. (1949). A theory of cooperation and competition. Human Relations, 2, 129-152.

Deutsch, M. (1962). Cooperation and trust: Some theoretical notes. In M. Jones (Ed.), Nebraska symposium on motivation. Lincoln: University of Nebraska Press, 275-319.

Deutsch, M. (1973). The resolution of conflict. New Haven, CT: Yale University Press.

Deutsch, M. (1985). Distributive justice. New Haven, CT: Yale University Press.

Deutsch, M., & Krauss, R. (1960). The effect of threat upon interpersonal bargaining. Journal of Abnormal and Social Psychology, 61, 181-189.

Eisenberg, N. & Mussen, P. H. (1995). The roots of prosocial behavior in children. Cambridge, MA: Cambridge University Press.

Fisher, R., & Ury, W. (1981). Getting to yes. New York: Penguin.

Flanders, N. (1964). Some relationships among teacher influence, pupil attitudesand achievement. In B. Biddle &W. Eilena (Eds.), Contemporary research on teacher effectiveness. New York: Holt, Rinehart, & Winston.

Follet, M. (1940). Constructive conflict. In H. Metcalf & L. Urwick (Eds.), Dynamic administration: The collected papers of Mary Parker Follet (pp. 30-49). New York: Harper.

Fullan, M. (2001). The new meaning of educational change (3rd Ed.). New York: Teachers College Press.

Garofalo, J., Siegel, L., & Laub, J. (1987). School-related victimizations among adolescents: An analysis of National Crime Survey (NCS) narratives. Journal of Quantitative Criminology, 3, 321-338.

Glasser, W. (1984). Control theory. New York: Harper & Row.

Gump, P. (1964). Environmental guidance of the classroom behavioral system. In B. Biddle &W. Eilena (Eds.), Contemporary research on teacher effectiveness. New York: Holt, Rinehart, & Winston.

Janz, T. & Tjosvold, D. (1985). Costing effective vs. ineffective work relationships. Canadian Journal of Administrative Sciences, 2, 43-51.

Johnson, D. W. (1967). Use of role reversal in intergroup competition. Journal of Personality and Social Psychology, 7, 135-141.

Johnson, D. W. (1970). The social psychology of education. New York: Holt, Rinehart, & Winston.

Johnson, D. W. (1971). Role reversal: A summary and review of the research. International Journal of Group Tensions, 1, 318-334.

Johnson, D. W. (1974). Communication and the inducement of cooperative behavior in conflicts: A critical review. Speech Monographs, 41, 64-78.

Johnson, D. W. (1978/1991). Human relations and your career (3rd Ed.). Boston: Allyn & Bacon.

Johnson, D. W. (1972/2003). Reaching out: Interpersonal effectiveness and self-actualization (8th Ed.). Boston: Allyn & Bacon.

Johnson D. W., & Johnson, F. (1975/2003). Joining together: Group theory and group skills (8th Ed.). Boston: Allyn & Bacon.

Johnson, D. W., & Johnson, R. (1979). Conflict in the classroom: Controversy and learning. Review of Educational Research, 49, 51-61.

Johnson, D. W., & Johnson, R. (1989). Cooperation and competition: Theory and research. Edina, MN: Interaction Book Company.

Johnson, D. W., & Johnson, R. (1994). Leading the cooperative school (2nd Ed.). Edina: Interaction Book Company.

Johnson, D. W., & Johnson, R. (1995a). Creative controversy: Intellectual challenge in the classroom (3rd Ed.). Edina: Interaction Book Company.

Johnson, D. W., & Johnson, R. (1995b). Teaching students to be peacemakers: Results of five years of research. Peace and Conflict: Journal of Peace Psychology, 1(4), 417-438.

Johnson, D. W., & Johnson, R. (1996). Conflict resolution and peer mediation programs in schools: A review of the research. Review of Educational Research, 66(4), 459-506.

Johnson, D. W., & Johnson, R. (1999). Learning together and alone: Cooperative, competitive, and individualistic learning (5th Ed.). Boston: Allyn & Bacon.

Johnson, D. W., & Johnson, R. (2003). Controversy and peace education. Journal of Research in Education, 13(1), 71-91.

Johnson, D. W., Johnson, R., & Holubec, E. (1998b). Advanced cooperative learning (3rd Ed.). Edina, MN: Interaction Book Company.

Johnson, D. W., Johnson, R., & Holubec, E. (1998a). Cooperation in the classroom (6th Ed.). Edina, MN: Interaction Book Company.

Johnson, D. W., Johnson, R., & Smith, K. (1998). Active learning: Cooperation in the college classroom (2nd Ed.). Edina, MN: Interaction Book Company.

Johnson, D. W., McCarty, K., & Allen, T. (1976). Congruent and contradictory verbal and nonverbal communications of cooperativeness and competitiveness in negotiations, Journal of Educational Psychology, 3, 275-292.

Johnson, R., & Johnson, D. W. (2002). Teaching students to be peacemakers: A meta-analysis. Journal of Research in Education. 12(1), 25-39.

Opotow, S. (1991). Adolescent peer conflicts: Implications for students and for schools. Education and Urban Society, 23(4), 416-441.

Patterson, G., DeBaryshe, B., & Ramsey, E. (1989). A developmental perspective on antisocial behavior. American Psychologist, 44(2), 329-335.

Prothrow-Stith, D., Spivak, H., & Hausman, A. (1987). The violence prevention project: A public health approach. Science, Technology, and Human Values, 12, 67-69.

Pruitt, D. (1981). Negotiation behavior. New York: Academic Press.

Rafalides, M., & Hoy, W. (1971). Students sense of alienation and pupil control orientation of high schools. The High School Journal, 55(3), 102.

Rubin, J., Pruitt, D., & Kim, S. (1994). Social conflict. New York: McGraw Hill.

Seligman, M. (1975). Helplessness: On depression, development, and death. San Francisco: W. H. Freeman.

Seligman, M. (1995). The Optimistic Child. New York: Houghton Mifflin Co. (1995).

Stevahn, L. (2003). Integrating conflict resolution and peer mediation training into the curriculum. Theory into Practice, 43(1), 50-58.

Stevahn, L., Johnson, D. W., Johnson, R., & Schultz, R. (2002). Effects of conflict resolution training integrated into a high school social studies curriculum. Journal of Social Psychology, 142(3), 305-331.

Tjosvold, D., & Johnson, D. W. (Eds.). (1983). Productive conflict management: Perspectives for organizations. Edina, MN: Interaction Book Company.

van de Vliert, E. (1990). Positive effects of conflict: A field assessment. The International Journal of Conflict Management, 1, 69-80.

van de Vliert, E., & Prein, H. (1989). The difference in the meaning of forcing in the conflict management of actors and observers. In M. Rahim (Ed.), Managing conflict: An interdisciplinary approach (pp. 51-63). New York: Praeger.

Walton, R. (1987). Managing conflict. Reading, MA: Addison-Wesley.

Watson, G., & Johnson, D. W. (1972) Social psychology: Issues and insights. Philadelphia: Lippincott.

References: Peacemaker Studies

1. Dudley, B. S., Johnson, D. W., & Johnson, R. (1996). Conflict-resolution training and middle-school students' integrative negotiation behavior. Journal of Applied Social Psychology, 26, 2038-2052.

2. Johnson, D. W., & Johnson, R. (2001). Peer mediation in an inner city elementary school. Urban Education, 36(2), 165-178.

3. Johnson, D. W., Johnson, R., & Dudley, B. (1992). Effects of peer mediation training on elementary school students. Mediation Quarterly, 10, 89-99.

4. Johnson, D. W., Johnson, R., Dudley, B., & Acikgoz, K. (1994). Peer mediation: Effects of conflict resolution training on elementary school students. Journal of Social Psychology, 134, 803-817.

5. Johnson, D. W., Johnson, R., Dudley, B., Mitchell, J., & Fredrickson, J. (1997). The impact of conflict resolution training on middle school students. Journal of Social Psychology, 137(1), 11-22.

6. Johnson, D. W., Johnson, R., Cotten, B., Harris, D., & Louison, S. (1995). Using conflict managers to mediate conflicts in an elementary school. Mediation Quarterly, 12(4), 379-390.

7. Johnson, D. W., Johnson, R., Dudley, & Magnuson, D. (1995). Training of elementary school students to manage conflict. Journal of Social Psychology, 135(6), 673-686.

8. Johnson, D. W., Johnson, R., Dudley, B., Ward, M., & Magnuson, D. (1995). Impact of peer mediation training on the management of school and home conflicts. American Educational Research Journal, 32(4), 829-844.

9. Johnson, D. W., Johnson, R., Mitchell, J., Cotten, B., Harris, D., & Louison, S. (1996). The effectiveness of conflict managers in an inner-city elementary school. Journal of Educational Research, 89(5), 280-285.

10. Stevahn, L., Johnson, D. W., Johnson, R. T., Green, K., & Laginski, A. M. (1997). Effects on high school students of conflict resolution training integrated into English literature. Journal of Social Psychology, 137(3), 302-315.

11. Stevahn, L., Johnson, D. W., Johnson, R. T., Laginski, A. M., & O'Coin, I. (1996). Effects on high school students of integrating conflict resolution and peer mediation training into an academic unit. Mediation Quarterly, 14(1), 21-36.

12. Stevahn, L., Johnson, D. W., Johnson, R., Oberle, K., & Wahl, L. (2000). Effects of conflict resolution training integrated into a kindergarten curriculum. Child Development, 71(3), 772-784.

13. Stevahn, L., Johnson, D. W., Johnson, R., & Real, D. (1996). The impact of a cooperative or individualistic context on the effectiveness of conflict resolution training. American Educational Research Journal, 33, 801-823.

14. Stevahn, L., Johnson, D. W., Johnson, R., & Schultz, R. (2002). Effects of conflict resolution training integrated into a high school social studies curriculum. Journal of Social Psychology, 142(3), 305-331.

15. Stevahn, L., Munger, L., & Kealey, K. (1999). First-year effects of teaching all students conflict resolution in a French Immersion elementary school. Paper presented at the Annual Meeting of the American Educational Research Association, Montreal, Quebec, April. Journal of Educational Research, in press.

16. Stevahn, L., & Oberle, K. (2003). Effects of perspective reversal training and conflict resolution based classroom management in kindergarten. Journal of Research in Education, 13(1), 62-72.